Weaving Services and People on the World Wide Web

Irwin King · Ricardo Baeza-Yates
Editors

Weaving Services and People on the World Wide Web

Editors
Prof. Irwin King
The Chinese University of Hong Kong
Dept. Computer Science & Engineering
Shatin, New Territories
Hong Kong, P. R. China
king@cse.cuhk.edu.hk

Prof. Ricardo Baeza-Yates
Yahoo! Research Barcelona
Ocata, 1
08003 Barcelona
1st Floor
Spain
ricardo.baeza@upf.edu

ISBN 978-3-642-42562-2 ISBN 978-3-642-00570-1 (eBook)
DOI 10.1007/978-3-642-00570-1
Springer Dordrecht Heidelberg London New York

ACM Computing Classification (1998): H.3.3, H.3.5, H.5.3, H.4.3

Cover design: KünkelLopka, Heidelberg

Printed on acid-free paper

Springer is part of Springer Science+Business Media (www.springer.com)

Preface

Ever since its inception, the Web has changed the landscape of human experiences on how we interact with one another and data through service infrastructure via various computing devices. This interweaving environment is now becoming ever more embedded into devices and systems that integrates seamlessly on how we live, in our working or leisure time.

This special volume on "Weaving Services and People on the WWW", features some of the cutting-edge research work that were presented at the Workshop Track of the 17th International World Wide Web Conference (WWW2008) held at Beijing, China, from April 21–25, 2008. The Workshop Track received 24 proposals and after a rigorous reviewing process ten full-day workshops were selected, of which two workshops were half-day workshops. They were:

- WS1 – Web Science Workshop (WSW2008) by Wendy Hall, Nigel Shadbolt, Tim Berners-Lee, Daniel Weitzner, and James Hendler.
- WS2 – Location and the Web (LocWeb) 2008 by Susanne Boll, Christopher Jones, Eric Kansa, Puneet Kishor, Mor Naaman, Ross Purves, Arno Scharl and Erik Wilde.
- WS3 – International Workshop on Context Enabled Source and Service Selection, Integration and Adaptation (CSSSIA 2008) by Ullas Nambiar and Michael Sheng.
- WS4 – Linked Data on the Web (LDW2008) by Tim Berners-Lee, Christian Bizer, Tom Heath, and Kingsley Idehen.
- WS5 – Fourth International Workshop on Adversarial Information Retrieval on the Web (AIRWeb 2008) by Dennis Fetterly, Carlos Castillo and Kumar Chellapilla.
- WS6 – Targeting and Ranking for Online Advertising by Ewa Dominowska and Vanja Josifovski.
- WS7 – MobEA VI: Personal Rich Social Media by Rittwik Jana, Daniel Appelquist, Galit Zadok, and Bin Wei.
- WS8 – Semantic Web for Health Care and Life Sciences by Huajun Chen, Kei Cheung, Michel Dumontier, Eric Prud'hommeaux, Alan Ruttenberg, Susie Stephens and Yimin Wang.

- WS9A – Workshops on Language-centric Web Applications:
  - WS9A – International Workshop on Question Answering on the Web (QAWeb2008) by Wenyin Liu, Qing Li and Xuedong Huang.
  - WS9P – NLP Challenges in the Information Explosion Era (NLPIX 2008) by Hiroshi Nakagawa, Masaru Kitsuregawa and Kentaro Torisawa.
- WS10A – Workshops on the Social Web (SW2008):
  - WS10A – Workshop on Social Web and Knowledge Management (SWKM2008) by Peter Dolog, Sebastian Schaffert, Markus Krotzsch, and Denny Vrandecic.
  - WS10P – Workshop on Social Web Search and Mining (SWSM2008) by Juanzi Li, Gui-Rong Xue, Michael R. Lyu, Jie Tang, and Zheng Chen.

After the completion of the conference, we invited authors from the top 20% of the presented papers from selected workshops to resubmit their work with a minimum of 30% extended material from their original workshop manuscripts to be considered for this volume. After a second-round of reviews and selection, 14 manuscripts were accepted including a selected number of workshop organizers who prepared an overview of their workshop. These papers are presented here to highlight the state of the art being done in the World Wide Web community.

Although the Workshop Track covered a wide range of interests, this volume highlights two of these emerging topics that we believe are important and will continue to play an ever increasing role in the future development of the Web. They are Web Services and Social Computing.

The first ten chapters are dedicated to Web Services. They range from semantic services for Web communities and Wikipedia to aggregation policies for RSS services. In addition, we highlight the mobile services and location-based services as they are becoming more important and relevant on the Web. In particular, Chaps. 5–7 focus specifically on Web services for mobile users by examining personalized services and user interface issues, while Chaps. 8–10 underscore the importance of location-based services by presenting ways to process vernacular places and regions from Web sources.

The remaining six chapters deal with issues in Social Computing. The first chapter presents a survey of topics related to knowledge management on the social web, while other chapters address topics ranging from security issues in trusted network, collaborative tagging, ranking strategies in folksonomies, to studies on behavior editing patterns in wikis.

The work within this volume represents the tip of an iceberg of the many exciting advancements on the WWW. It is our hope that these chapters will stimulate new discussions and generate original ideas that will make these technologies even more integrated into our social tapestry.

The volume editors would like to thank the authors for their contributions, the WWW2008 Workshop Track Program Committee members for their professionalism in selecting the workshops, and the first- and second-round reviewers for their expertise to improve the manuscripts. Moreover, we are grateful to Springer for the opportunity to publish this volume and their wonderful editorial support. Lastly, thanks to Mr. Kam Tong Chan for his administrative assistance in organizing the book.

Hong Kong, P. R. China | Irwin King
Barcelona, Spain | Ricardo Baeza-Yates
January 2009

Contents

Part I Web Services

Contributors

Alia I. Abdelmoty Cardiff University, UK, a.i.abdelmoty@cs.cf.ac.uk

Fabian Abel IVS – Semantic Web Group, Leibniz University Hannover, Appelstr. 4, D-30167 Hannover, Germany, abel@kbs.uni-hannover.de

Daniel Appelquist Vodafone Group, daniel.appelquist@vodafone.com

Ching-man Au Yeung Intelligence, Agents, Multimedia Group, School of Electronics and Computer Science, University of Southampton, Southampton, SO17 1BJ, UK, fcmay06r@ecs.soton.ac.uk

Leif Azzopardi DCS, University of Glasgow, UK, leif@dcs.gla.ac.uk

Krisztian Balog ISLA, University of Amsterdam, The Netherlands, kbalog@science.uva.nl

Djamal Benslimane LIRIS laboratory, Lyon 1 University, France, dbenslim@liris.cnrs.fr

Philip Boulain Intelligence, Agents, Multimedia Group, School of Electronics and Computer Science, University of Southampton, Southampton SO17 1BJ, UK, prb@ecs.soton.ac.uk

Greg Buehrer Microsoft Corp, 1 Microsoft Way, Redmond, WA 98052, buehrer@microsoft.com

Kumar Chellapilla Microsoft Corp, 1 Microsoft Way, Redmond, WA 98052, kumarc@microsoft.com

Maarten de Rijke ISLA, University of Amsterdam, The Netherlands, mdr@science.uva.nl

José M. del Álamo Departamento de Ingenier'ıa de Sistemas Telem'aticos, Universidad Polit'ecnica de Madrid, Spain, jmdela@dit.upm.es

Stefan Dietze Knowledge Media Institute, The Open University, Milton Keynes, UK, s.dietze@open.ac.uk

Peter Dolog Aalborg University, Computer Science Department, Selma Lagerlöfs Vej 300 DK-9220 Aalborg, Denmark, dolog@cs.aau.dk

Paolo Falcarin Department of Control and Computing Engineering, Politecnico di Torino, Italy, paolo.falcarin@polito.it

Qiangze Feng NEC Laboratories, China, 14/F, Bldg. A, Innovation Plaza, Tsinghua Science Park, Beijing 100084, China, fengqiangze@research.nec.com.cn

Linyun Fu Department of Computer Science & Engineering, Shanghai Jiao Tong University, Shanghai, 200240, China, fulinyun@apex.sjtu.edu.cn

Toshikazu Fukushima NEC Laboratories, China, 14/F, Bldg. A, Innovation Plaza, Tsinghua Science Park, Beijing 100084, China, fukushima@research.nec.com.cn

Chirine Ghedira LIRIS laboratory, Lyon 1 University, France, cghedira@liris.cnrs.fr

Nicholas Gibbins Intelligence, Agents, Multimedia Group, School of Electronics and Computer Science, University of Southampton, Southampton, SO17 1BJ, UK, nmg@ecs.soton.ac.uk

Young Geun Han School of Computing, Soongsil University, Seoul, Korea, younggeun@gmail.com

Andreas Henrich University of Bamberg, Germany, andreas.henrich@uni-bamberg.de

Nicola Henze IVS – Semantic Web Group, Leibniz University Hannover, Appelstr. 4, D-30167 Hannover, Germany, henze@kbs.uni-hannover.de

Dan Hong Department of Computer Science and Engineering, Hong Kong University of Science and Technology, Hong Kong, csdhong@cse.ust.hk

Rittwik Jana AT&T Labs Research, Bldg 103, Rm B229, 180 Park Ave, Florham Park, NJ, 07932, USA, rjana@research.att.com

Christopher B. Jones Cardiff University, UK, c.b.jones@cs.cf.ac.uk

Jae Hwi Kim School of Computing, Soongsil University, Seoul, Korea, oasisdle@gmail.com

Martin Kofahl University Rostock, Geodesy and Geoinformatics, Germany, m.kofahl@gmx.de

Daniel Krause IVS – Semantic Web Group, Leibniz University Hannover, Appelstr. 4, D-30167 Hannover, Germany, krause@kbs.uni-hannover.de

Matthias Kriesell Department of Mathematics, University of Hamburg, Bundesstraße 55 D-20146 Hamburg, Germany, kriesell@math.uni-hamburg.de

Markus Krötzsch Institute AIFB, Universität Karlsruhe D-76128 Karlsruhe, Germany, mak@aifb.uni-karlsruhe.de

Sang Ho Lee School of Computing, Soongsil University, Seoul, Korea, shlee199@gmail.com

Qiaoling Liu Department of Computer Science & Engineering, Shanghai Jiao Tong University, Shanghai, 200240, China, lql@apex.sjtu.edu.cn

Volker Lüdecke University of Bamberg, Germany, volker.luedecke@uni-bamberg.de

Zakaria Maamar College of Information Technology, Zayed University, UAE, zakaria.maamar@zu.ac.ae

Michael Mrissa PReCISE Research Center, University of Namur, Belgium, mmrissa@fundp.ac.be

Thomas Penin Department of Computer Science & Engineering, Shanghai Jiao Tong University, Shanghai, 200240, China, tpenin@apex.sjtu.edu.cn

John C. Platt Microsoft Corp, 1 Microsoft Way, Redmond, WA 98052, jplatt@microsoft.com

Hongwei Qi NEC Laboratories, China, 14/F, Bldg. A, Innovation Plaza, Tsinghua Science Park, Beijing 100084, China, qihongwei@research.nec.com.cn

Sebastian Schaffert Salzburg Research Forschungsgesellschaft, Knowledge Based Information Systems, Jakob-Haringer Strasse 5/II, A-5020 Salzburg, Austria, sebastian.schaffert@salzburgresearch.at

Nigel Shadbolt Intelligence, Agents, Multimedia Group, School of Electronics and Computer Science, University of Southampton, Southampton, SO17 1BJ, UK, nrsg@ecs.soton.ac.uk

Vincent Y. Shen Department of Computer Science and Engineering, Hong Kong University of Science and Technology, Hong Kong, shen@cse.ust.hk

Quan Z. Sheng School of Computer Science, The University of Adelaide, Australia, qsheng@cs.adelaide.edu.au

Jack W. Stokes Microsoft Corp, 1 Microsoft Way, Redmond, WA 98052, jstokes@microsoft.com

Philippe Thiran PReCISE Research Center, University of Namur and Louvain School of Management, Belgium, pthiran@fundp.ac.be

Florian A. Twaroch Cardiff University, UK, f.a.twaroch@cs.cf.ac.uk

Denny Vrandečić Institute AIFB, Universität Karlsruhe D-76128 Karlsruhe, Germany, dvr@aifb.uni-karlsruhe.de

Haofen Wang Department of Computer Science & Engineering, Shanghai Jiao Tong University, Shanghai, 200240, China, fwhfcarter@apex.sjtu.edu.cn

Erik Wilde School of Information, UC Berkeley, Berkeley, CA, USA, dret@berkeley.edu

Guirong Xue Department of Computer Science & Engineering, Shanghai Jiao Tong University, Shanghai, 200240, China, grxue@apex.sjtu.edu.cn

Yong Yu Department of Computer Science & Engineering, Shanghai Jiao Tong University, Shanghai, 200240, China, yyug@apex.sjtu.edu.cn

Jian Yu School of Computer Science, The University of Adelaide, Australia, jyu01@adelaide.edu.au

Part I
Web Services

Classification of Automated Search Traffic

Greg Buehrer, Jack W. Stokes, Kumar Chellapilla and John C. Platt

Abstract As web search providers seek to improve both relevance and response times, they are challenged by the ever-increasing tax of automated search query traffic. Third party systems interact with search engines for a variety of reasons, such as monitoring a web site's rank, augmenting online games, or possibly to maliciously alter click-through rates. In this paper, we investigate automated traffic (sometimes referred to as *bot* traffic) in the query stream of a large search engine provider. We define automated traffic as any search query not generated by a human in real time. We first provide examples of different categories of query logs generated by automated means. We then develop many different features that distinguish between queries generated by people searching for information, and those generated by automated processes. We categorize these features into two classes, either an interpretation of the physical model of human interactions, or as behavioral patterns of automated interactions. Using the these detection features, we next classify the query stream using multiple binary classifiers. In addition, a multiclass classifier is then developed to identify subclasses of both normal and automated traffic. An active learning algorithm is used to suggest which user sessions to label to improve the accuracy of the multiclass classifier, while also seeking to discover new classes of automated traffic. Performance analysis are then provided. Finally, the multiclass classifier is used to predict the subclass distribution for the search query stream.

1 Introduction

The Web has quickly become the *de facto* method for general information gathering. This transition has allowed web search to grow into a multi-billion dollar industry in only a few years. In addition, the proliferation of the web has allowed web search to become an environment for cultivating advancements along many dimensions of research. One such dimension is adversarial informal retrieval, and in particular spam detection. Two common types of spam are email spam and link

G. Buehrer (✉)
Microsoft Corp, 1 Microsoft Way, Redmond, WA 98052
e-mail: buehrer@microsoft.com

I. King, R. Baeza-Yates (eds.), *Weaving Services and People on the World Wide Web*,
DOI 10.1007/978-3-642-00570-1_1,

spam. Email spam is designed to return the receiver to a location in which he would then be coaxed into purchasing a product, relinquishing his bank passwords, etc. This type of email is almost always automated. One study suggested that 85% of all email spam, which constitutes well more than half of all email, is generated by only six botnets.[1] With link spam, the generator is attempting to manipulate the search engine towards the end goal of improving its rank in the search results. The generator adds hyperlinks on web pages so as to imply the target page is important, since many since engines use PageRank [4] as an importance metric. For example, a high number of automatically generated web pages can be employed to redirect static rank to a small set of paid sites [7].

In this paper, we focus our attention on an understudied form of automation, namely automated web search engine queries. We define legitimate search queries as those queries entering the system which are typed by a human to gather information. Then, all other traffic is deemed automated traffic. Automated search traffic is of significant concern because it hampers the ability of large scale systems to run efficiently, and it lowers patron satisfaction by hindering relevance feedback. Because search engines are open for public consumption, there are many automated systems which make use of the service.

A *bot* – the entity generating the automated traffic – may submit queries for a variety of reasons, most of which are benign and not overly monetizable. As an example, rank bots periodically scrape web pages to determine the current ranking for a <query,URL> pair. A Search Engine Optimization company (SEO) may employ a rank bot to evaluate the efficacy of his web page ranking optimizations for his clients. If a client's current rank is low, a user may need to generate many *NEXT_PAGE* requests to find it in the search engine's results. Since SEOs can have many clients, this practice can result in a significant amount of traffic for a single userId. The traffic of a typical bot is depicted in Fig. 1. This bot queries approximately every 7 s from midnight to about 6A.M., then at a slightly slower rate (approximately every 30 s) for the rest of the day. The total number of queries is about 4,500, far more than a human would do in normal browsing.

Correctly separating legitimate queries from automated queries can improve the end user experience in a number of ways. First, search latency can be reduced for legitimate queries; the search engine company may wish to throttle users to improve the Quality of Service (QoS) for interactive users. By reducing the total traffic serviced, or by reordering requests, response times for human users could be lowered (or maintained with less hardware). In addition, some search engines may consider click-through data implicit feedback on the relevance of a URL for a given query [13, 14]. This feedback may then be used to modify the rankings of the associated URLs. This may extend beyond explicit clicks, and include the absence of a click, such as to demote the URL of all results which were not clicked. Conversely, if the fourth result is clicked three times as often as the first result for a given query, it may imply that the fourth result is ranked too low. However, this

[1] http://computerworld.co.nz/news.nsf/scrt/C70ED4E3A608806CCC25740100186FC6

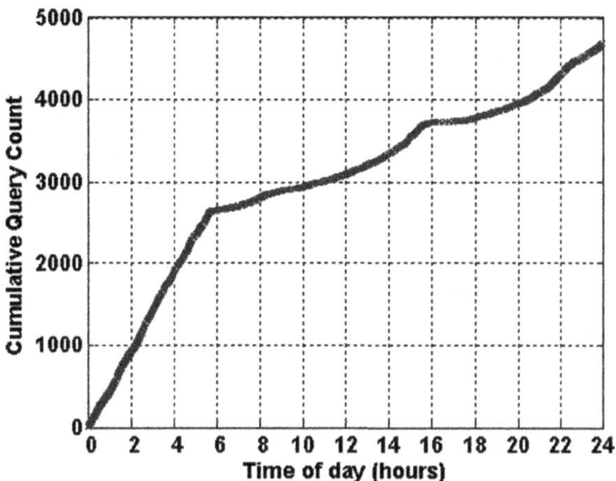

Fig. 1 A graph depicting *time of day* vs. *aggregate queries* for a typical bot

form of ranking is as susceptible to malicious behavior as link ranking algorithms – an SEO could easily generate a bot to click on his clients' URLs. This form of automatically clicking links is commonly referred to as click fraud. Click fraud for paid search results has been a challenge for some time [5, 11, 13]. This activity may involve rival companies automating click activity on paid search results and banner ads in an attempt to increase an opponent's marketing costs. Another source of click fraud occurs when illegitimate businesses attempt to pose as intermediate search engines who host ads and forward illegitimate click traffic. Recently, a study by Click Forensics reported that click fraud for paid results in the 4th quarter of 2007 represents over 16% of all ad click traffic, up 15% from the same quarter of 2006.[2] In particular, the report notes that search engine ads experience a fraud rate of 28.3%. Other reports suggest a lower fraud rate, closer to 6% [5], which is still rather high.

In this paper, we target automated traffic and clicks for unpaid results, which do not have the potential benefit of using conversion rates (e.g. Cost-Per-Action metrics) as secondary indicators [11] for legitimate activity. Detecting automated traffic can be difficult for several reasons. To begin with, the identification of user sessions is not trivial. One method to achieve this is through the use of cookies. A cookie is placed on the user's machine whenever the browser visits the site. Some users do not allow cookies, so each visit to the site appears to be a new user. In this case, the IP address of the request can be used, if there is sufficient confidence that the IP address is not a shared resource. In this work, we assume the ability to identify sessions. A second challenge in detecting automated traffic is that it may not be clear, even to a panel of experts viewing the queries, whether the source is automated. Although current techniques used to automatically query search engines can be relatively simple, sophisticated botnets certainly improve the ability of the programmer to mimic human traffic patterns [6]. Finally, as with most adversarial

[2] http://www.clickforensics.com/Pages/Releases.aspx?r=01312008

challenges, the behavior of the adversary changes over time. This suggests that specific signature-based solutions are only effective in the near term. For example, a bot may use the same IP address for an extended period of time, permitting a short term solution of ignoring traffic from that address. These types of practical solutions lead to black lists for IP addresses, user agents, referrers, etc., which must be constantly updated by the search engine. However, if the bot is run from a different IP address, may be incorrectly labeled as normal traffic.

In this paper, we investigate both binary classification as well as multiclass classification, via subgroups of both normal and bot traffic (e.g. *SpamBot*, *AdultBot*). The goal of this work is to quickly discover new classes of query streams while simultaneously improving the accuracy of the resulting classifiers. Active learning is combined with multimodal anomaly detection to achieve this goal. In active learning for classifier training, a ranked list of items is provided for the analyst to label; labeling the samples at the top of the list improves the performance of the algorithm by some measure. In the past, active learning has been to shown to significantly increase the accuracy of a classifier by having the analyst label samples which are closest to one of the decision boundaries. A classifier is least certain of the class label of these samples – labeling them provides the most information for the next round of classifier training.

Instead of trying to learn a classifier to detect automated bot traffic, we could instead use anomaly detection. In typical anomaly detection algorithms, a model of the "Normal" behavior is learned. For the problem addressed in this paper, traffic which does not belong to the normal class is assigned to the automated bot traffic class. Typical anomaly detection algorithms often fail when it is difficult to learn a model which adequately describes all normal traffic. Instead, we learn separate models for each class of search query traffic. To discover new classes, active anomaly detection is also used. In active anomaly detection, samples are labeled which are the most anomalous for each class of traffic. By searching for new classes of traffic, we seek to quickly discover new ways that automated bots are querying the system. For malicious bot traffic, query patterns can change quickly. In the final algorithm (presented in Sect. 6), we combine active learning for classifier training and active anomaly detection to yield an algorithm which both discovers new classes of search query traffic and also produces individual classifiers which are highly accurate.

This paper makes the following contributions.

- A large-scale study of search engine traffic (100M requests) is performed.
- Several real-world bot patterns are described.
- Based on the study, a set of discriminating features is presented, designed to separate automated traffic from human traffic.
- A preliminary evaluation is performed, using both binary classification as well as multiclass classification.

The remainder of the paper is organized as follows. Related work is provided in Sect. 2. In Sect. 3, we describe the search query data used in this study. Sect. 4 describes behavioral features of current-day bots. In Sect. 5, we provide details of our proposed features. We partition the features into two groups, namely physical model features and behavioral features. In Sect. 6, we describe an algorithm based on active learning which can be used to label search query traffic in order to both increase a multiclass classifier's accuracy as well as discover new types of traffic. Experimental results are provided in Sect. 7. We then conclude in the final section.

2 Related Work

Relatively little work has specifically targeted classification of automated traffic in query logs. Agichtein, Brill, Dumais and Ragno developed models depicting user behavior for web search [1]. In this work, the authors are primarily interested in modeling users to guide relevance rankings, but some of these features could be used to partition humans from automated traffic as well. They point out that users provide more than click-through data when interacting with search engines. The authors consider deviations from normal behaviors, such as large increases in click-through rates for <query,URL> pairs. In addition, they incorporate page dwell time, query reformulation, and query length, among other features.

Research which studies click fraud in sponsored search results has examined traffic patterns and user behavior. These works do not address bot traffic with respect to organic results, but they do offer insight into the nature of the query stream. Daswani, et al. [6] dissect a large click botnet called ClickBot.A and describe its functionality and technique in detail, with accompanying source code. The botnet is of particular interest because it exhibits controlled execution so as to avoid detection, while still generating significant fraudulent impact. It replicates client bots on over 100,000 machines, each of which have a separate IP address and only click on at most 20 items. The authors do not provide a detection method.

A report by Tuzhilin [13] describes the challenges and issues with click fraud detection. In the report, the author concludes that Google, Inc is taking sufficient steps towards mitigating click fraud. Techniques include both static analysis and dynamic analysis, although exact measures are not described. The report also discusses an alternate reward system, in which rather than employing a system based on click-through rates, it is more advantageous for both parties if conversion rates were employed instead. Schluessler, Goglin and Johnson [11] develop a client-side framework for detecting whether input data has been automatically generated. The technique targets online gaming, but also mentions that it can be used to address some forms of click fraud in online advertising.

Fetterly, Manasse and Najork [7] perform a similar study to our work to discover web link spam. They illustrate that statistical analysis of web page properties, in particular features such as out degree distributions, host-machine ratios, and near duplicate document clusters can provide significant lift in labeling portions of the web as spam or legitimate material. Anick [2] removes both known and suspected bots coming from internal AltaVista addresses for a study on web searcher behavior using terminological feedback. To eliminate bots traffic from a study on mobile web search, Kamvar and Baluja only considered traffic from a single large wireless carrier [9]. Karasaridis, Rexroad and Hoeflin [10] analyze the transport layer to discover IRC-based botnets attempting Denial-of-service attacks, among other malicious behavior. The method does not use signatures, instead monitoring ports for controller traffic patterns. The work does not investigate botnets attacking search engines.

The active learning algorithm used to label subclasses of search query traffic was originally proposed by Stokes et al. [12]. In this paper, subclasses of network traffic were analyzed using a multiclass classifier in order to discover new forms of malware running on computers in a large corporate network: the malware is detected from anomalous network packet transmissions to machines located on the global internet.

3 Data Set Description

In this section, we describe the data used in our study. We obtained a random sample of approximately 100M requests to a popular search engine from a single day (August 7, 2007). We sampled user queries, such that if a user is in our sample, then all his queries from that day are also included the sample. For this study, we further prune the data to include only users who query at least five times in the day, resulting in 46M requests.

In this study, users are sessionized with a cookie and assigned a userId. Thus, at times we will refer to a userId and the underlying query stream interchangeably. The same applies for the term *bot*, although in this case the stream has been deemed automated. It is also common to sessionize by the requesting IP address. Although in some cases a single IP will service multiple users (i.e. proxies), and in some cases a single user may request from several IPs (see Fig. 3), the technique of sessionizing by IP can be the basis for useful sessionization. It is possible for a single machine to produce both bot and human search engine traffic. In these cases, we do not attempt to separate multiple signals from a single cookie.

Finally, we offer some nomenclature. A query is an ordered set of keywords sent to the search engine. The engine then provides as a response an impression set (or simply impressions), which is a set of displayed results (both sponsored and organic). A query may have multiple requests, such as for result page two, upon which the engine will respond with additional impressions, e.g. the results for page two. Thus, the total number of requests may be more than the total number of queries. A click is always with respect to the impression presented to the user.

4 Qualitative Analysis

We now describe several bots discovered through the course of studying the query stream. While these are not inclusive, they are meant to present the reader with common forms of automated traffic. The first bot that we present scans the index for top spam words. Typically, the goal of improving a web site is to offer goods or services for financial gain; thus, a metric relating the query term to the other

Table 1 An example of a simple spam bot

Queries	
Managing your internal communities	Find your true love
Mailing list archives	Book your mountain resort
Studnet loan bill	Agreement forms online
Your dream major	Based group captive convert video from
Computer degrees from home	Products from thousands
Free shipping coupon offers	mtge market share slips

terms often found in email and/or web spam may be an indication that the query is generated by a bot. This class of bot rarely clicks, often has many queries, and most words have high correlation with typical spam. An example of 12 queries from one particular spam bot are presented in Table 1.

A second bot, which has a similar pattern of a large number of queries without clicking, but a different bag of words is a finance bot. Eighteen sample queries are presented in Table 2. Most of the keywords in the query are associated with mortgages, credit, money and the housing industry in general. The goal of this bot is to ascertain which web sites are most correlated with these finance terms in the search index.

Some bot activity implies less benign intent. The bot whose queries appear in Table 3 seems to be querying the system for various URLs which are either web sites owned by spammers and operated as spam sites (e.g. http://adulthealth.longlovetabs.biz/cialis.htm) or web sites on legitimate, hijacked domains (e.g. http://astro.stanford.edu/form_1/buy_cialis_oneline.html) created to host spam. Presumably, the bot is attempting to boost its search engine rank. In the next example in Table 4, the

Table 2 An example of a finance bot

Queries		
2ndmortgage	Bestmortgagerate	2ndmortgage
1sttimehomebuyer	Badcreditloan	Equity
1sttimehomebuyer	Badcreditrefinance	Equityloans
Financinghouse	Debtconsolidation	Banks
Badcredithomeloan	Debtconsolidationloan	Financing
Badcreditmortgage	Financinghouse	Firstmortgage

Table 3 An example of a URL bot

Queries
http://astro.stanford.edu/forum/1/buy.cialis.online.html
http://adulthealth.longlovetabs.biz/cialis.htm
http://www.bigdrugstoreforyou.info?Viagra.cialis
http://www.cheap.diet.pills.online.info/drugs/pagemaker.html
http://dosap.info/d.php?search=ed,viagra,levitra,cialis
http://www.generic.viagra.cialis.levitra.info/index/cialis.php
http://www.pharmacydirectory.biz/submitlink5.html
http://www.get.prescriptions.online.biz/buy.viagra.online.htm
http://www.redloungebiz.section.gb?page=5

Table 4 An example of a real estate bot

Queries	
Maricopa kern broker	Monrovia los angeles broker
Martinez contra costa broker	Montague siskiyou broker
Mcfarland kern broker	Moorpark ventura broker
Mendota fresno broker	Moreno valley riverside broker
Menifee riverside broker	Moreno valley riverside broker
Menifee riverside broker	Newport beach orange broker
Merced merced broker	Norwalk los angeles broker
Mill valley marin broker	Orange orange broker
Millbrae san mateo broker	Orland glenn broker
Milpitas santa clara broker	Oroville butte broker

bot queries the search engine for mortgage broker keywords. The bot is attempting to find the top ten broker results for a large set of cities. This bot queried the search engine over 2,000 times in our one day random sample.

Some bots not only repeatedly query the system for information with respect to a particular category, but query in such a way that provides an unnatural signature. For example, the stock bot queries in Table 5 almost all are single keywords, and those keywords are primarily of length three or four. This bot appeared to be searching for financial news related to particular companies.

Another common bot scenario is when a userId sends queries from many different cities within a short amount of time. An example is shown in Table 6 (IP addresses have been coded to preserve anonymity). This userId sent 428 requests over a 4-h period, from 38 different cities. Also, the bot always uses the *NEXT_PAGE* button when available and never clicks on algorithmic results (search engine results).

Table 5 An example of a stock bot

Queries								
pae	cln	eu3	eem	olv	oj	lqde	igf	ief
nzd	rib	xil	nex	intc	tei	wfr	ssg	sqi
nq	trf	cl	dax	ewl	bbdb	csco	pl	idti
nesn	edf	intl	spx	ewj	tasr	ibkr	lat	hb1
mesa	edl	dram	iev	sndk	rukn	ifg	igv	ms

Table 6 An example of a bot with a single cookie but whose queries originate from many cities

Time	IP Address	City of origin
4:18:34 AM	IP1	Charlottesville, Virginia
4:18:47 AM	IP2	Tampa, Florida
4:18:52 AM	IP3	Los Angeles, California
4:19:13 AM	IP4	Johnson City, Tennessee
4:22:15 AM	IP5	Delhi, Delhi
4:22:58 AM	IP6	Pittsburgh, Pennsylvania
4:23:03 AM	IP7	Canton, Georgia
4:23:17 AM	IP8	St. Peter, Minnesota

The bot's queries had an unusually high number of adult terms. We suspect the userId is automating traffic through anonymous browsing tools, but oddly those tools did not account for machine cookies. It is not uncommon for a source of automated traffic and a legitimate user to originate from the same machine. In some cases, it may be botnet-related activity. However, a second common scenario is that the originator of the bot program is also using the search engine, possibly to set up the program. For example, a particular userId issued 6,534 queries, with only four clicks. Upon inspection, the four clicks were from the first five queries in the day, namely "pottery barn", "pottery barn kids", "pottery barn kids outlet", "pottery barn kids outlet store", and "pier 1". These queries spanned about 7 min, which is a typical usage pattern. The userId then issued 6,529 queries over the course of 3 h without a click - clearly bot activity.

In a final example, one userId issued the same query 1,892 times over the course of the day. Of those requests, 1,874 had click responses. A possible motive for a very high click rate is to glean why the top results are so ranked. Then, the user can improve the rank of his page by incorporating the discovered attributes. For example, if a user queries the index for "best flowers in San Francisco" and then scrapes the html of the top 1,000 impressions, he can find the most common keywords in those pages, their titles, etc. and incorporate them into his own site.

5 Quantitative Analysis

Table 7 provides an overview of our set of features for detecting automated traffic in the query stream. We generally classify these features into two groups. The first group is the result of considering a physical model of a human. The second group is a set of observed behaviors of current-day automated traffic. In the following two subsections, we investigate each feature in some detail. Histograms are built for each feature, which are normalized to 100,000 users. Areas of high bot class lift in

Table 7 A summary of the proposed query stream feature set

Name	Description	Type
Number of requests, queries, clicks	Number of requests, queries, clicks	Physical
Query rate	The max number of queries in any 10-s period	Physical
Number of IPs/location	Number of originating IPs/cities	Physical
Click-through rate	Ratio of queries to clicks	Behavioral
Alphabetical score	Alphanumeric ordering of queries, etc.	Behavioral
Spam score	Indicator that the keywords are associated with spam	Behavioral
Adult content score	Indicator that the keywords are pornographic	Behavioral
Keyword entropy	Informational entropy of query terms	Behavioral
Keyword length entropy	Informational entropy of query term lengths	Behavioral
Request time periodicity	Periodicity of requests, queries, clicks	Behavioral
Advanced syntax score	Number of advanced syntax terms in requests	Behavioral
Category entropy	Informational entropy of categories of queries	Behavioral
Reputation	Blacklisted IPs, user agents, country codes, etc.	Behavioral

the graphs are then circled. Thus, in the figures presented in this section, the vertical axes are counts of users for the feature, and the horizontal axes are discretized ranges of the values of that feature. In a few cases, we normalized to one million users to allow the areas of interest to be sufficiently displayed.

5.1 Physical Model Feature Set

In this section, we discuss several features which are designed to model the interaction of a user and the search engine. Humans have physical limitations for entering queries, reading the results, and clicking on URLs. For example, a typical person can only issue and absorb a few queries in any 10-s period. A user with 100 distinct requests in 10 s would lie outside the boundary of normal use. Search query traffic entered by automated means are not subject to these physical limitations. Thus, the following features may be used to discriminate between web search traffic from humans and automated bots.

5.1.1 Number of Queries, Clicks, Pageviews, Etc.

A strong first indicator of automated traffic is volume. Bots often submit many more queries (and possibly clicks) in a given day than the typical person. Volume represents a class of features for which simple aggregate statistics can provide insight into the class of a userId. For example, in Fig. 2 (left) we plot the distribution of the number of search queries from each unique user in our sample. While it is possible that a human user submits more than 200 queries in a given day, the histogram suggests it occurs with an unnatural probability. Upon inspection, we found that most of the traffic at this volume appeared automated. As an example, one userId queried the search engine for the term *mynet* 12,061 times during this day.

5.1.2 Query Rate

Since bots are automated, they often enter queries at a much higher rate than queries which have been entered on a keyboard by a human. Various statistics of the query rate such as the average, median, and maximum can help distinguish queries generated by bots versus humans. We studied the query rates for human traffic and

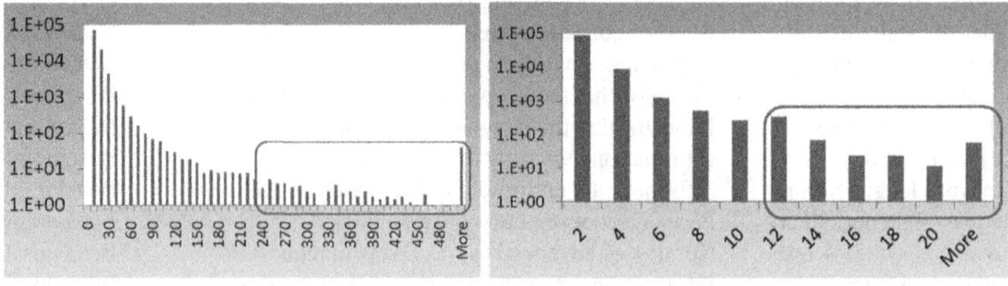

Fig. 2 Number of requests (*left*), and maximum requests in any 10 s interval (*right*)

concluded that humans rarely submit more than 7 requests in any 10-s interval. In Fig. 2 (right), we plot the distribution of the maximum queries for a user in any 10-s interval over the course of the day. The users falling into the circled area were by and large bot traffic.

5.1.3 Number of IP Addresses / Locations

A human cannot be in two distant places at the same time. We maintain a list of requester IP addresses used by each userId. The motivation is to discover potential bot nets. If a user's cookie is compromised by miscreants and is used to make queries from two or more IP addresses, possibly located across large geographical distances, or is used in an interleaved fashion from two IP locations again separated by significant distances, then the unique Id likely belongs to two or more computers each of which are owned by a botnet.[3] A second usage scenario is when a userId is querying the system through an anonymous browsing tool, but has not disabled cookies. When correlating IP addresses, care must be taken to allow for mobile computers and devices which are used in the morning in one city, but later in the day at one or more additional cities. Also, users accessing the internet via a dial-up modem are often assigned a new IP address by the internet service provider (ISP) each time the user logs into the internet service. As a result the feature must ignore small variances in geographic location. In Fig. 3 (left), we show a histogram of the number of users employing Multiple IP addresses (normalized to one million users). Figure 3 (right) depicts the same users wherein only the first two octets of an IP address are considered. This allows for multiple IP addresses in the same geographical region. We have highlighted the region where we moderate significant lift in bot classification. As an example, the bot in Table 6 would be flagged by this feature.

5.2 *Behavioral Feature Set*

The previous subsection introduces physical features that attempt to discriminate traffic generated by humans from that produced by automated means. However, automated search query traffic can be modeled to mimic human input. For these

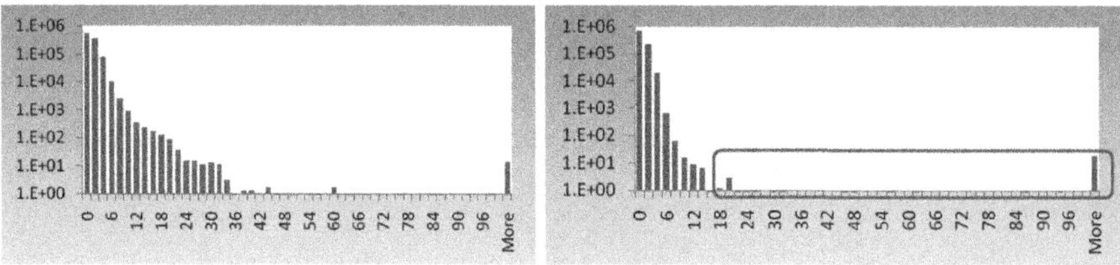

Fig. 3 Distinct IP address (all four octets) (*left*), and distinct IP address (first two octets) (*right*)

[3] http://www.hitslink.com/whitepapers/clickfraud.pdf

reasons we now provide additional features which seek to classify legitimate web search traffic generated by typical users from illegitimate traffic generated by automated means. In many cases, we will illustrate the efficacy of the feature with an example of a discovered bot.

5.2.1 Click-Through Rate

Much of automated traffic is likely used for informational gathering purposes, either to examine the search engine's index, or to collect data for self-use, and thus exhibits lower than typical click-through rates. Previously published click-through rates for humans vary, but most show that most users click at least once in ten queries. Our own inspection of the data suggests that many of the zero-click users are automated. Further, when used in conjunction with the total number of queries issued over the day, the feature provides very good lift. We illustrate this principle with two distributions, Fig. 4 (left and right, neither are log plots). In Fig. 4 (left), we plot click-through rates for all users in the sample with at least a modest number of queries. We then further prune the data to those users with ten times as many queries, shown in Fig. 4 (right). Clearly, as the number of queries increases, the percentage of zero-click users increases. This is counter-intuitive if we limit the study to human users, since each query has a non-zero probability for clicking. However, if we consider automated traffic, we can reason about this increase; most bots do not need to click on the results. Even in the case where the bot requires extended information about the URL target, the bot can be programmed to load this URL directly. Thus there are three typical bot click through rates; a bot that clicks on no links, a bot that clicks on every link, and a bot that only clicks on targeted links. Of these, the first is the most common by a wide margin.

As an example, one userId queried for 56,281 times without a single click. On the other extreme, a second userId made 1,162 requests and clicked each time. Upon inspection of the queries, it appeared the userId was downloading the html for each impression in the index for the keywords *168.216.com.tw*. Also, the userId in Sect. 4 who clicked on 1,874 out of 1,892 requests would also be discovered by this feature.

5.2.2 Alphabetical Ordering of Queries

We have identified a number of instances of bot-generated queries which have significant alphabetical ordering. It may be that the authors of the programs use the

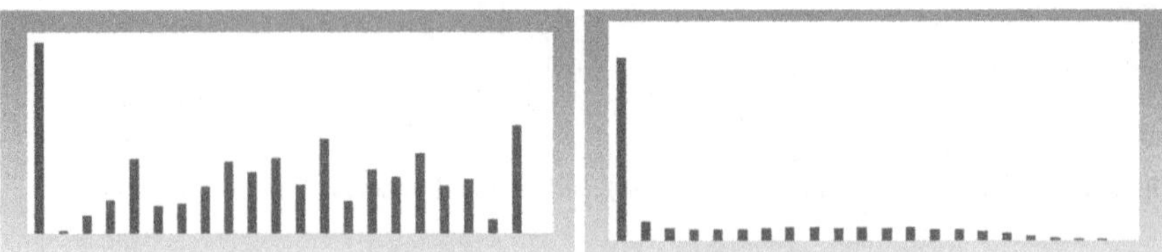

Fig. 4 Click-through rates, low minimum queries (*left*), and click-through rates, 10X minimum queries (*right*)

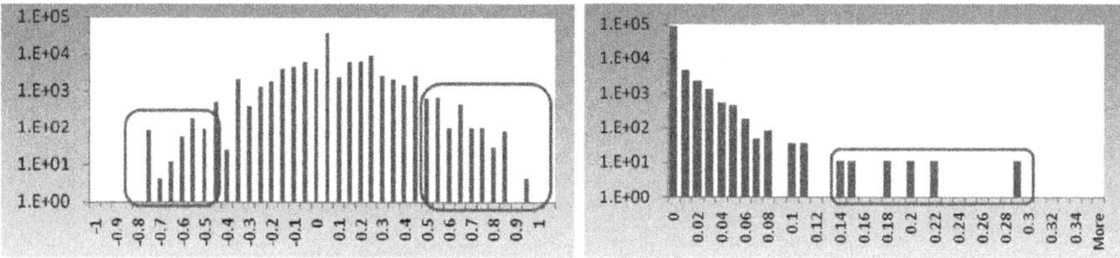

Fig. 5 Alphabetical scores (*left*), and spam scores (*right*)

alphabetical ordering for improved searching or analyzing. When submitted to the search engine, it is quite detectable. Returning to the bot in Table 4, we witness this behavior. To calculate an alphabetical score for a user, we order the queries chronologically and for each query pair $< i, i + 1 >$, we add 1 if $i + 1$ sorts after i, and subtract 1 if $i + 1$ sorts before i. This number is then normalized by the total number of queries. In the majority of cases, the alphabetical score is near zero, as shown in Fig. 5 (left). The discretization [−0.05,+0.05] has contains more than 50% of the mass in the distribution. In almost all cases where the user Id has more than a couple queries and the alphabet score was outside [−0.30,+0.30], we believe the traffic to be automated.

5.2.3 Spam Score

Spam bots submit spam words to a search engine such as the queries shown in Table 4. Consequently, a feature which estimates the amount of spam words in the search queries can be useful for detecting queries from spam bots. We compute a spam score as a feature using a bag of <spam word,weight> pairs for all queries for each userId. The weight assigns a probability that a given keyword is spam. For example, the term *Viagra* has a higher probability of being spam than the term *coffee*. In Fig. 5 (right) we show a normalized histogram of the spam score for queries received from individual cookies. The circled region in the histogram indicates userIds submitting queries containing large numbers of spam terms. Per user scores are generated by summing the keyword spam score for their queries.

5.2.4 Adult Content Score

The adult entertainment industry has taken to the web with vigor. Many in this industry attempt to attract new customers by directing users to web sites containing pornography. Adult content enterprises may employ bots to measure the ranking of their web site or try to boost their web site's rank in the search engine. Although it is also a common human query space, there is lift in relative adult query counts. Thus, bot generated queries often contain words associated with adult content. As with the spam score, we use another bag of <adult word,weight> pairs to compute an adult score for each userId. A normalized histogram is presented in Fig. 6 (left) where we have circled the region in the figure which offers significant lift for bot detection. Examples of discovered bots for this feature are omitted due to space constraints.

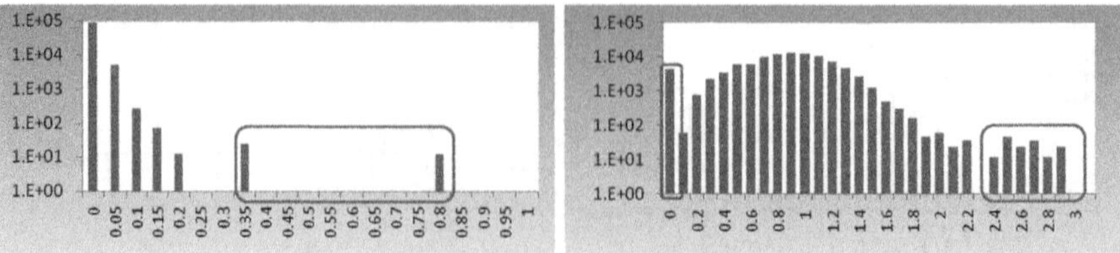

Fig. 6 Adult content scores (*left*), and query term entropy (*right*)

5.2.5 Query Keyword Entropy

Many bots enter queries that are extremely redundant; as a result, bot queries tend to have keyword entropies which fall outside normal usage patterns. We calculate a map of <word,count> pairs for each userId. We then use traditional informational entropy, H(k), to assign a score to each user

$$H(k) = E(I(k)) = -\sum_{i}\sum_{j} p(k_{ij}) \log_2 p(k_{ij}) \tag{1}$$

where k_{ij} is the jth keyword (i.e. query term) in the ith query submitted by a single userId. In Fig. 6 (right), we plot the distribution of the entropy of keywords in the set of queries issued by users. In one example of a low keyword entropy bot, a user queried *mynet* 10,497 times, generating an entropy of zero.

5.2.6 Query Word Length Entropy

Typical query terms have a natural word length entropy distribution, as does the length of a typical query. Some bots query for specific classes of words which are outliers of this distribution. For example, the word length entropy for the stock bot shown in Table 5 will have a lower word length entropy compared to that for a typical human. The word length entropy WLE is calculated as

$$WLE(l_{ij}) = -\sum_{i}\sum_{j} l_{ij} \log_2(l_{ij}) \tag{2}$$

where i is the index for each separate query submitted to the search engine by a single userId and l_{ij} is the length of the individual query term j in the ith query. The word length entropy is shown in Fig. 7 (left, normalized to 1M users). One could also have as a feature the longest query in the session.

5.2.7 Query Time Periodicity

It is not uncommon for a bot to generate traffic at regular intervals, such as every 15 min [6]. To capture this property, we sort requests by request time for each user, and calculate the difference in time between successive entries. For each observed

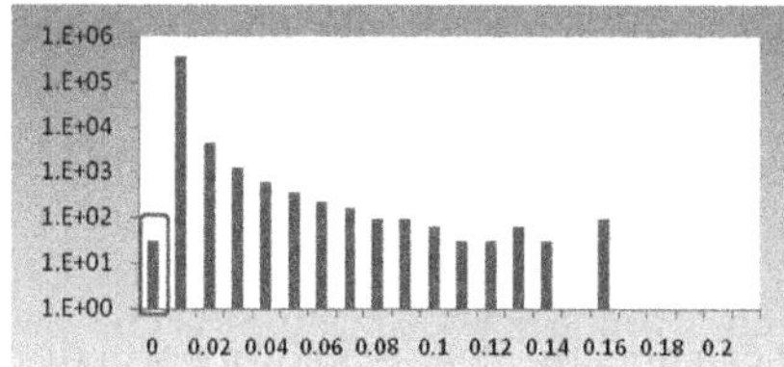

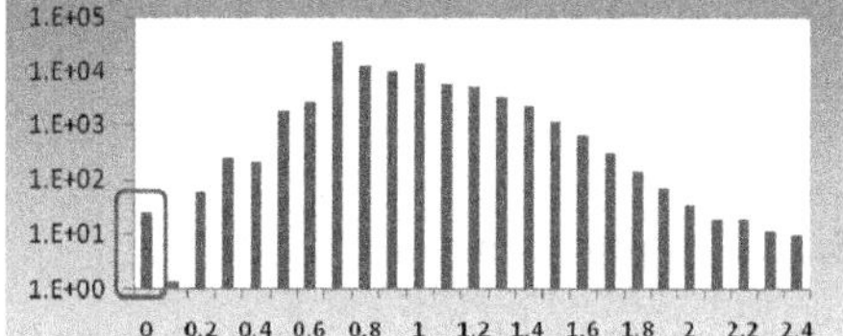

Fig. 7 Keyword length entropy (*left*), and query period entropy (*right*)

delta, we record the number of occurrences for each user. We then calculate the informational entropy of the deltas (a second option would be to calculate an FFT score for each user). This can be done at a variety of granularities for time deltas (seconds, 10 s, minutes, etc). The distribution for seconds can be seen in Fig. 7 (right). This feature can be used to investigate dwell time (the number of seconds spent on a clicked URL) [1]. When combined with other features, such as the number of requests, it has the potential to provide significant lift. For example, a userId with 30 queries may not appear automated based on request count alone, but if the entropy for time deltas is zero, it is much more likely to be a bot.

5.2.8 Advanced Query Syntax

Some bots use advanced syntax to probe particular features of the index. For example, prefixing a query with "*intitle:* for many search engines will force results to have the listed keywords as part of the title of the web page. Similarly, *inURL:* will restrict results to those URLs which have the keywords embedded into the URL. To discover bots which use advanced query syntax, we keep a total count of all advanced terms for each user throughout the day. A histogram is shown in Fig. 8. Less than 1/10th of 1% of users use more than 5 advanced terms in the sample. As an example of a bot, one user had 110 queries, all of which requested the terms appear in the title of the web page.

5.2.9 Category Entropy

As a generalization of both adult content score and spam score, we can define a feature which captures the number of distinct categories associated with a userId.

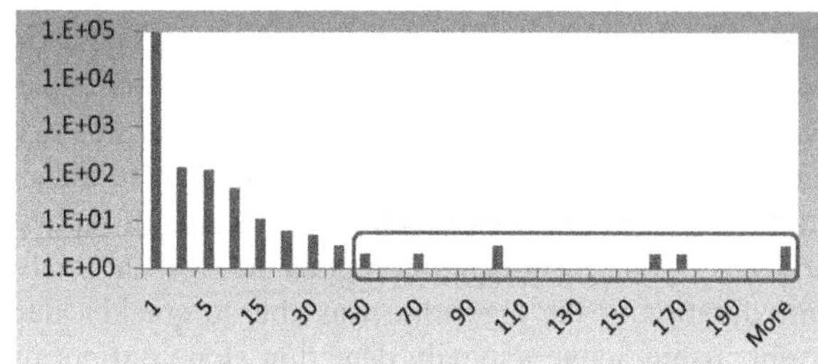

Fig. 8 Advanced query term scores

We use a category hierarchy to assign a category to each query. We then track the category entropy for each userId.

5.2.10 Reputations and Trends

There are several fields in the query logs that can directly identify known bot activity. Examples include blacklisted IP addresses, blacklisted user agents, and particular country codes. Tables are built for each property using domain expertise. For these cases, we simply perform a lookup into these tables at runtime. In less direct cases, query and query-click probability lists are used. For example, some bots search rare queries inordinately often. We often see sessions where each query is nonsensical. To detect these bots, a table of query-frequency pairs can be used to evaluate the popularity of the sessions queries. Finally, a table of <query,URL> click pairs can be stored to evaluate the probability that the user will click on a particular page. Users who often click on very low probability pairs are then deemed suspect. A potential weakness of these last two features is that a separate process is required to update the tables on a regular basis, and the tables can be somewhat large.

6 Active Learning for High Classifier Accuracy and Rare-Class Discovery

In the previous sections, we provide numerous physical and behavioral features which can discriminate human from automated search query traffic. In this section, we discuss an algorithm based on active learning which can be used to provide labeled queries to train a multiclass classifier in order to detect subclasses within the search query stream. In general, an active learning algorithm is simply one that can make oracle queries as to the labels of a small number of data points. While it may be expensive to label a "large" set of data, we assume an analyst is available to label a limited number of queries. The proposed algorithm seeks to quickly identify new subclasses of *Normal* and *Bot* traffic while simultaneously improving the accuracy of the resulting multiclass classifier. Using active learning, a ranked list of items is provided to the analyst to label; labeling the samples at the top of the list improves the performance of the algorithm by some measure. Active learning is typically used to reduce the number of samples needed to train a classifier and has been shown to outperform classifier training based on randomly sampled items. The active learning algorithm used in this paper was originally proposed to discover new forms of malware based on outbound network behavior on a large corporate network [12]. In the earlier work, the original goal was to combine active learning and anomaly detection (active anomaly detection) to discover new classes of network traffic which might correspond to new forms of malware transmitting information collected from an infected computer back to the malware host server. While the first iteration of the algorithm was able to quickly identify new forms of network traffic, using active anomaly detection alone did not produce classifiers with high accuracy for small amounts of labeled data for a particular class. To overcome this problem, active anomaly detection was combined with standard active learning to produce a framework which both discovers new classes in a data set while learning a multiclass classifier with high classification accuracy.

By discovering new classes of queries, we seek to gain the following:

- Discover new forms of automated bot and normal search query activity in the vast amounts of data processed by a production search engine.
- Understand the distribution of different types of bot activity in a typical day of search engine queries.
- Train a multiclass classifier and compare the performance with a simpler, binary classifier (i.e. two-class *Normal, Bot*).

As described in Sect. 3, a day's worth of search traffic was collected from a production search engine and converted into a set of items (feature vectors) corresponding to each userId. Each item, **x**, is composed of a subset of the individual search query features described earlier. For this problem, all of the features are continuous quantities and the log of each feature is modeled with a univariate Gaussian distribution.

The algorithm described in Figs. 9 and 10 with pseudo code provided in Fig. 11 is now briefly reviewed for the problem of discovering new classes of normal and automated search queries; interested readers should consult [12] for additional details. A classifier is first trained using a set of labeled items (i.e. aggregated search query feature vectors) indicated by the larger dots in Fig. 10. In this work, we use multiclass logistic regression [3] trained with stochastic gradient descent, although other supervised algorithms (e.g. Support Vector Machine (SVM), naive Bayes) could be

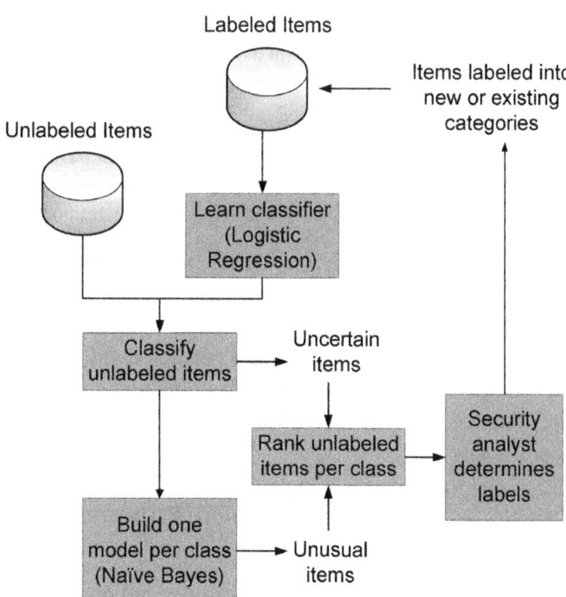

Fig. 9 The algorithmic architecture for discovering new classes of search query traffic

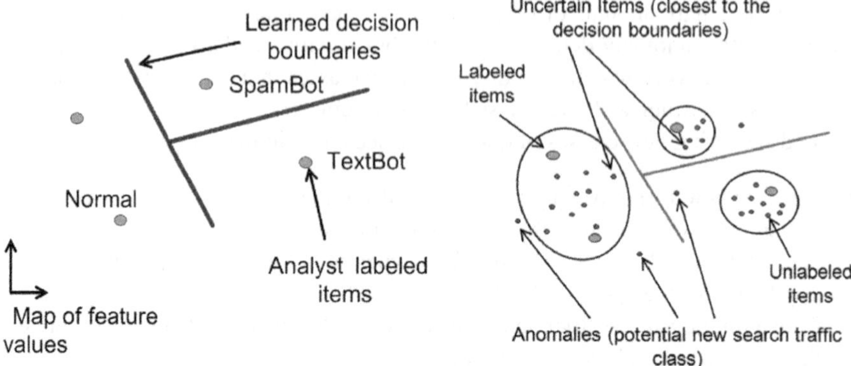

Fig. 10 The *left figure* shows the result of training a classifier: decision boundaries in input space are hyperplanes. The *right figure* shows the selection of the anomalies and uncertain items by the per-class models

---

1. Learn a classifier on the labeled samples
2. Evaluate the classifier and a certainty score C, (i.e. the margin), for each of the unlabeled samples
3. Assign all unlabeled samples to the most likely category
4. Compute the model parameters (mean, variance, or histogram) for every $P(\mathbf{x}|c)$
5. Compute an anomaly score A, how likely the sample is to belong to the class, for all unlabeled samples
6. Select the next group of samples to be labeled choosing as follows, sweeping through the categories:

   a. select the next, most anomalous unlabeled sample with the highest anomaly score in each class
   b. OR, select the sample with the smallest certainty score for each class
   c. if not enough samples for a class are found from 6a) or 6b) select the unlabeled sample with the next highest output probability $P(c|\mathbf{x})$ corresponding to the desired class c

7. Repeat step 6 until the desired number of samples have been labeled for the iteration

---

Fig. 11 One iteration of the proposed active-learning training algorithm, as pseudo code

used for this step. Multiclass logistic regression produces a set of linear hyperplanes which partitions the high-dimensional feature space. Once the multiclass classifier has been learned, the class labels for all of the unlabeled items, indicated by the smaller dots in Fig. 10, are then predicted. In addition, an certainty score C (i.e. the margin) is computed for each unlabeled sample which provides a measure of the distance from the labeled sample to the closest decision boundary. The certainty score is given by

$$C = \min_{i,j \neq i} |P(i|\mathbf{x}) - P(j|\mathbf{x})|, \qquad (3)$$

for item $\mathbf{x}$ and classes i and j where $i = \arg\max_k(P(k|\mathbf{x}))$.

Afterwards, a generative model is learned *for each class* by combining labeled items with the predicted labels from the unlabeled items belonging to the class. In our work, we learn a naive Bayes model for each class allowing us to compute an anomaly score A which estimates how likely each unlabeled item is to belong to its model. For naive Bayes, the anomaly score can be computed for item $\mathbf{x}$ predicted to belong to class c by taking the negative of the sum of the log of the probabilities (i.e. log-likelihood) for each feature f, as

$$A = -\log P(\mathbf{x}|\text{class } c) = -\sum_{f} \log P(x_f|\text{class } c), \tag{4}$$

where a large anomaly score indicates a low probability (anomalous) item. The unlabeled items are then ranked for an analyst to label. The ranking is performed in a round-robin fashion where a set containing a single item from each class is chosen during one iteration of the algorithm for an analyst to review. The round-robin nature of the algorithm (i.e odd, even iterations) is illustrated by the two output arrows emerging from the "Classify unlabeled items" block in Fig. 9, and the ranking metrics are illustrated on the right side of Fig. 10. For the odd iterations, a set of queries containing one anomaly for each class (the sample with the next highest anomaly score) is presented to the analyst. The anomalies for each class are unlabeled items which may belong to a new class of bot or human search query traffic; this iteration facilitates new class discovery. For the even iterations of the labeling process, the set containing the most uncertain item for each class is then presented to the analyst for labeling. These unlabeled, uncertain items lie closest to one of the decision boundaries and are indicated by the sample with the next smallest certainty score. If the decision boundaries are incorrect, these uncertain items may actually belong to another class. Labeling these items will improve classification accuracy compared to labeling a random unlabeled item predicted to belong to the class.

After the weights for the classifier have been trained using logistic regression, new incoming search queries can be then evaluated. Evaluation for logistic regression is extremely fast and is easily parallelizable. As a result downstream processing can have an accurate prediction of the type of normal or bot traffic received from a userId.

7 Experimental Results

In this section, we investigate the experimental performance of both the binary (i.e. *Normal*, *Bot*) and well as the multiclass search query classifier. We labeled 370 different user sessions using the active learning framework described in Sect. 6. The process discovered eight classes of search traffic shown in Table 8. Using the 370 labeled user sessions as an oracle, we simulate how fast the active learning system would discover all of the classes in Fig. 12. We first randomly select 10 sessions which yields 3 classes of search query traffic. Having the oracle label 20 sessions

Table 8 The labeled multiclass data set – note that the amounts are distinct

Class	Type	Amount
Base Normal	Normal	205
AdultSurfer	Normal	12
Base Bot	Bot	100
TrackBackBot	Bot	7
TextBot	Bot	15
SpamBot	Bot	10
AlphaBot	Bot	12
AdultBot	Bot	9

per iteration, we see that the algorithm has identified the remaining 5 classes in 3 iterations (i.e. 60 labeled sessions).

From Table 8, the *AdultSurfer* class contains search queries from a human searching for adult content; the Adult Content feature is useful for detecting items belonging to the *AdultSurfer* class. The remainder of the search queries entered by typical human users are represented by the *Normal* class. Including the main *Bot* class, there are six bot types. The *AlphaBot* contains queries which have a large number of consecutive searches which are in alphabetical order and use the Alphabet Score as the primary feature for detection. A *TextBot* contains large amounts of random text submitted to the search engine: the keyword entropy feature is highly indicative of a *TextBot*. In addition to being a strong feature for the *AdultSurfer* class, the Adult Content feature is useful for detecting *AdultBots*: bots which typically submit a large number of queries containing adult keywords. Other physical and behavioral features also help to further separate instances of these two classes. The Spam Content feature is helpful for detecting *SpamBots* which submit queries containing many different types of spam terms. A *TrackBackBot* contains queries which usually contain the terms *trackback address* or *trackback from your own site*. Adding additional features to detect these specific keywords would significantly improve

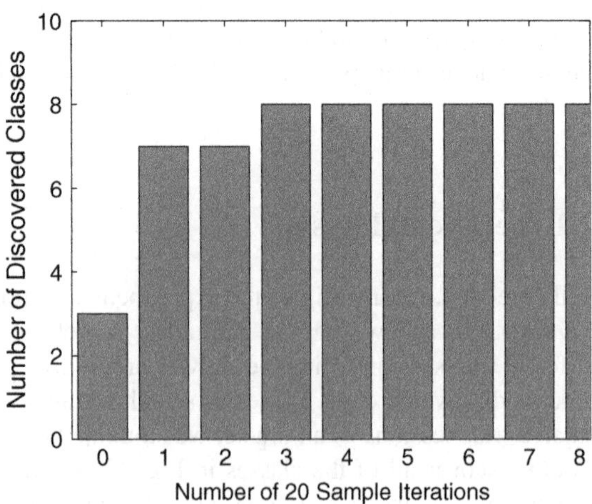

Fig. 12 The number of discovered classes using proposed active learning algorithm

the accuracy of detecting the *TrackBackBot* class. Finally, all remaining automated traffic is currently grouped in the *Bot* class. It is noted that not all of the Bot types described in Sect. 4 were discovered by this process, most likely due to insufficient labeled data.

We note that this distribution is artificially skewed towards an equal amount of Bot and Normal traffic because the active learning suggests userIds for labeling which do not lie in the mass of previously discovered classes. Also, a larger set of labeled sessions would improve confidence.

7.1 Binary Classification Results

We report binary classification results provided by the publicly available Weka toolset [8] (default options in all cases), as shown in Table 9. In all cases, we used 10-fold cross validation. We consider automated traffic labeled as automated traffic to be a true positive, noted as TP. Most of the classifiers chosen afforded about 90% accuracy on this small labeled, data set. Bagging with trees was the most accurate at 93%.

We also used Weka's attribute evaluator to gain insight into the relative benefits of each feature, namely Information Gain using the Ranker search method. The top four features in order were query count, query entropy, max requests per 10 s, click through rate, and spam score, with ranks of 0.70, 0.39. 0.36, 0.32, and 0.29. As suspected, volume is a key indicator of present-day automated activity.

Table 9 The binary classification results using proposed feature set and Weka

Classifier	TP	TN	FP	FN	Percent correct
AdaBoost	123	207	10	30	89
ADTree	131	201	16	22	90
BaggingTrees	135	209	8	18	93
Bayes Net	130	202	15	23	90
Logistic Regression	126	211	6	26	91
Nave Bayes	131	201	16	22	90
PART	129	199	18	24	87

7.2 Multiclass Classification Results

We now employ Weka to classify in the multiclass case. If we consider exact class matches, then the accuracy is lowered considerably, as is shown in Table 10. The highest accuracy is 83% afforded by Logistic Regression.

However, as shown in the confusion matrix[4] in Table 11, the accuracy of Logistic Regression is 89% if we consider any Bot userId labeled as any Bot type as correct.

[4] A confusion matrix shows the count of the correctly classified instances (values on the diagonal) as well as the count of the misclassified instances (values off the diagonal).

Table 10 The multiclass classification results using proposed feature set and Weka

Classifier	Percent correct
AdaBoost	76
BaggingTrees	81
Bayes Net	78
Logistic Regression	83
Nave Bayes	71
PART	82
RandomForest	82

Table 11 The confusion matrix for the multiclass case, using logistic regression as the classifier

A	B	C	D	E	F	G	H	← Classified As
6	1	0	0	3	0	0	0	**A = SpamBot**
1	5	0	0	1	0	2	0	**B = AdultBot**
0	0	3	0	2	0	0	1	**C = TrackBack**
0	0	0	195	6	0	2	2	**D = Normal**
2	1	2	19	71	2	1	2	**E = Bot**
0	0	0	0	2	13	0	0	**F = TextBot**
0	1	0	1	0	1	9	0	**G = AdultSurfer**
0	0	0	3	4	0	1	4	**H = AlphaBot**

For example, examining row E, the Bot row, we can see that of the 29 misclassified elements, 9 are actually classified as a Bot subclass. Similarly, 4 of the 8 misclassified Alphabots were classified as some other Bot type. We then ran the classifier on a large subset of the data described in Sect. 3. The relative Bot distribution is shown in Fig. 13 (scaled to 1M userIds); the vast majority of bots were not classified as a distinct Bot subclass. It is reasonable to argue that for many of the Bot subclasses, there are insufficient samples to predict accurately. One avenue for further study would be to label much more data, and retrain the classifier.

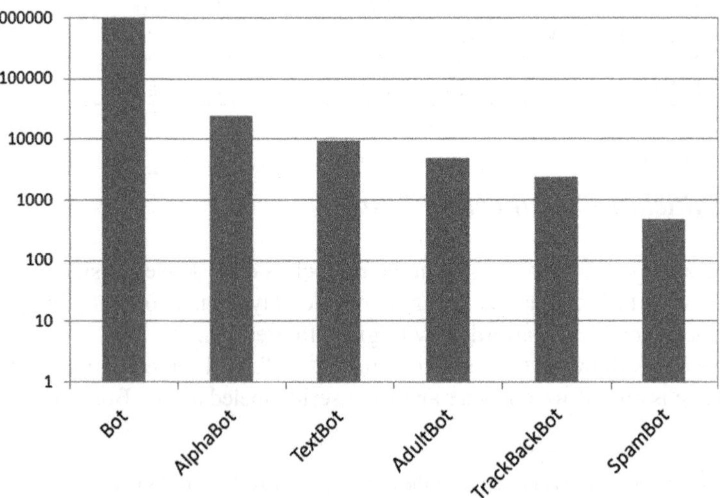

Fig. 13 The predicted distribution of bot traffic for sessionized userIds

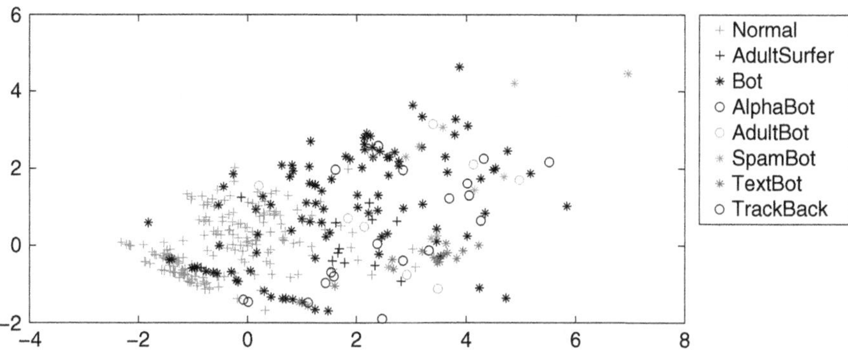

Fig. 14 The multiclass query projection using principle component analysis

We now investigate how well the multiple classes separate when projected onto the two largest basis functions using principle component analysis (PCA). The covariance matrix was first computed using all of the samples from both the labeled and unlabeled collections. The resulting projection of the labeled data is shown in Fig. 14. The items from the *Normal* class and the *AdultSurfer* do cluster relatively well on the left side of the figure, but overall there is not significant correlation. For PCA, the different classes of automated traffic tend to overlap.

8 Conclusions

In this paper, we provided an investigation of web query traffic received from a large-scale production search engine. Separating automated traffic from human traffic is useful from both a relevance perspective as well as a performance perspective. To this end, a set of repurposeable features has been proposed to model the physical interaction of a user as well as the behavior of current day automated traffic. An analysis of the distributions of these features indicated they can be used as a basis for labeling search engine query streams accordingly. We then described a framework for active anomaly detection, which can be used to discover distinct subclasses of automated traffic. An empirical study suggests that while classification is more accurate in the binary case, information can be gleaned by investigating subclasses. We are investigating several avenues which may improve the proposed feature set, for example analysis over a longer time range (one month), and the evolution of a user's query stream over time.

References

1. Agichtein, E., Brill, E., Dumais, S., and Ragno, R.: Learning User Interaction Models for Predicting Web Search Result Preferences, In *SIGIR'06*, 29th International ACM Conference on Research and Development on Information Retrieval, 2006. (ACM, New York, NY) pp 3–10.
2. Anick, P.: Using Terminological Feedback for Web Search Refinement – A Log-based Study., In *SIGIR'03*, 26th International ACM Conference on Research and Development on Information Retrieval, 2003. (ACM, New York, NY) pp 88–95.

3. Bishop, C.: *Pattern Recognition and Machine Learning*. (Springer, New York, NY, 2006).
4. Brin, S., and Page, L.: The Anatomy of a Large-scale Hypertextual Web Search Engine, In *WWW'98*, 7th International Conference on World Wide Web, 1998. (Elsevier Science Publishers B. V., Amsterdam, The Netherlands) pp 107–117.
5. Click Quality Team, Google, Inc. How Fictitious Clicks Occur in Third-Party Click Fraud Audit Reports. http://www.google.com/adwords/ReportonThird-PartyClickFraudAuditing.pdf, 2006.
6. Daswani, N., Stoppelman, M., and the Google Click Quality and Security Teams: The Anatomy of Clickbot.A, In *HOTBOTS'07*, 1st Workshop on Hot Topics in Understanding Botnets, 2007. (USENIX Association, Berkeley, CA) pp 11–11.
7. Fetterly, D., Manasse, M., and Najork, M.: Spam, Damn Spam, and Statistics: Using Statistical Analysis to Locate Spam Web Pages, In *WebDB'04*, 7th International Workshop on the Web and Databases, 2004. (ACM, New York, NY) pp 1–6.
8. Frank, E., Hall, M., Trigg, L., Holmes, G., and Witten, I. H.: Data Mining in Bioinformatics Using Weka. Bioinformatics, 20(15), 2479–2481, 1994.
9. Kamvar, M., and Baluja, S.: A Large Scale Study of Wireless Search Behavior: Google Mobile Search, In *CHI'06*, CHI Conference on Human Factors in Computing Systems, 2006. (ACM, New York, NY) pp 701–709.
10. Karasaridis, A., Rexroad, B., and Hoeflin, D.: Wide-scale Botnet Detection and Characterization, In *HOTBOTS'07*, 1st Workshop on Hot Topics in Understanding Botnets, 2007. (USENIX Association, Berkeley, CA) pp 7–7.
11. Schluessler, T., Goglin, S., and Johnson, E.: Is a Bot at the Controls? Detecting Input Data Attacks, In *NetGames'07*, 6th Workshop on Network and System Support for Games, 2007. (ACM, New York, NY) pp 1–6.
12. Stokes, J. W., Platt, J. C., Kravis, J., and Shilman, M.: ALADIN: Active Learning of Anomalies to Detect Intrusions, Microsoft Research Technical Report MSR-TR-2008-24, March 4, 2008.
13. Tuzhilin, A.: The Lane's Gifts v. Google Report. http://googleblog.blogspot.com/pdf/Tuzhilin_Report.pdf.
14. Wu, K.-L., Yu, P. S., and Ballman, A.: SpeedTracer: A Web Usage Mining and Analysis Tool. http://www.research.ibm.com/journal/sj/371/wu.html, 1998.

Semantic Services for Wikipedia

Haofen Wang, Thomas Penin, Linyun Fu, Qiaoling Liu, Guirong Xue and Yong Yu

Abstract Wikipedia, a killer application in Web 2.0, has embraced the power of collaborative editing to harness collective intelligence. It features many attractive characteristics, like entity-based link graph, abundant categorization and semi-structured layout, and can serve as an ideal data source to extract high quality and well-structured data. In this chapter, we first propose several solutions to extract knowledge from Wikipedia. We do not only consider information from the relational summaries of articles (infoboxes) but also semi-automatically extract it from the article text using the structured content available. Due to differences with information extraction from the Web, it is necessary to tackle new problems, like the lack of redundancy in Wikipedia that is dealt with by extending traditional machine learning algorithms to work with few labeled data. Furthermore, we also exploit the widespread categories as a complementary way to discover additional knowledge. Benefiting from both structured and textural information, we additionally provide a suggestion service for Wikipedia authoring. With the aim to facilitate semantic reuse, our proposal provides users with facilities such as link, categories and infobox content suggestions. The proposed enhancements can be applied to attract more contributors and lighten the burden of professional editors. Finally, we developed an enhanced search system, which can ease the process of exploiting Wikipedia. To provide a user-friendly interface, it extends the faceted search interface with relation navigation and let the user easily express his complex information needs in an interactive way. In order to achieve efficient query answering, it extends scalable IR engines to index and search both the textual and structured information with an integrated ranking support.

H. Wang (✉)
Department of Computer Science and Engineering, Shanghai Jiao Tong University, Shanghai, 200240, China
e-mail: whfcarter@apex.sjtu.edu.cn

I. King, R. Baeza-Yates (eds.), *Weaving Services and People on the World Wide Web*, DOI 10.1007/978-3-642-00570-1_2, © Springer-Verlag Berlin Heidelberg 2009

1 Introduction

The Web 2.0 is characterized by community-based collaboration and information sharing. End users are not only information consumers but also its producers. One of the best-known example is Wikipedia, the largest free online encyclopedia, authored by a broad community of volunteers. Up to November 2008, the contributors have developed editions in 264 languages,[1] among which the English version contains more than 2,600,000 articles.[2] The huge impact of Wikipedia has propelled it into the top 10 of the most popular Web sites of the planet.[3]

Recent research [2] has shown that the accuracy of Wikipedia can compete with that of commercial encyclopedias such as Encyclopedia Britannica. Its high quality and popularity is probably due to the so-called "wiki way", characterized by openness, collaboration, democracy and absence of hard restrictions. These qualities are appealing for other actors like the Semantic Web, a concept that aims at expliciting knowledge to make it accessible and understandable by machines (e.g. agents, services). There are interesting opportunities to provide semantic services for Wikipedia with the help of the Semantic Web technologies.

In this chapter, we first propose several solutions to extract knowledge from Wikipedia, respectively based on Wikipedia's infoboxes and on the text of the articles. Besides typical challenges encountered when extracting data from the Web, particular issues are also dealt with, such as the non-redundancy in Wikipedia and the small amount of available labeled data. We tackle these issues by adapting traditional machine learning algorithms. However, Infobox-based solutions suffer from the problem of a low article coverage, as according to the statistics in Wikipedia, only 44.2% of articles have infoboxes while more than 80.6% are annotated with at least one category. Thus, we propose to automatically extract knowledge from Wikipedia categories as a complementary method.

The derived knowledge can be further used to improve editing in Wikipedia. Eighty Percent of the articles are edited by only 10% of the contributors [9], a situation that the "wiki way" was supposed to avoid. Editing requires to find out if a hyperlink should be provided, which category an article should belong to, or which items should be filled in an infobox. A semantic authoring interface can help bring solutions and lower the barrier to improve an article, making possible for non-expert users to produce high-quality articles. We propose a *link suggestion* module to reuse existing article hyperlinks, a *category suggestion* module to borrow relevant categories from similar articles, and a *infobox content suggestion* module to help fill in the infoboxes.

---

[1] http://meta.wikimedia.org/wiki/List_of_Wikipedias

[2] http://en.wikipedia.org/

[3] http://www.alexa.com/site/ds/top_sites?ts_mode=global&lang=none

Although searching Wikipedia is a fundamental required service, the existing solutions (e.g. Google, Clusty-Wikipedia[4] and FUTEF[5]) are not well adapted, the structured information being partially or even not considered. How to process this huge volume of information remains a challenge: integrating database and information retrieval (IR) technologies usually results in decreased performance. We propose an enhanced search system for Wikipedia with integrated ranking that extends IR engines to harness optimizations on the physical storage and achieves good scalability. From a user interaction point of view, the traditional "keywords → result list→ click" model is not enough to benefit from using the structured information. We extend faceted search paradigm [7] with relation navigation to allow expressing complex information needs.

The rest is organized as follows. Wikipedia is first introduced in Sect. 2. The extraction solutions are described in Sect. 3. We then present the suggestion and search services in the following sections.

2 Wikipedia

In this section, we will detail the different features of Wikipedia (Fig. 1) that will be useful for our proposed semantic services.

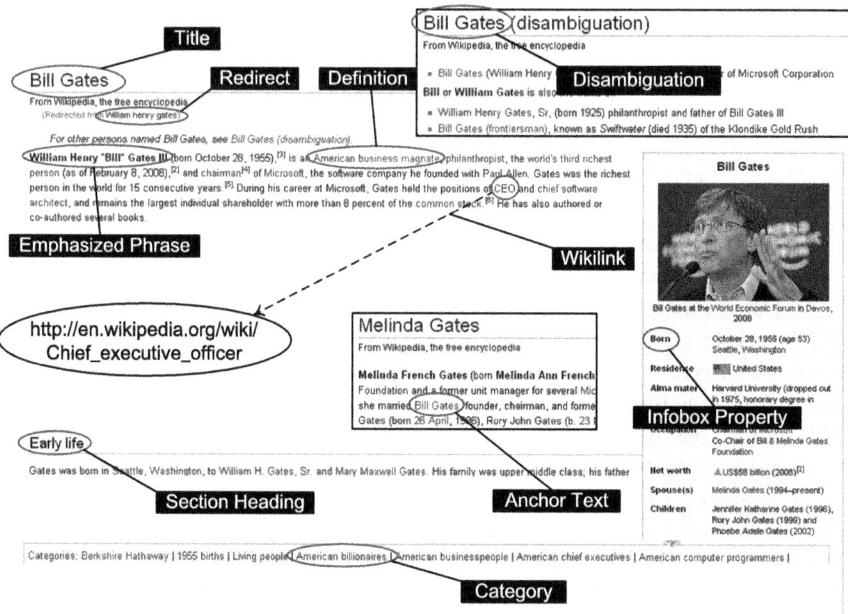

Fig. 1 Important features in Wikipedia

[4] http://wiki.clusty.com/

[5] http://futef.com/

Title. The *title* serves as the name and unique identifier of the article, like "Bill Gates" for the Wikipedia entry http://en.wikipedia.org/wiki/Bill_Gates.

Definition and Definition Features. The first sentence of an article usually serves as the *definition* of the topic entity. For example, the definition of the article "Bill Gates" is "***William Henry 'Bill' Gates III** (born October 28, 1955), is an American business magnate, philanthropist, ...* ". The *definition features* denote the classes to which the described entity belongs. Here, the features are: "American business magnate", "business magnate", "philanthropist", etc.

Wikilink. *wikilinks* can be *incoming links* (entries linking to the current article) or *outgoing links* (entries that the current article links to). They form an implicit semantic network and are used to navigate Wikipedia. In the wiki code, a link is written between two doubles "[", like "[[Chief executive officer|CEO]]".

Synonym (Redirect, Emphasized Phrase and Anchor Text). A *redirect* is an empty article that transfers to an equivalent entry. For example, "William Henry Gates" redirects to the article "Bill Gates". The *emphasized phrase* (*bold phrase*) in the definition is a self-reference to the topic entity. "William Henry 'Bill' Gates III" is the full name of "Bill Gates". An *Anchor text* is the name of a wikilink as it is visible on the page. For "[[World Wide Web]]" and "[[World Wide Web|WWW]]", the anchor text is respectively "World Wide Web" and "WWW". Redirects, emphasized phrases, and anchor texts build up the *synonym features* of an article.

Polysemy (Disambiguation). A *disambiguation* page links to the different articles that could use the same titles. From the page "Bill Gates (disambiguation)", we can see that "Bill Gates" might refer to the Microsoft Founder or his father. Thus "Bill Gates" serves as a *disambiguation feature* for both articles.

Category. Each article is annotated with one or more *categories*. Category names are noun phrases and most of them represent the classes of the current article's topic entity. We heuristically consider them to represent the classes if the head of their names is a plural. For example, "American billionaires" is a class for "Bill Gates" while "Berkshire Hathaway" is not. We can extract "American billionaires" and "billionaires" as *category features*.

Section Heading. *Sections* denote sub-topics which depict some attributes of the topic entity. The *section headings* are the most representative identifiers among them. For example, the article "Bill Gates" has "Early life" and "Microsoft" as section headings.

Infobox. Certain articles contain an *infobox* describing some properties of the topic entity. For example, the article "Bill Gates" proposes an infobox containing fields common to "Person" entities, such as "Occupation" and "Net Worth". The former has a value in the wikilink form of "[[Chairperson| Chairman]]", associating "Bill Gates" with "Chairperson" through the "Occupation" relation. The latter can be regarded as an attribute of Bill Gates with the text value "US$56 billion".

3 Knowledge Extraction from Wikipedia

In this section, we investigate three solutions to extract knowledge from Wikipedia. These methods are based on particular characteristics of Wikipedia presented in Sect. 2, respectively infoboxes, free text and categories.

3.1 Relation Extraction Using Infoboxes

As presented in Sect. 2, numerous wikipedia articles are associated with an *infobox*, usually defined according to a template proper to a type of article (about a person, a location, etc.), that proposes structured information in the form of an array of attribute-values couples.

The Wikipedia syntax makes it easy for machines to extract infoboxes from the article wiki code and to access the different data fields of the template. The following example is an extract of the code of an infobox:

```
{{Infobox Person
| name          = Bill Gates
| birth_date    = {{birth date and age|1955|10|28}}
| birth_place = [[Seattle]], [[Washington]]
| occupation    = Chairman of [[Microsoft]] (...)
| spouse        = [[Melinda Gates]] (1994-present)
| residence     = {{flagicon|USA}} United States
| footnotes     =
 }}
```

The structure of infoboxes make them valuable to extract machine-processable information at a relatively low complexity cost and this approach is often followed by the related work. This is for example the case of DBPedia,[6] a community effort to extract structured information from Wikipedia which latest version (November 2008) contains no less than 274 million pieces of information (triples).

3.1.1 Method

A triple is the basic piece of information to be extracted, composed of three elements: a subject, a predicate (relation) and an object. The predicate is the semantic relationship between the subject and the object. For instance, ("Bill Gates", Occupation, "Chairman of Microsoft") is a triple which explains that "Chairman of Microsoft" is the "Occupation" of the entity "Bill Gates".

In the case of infoboxes, a traditional approach to extract triples considers the article title as the subject and the infobox elements as the predicate-object parts of the extracted triple. This is possible because each article represents a single

---

[6] http://wiki.dbpedia.org

entity. For the "Bill Gates" article, it is possible to extract triples like ("Bill Gates", Birth_Place, Seattle) or ("Bill Gates", spouse, "Melinda Gates").

3.1.2 Discussion

Although information extraction from infoboxes is often considered as being the easiest way to obtain semantic information from Wikipedia articles, it still faces several disadvantages. Some of them are the following:

- The coverage of infoboxes is far from complete. According to our statistics,[7] only 44.2% of articles have infoboxes, which limits the quantity of triples that can be extracted.
- Infoboxes themselves are not already complete, due to the unavailability of data or to the fact that contributors did not fill in all fields proposed by the infobox template. In our previous example, the field "footnotes" was left empty.
- Sometimes the value part contains several pieces of information. In our example, the field "spouse" contains the name "Melinda Gates", as well as the date range "(1994-present)". Since the contributors are not always following the syntactic recommendations, it may be a challenge, that is usually addressed thanks to heuristic rules.
- The related problem of units. Depending on the localization of the Wikipedia version considered, different types of units can be used, and sometimes a field can even contain the same value expressed in several units.

Besides these drawbacks, the limitation to the infobox content is also forgetting the article text, that usually contains much more information. We will now introduce another solution to address this shortcoming and consider triple extraction from the article text itself.

3.2 Relation Extraction Using Full Text

In this section, we will see how it is possible to extract triples from the article text in Wikipedia.

3.2.1 Method

The proposed method benefits from the relations already defined in the infoboxes, along with their value. It will constitute the starting point of a machine learning problem that in turn will extract pairs of entities from the article text also linked by these relations. However, as mentioned before, missing data value is a common issue which causes not adequate structured information to be available as labeled data for learning an extractor. Furthermore, the articles do not explicitly state that they do not belong to a class associated with a specific infobox, which causes negative examples to be missing, leading to a positive-only approach.

[7] Obtained from the English Wikipedia database dump on January 2008.

3.2.2 The B-POL Algorithm

Due to space limitation, we will not present here the details of the algorithm but rather give a general description of the way it works. Readers interested to go further can refer to [6].

The core algorithm, called B-POL, builds on top of a state-of-the-art positive-only learning (POL) approach [3] that initially identifies strong negative examples from unlabeled data and then iteratively classifies more negative data until convergence. B-POL makes several extensions to POL to work with fewer positive examples without sacrificing too much precision. Specifically, a conservative strategy is made to generate strong initial negative examples, resulting in high recall at the first step. The newly generated positive data identified by POL is added for training. The method iterates until no positive data can be generated anymore. It exploits unlabeled data for learning and is transformed to a transductive learning method[8] that works better with sparse training data.

B-POL is fed with a set of positive examples for a given relation and a set of unlabeled subject-object pairs. It outputs those having this relation as their predicate.

3.2.3 The Relation Extraction System

The extraction system works as follows:

1. **Three types of features are extracted from Wikipedia (see Sect. 2):**
   - *Definition features*. We heuristically extract the head word of the first noun phrase following a be-verb in the definition of the article. For example, in the sentence "Annie Hall is an Academy Award-wining, 1997 romantic comedy film directed by Woody Allen.", the word "film" and the augmented word "comedy_film" are extracted as definition features for "Annie Hall".
   - *Category features*. Since the name of each category is generally a noun phrase, the head word is extracted. For example, "Annie Hall" belongs to the category "Romantic comedy films". "film" and the augmented version "comedy_film" are extracted.
   - *Infobox features*. The predicates are extracted, with each white space character replaced by an underscore (e.g. "produced_by", "written_by", etc.).
2. **The entity-pair co-occurrence context is extracted from Wikipedia text.** For instance, in the sentence "In the film *Heavenly Creatures*, directed by *Peter Jackson*, *Juliet Hulme* had TB, and her fear of being sent ...", there are three wikilinked entities (represented here in italic). For each pair of entities, e.g. (*Heavenly Creatures*, *Peter Jackson*), tokens to the left of *Heavenly Creatures*, those to the right of *Peter Jackson*, and those between the two entities are extracted and encoded as the *context features*.
3. **For each relation, irrelevant instances are filtered out using the positive training data.** We first define a feature selection method. We denote the

[8] http://en.wikipedia.org/wiki/Transductive_learning

complete set of data as C and the positive set in C as P. To define a score of a feature f, we further denote the set of data from P containing f as P_f and the set of data from C containing f as C_f . The scoring function is shown in Eq. (1).

$$score(f) = |P_f| \times \log(|C|/|C_f|). \tag{1}$$

Features usually express different aspects of an entity. Nevertheless, it is reasonable to assume that entities in a given relation at a given argument position (subject or object) share a certain degree of commonality. We use Eq. (1) to rank features of entities at each argument position and select the top k features.

The selected features are called Salient Entity Features. For convenience, the salient features of entities at subject (object) position are called Salient Subject (Object) Features. The set of entity pairs from which features of the left-hand-side (right-hand-side) entity intersect with the Salient Subject (Object) Features are kept. We denote the set of entity pairs finally kept as C', and then the unlabeled set $U = C' - P$.

In the previous example, although there are several pairs of entities, pairs such as *<Peter Jackson, Juliet Hulme>*, *<Heavenly Creatures, Juliet Hulme>*, etc. will be filtered out when we are extracting the "filmdirector" relation. This is because the Salient Subject (Object) Features are <film, drama_film, movie, ... > and <director, film_director, ... >, respectively, which do not have intersection with those of the filtered-out pairs.

4. **A relation extractor is conducted on the filtered set of subject-object pairs using B-POL.**

3.2.4 Discussion

Experimental results show that B-POL significantly outperforms the multi-class classification approach especially when the amount of labeled data is small. Although the solution is applied in the context of Wikipedia, the core algorithm B-POL can also be adapted to other domains. Readers are invited to refer to [6] for a detailed evaluation .

3.3 Relation Extraction Using Categories

Although infoboxes bring about promising results, we have seen that they suffer from one major disadvantage: their low article coverage. Triples extraction from categories appears as an interesting path to follow. However, previous category-based methods (e.g. [5]) relied on manually specifying regular expressions for each relation to match category names. This is very effort-consuming. As a result, a large portion of knowledge in the categories remains unexplored. We focus on *automatically* extracting predicates and triples from categories to achieve a wider coverage with less effort.

3.3.1 Method

In the example "Category:Songs by Pat Ballard", it is difficult for machines to understand that the songs are written by Pat Ballard. However, the category hierarchy provides some clues. Given that "Category:Songs by Pat Ballard" has a parent category "Category:Songs by songwriter", it is easier to extract "songwriter" as predicate and "Pat Ballard" as value for those songs. Then, we can obtain triples like ("Mr. Sandman", songwriter, "Pat Ballard"). The syntax and semantics brought by parent-child category pairs make it possible to automatically extract structured data from category names. This process to extract triples from categories is described as follows:

Step 1: Recognize Useful Patterns

We analyze the category names based on natural language processing (NLP) technologies to discover useful patterns using predicate-contained category names (PCCN) and value-contained category names (VCCN), thanks to the following name patterns:

- Pattern1: by-prep, which means the parent category is a PCCN with by-phrase and the child category is a VCCN with prepositional phrase, e.g. "Category:Songs by theme"-"Category:Songs about divorce".
- Pattern2: by-noun, which means the parent category is a PCCN with by-phrase and the child category is a VCCN with noun phrase, e.g. "Category:Songs by artist"-"Category:The Beatles songs".
- Pattern3: *-prep **except** by-prep, which means the child category is a VCCN with prepositional phrase and the parent category is not a PCCN, e.g. "Category:Songs"-"Category:Songs from films".
- Pattern4: *-noun **except** by-noun, which means the child category is a VCCN with noun phrase and the parent category is not a PCCN, e.g. "Category:Rock songs"-"Category:British rock songs".

Step 2: Extract Explicit Predicates and Values

Several rules are proposed to extract the explicit predicates and values for categories.

- Rule-p: for Pattern1 and Pattern2, extract the by-phrase in the parent category as predicate, e.g. "theme" in "Category:Songs by theme".
- Rule-v1: for Pattern1 and Pattern3, extract the prepositional phrase in the child category as value, e.g. "divorce" in "Category:Songs about divorce".
- Rule-v2: for Pattern2 and Pattern4, extract the extra modifier of the head of the child category compared with the parent category as value, e.g. "The Beatles" in "Category:The Beatles songs" w.r.t. "Category:songs".

Special cases need to be considered. In Rule-v1, the prepositional phrase in the child category may be a by-phrase. Some by-phrases are useful to extract values, e.g. "Category:Songs by songwriter"-"Category:Songs by Richard Adler", while others are not, e.g. "Category:Songs by genre"-"Category:Rock songs by subgenre". We judge the by-phrase useful if two conditions are satisfied: (1) the number of its articles is larger than ten times the number of its child categories. (2) the by-phrase is not contained in the predicates collected from infobox triples.

Step 3: Vote Implicit Predicates

To derive predicates for child categories in Pattern3 and Pattern4, we encounter a problem when discovering the implicit predicate given the explicit value for a category. We propose a voting strategy, which elects the predicate with the maximum frequency in existing triples for this category. This can be considered as a narrow voting. We further propose a broad voting strategy that improves it by considering more contextual information.

Step 4: Generate Triples for Articles

Until now, we have derived predicate-value pairs for the child categories in all four patterns. Based on these, we generate triples for articles belonging to these categories.

3.3.2 Discussion

The evaluation results [4] show the strengths of our method. We find that using parent-child category pairs for triple extraction is effective by leveraging the Wikipedia category system.

4 Semantic Editing for Wikipedia

In this section, we present our solution to the editing problem. We equip the current Wikipedia with a link suggestion module that seamlessly integrates search and authoring to provide the user with proper wikilinks, a category suggestion module that helps the user to find appropriate categories for her article, and an infobox content suggestion module that proposes reasonable infobox fields for the article.

4.1 A Unified Suggestion Method

In this section, we introduce a unified suggestion method which focuses on modeling Wikipedia articles and the inputs for those suggestion modules, and a variety of similarity measurements to evaluate their relevance.

4.1.1 Resource and Query Graph Models

We model each article as a *resource graph* according to the features mentioned in Sect. 2, illustrated in Fig. 2 (a), where oval nodes denote *resource features* and

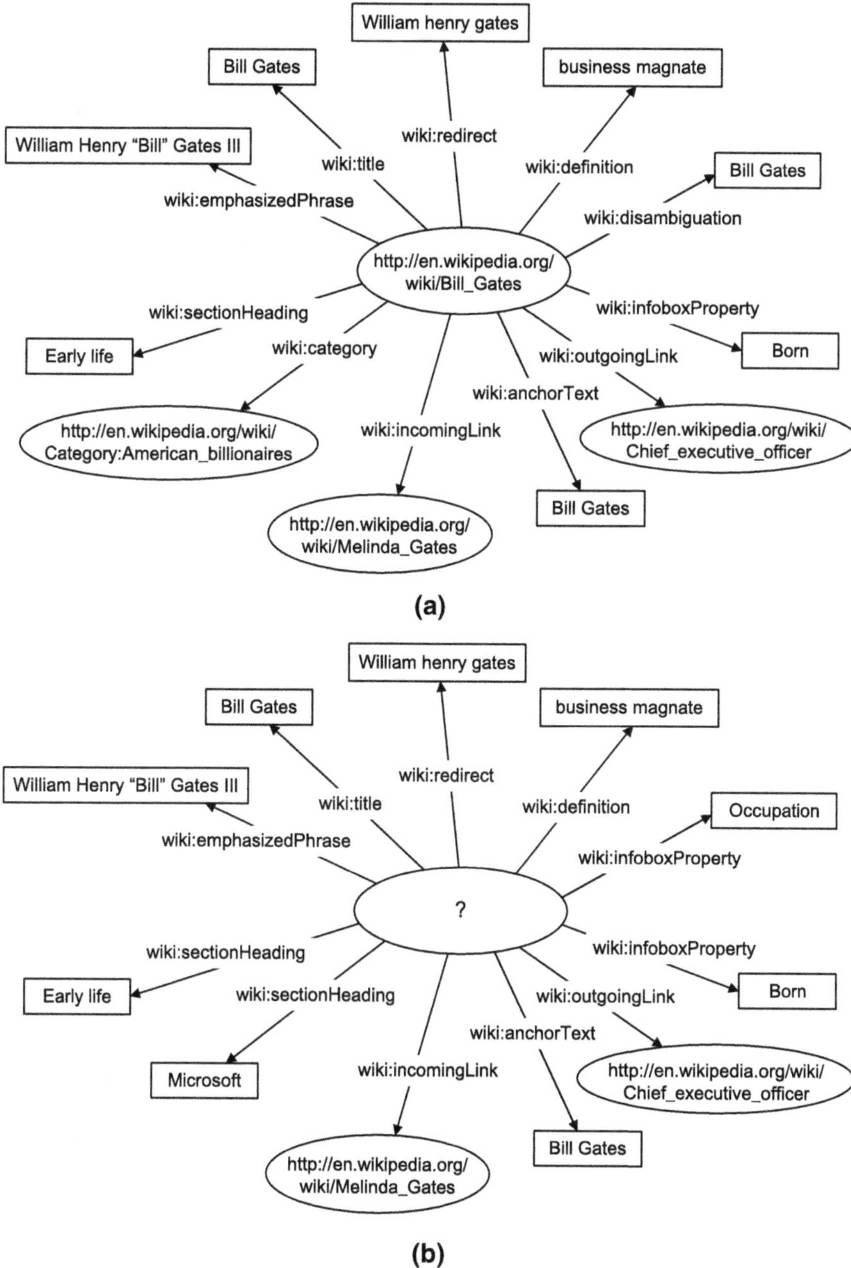

Fig. 2 (**a**) A resource graph for an article in Wikipedia. (**b**) A sample query graph

rectangular nodes denote *literal features*. Note that each feature of an article may have multiple values that form a *feature vector*. The resource graph of each article can be connected to form a huge graph for the whole Wikipedia corpus. We limit the graph representation to the *Concise Bounded Descriptions* (CBD)[9] of articles to guarantee efficiency of our matching algorithm.

In order to find the most relevant target articles w.r.t. the inputs, we convert each input into a *query graph* as shown in Fig. 2 (b). A query graph is quite similar to a resource graph. The only difference is that the central node is always a blank node, indicated by a question mark. Since a query graph is used to find articles whose CBDs are similar, it contains only one blank node at the center.

4.1.2 Similarity Measurements

Similarity between a query graph and a resource graph is derived from similarity between each query feature vector and the corresponding resource feature vector. Similarity between a pair of feature vectors can be defined according to the need of a specific application. We use the following two kinds of similarities for our tasks:

Prefix Similarity. It is used for link suggestion, defined by $Sim_{pre}(l_q, \mathbf{V}_r)$, where l_q is the literal feature of the query graph and $\mathbf{V}_r$ is the corresponding feature vector of the resource graph. The simplicity of Eq. (2) makes the link suggestion efficient enough to assist a real-time authoring.

$$Sim_{pre}(l_q, \mathbf{V}_r) = \sum_{l_r \text{ in } \mathbf{V}_r \wedge l_q \text{ is prefix of } l_r} tfidf(l_r \text{ in } \mathbf{V}_r) \tag{2}$$

Exact Similarity. It is used for category and infobox content suggestions, defined by $Sim_{ex}(\mathbf{V}_q, \mathbf{V}_r)$, where $\mathbf{V}_q$ and $\mathbf{V}_r$ are respective feature vectors of the query graph and the resource graph. It is a cosine similarity as shown in Eq. (3).

$$Sim_{ex}(\mathbf{V}_q, \mathbf{V}_r) = \mathbf{V}_q \cdot \mathbf{V}_r / |\mathbf{V}_q||\mathbf{V}_r| \tag{3}$$

The similarity between a query graph q and a resource graph r, denoted by $Similarity(q, r)$, is defined as the weighted sum of the similarities of their corresponding feature vectors, as shown in Eq. (4).

$$Similarity(q, r) = \sum_{f \in F(q) \cap F(r)} w_f \cdot Sim_f(\mathbf{V}_f(q), \mathbf{V}_f(r)) \tag{4}$$

Here $F(g)$ denotes the set of feature vectors of a graph g, $\mathbf{V}_f(g)$ denotes the vector of a feature f in the graph, and w_f is the weight for the feature f to indicate its importance. Note that Sim_f can be either Sim_{pre} or Sim_{ex}.

[9] http://www.w3.org/Submission/CBD

4.2 Applications of the Method

In this section, we present three applications to recommend possible links, categories and infobox contents respectively during Wikipedia authoring based on our proposed suggestion method.

4.2.1 Link Suggestion

The link suggestion module takes the phrase typed by the user as its input. It first converts the phrase into a query graph, then matches all the articles along with similarity scores w.r.t. the query graph, and finally displays the ranked articles with close similarities. The query graph for a phrase contains five feature vectors: Title, Redirect, Emphasized Phrase, Anchor Text and Disambiguation, each containing the same value as the input phrase. These features are selected as they are usually used as the title of articles to refer to the topic entity. Figure 3 (a) shows an example query graph when inputting "William Henry".

4.2.2 Category Suggestion

The process of category suggestion can be divided into two steps. First, the article to be categorized is converted into a query graph. It is matched against resource graphs of other articles to find the most similar articles. Then we use these articles to vote on the categories they belong to and decide the rank positions of the suggested categories. The amount of votes a category gets is counted by Eq. (5), where S denotes the set of these similar articles, $A(c)$ represents the set of articles that belong to category c, and $Similarity(q, a)$ is defined in Eq. (4).

$$Vote(c) = \sum_{a \in S \wedge a \in A(c)} Similarity(q, a) \tag{5}$$

The query graph considers six kinds of features: Incoming Link, Outgoing Link, Section Heading, Category, Definition, and Infobox. They depict the structure of the article and we notice that structurally similar articles usually belong to the same categories. Figure 3 (b) shows a sample query graph for the article "Bill Gates".

4.2.3 Infobox Content Suggestion

Suggesting fields in the infobox of an article is similar to that of category suggestion, except that we use a different set of features, namely Category, Definition and Infobox. A query graph of the same article is presented in Fig. 3 (c).

4.2.4 Discussion

According to experiment results [1], link suggestion outperformed the existing title matching approaches, especially when the input is not the prefix of or is totally

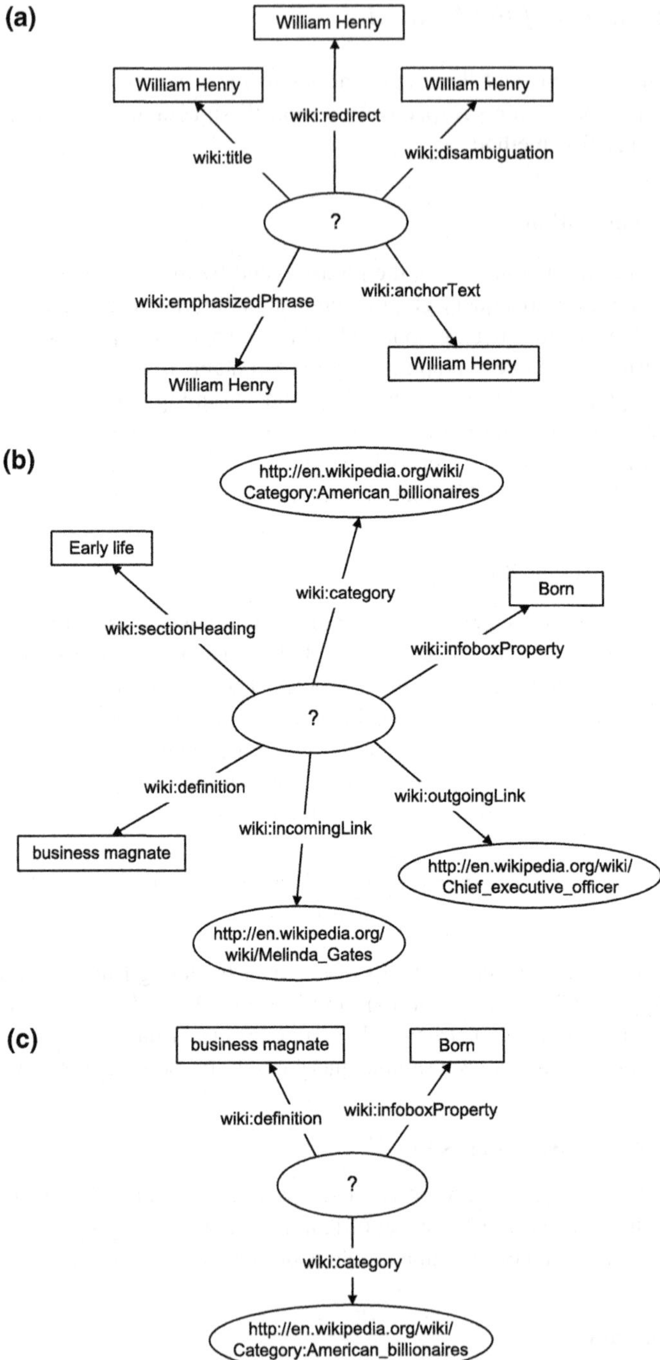

Fig. 3 Three kinds of query graphs. (**a**) Query graph for link suggestion. (**b**) Query graph for category suggestion. (**c**) Query graph for infobox content suggestion

different from the title of the target article. The average time (within 100 ms) makes it suitable for a real-time use. The category suggestion succeeded in finding missing categories, discovering improper categorizations, and classifying articles to proper levels of abstraction in Wikipedia. Finally, the infobox content suggestion also gave promising results in terms of mean average precision (MAP).[10]

4.3 Demonstration

Figure 4 gives four snapshots of our prototype system EachWiki.[11] When a user types an (incomplete) phrase in the Wikipedia editor and pauses for a short time, the link suggestion module will be triggered and pop up a list of suggested links. The user can select the intended wikilink, as shown in Fig. 4 (a). When the user

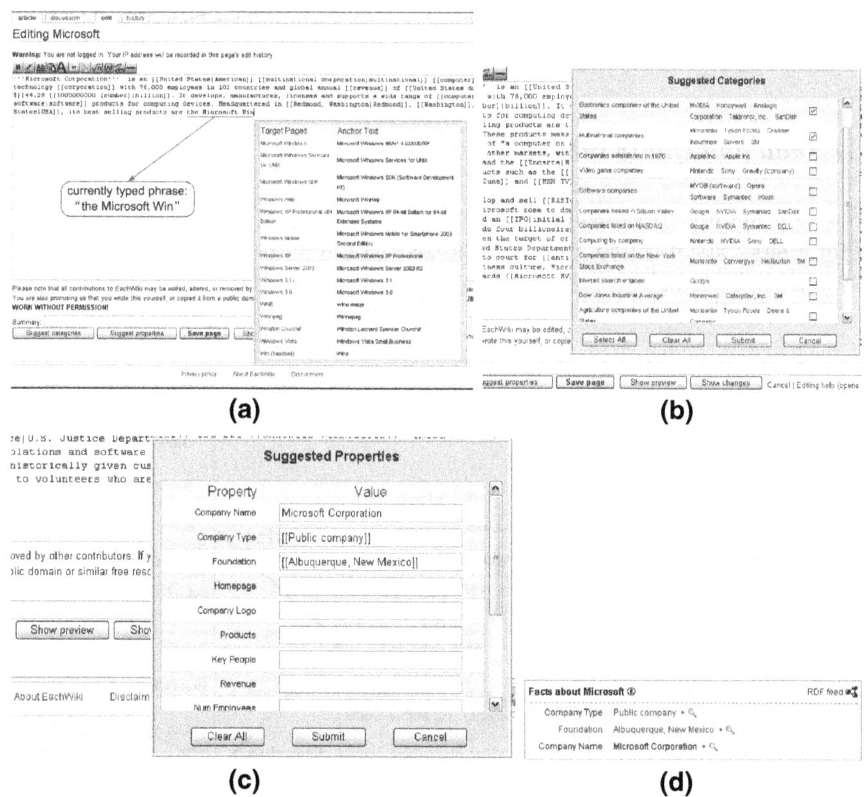

Fig. 4 Snapshots of our prototype system. (**a**) Link suggestion interface. (**b**) Category suggestion interface. (**c**) Infobox content suggestion interface. (**d**) Page view of the annotated relations

[10] http://en.wikipedia.org/wiki/Information_retrieval#Average_precision_of_precision_and_recall
[11] http://eachwiki.apexlab.org

clicks the “Suggest categories” button, the system analyzes the edited article and provides a list of suggested categories. The user can select several proper categories from the list, as shown in Fig. 4 (b). Similarly, when the user clicks the “Suggest properties” button, a list of infobox fields to be suggested pops up, as shown in Fig. 4 (c). Finally, when the user finishes editing, he can see annotated relations rendered in the article page (Fig. 4 (d)).

5 Enhanced Search for Wikipedia

In this section, we present an enhanced search system called RelSE for Wikipedia which supports hybrid queries containing both keywords and semantic information. We extend the well-known IR index for storing textual information as well as structured data. A scalable retrieval algorithm with integrated ranking is proposed to support the above search capability. Besides, we provide a faceted browsing interface towards exploratory search for end users.

5.1 *Data and Query Model*

Thanks to knowledge extraction, the triples from infoboxes, free text and categories form a large graph across Wikipedia articles as a knowledge base (KB). A segment of such a graph is shown in Fig. 5. We use d, C, R to represent an article, a category and a relation respectively. Moreover, $(d, type, C)$ represents that the

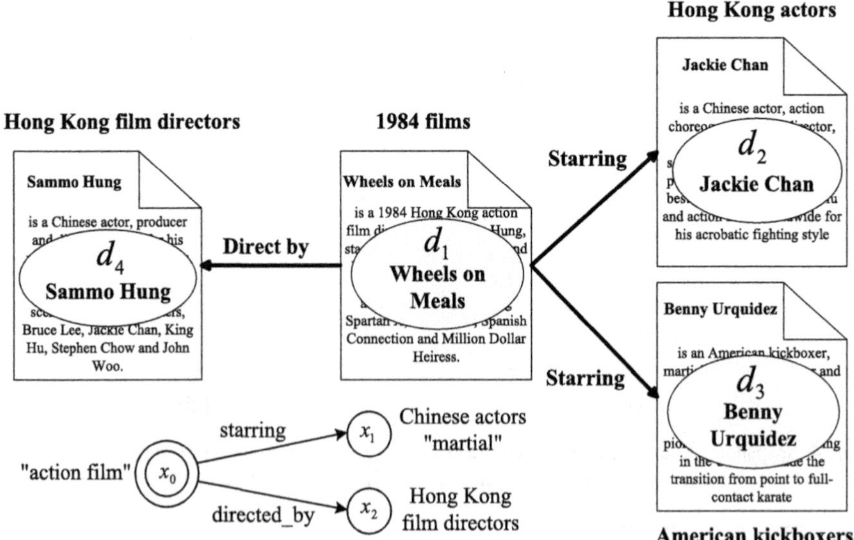

Fig. 5 A segment of Wikipedia knowledge base and an example hybrid query

article d belongs to category C, (s, R, o) indicates that two articles s and o are connected through relation R, and $(d, about, K)$ denotes that the article d matches keyword K.

We further introduce *hybrid queries*, defined as a directed labeled tree $Q(v_t) = (V, v_t, E, L_K, L_C, L_R)$. V is a finite set of vertices, each representing an article variable. $v_t \in V$ specifies the target variable of the query. $E \subseteq V \times V$ represents a finite set of edges, each denoting a relation between two variables. Each vertex $u \in V$ has a keyword label $L_K(u)$ and a category label $L_C(u)$. Each edge $(u, v) \in E$ has a relation label $L_R(u, v)$. A keyword query can be viewed as a special case with a single vertex. Figure 5 shows an example query $Q(x_0)$, which aims at finding action films cooperated by martial arts actors and Hong Kong directors.

Let f denote a valuation function mapping variables in V onto articles. A valuation f satisfies the query $Q(v_t)$, written as $f \models Q(v_t)$, if for each $v \in V$, we have $(f(v), \texttt{about}, L_K(v))$ and $(f(v), \texttt{type}, L_C(v))$, and for each $(u, v) \in E$, we have $(f(u), L_R(u, v), f(v))$. The results of $Q(v_t)$ are a set of articles defined by $\{f(v_t) \mid f \models Q(v_t)\}$. According to Fig. 5, the article d_1 "Wheels on Meals" is among the search results for query $Q(x_0)$.

5.2 System Overview

Figure 6 shows the architecture of RelSE. During the offline index stage, both the textual and structured information are indexed. During the online search stage, users can interact with the interface to create hybrid queries. The search layer then processes the queries and finally returns the ranked results.

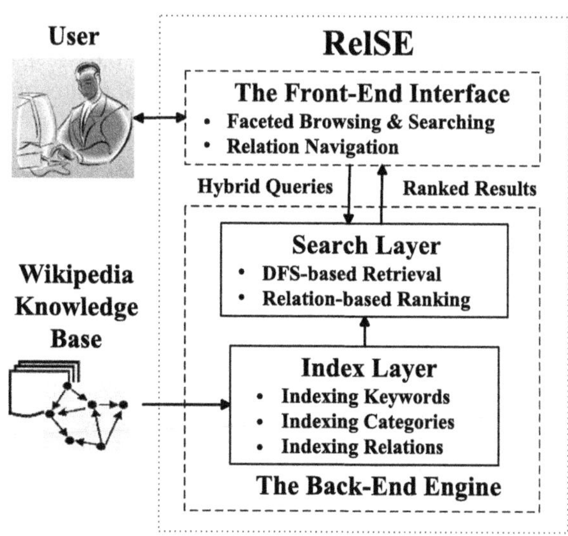

Fig. 6 System architecture of RelSE

5.2.1 Index Layer

An IR index [10], widely used for keyword search, consists of a collection of posting lists, one per term, recording its documents. The posting list for a term t is composed of the document frequency f_t and a list of records in the form of $\langle d, f_{d,t}, \langle p_1, \ldots, p_{f_{d,t}}\rangle\rangle$ with length f_t, where d is a document identifier, $f_{d,t}$ is the number of occurrences of t in d, and p_i is the word positions at which t occurs in d.

We transform triples into artificial documents with fields and terms, and extend IR index structure to store data in such a KB. Figure 7 gives an example of the extended index for the data shown in Fig. 5. All $(d, \texttt{about}, K)$ triples can be indexed. Similarly, we can index triples in the form of $(d, \texttt{type}, C)$ by regarding category C as a special term for article d. In order to index relation triples in the form of (s, R, o), we regard the relation R as a special term for the subject s, and store the object o as a "position", i.e. the position list can be used to store the objects of relation R for subject s.

This way, for the physical storage and access of the index structure, we harness all the optimizations from IR engines, such as byte-aligned index compression and self-indexing [10]. Furthermore, since positions of the same term are usually physically stored together in IR engines, the objects of a relation enjoy the benefit of spatial locality for fast access.

5.2.2 Search Layer

Based on the above index, RelSE can efficiently answer a tree-shaped hybrid query using a DFS-based retrieval algorithm. The basic idea is to decompose query evaluation into simple IR operations over posting lists. As an improvement to our previous work [8], scoring functions are specified for the basic operations according to probability theory, and thus a relation-based ranking scheme is integrated.

We generalize the notion of posting list to a Scored Ascending Integer Stream (SAIS), which is accessed from the smallest integer to the largest one. For example, given a SAIS $S = \{\langle d_1, 0.4\rangle, \langle d_3, 0.8\rangle, \langle d_4, 0.6\rangle, \ldots\}$, we represent the score of d_1 by $S[d_1] = 0.4$. Then the three basic operations are efficiently supported:

Field	Term t	f_t	Inverted list for t
text	Benny	1	$\langle d_3, 1, \langle 1\rangle\rangle$
text	Chan	1	$\langle d_2, 1, \langle 2\rangle\rangle$
text	Hung	1	$\langle d_4, 1, \langle 2\rangle\rangle$
text	Jackie	1	$\langle d_2, 1, \langle 1\rangle\rangle$
type	1984_films	1	$\langle d_1, 1, \langle 1\rangle\rangle$
type	American_kickboxers	1	$\langle d_3, 1, \langle 1\rangle\rangle$
type	Hong_Kong_actors	1	$\langle d_2, 1, \langle 1\rangle\rangle$
type	Hong_Kong_directors	1	$\langle d_4, 1, \langle 1\rangle\rangle$
subjOf	directed_by	1	$\langle d_1, 1, \langle d_4\rangle\rangle$
subjOf	starring	1	$\langle d_1, 2, \langle d_2, d_3\rangle\rangle$
objOf	directed_by	1	$\langle d_4, 1, \langle d_1\rangle\rangle$
objOf	starring	2	$\langle d_2, 1, \langle d_1\rangle\rangle\langle d_3, 1, \langle d_1\rangle\rangle$

Fig. 7 Sample extended IR index (It indexes keywords in the "text" field, categories in the "type" field, and relations in the "subjOf" and "objOf" fields)

Basic-retrieval $b(f, t)$**.** Given a field f and a term t, it retrieves the corresponding posting list from the inverted index as a SAIS. Each item in the result SAIS is scored by

$$b(f, t)[d] = \begin{cases} RSV(t, d) \cdot \alpha & \text{if } f = \textit{text} \\ \beta & \text{if } f = \textit{type} \\ 1 & \text{else} \end{cases} \tag{6}$$

where $RSV(t, d)$ computes the relevance of the document d with respect to the term t according to the tf-idf principle and returns a degree within [0,1]. α, β are two parameters in [0,1] used to give different weights to keywords and categories.

Merge-sort $m(S_1, \cap, S_2)$**.** Given two SAISs S_1 and S_2, it computes $S_1 \cap S_2$ and returns a new SAIS, in which each item is scored by

$$m(S_1, \cap, S_2)[d] = S_1[d] \cdot S_2[d] \tag{7}$$

Mass-union $u(S, R)$**.** Given a relation R and a SAIS S, it computes the set as $\{o \mid \exists s : s \in S \wedge (s, R, o)\}$ and returns a new SAIS. Each item in the result SAIS is scored by

$$u(S, R)[o] = 1 - \prod_{s:s \in S \wedge (s,R,o)} (1 - S[s]) \tag{8}$$

The DFS-based retrieval algorithm can be visually imagined as traversing the query tree in the depth-first order while conducting the basic operations at the same time. The traversal will terminate in $|V|$ steps. Finally, the result of each vertex v is computed as a scored set:

$$\begin{aligned} res[v] = & \, b(\texttt{text}, L_K(v)) \cap b(\texttt{type}, L_C(v)) \\ & \cap \bigcap_{(u,v) \in E} u(res[u], L_R(u, v)) \end{aligned} \tag{9}$$

$$\begin{aligned} res[v][d] = & \, b(\texttt{text}, L_K(v))[d] \cdot b(\texttt{type}, L_C(v))[d] \\ & \cdot \prod_{(u,v) \in E} u(res[u], L_R(u, v))[d] \end{aligned} \tag{10}$$

Hence, a ranking scheme is seamlessly integrated into the retrieval process. Firstly, each vertex will be assigned an initial score with respect to its keyword label and category label. We choose $\alpha = 0.9$ and $\beta = 0.1$ so that keyword matches are weighed much higher than category matches. Then, these scores will propagate along the edges from leaf vertices to the root vertex (the target vertex). The propagation can take advantage of the semantic information and the tree-shaped hybrid query to improve the quality of search results.

5.3 Demonstration

The interface of RelSE[12] is shown in Fig. 8. It consists of three panels: the *Query Tree* to let users input their information needs, the *Navigator* where users view and select facets, and the *Result Panel* to display the ranked results.

Assuming that Lucy intends to watch "an action film starring Chinese martial arts actors" while she has little knowledge of these films. She uses RelSE to give her some recommendations. She first types in the keywords "action film" and gets ranked articles about action films together with a suggested category list and relation list. By selecting a category she can restrict current results. Besides, she can select a relation to navigate to a new set of results having the specific relation with current results. In our case, she then clicks the relation "starring". Subsequently, a list of actors playing a role in those action films is shown. Meanwhile, a row representing the actors is inserted to the query tree panel, below the first row representing the action films. She further types in a second keyword "martial" and selects the category "Chinese actors". The range of actors is now confined with these two conditions. To switch the target, she clicks the first row "action film" in the query tree panel to highlight the films again which shows the films that she wants in the result panel.

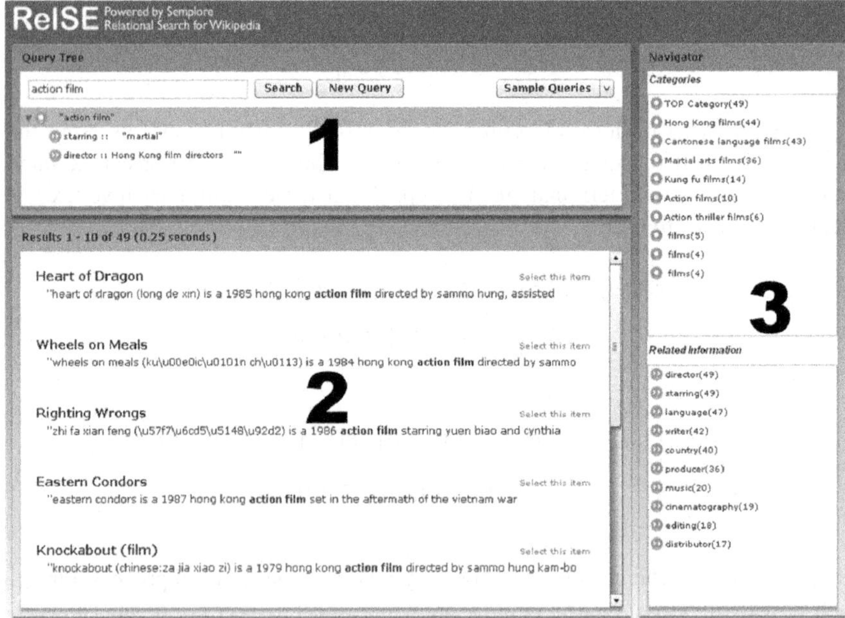

Fig. 8 The faceted browsing and search interface

---

12 http://relse.apexlab.org

6 Conclusion

In this chapter, we have proposed several solutions benefiting from Wikipedia characteristics to improve the user interaction with the world's largest encyclopedia.

We have started by describing three scenarios to extract knowledge, respectively from infoboxes, article text and category hierarchy, and shown several solutions to tackle the difficulties faced by the different systems. Knowledge extraction can in turn benefit to the user interaction through the two other applications that we proposed, namely an editing system and an enhanced search engine. The former provides the contributor with suggestions of links, categories and infobox elements during the edition process, thus lowering the barrier needed to contribute to Wikipedia. The latter allows a better search experience through faceted browsing.

Every solution was useful to illustrate particular challenges and the choices that were made to address them. Through our review, we have also seen how different research fields, such as Semantic Web, User Interaction, IR Search or Machine Learning could be leveraged to deal with the challenges faced when working at improving the availability of new services for the Wikipedia user.

References

1. Fu, L., Wang, H., Zhu, H., Zhang, H.,Wang, Y., Yu, Y.: Making more wikipedians: Facilitating semantics reuse for wikipedia authoring. Lecture Notes in Computer Science 4825, 128 (2007)
2. Giles, J.: Special Report–Internet encyclopaedias go head to head. Nature 438(15), 900–901 (2005)
3. Li, X., Liu, B.: Learning to classify texts using positive and unlabeled data. In: International Joint Conference on Artificial Intelligence. Lawrence Erlbaum Associates Ltd vol. 18, pp. 587–594 (2003)
4. Liu, Q., Xu, K., Zhang, L., Wang, H., Yu, Y., Pan, Y.: Catriple: Extracting Triples from Wikipedia Categories. In: Proceedings of the 3rd Asian Semantic Web Conference on The Semantic Web. Springer pp. 330–344 (2008)
5. Suchanek, F., Kasneci, G.,Weikum, G.: Yago: a core of semantic knowledge. In: Proceedings of the 16th international conference on World Wide Web. ACM New York, NY, USA pp. 697–706 (2007)
6. Wang, G., Yu, Y., Zhu, H.: Pore: Positive-only relation extraction from wikipedia text. Lecture Notes in Computer Science 4825, 580 (2007)
7. Yee, K., Swearingen, K., Li, K., Hearst, M.: Faceted metadata for image search and browsing. In: Proceedings of the SIGCHI conference on Human factors in computing systems. ACM New York, NY, USA pp. 401–408 (2003)
8. Zhang, L., Liu, Q., Zhang, J., Wang, H., Pan, Y., Yu, Y.: Semplore: An ir approach to scalable hybrid query of semantic web data. Lecture Notes in Computer Science 4825, 652 (2007)
9. Zlatić, V., Božičević, M., Štefančić, H., Domazet, M.: Wikipedias: collaborative web-based encyclopedias as complex networks. SIAM Rev Phys Rev E 74, 016, 115 (2003)
10. Zobel, J., Moffat, A.: Inverted files for text search engines. ACM Computing Surveys (CSUR) 38 (2) (2006)

Context-based Semantic Mediation in Web Service Communities

Michael Mrissa, Stefan Dietze, Philippe Thiran, Chirine Ghedira, Djamal Benslimane and Zakaria Maamar

Abstract Communities gather Web services that provide a common functionality, acting as an intermediate layer between end users and Web services. On the one hand, they provide a single endpoint that handles user requests and transparently selects and invokes Web services, thus abstracting the selection task and leveraging the provided quality of service level. On the other hand, they maximize the visibility and use rate of Web services. However, data exchanges that take place between Web services and the community endpoint raise several issues, in particular due to semantic heterogeneities of data. Specific mediation mechanisms are required to adapt data operated by Web services to those of the community. Hence, mediation facilititates interoperability and reduces the level of difficulty for Web services to join and interact with communities. In this chapter, we propose a mediation approach that builds on (1) context-based semantic representation for Web services and the community; and (2) mediation mechanisms to resolve the semantic heterogeneities occuring during data exchanges. We validate our solution through some experiments as part of the WSMO framework over a test community and show the limitations of our approach.

Keywords Context · Community · Mediation · Semantics · Web services · WSMO

1 Introduction

The service-oriented paradigm is gaining momentum as a way to interconnect applications across distributed organizations. Especially on the World Wide Web, the advent of Web services provides a framework to interconnect applications. Web services are remotely accessible software components providing a specific functionality. They rely on well-defined Web protocols such as HTTP for transport, which are coupled to some XML-based languages for supporting message

M. Mrissa (✉)
PReCISE Research Center, University of Namur, Belgium
e-mail: mmrissa@fundp.ac.be

I. King, R. Baeza-Yates (eds.), *Weaving Services and People on the World Wide Web*, DOI 10.1007/978-3-642-00570-1_3,

exchange (SOAP [7]), functional service description (WSDL [10]), and discovery (UDDI [27]). The main advantage of Web services is their capacity of being composed. A composition consists of combining several Web services into the same business process, in order to address complex user's needs that a single Web service could not satisfy.

Due to the increasing number of services available on the Web, the discovery and selection steps are becoming of major importance. They will later determine the relevancy of a composition for fulfilling a specific goal in a specific situation and also contribute to its successful achievement. As stated in the work of Al-Masri et al. [1], the common practice nowadays is to manually search for and select Web services depending on several Quality of Service (QoS) characteristics such as availability, price, efficiency, reliability, etc.

Gathering Web services into communities facilitates the discovery and selection tasks by providing a centralized access to several functionally-equivalent Web services via a unique endpoint. Community-based frameworks thus enhance Web services availability and improve the success rate of compositions. They also improve the confidence level as they select independent Web services according to a set of criteria (price, availability, speed, response quality, etc.). Several research works propose to use communities for easing the management and access to Web services [3, 4, 15, 16, 23, 26].

However, several heterogeneities between Web services and the community hamper straightforward integration. At the semantic level, discrepancies between the data representations of Web services and the data representation of the community must be resolved in order to allow transparent invocation of services via the community. Indeed, when a user request is sent to the community endpoint, the semantics of this request is organized according to the community semantics. This request is forwarded to some Web service of the community. However, each Web service already has its own semantics chosen at design time, prior to subscribing to the community. A mediation is required between the semantics of the Web services that answer the request and those of the community endpoint.

In this chapter, we address the interoperability problems raised by semantic heterogeneities in Web services communities. Our motivation, and what makes the originality and main contribution of this chapter, is to demonstrate how context-based mediation is relevant to the domain of Web service communities, and to illustrate the feasibility of our proposal via a concrete implementation. To do so, we develop a mechanism for semantic mediation that relies on a context-based model for data representation proposed in previous work [19]. We show in the following how to solve semantic discrepancies and enable seamless invocation of Web services in communities, and we illustrate our work by implementing our proposal within the WSMO framework.

This chapter is organized as follows: Sect. 2 introduces the notion of community for gathering Web services and summarizes the context-based model we rely on for describing data semantics. Section 3 discusses how the deployment of a semantic mediation module helps solve semantic inconsistencies of data between Web services and communities. Further details on the functioning of the mediation module and how it takes advantage of our context-based model are given in this section. Moreover, an implementation alternative based on the WSMO framework is proposed in Sect. 4. Section 5 presents related work on semantic mediation in communities, and Sect. 6 discusses the limitations of our work and presents some insights for future work.

2 General Architecture

2.1 Communities of Web Services

A community is typically a group of people living together or united by shared interests, cultural, religious or political reasons. In the domain of Web services, communities help gather Web services that provide a common functionality, thus simplifying the access to Web services via a unique communication endpoint, that is the access point to the community.

In previous work, we proposed an approach that supports the concepts, architecture, operation and deployment of Web service communities [23]. The notion of community serves as a means for binding Web services. A community gathers several *slave* Web services that provide the same functionality. The community is accessed via a unique *master* Web service. Users bind to the master Web service that transparently calls a slave in the community. On top of forwarding calls back and forth between users and slave Web services, the master also manages its community at a higher level. Our previous work details the management tasks a master Web service is responsible for. Such tasks include among other things registering new Web services into the community, tracking bad Web services, and removing ineffective Web services from the community.

A *master* Web service represents the community and handles users' requests with slave Web services with the help of a specific protocol. In our previous work we rely on a slightly extended version of the Contract Net protocol (CNProtocol) [25], as illustrated in Fig. 1:

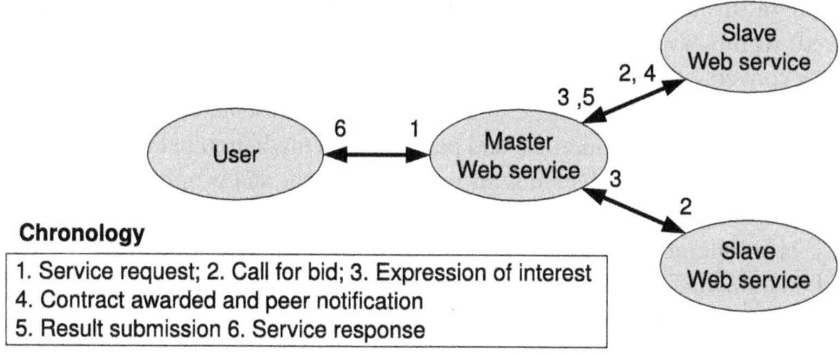

Fig. 1 Contract-Net protocol interactions

1. The master Web service sends a call for bids to the slave Web services of the community.
2. Slave Web services assess their current status and availability to fulfil the request of the master Web service, and interested Web service reply to the call.
3. The master Web service examines the received proposals and chooses the best Web services according to its preferences (QoS, availability, cost, fairness...). Then, it notifies the winner slave Web service.
4. Slave Web service that answered the call for bids but were not selected are notified too.

In this chapter, we provide a context-based semantic mediation architecture for Web service communities. Indeed, the applicability of our mediation proposition goes beyond this domain. However, we specifically focus here on its deployment with communities as defined in [23], where semantic mediation is performed between the community master and slave Web services.

2.2 Context Representation

The notion of context has for a while been a hot topic in the database field [12], and has been specifically adapted in previous work to the description and mediation of data semantics for Web services [19]. In this specific work [19], context-based representation of data semantics is particularly relevant and specifically designed to data exchange between Web services engaged in a composition. It distinguishes two concerns at different levels, where existing knowledge representation approaches see one concern only.

At the conceptual level, context-based approach encompasses matching the different domain concepts used by the actors involved in the data exchange. While semantic differences (such as different granularities of the domain concepts) may hamper straightforward matching between world representations, we assume that correspondences can be established between the domain concepts used.

At the contextual level, context-based approach encompasses the description and mediation of the different data interpretations attached to the domain concepts, which are intrinsically related to the (heterogeneous) local assumptions of the actors involved. At this level, more complex conversion rules are required to enable accurate data conversion and interpretation.

Thus, while typical approaches on knowledge representation visualize domain concepts with attached properties, and perform data mediation in an all-in-one fashion, context-based approach distinguishes two concerns and simplifies the mediation steps by dividing the complex mediation task into two distinct subtasks. The first subtask is to interconnect domain concepts at the semantic level, and the second subtask is to mediate data between different contexts using conversion rules.

Context description involves pushing data up to the level of *semantic objects*. A semantic object is a data object with an explicit semantics described through its context. A semantic object S is a tuple $S = (c, t, v, C)$ that holds a concept c

described in a domain ontology, a type t that is the XML Schema type of the data, a value v that is the data itself and a context C that is a set of semantic objects called modifiers.

Modifiers are semantic objects that participate in a context. Therefore, context is seen as a tree of modifiers where the leaves are modifiers with a *null* context. Modifiers can be of type static or dynamic. The main characteristic of dynamic modifiers is their capacity to have their value inferred from the values of static modifiers. For instance, as shown in Fig. 2, if a *price* semantic object is attached to the country *France* and to the date May 15, 2005, then it can be inferred that the *currency* modifier, which describes the currency of this price, has *Euro* as a value, making *currency* a dynamic modifier. Static modifiers have to be made explicit in order to describe the meaning of the semantic object.

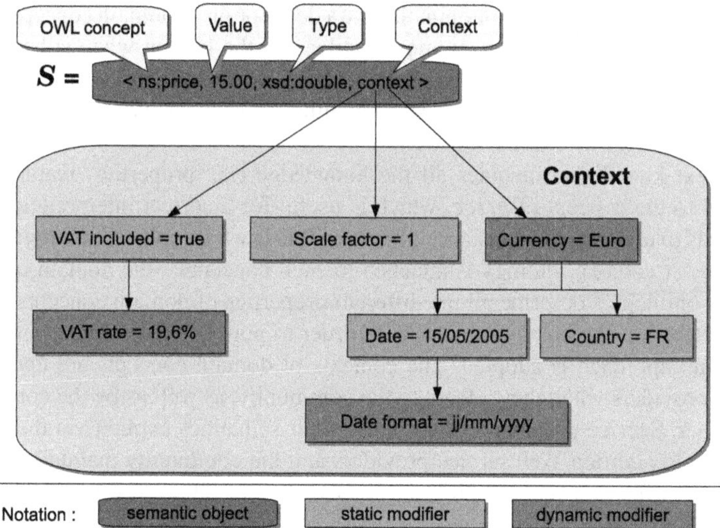

Fig. 2 Description of the *price* semantic object

2.3 Domain and Context Ontologies

The use of context comes from a simple assumption: Web services adhere to communities with difficulty. Several reasons such as strategic and economic aspects are involved, but are out of the scope of this chapter. Another reason is semantic incompatibility. In fact, each community follows a specific knowledge representation that is not always compliant with other communities' knowledge representations, and Web services already have, either implicitly or explicitly, their providers' local semantics.

Therefore, the adhesion of a Web service to a new community requires either a hard-coded change in the service implementation or the design of a wrapper that acts on behalf of the original Web service, in order to comply with the community's knowledge representation. Such tedious requirement applies to each new community a Web service wishes to adhere to. Our context-based model has for objective to ease the task of Web service providers when they decide to adhere to new communities, by scaling domain ontologies down to the minimum, and providing additional context ontologies to handle the different local semantics of service providers. To do so, our context-based model makes the distinction between domain knowledge and context knowledge.

Domain knowledge includes main concepts that are assumed to be (or should be) common to all parties. For instance, the concept of *price* might be part of a domain knowledge and included in domain ontologies. We deem appropriate to limit the application of domain ontologies to the concepts and relationships that can be devised in a top-down way. Experts in the knowledge domain should specify domain ontologies and limit to the minimum the extra description of domain concepts. Thus, domain ontologies should be the most similar and the burden when adhering to a community should be limited. An ideal situation is the design of a unique domain ontology that all communities could adopt, although such a situation is not likely to happen in an open world like the Web.

Context knowledge includes all the knowledge (i.e. properties, features, etc.) attached to the concept of *price*, which is useful for a correct interpretation when one needs to understand an instance of *price*. This is where context ontologies come into play. A context ontology is attached to each concept of the domain ontology. Context ontologies describe all the different properties of domain concepts that are not described in the domain ontology. In order to populate the context ontology, a bottom-up approach is adopted. The contexts of domain concepts are updated by service providers when they adhere to the community, as well as by the community maintainer. Service providers should make their semantics explicit via the context ontology. In addition Web service providers and the community maintainer should describe the links between the different context representations that populate context ontologies.

Separation of concerns has proven to be an efficient way to solve complex problems in the field of software engineering, and the separation of concerns we propose between domain and context ontologies follows such a well-established practice in order to facilitate semantic interoperability between Web services.

2.4 Context Annotation of WSDL

Propelling input and output data of Web services (described in the WSDL documents) to the level of semantic objects requires additional information. In WSDL documents, `<message>` elements describe data exchanged for an operation. Each message consists of one or more `<part>` elements. We also refer to `<part>` elements as "parameters" in the rest of this chapter. Each parameter has a `<name>` and a `<type>` attribute, and allows additional attributes.

In [20], we proposed a WSDL annotation that enriches input and output parameters contained in WSDL documents with a concept from a domain ontology and static modifiers from the context ontology attached to the concept. Our annotation takes advantage of the extension proposed in the WSDL specification [10], so that annotated WSDL documents operate seamlessly with both classical and annotation-aware clients. `<part>` elements are annotated with a `context` attribute that describes the names and values of static modifiers using a list of qualified names. The first qualified name of the list specifies the domain ontology concept of the semantic object (c). Additional elements refer to context ontology concept instances to describe the names and values of static modifiers. These concept instances are OWL individuals, thus they allow specifying the name and value of context attributes at the same time.

With the help of such annotation, a value v and its data type t described in the WSDL document are enriched with the concept c and the necessary modifiers to define the context C, thus forming a semantic object (c, v, t, C). To keep this chapter self-contained, we provide a simplified structure of the annotated WSDL document in Listing 1.

```
<? xml version ="1. 0"  encoding ="UTF–8"?>
<wsdl : definitions . . .>
. . .
<wsdl:message name="checkPriceReq">
   <wsdl:part name="price"  type="xsd:double"
   ctxt:context="dom:Price  ctx1:ScaleFactorOne
   ctx1:dateValue  ctx1:VATIncluded ctx1: France"/>
</wsdl:message>
. . .
</wsdl:definitions>
```

Listing 1 Annotated WSDL Snippet

A context C is populated at runtime, using logical rules. Logical rules infer the values of dynamic modifiers from the information provided by static modifiers of the WSDL annotation. Using rules offers several advantages: rules are easily modifiable, making this solution more adaptable to changes in the semantics. Often-changing values of dynamic modifiers could not be statically stored, so using rules simplifies the annotation of WSDL. Furthermore, rules separate application logic from the rest of the system, so updating rules does not require rewriting application code. In this chapter, we rely on our annotation and rule-based mechanisms in order to provide the semantic information required to perform semantic mediation within a community.

Our annotation of WSDL is a way to add semantics to the standard description language for Web services. While in our implementation (Sect. 4) we use another language (OCML) for describing Web services, our WSDL annotation allows existing Web services to comply with the requirements of context-based representation with few simple changes in the original WSDL file of the Web service.

3 Semantic Mediation for Web Service Communities

Our mediation architecture for Web service communities is built on a master Web service that contains a mediation module. This mediation module enables the master Web service to handle incoming requests from outside the community.

Thanks to the mediation module, the master Web service can act as a mediator. Upon reception of a user's request, it uses the mediation module to convert the message into the slave Web service's semantics. Upon reception of an answer from a slave Web service, the master Web service uses the mediation module again to convert the message into the semantics of the community before sending it back to the user. Our master Web service is also responsible for other tasks, such as selecting a slave Web service upon reception of a request or managing the community, as described earlier.

3.1 Accessing the Community

Typically, a user that wishes to interact with a community for fulfilling his/her goals discovers and selects the WSDL file of the community via a UDDI registry. Then, the client program uses this WSDL file to build a query and send it to the community endpoint, i.e. the master Web service. The latter handles the interactions with the client in order to hide the community complexity. Then, a community-based architecture is completely transparent from the user's point of view.

However, the master Web service does not implement the community functionality itself. Its role is to select one of the slave Web services that belong to the community according to the user's preferences, and to forward the client's request to this slave Web service. Then, it must forward back the answer from the slave Web service to the client. We detail the functioning of the master Web service hereafter.

3.2 Details on Context-Based Mediation

When it comes to the mediation aspect, our master Web service behaves as a proxy for the community. It handles and transfers incoming requests from users and outgoing answers from slave Web services. On reception of an incoming request, it uses the mediation module to perform the following actions in order to solve semantic heterogeneities using our context-based approach. The mediation module contains several components:

- an interface to communicate with the master Web service,
- a core component called *mediator* that orchestrates the different steps of the mediation process described below,
- a component called *WSDL context reader* to read WSDL annotations,
- repositories for domain and context ontologies for the community,
- a rule engine and a knowledge repository to store rules for data conversion and context building.

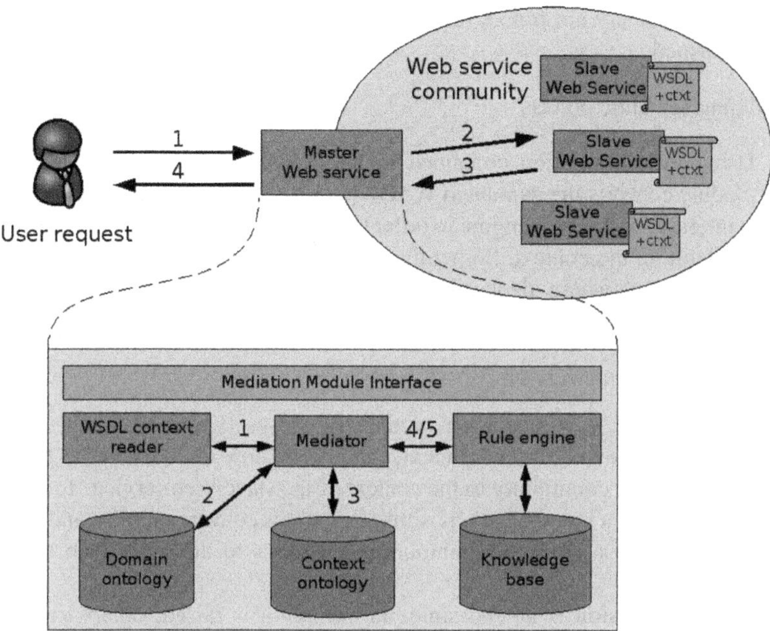

Fig. 3 Overview of the mediation process

All these components participate in the semantic mediation process in the following way, as illustrated in Fig. 3:

1. Reading WSDL annotation
   a. It selects a slave Web service and fetches its WSDL description.
   b. Then, it parses the input and output parameters of the selected WSDL operation of this slave Web service.
   c. For each parameter, it extracts the domain concept and static modifiers contained in the WSDL annotation. We assume our semantic mediation module is configured for a specific community and already has in-memory representations of the input/output parameters of the community as semantic objects, so there is no need to fetch the WSDL file proposed by the community.
2. Identifying domain vocabulary
   a. It communicates with the domain ontology to identify the domain concepts contained in the annotation.
   b. If the terms are not found, an exception is raised, otherwise the next step is confirmed.
3. Identifying context
   a. It communicates with the context ontology to identify the modifiers contained in the annotation.

   b. If the terms are not found, an exception is raised, otherwise the next step is confirmed.

4. Building semantic objects

   a. Using the information contained in the WSDL annotation, our mediation module converts the annotated WSDL parameters into semantic objects.
   b. It interacts with a rule engine in order to infer the values of dynamic modifiers available in the context. Sometimes not all dynamic modifiers can be populated. In such a case, data semantic conversion is still possible over a limited context.

5. Performing data conversion

   a. At this stage, our mediation module possesses two in-memory semantic objects that have different contexts, and needs now to convert data from the context of the community to the context of the slave Web service. To do so, it interacts with a knowledge repository that stores conversion rules and enables data conversion from the community semantics to the slave Web service's semantics.
   b. If the conversion is not possible, an exception is raised, otherwise data is forwarded to the slave Web service.

On reception of an outgoing answer, the task of our mediation module is reversed:

1. It reads the WSDL description of the slave service it interacts with, identifies the domain and context information contained in the annotation, and builds semantic objects.
2. It interacts with the rule engine that converts data from the slave Web service's semantics back to the community semantics.
3. It raises an exception if the conversion does not succeed or forwards the converted data back to the client of the community.

4 Interoperability with Semantic Web Services Frameworks: The Case of WSMO

In order to demonstrate the applicability of our approach, we consider the implementation of the conceptual approach proposed in this chapter through established Semantic Web Service (SWS) frameworks. Particularly, we discuss in the following its implementation through the established Web Service Modelling Ontology (WSMO) framework.

4.1 Semantic Web Services and WSMO

SWS frameworks aim at the automatic discovery, orchestration and invocation of distributed services for a given user goal on the basis of comprehensive semantic descriptions. SWS are supported through representation standards such as WSMO [2] and OWL-S [14]. In this chapter, we refer to the Web Service Modelling Ontology (WSMO), a well established SWS reference ontology and framework. The conceptual model of WSMO defines the following four main entities:

- Domain Ontologies provide the foundation for describing domains semantically. They are used by the three other WSMO elements. WSMO domain ontologies not only support Web services related knowledge representation but semantic knowledge representation in general.
- Goals define the tasks that a service requester expects a Web service to fulfill. In this sense they express the requester's intent.
- Web service descriptions represent the functional behavior of an existing deployed Web service. The description also outlines how Web services communicate (choreography) and how they are composed (orchestration).
- Mediators handle data and process interoperability issues that arise when handling heterogeneous systems.

WSMO is currently supported through several software tools and runtime environments, such as the Internet Reasoning Service IRS-III [9] and WSMX [28]. IRS-III is a Semantic Execution Environment (SEE) that also provides a development and broker environment for SWS following WSMO. IRS-III mediates between a service requester and one or more service providers. Based on a client request capturing a desired outcome, the goal, IRS-III proceeds through the following steps utilizing the set of SWS capability descriptions:

1. Discovery of potentially relevant Web services.
2. Selection of a set of Web services which best fit the incoming request.
3. Invocation of selected Web services whilst adhering to any data, control flow and Web service invocation constraints defined in the SWS capabilities.
4. Mediation of mismatches at the data or process level.

In particular, IRS-III incorporates and extends WSMO as core epistemological framework of the IRS-III service ontology which provides semantic links between the knowledge level components describing the capabilities of a service and the restrictions applied to its use. IRS-III utilizes OCML [18] as knowledge modelling language to represent WSMO-based service models.

4.2 Implementing Context-Based Mediation Through WSMO and IRS-III

Particularly with respect to mediation, the use of WSMO and IRS-III provides several advantages, since mediation is an implicit notion of WSMO with explicit support through dedicated mediators [8]. Mediators are often classified as OO-, GG-, WG- and WW-mediators [22]. Whereas OO-mediators resolve mismatches between distinct WSMO ontologies, GG-mediators refine a WSMO goal. WG-mediators mediate between heterogeneous goals and SWS specifications whereas

WW mediators resolve heterogeneities between distinct Web service implementations. Whereas OO-, GG-, and WG-mediators primarily support SWS discovery, WW mediators are related to orchestration and invocation. However, mediation usually involves a set of multiple different mediators. For instance, a WG-mediator usually requires OO-mediation as well in order to align distinct vocabulary formalizations. Therefore, we use the generic term mediator throughout the remaining sections instead of explicitly separating between different sorts of mediators.

The conceptual model of WSMO is well-suited to support the conceptual approach proposed in this chapter, since the representation of distinct service provider perspectives, i.e., their contexts, is an implicit element of WSMO. Moreover, distinct contexts are addressed through the notion of mediation, which aims at resolving heterogeneities which will definitely occur between distinctive Web service implementations and representations. Particularly, regarding the conceptual approach proposed in this chapter, we propose an implementation of the mediation scenario (Sect. 3) utilizing WSMO and IRS-III as follows:

1. Representation of slave Web services as SWS following WSMO.
2. Representation of context ontologies utilized by each provider as WSMO ontologies associated with each SWS.
3. Aligning the WSMO ontologies to a common upper-level domain ontology.
4. Representation of a common WSMO goal expressing the community request.
5. Description of WSMO mediators linking WSMO SWS to the WSMO goal by defining appropriate mediation rules.

Given these semantic representations, IRS-III is able to select appropriate services, which are orchestrated and invoked, whereas the mediator resolves heterogeneities at runtime. In that, by referring to the description of the functionalities of the master Web service (Sect. 3.2), it can be stated, that the built-in reasoning of IRS-III facilitates steps 1–4 as proposed in Sect. 3.2, while the implemented WSMO mediator (Med.1 in Fig. 4) aims at resolving data heterogeneities (step 5 of Sect. 3.2). Figure 4 depicts the created WSMO goal, mediator and SWS descriptions which implement the use case described in Sect. 3.

Please note, that the context ontologies, representing the context of each Web service provider are now explicit parts of the WSMO SWS descriptions, i.e., WS.1 and WS.2, whereas the domain ontology is implemented as an independent upper-level WSMO ontology, which is derived for certain contexts through the WSMO SWS descriptions, respectively the context ontologies. Indeed, the context and domain ontologies as mentioned in Sect. 2.2 are not physically separated, but the context-based approach still holds as the two levels (domain concept matching and data interpretation/conversion) remain clearly distinct via WSMO ontologies and SWS descriptions. Apart from that, we would like to point out that following the proposed WSMO-based approach, the previously introduced slave services are now supported through WSMO-compliant SWS, whereas the functionality

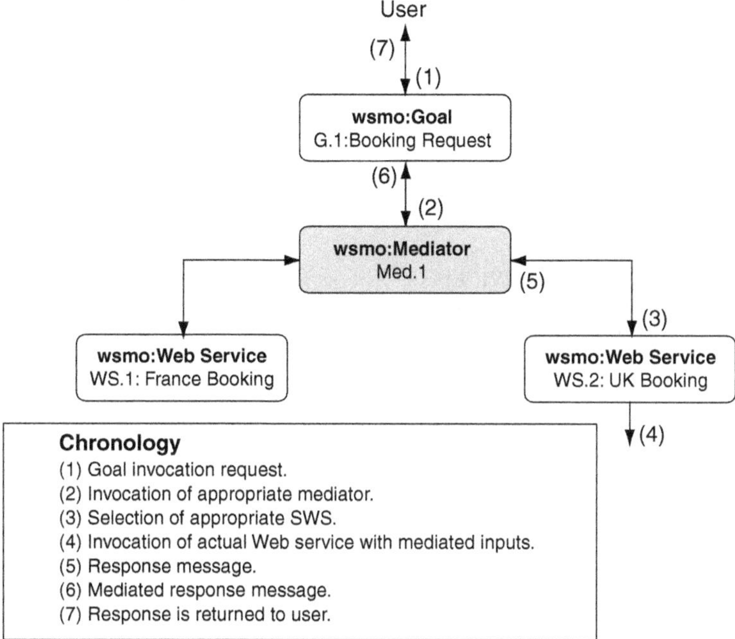

Fig. 4 WSMO goal linked to Semantic Web Services through common mediator

of the master Web service is provided by the WSMO reasoning mechanisms of IRS-III together with the mediation rules defined in the corresponding WSMO mediator.

Referring to the previously given definition of a semantic object $S = (c, v, t, C)$, c is defined as part of the upper-level WSMO domain ontology, while t is defined as part of the WSMO SWS, describing on the one hand the XML binding of the actual input message of the Web service and its expression following the used modelling language (OCML) on the other hand. The value v represents the actual value of an input parameter chosen to invoke the WSMO goal while the context C is represented as part of the WSMO SWS descriptions. Moreover, please take into account, that the WSMO descriptions proposed above not only enable the mediation between distinct data formats, i.e., currencies and date formats, but also the selection of the most appropriate Web service, either WS.1 or WS.2, based on the input values used to invoke the goal G.1. Particularly, the requested departure country is utilized with this respect, i.e., WS.1 is selected in case the requested booking departs from any European country other than UK, while in the case of UK, WS.2 is automatically invoked. The Web service selection is based on the semantic capability descriptions provided through WSMO. Listing 2 shows a simple SWS capability of WS.2 enabling the selection proposed above:

```
wsmo:WebService WS.2

(DEF–CLASS Get–UK–BOOKING–REQUEST–WS–CAPABILITY
        (CAPABILITY)
        ?CAPABILITY
        ((USED–MEDIATOR :VALUE GET-BOOKING–REQUEST–MED)
                (HAS–ASSUMPTION
                :VALUE
                (KAPPA
                  (?WEB–SERVICE)
(= (WSMO–ROLE–VALUE ?WEB–SERVICE HAS–DEPARTURE–COUNTRY) "Uk")))
        (HAS–NON–FUNCTIONAL–PROPERTIES
:VALUE
Get–UK–BOOKING–REQUEST–WS–CAPABILITY–NON–FUNCTIONAL–PROPERTIES)))
```

Listing 2 SWS capability description of WS.2

It can be summarized, that basing the conceptual approach proposed in this chapter on a common SWS framework, i.e., WSMO, and an established execution environment and reasoning engines, namely IRS-III, provides the opportunity of reusing predefined functionalities related to SWS representation, discovery and orchestration. Particularly, it could be shown, that the WSMO-based implementation enabled the reuse of IRS-III in order to deal with the master service functionalities 1-4 (Sect. 3.2). Moreover, the approach of aligning distinct context representations, being implicit part of SWS descriptions, to a common upper-level ontology is well-suited to facilitate interoperability between distinct SWS representations [11].

5 Related Work

To the best of our knowledge, there are no existing works on semantic mediation within the context of Web service communities as defined in [23]. However, our approach is inspired by several works on semantic mediation for Web services and communities of Web services, that we detail hereafter.

5.1 Semantics and Mediation for Web Services

Semantic description and mediation for Web services is a very active research topic, as the many works on the subject [2, 5, 6, 8, 13, 14, 17, 21] prove. In the following, we describe the most important works that inspired us for this chapter.

In [21], Nagarajan et al. classify the different semantic interoperability concerns that apply to Web services. They distinguish several aspects that are particularly useful for the purpose of semantic mediation.

OWL-S [14] is a language for semantic description of Web services, relying on the OWL language [24], OWL-S enables explicit semantic description of Web services input an output parameters via references to concepts described in OWL domain ontologies. With [17], Miller et al. propose an annotation to the standard description language WSDL in order to facilitate the semantic description of Web services. However, OWL-S is a full language and does not offer the benefits of WSDL annotation, and the WSDL-S annotation typically relies on domain ontologies and does not support additional context attributes nor the use of context ontologies.

With WSMX [13], Haller et al. propose a solution that is a part of the WSMO framework (WSMX is the reference implementation of WSMO). In this work, the semantics of the terms used are encoded into the WSMO description files of the services. Semantic heterogeneities between Web services are solved by reasoning on the content of a common domain ontology that has for purpose to explicitly describe reference vocabulary. The mediation process is not about converting data but more about matching the semantic description stored in the ontologies.

In [5], Dogac et al. propose an interoperability framework for the healthcare domain. This framework relies on the notion of archetype to describe data semantics. An archetype is a formal way to describe domain concepts via constraints on data. Data instances are constrained instances of a reference domain model. This work is similar to our context-based approach in the sense that a common agreement is made on a domain concept, and the different views of Web services are represented under the form of constraints over the instances of these domain concepts. However, the work of Dogac et al. requires the domain concept to encompass all the different views of Web services, which is feasible in the healthcare domain where predefined models are agreed on, but not in a more general context as presented in this chapter.

In [6], Bowers and Ludäscher propose a semantic mediation framework for scientific workflows. Their work relies on the notion of semantic type and structural type, defined on a global ontology shared by all the users. The semantic type corresponds to the abstract concept that characterizes data, and the structural type is the schema that describes data structure. For a single semantic type, the objective is to adapt the different structural data representations of Web services. This paper relies on typical semantic matching methods before performing structural-level data mediation. In the present work, we propose context-based, semantic-level data mediation for Web services.

5.2 Communities of Web Services

Several works gather functionally-similar Web services into communities that are accessed via a common interface. Benatallah et al. propose such a solution with SELF-SERV [3]. In this work, several mediators establish correspondences between the community interface and Web services that implement the functionality of the community.

Benslimane et al. [4], also group Web services into communities. The community is accessed via an interface implemented as an abstract Web service that describes the provided functionality in an abstract fashion and a set a concrete Web services that implement the functionality. A generic driver called Open Software Connectivity (OSC) handles the interactions between clients and the community.

Building upon this work, Taher et al. [26] address the problem of Web service substitution in communities. Web service substitution consists of replacing a non-functioning or non-responding Web service with a functionally equivalent one, in order to find an alternative way to enable a composition in case of exception. Substituting a service with another requires the mediation of communications between the replacing service and the original client. Mediator Web services communicate with the concrete Web services that implement the functionality, each mediator connects to a specific service.

In Taher et al.'s work, Web service selection is performed according to a set of QoS criteria (speed, reliability, reputation, etc.). The community is also in charge of administrative tasks such as addition and suppression of services to and from the community.

Medjahed and Bouguettaya proposes a community-based architecture for semantic Web services in [16]. In this work, communities gather services from the same domain of interest and publish the functionalities offered by Web services as generic operations. A community ontology is used as a general template for describing semantic Web services and communities. A major advantage of this work that relates to our proposal is the peer-to-peer community management solution that addresses the problems of centralized approaches.

6 Conclusion

Communities facilitate the discovery and selection of several functionally-equivalent Web services. Nevertheless, researches on communities usually impose a unique ontology that Web services must bind to, or require users to adapt to the semantic requirements of Web services belonging to the community. In this work, we present a trade-off between these approaches by using a context-based approach that separates shared knowledge from the local contexts of Web service providers. We demonstrate the significance of our proposal and develop mediation mechanisms that handle semantic data discrepancies between Web services and communities, thus enabling seamless interoperation at the semantic level. Short-term future work includes studying other aspects related to mediation in Web service communities such as transactional or security aspects.

However, we noticed from our experimentation that creating and using several ontologies is a difficult task, the hardest task being the update of context ontologies. Indeed, it is required that providers correctly update their context ontologies with their own context representations, but also they must provide the correspondences between their context and the contexts of other providers. Making such knowledge explicit is a hard task for providers, particularly on a large scale.

In that way, it would be interesting to find suitable solutions to avoid such constraints on providers. Therefore, long-term future work includes studying how to reduce this task by proposing advanced reasoning mechanisms that could help interconnect the different contexts of providers.

References

1. E. Al-Masri and Q. H. Mahmoud. Investigating web services on the world wide web. In J. Huai, R. Chen, H.-W. Hon, Y. Liu, W.-Y. Ma, A. Tomkins, and X. Zhang, editors, *WWW*, pages 795–804. ACM, 2008.
2. S. Arroyo and M. Stollberg. WSMO Primer. WSMO Deliverable D3.1, DERI Working Draft. Technical report, WSMO, 2004. `http://www.wsmo.org/2004/d3/d3.1/`.
3. B. Benatallah, Q. Z. Sheng, and M. Dumas. The self-serv environment for web services composition. *IEEE Internet Computing*, 7(1):40–48, 2003.
4. D. Benslimane, Z. Maamar, Y. Taher, M. Lahkim, M.-C. Fauvet, and M. Mrissa. A multi-layer and multi-perspective approach to compose web services. In *AINA*, pages 31–37. IEEE Computer Society, Washington, DC 2007.
5. V. Bicer, O. Kilic, A. Dogac, and G. B. Laleci. Archetype-based semantic interoperability of web service messages in the health care domain. *International Journal of Semantic Web and Information Systems (IJSWIS)*, 1(4):1–23, October 2005.
6. S. Bowers and B. Ludäscher. An ontology-driven framework for data transformation in scientific workflows. In E. Rahm, editor, *DILS*, volume 2994 of *Lecture Notes in Computer Science*, pages 1–16. Springer, 2004.
7. D. Box, D. Ehnebuske, G. Kakivaya, A. Layman, N. Mendelsohn, H. F. Nielsen, S. Thatte, and D. Winer. Simple object access protocol (SOAP) 1.1. Technical report, The World Wide Web Consortium (W3C), 2000. `http://www.w3.org/TR/SOAP/`.
8. L. Cabral and J. Domingue. Mediation of semantic web services in IRS-III. In *First International Workshop on Mediation in Semantic Web Services (MEDIATE 2005) held in Conjunction with the 3rd International Conference on Service Oriented Computing (ICSOC 2005), Amsterdam, The Netherlands*, December 12th 2005.
9. L. Cabral, J. B. Domingue, S. Galizia, A. Gugliotta, B. Norton, V. Tanasescu, and C. Pedrinaci. IRS-III: A broker for semantic web services based applications. In *Proceeding of the 5th International Semantic Web Conference (ISWC2006)*, Athens, GA, USA, 2006.
10. E. Christensen, F. Curbera, G. Meredith, and S. Weerawarana. Web Services Description Language (WSDL) 1.1. W3c note, The World Wide Web Consortium (W3C), March 2001. `http://www.w3.org/TR/wsdl`.
11. S. Dietze, A. Gugliotta, and J. Domingue. A semantic web service oriented framework for adaptive learning environments. In E. Franconi, M. Kifer, and W. May, editors, *ESWC*, volume 4519 of *Lecture Notes in Computer Science*, pages 701–715. Springer, 2007.
12. C. H. Goh, S. Bressan, S. Madnick, and M. Siegel. Context interchange: new features and formalisms for the intelligent integration of information. *ACM Transactions on Information and Systems*, 17(3):270–293, 1999.
13. A. Haller, E. Cimpian, A. Mocan, E. Oren, and C. Bussler. Wsmx – a semantic service-oriented architecture. In I. C. Society, editor, *ICWS*, pages 321–328. IEEE Computer Society Washington, DC, 2005.
14. D. L. Martin, M. Paolucci, S. A. McIlraith, M. H. Burstein, D. V. McDermott, D. L. McGuinness, B. Parsia, T. R. Payne, M. Sabou, M. Solanki, N. Srinivasan, and K. P. Sycara. Bringing semantics to web services: the OWL-S approach. In J. Cardoso and A. P. Sheth, editors, *SWSWPC*, volume 3387 of *Lecture Notes in Computer Science*, pages 26–42. Springer Berlin, 2004.
15. B. Medjahed and Y. Atif. Context-based matching for web service composition. *Distrib. Parallel Databases*, 21(1):5–37, 2007.
16. B. Medjahed and A. Bouguettaya. A dynamic foundational architecture for semantic web services. *Distributed and Parallel Databases*, 17(2):179–206, 2005.
17. J. Miller, K. Verma, P. Rajasekaran, A. Sheth, R. Aggarwal, and K. Sivashanmugam. WSDL-S: Adding Semantics to WSDL - White Paper. Technical report, Large Scale Distributed Information Systems, 2004. `http://lsdis.cs.uga.edu/library/download/wsdl-s.pdf`.

18. E. Motta. An overview of the ocml modelling language. In *Proceedings KEML98: 8th Workshop on Knowledge Engineering Methods & Languages*, pages 21–22. Karlsruhe, Germany, 1998.
19. M. Mrissa, C. Ghedira, D. Benslimane, and Z. Maamar. A context model for semantic mediation in web services composition. In D. W. Embley, A. Olivé, and S. Ram, editors, *ER*, volume 4215 of *Lecture Notes in Computer Science*, pages 12–25. Springer, Berlin, 2006.
20. M. Mrissa, C. Ghedira, D. Benslimane, and Z. Maamar. Towards context-based mediation for semantic web services composition. In *Proceedings of the Eighteenth International Conference on Software Engineering and Knowledge Engineering (SEKE'2006)*, San Francisco, California, July 2006.
21. M. Nagarajan, K. Verma, A. P. Sheth, J. Miller, and J. Lathem. Semantic interoperability of web services – challenges and experiences. In *ICWS*, pages 373–382. IEEE Computer Society Washington, DC, 2006.
22. M. Paolucci, N. Srinivasan, and K. Sycara. Expressing WSMO mediators in owl-s. In *Proceeding of the Semantic Web Services Workshop (SWS) at the 3rd International Semantic Web Conference (ISWC)*, Hiroshima, Japan, 2004.
23. S. Sattanathan, P. Thiran, Z. Maamar, and D. Benslimane. Engineering communities of web services. In G. Kotsis, D. Taniar, E. Pardede, and I. K. Ibrahim, editors, *iiWAS*, volume 229 of *books@ocg.at*, pages 57–66. Austrian Computer Society, Wien, 2007.
24. G. Schreiber and M. Dean. Owl web ontology language reference. `http://www.w3.org/TR/2004/REC-owl-ref-20040210/`, February 2004.
25. R. G. Smith. The contract net protocol: high-level communication and control in a distributed problem solver. *IEEE Trans. Computers*, 29(12):1104–1113, 1980.
26. Y. Taher, D. Benslimane, M.-C. Fauvet, and Z. Maamar. Towards an approach for web services substitution. In P. Ghodous, R. Dieng-Kuntz, and G. Loureiro, editors, *IDEAS*, pages 166–173. IOS Press, Amsterdam, 2006.
27. UDDI Specification Technical Commitee. Universal Description, Discovery, and Integration of Business for the Web. Technical report, October 2001. `http://www.uddi.org`.
28. WSMX Working Group. The web service modelling execution environment, 2007. `http://www.wsmx.org/`.

An Effective Aggregation Policy for RSS Services

Jae Hwi Kim, Sang Ho Lee and Young Geun Han

Abstract RSS is the XML-based format for syndication of Web contents and users aggregate RSS feeds with RSS feed aggregators. As the usage of RSS service has been diffused, it is crucial to have a good aggregation policy that enables users to efficiently aggregate postings that are generated. Aggregation policies may determine not only the number of aggregations for each RSS feed, but also schedule when aggregations take place. In this paper, we first propose the algorithms of minimum missing aggregation policy which reduces the number of missing postings during aggregations. Second, we compare and analyze the experimental results of ours with the existing minimum delay aggregation policy. Our analysis shows that the minimum missing aggregation policy can reduce approximately 29% of the posts the existing minimum delay aggregation policy would miss.

1 Introduction

As blogs becomes popular recently, the use of RSS, which is the XML-based format for syndication and subscription of information, diffuses [6]. According to the Pew Internet [13], 6 million Americans get information through RSS aggregators in 2004 and it has been increasing rapidly. RSS stands for the Really Simple Syndication, Rich Site Summary, or RDF (Resource Description Framework) Site Summary. In particular, RSS is used to easily deliver up-to-date postings such as personal weblogs, news Web sites to their subscribers [3, 15]. RSS 0.90 was designed by Netscape in 1999. After the RSS team at Netscape evaporated, the RSS-DEV Working Group and the UserLand company have been working on standardization on RSS independently. The RSS-DEV Working Group has designed RSS 1.0 based on RDF. UserLand has designed RSS 2.0 based on RSS 0.90 [6, 8, 15, 18]. These two standards are currently available and our study is based on RSS 2.0.

J.H. Kim (✉)
School of Computing, Soongsil University, Seoul, Korea
e-mail: oasisdle@gmail.com

I. King, R. Baeza-Yates (eds.), *Weaving Services and People on the World Wide Web*,
DOI 10.1007/978-3-642-00570-1_4, © Springer-Verlag Berlin Heidelberg 2009

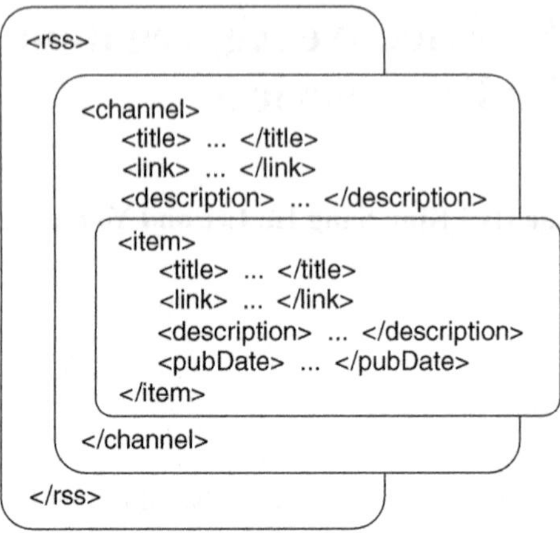

Fig. 1 Basic structure of RSS 2.0

Figure 1 shows the basic structure of RSS 2.0. The subordinate to the <rss> element is the <channel> element that contains metadata about RSS feeds. <item> is an element that has information on postings. A channel may contain any number of <item>s.

RSS does not run under a push-based protocol but does under a pull-based protocol in which individual subscribers are responsible for collecting information from Web sites. The basic syndication and subscription process of RSS feeds is shown in Fig. 2. Publishers generate postings into RSS feeds. Subscribers register RSS feed addresses to an RSS feed aggregator. An RSS feed aggregator aggregates registered RSS feeds and shows postings to subscribers. Unlike crawlers, RSS feed aggregators do not extract new URLs from the postings and use them as seeds. They only aggregate feeds that are previously registered by the users.

The role of RSS aggregator becomes more important in Web services. As the number of RSS feed that users want to subscribe grows, the number of RSS feeds that an RSS aggregator has to aggregate grows. In addition, postings dynamically appear and disappear over time [2, 4, 5, 9–12]. It is crucial to have a good aggregation policy that enables us to efficiently aggregate postings that are generated.

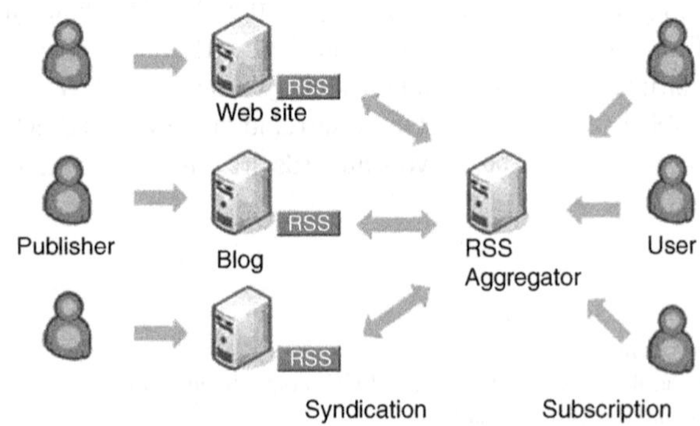

Fig. 2 Basic RSS feed syndication and subscription process

Aggregation policies may determine not only the number of aggregations for each RSS feed, but also schedule when aggregations take place. Sia and Cho [16, 17] proposed the framework of an information aggregator, and proposed the scheduling and resource allocation algorithm that exploits posting patterns and user browsing patterns.

RSS feeds are unlikely to store all generated postings. Instead, they store only a part of the most recently generated postings. It is possible for some postings in RSS feeds to be deleted (hence not to be aggregated by RSS aggregators). This paper proposes the aggregation policy that is likely to minimize the missing posting during aggregations. We present two aggregation algorithms, which we call minimum missing aggregation algorithms. We first present the initial algorithm of our policy that reduces missing postings. Then, we augment the algorithm with periodically rescheduling aggregations by analyzing previous aggregations. We compare our aggregation algorithms with existing ones. Our results show that our aggregation policy can reduce approximately 29% of the postings being missed in comparison with the minimum delay aggregation policy.

The rest of this paper is organized as follows: In Sect. 2, we review the existing aggregation policies, discuss problems in those polices. In Sect. 3, we present our policy. Section 4 describes our experimental results. Closing remarks are in Sect. 5.

2 Related Works

Let an RSS aggregator aggregate n RSS feeds. The simplest aggregation policy is to give each feed the same number of aggregations. This is called the uniform aggregation policy. The uniform aggregation policy is inefficient, because RSS feeds are aggregated equally no matter how many postings are stored in RSS feeds and how often postings are generated. They should be treated differently [14].

The aggregation delay is a widely-accepted metric that can evaluate an RSS aggregation policy [16]. The aggregation delay is the delay time between the generation time of a posting at an RSS feed and its aggregation time by an aggregator. Assume that an RSS feed F generates postings $p_1, \ldots, p_k$ at times $t_1, \ldots, t_k$ and the aggregator aggregates new postings from F at times $a_1, \ldots, a_m$. The delay associated with the posting p_i is defined as

$$D(p_i) = a_j - t_i, \tag{1}$$

where a_j is the minimum value of $a_1, \ldots, a_m$ with a_j greater than posting time t_i ($a_j >= t_i$). The delay time becomes bigger as a_j becomes more far away from t_i, as can be seen in Fig. 3. The total aggregation delay for all postings $p_1, \ldots, p_k$ of an RSS feed F is defined as follows.

$$D(F) = \sum_{i=1}^{k} D(p_i) = \sum_{i=1}^{k} a_j - t_i, where, t_i \in [a_{j-1}, a_j]. \tag{2}$$

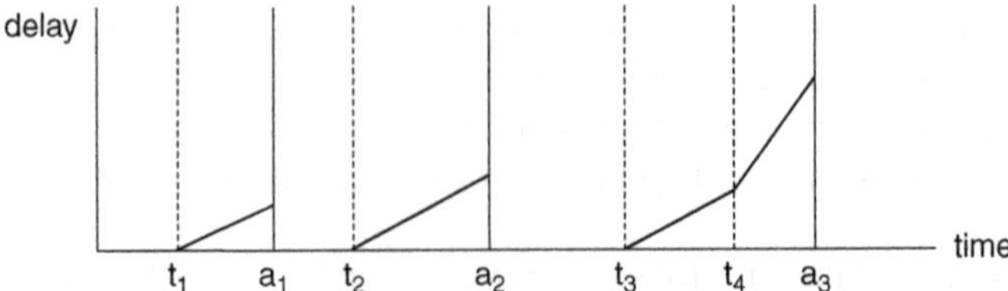

Fig. 3 Aggregation delay

We have the condition, $t_i \in [a_{j-1}, a_j]$, because the aggregation delay calculates the posting times that are generated between aggregation times a_j and a_{j-1}, where a_{j-1} denotes the immediately previous aggregation time of a_j. The total aggregation delay for all RSS feeds is defined as below:

$$D(A) = \sum_{i=1}^{n} D(F_i). \tag{3}$$

Example 1. As in Fig. 4, postings $p_1,\ldots, p_5$ are generated at $t_1,\ldots, t_5$ in a RSS feed and an aggregator aggregates at times a_1 and a_2. The aggregation delay is the difference between the aggregation time and the generation time. $D(p_1)$ is the difference between a_1 and t_1, therefore 3.

The total aggregation delay for all postings $p_1,\ldots, p_5$ of an RSS feed can be calculated:

$$\begin{aligned} D(F) = \sum_{i=1}^{5} D(p_i) = \sum_{i=1}^{k} a_j - t_i, \textit{ where}, t_i \in [a_{j-1}, a_j] \\ = D(p_1) + D(p_2) + D(p_3) + D(p_4) \\ = 11. \end{aligned} \tag{4}$$

In order to reduce the aggregation delay, Sia and Cho [16] proposed the minimum delay aggregation policy that allocates aggregation on the basis of the posting rate, which is the number of postings over a period of time. Let RSS feed F_i have the posting rate λ_i and the importance weight ω_i. Let M be the possibly maximum num-

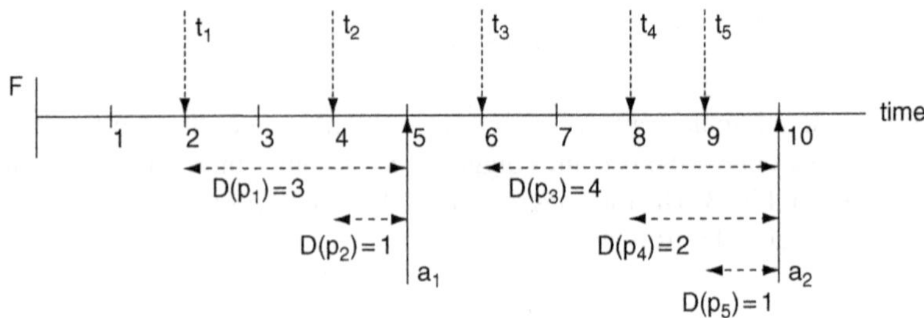

Fig. 4 Example of aggregation delay

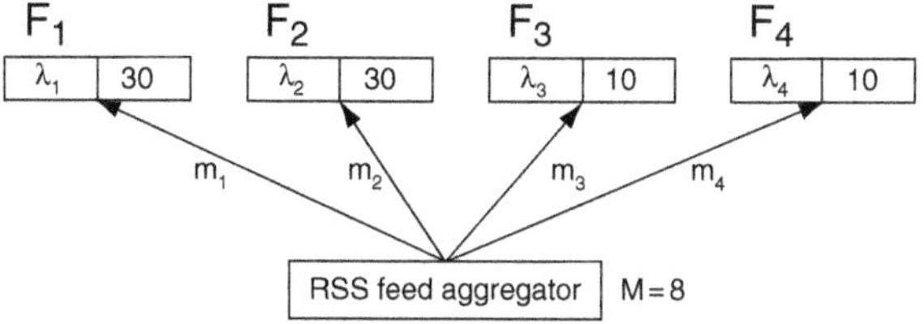

Fig. 5 Feeds and posting rates

ber of aggregations F_i can aggregate over time T. Then, the number of aggregation of F_i can be calculated as

$$m_i = k\sqrt{\omega_i \lambda_i}, \tag{5}$$

where k is a constant that satisfies $m_i = k\sqrt{\omega_i \lambda_i} = M$.

Example 2. Assume that there are RSS feeds F_1, F_2, F_3, F_4 that have the posting rates λ_1, λ_2, λ_3, λ_4 as 30, 30, 10, 10, respectively (see Fig. 5). Also assume that all RSS feeds have the same importance weight ($\omega_i = 1$) and M is 8.

Table 1 shows the allocation result. Since $\sum_{i=1}^{4} k\sqrt{\lambda_i} = 8$, the value of constant k is approximately 0.46 and the values of m_1, m_2, m_3, m_4 are 3, 3, 1, 1, respectively. Note that the values of m for RSS feeds under the uniform aggregation policy would be 2.

Table 1 Example of the minimum delay aggregation policy

F_i	λ_i	ω_i	$k\sqrt{\omega_i \lambda_i}$	m_i
F_1	30	1	2.54	3
F_2	30	1	2.54	3
F_3	10	1	1.46	1
F_4	10	1	1.46	1

3 Minimum Missing Aggregation Policy

In the previous approach, the performance criteria of RSS aggregation policy is the total aggregation delay of RSS feeds. The algorithm is devised to minimize the total aggregation delay of RSS feeds. In [7], we proposed a new performance criterion, missing postings. In this section, we propose the algorithms for minimum missing aggregation policy. There are two approaches; one that considers the storage capacity of RSS feeds and the posting rate, one that additionally exploits the aggregation rate.

The RSS feeds are unlikely to store all generated postings. Instead, they are likely to store only a part of the most recently generated postings. It is possible for some

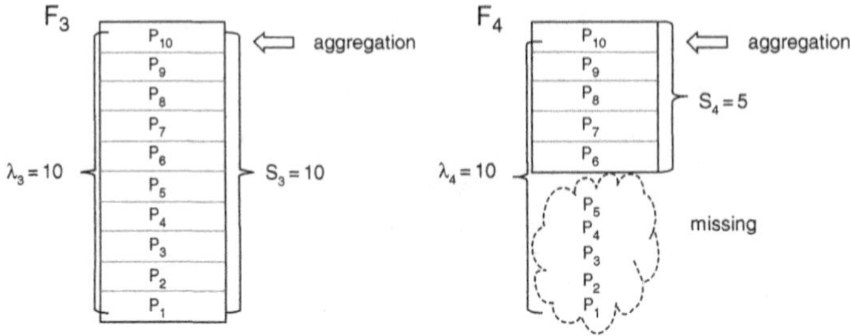

Fig. 6 Example of missing postings in RSS feeds

postings in RSS feeds to be deleted (hence not to be aggregated by RSS aggregators). Let S_i be a number of maximum postings that can be stored in the ith feed. Consider Fig. 6 where S_3 and S_4 are set to be 10 and 5, respectively. All 10 postings are stored in F_3, so an aggregator can aggregate all postings in a single aggregation.

However, postings $p_1,\ldots, p_5$ are deleted in F_4 as new postings $p_6,\ldots, p_{10}$ are generated, since S_4 is 5. An aggregator in a single aggregation can aggregate only 5 new postings, missing 5 postings that were previously generated. Postings that are generated in RSS feeds but are not aggregated (due to storage capacity of RSS feeds) by an aggregator are called missing postings.

We denote the number of postings that are expected to be aggregated at the jth aggregation in the ith RSS feed as $EPPA_{i,j}$ (expected postings per aggregation). The number of total missing postings in RSS feeds F_i, which we denote as $MP(F_i)$, is calculated as:

$$MP(F_i) = \lambda_i - \sum_{j=1}^{m_i} EPPA_{i,j}. \tag{6}$$

Then, the number of total missing postings in an RSS aggregator can be defined as

$$MP(A) = \sum_{i=1}^{n} MP(F_i). \tag{7}$$

We denote the number of the total postings that can be aggregated after the jth aggregation in the ith RSS feed as $TP_{i,(j+1)}$ (target postings). Then we have:

$$TP_{i,(j+1)} = TP_{i,j} - EPPA_{i,j}. \tag{8}$$

The total number of postings that can be aggregated before the aggregation (when $j = 0$) (i.e., $TP_{i,1}$) is λ_i, since the number of total postings generated in RSS feeds F_i is λ_i. The total number of target postings in RSS feed F_i when the aggregations are completed in RSS feed F_i (when $j = m_i$) (i.e., $TP_i, (m_{i+1})$) is $MP(F_i)$, since $MP(F_i)$ is the difference of λ_i and summation of $EPPA_{i,j}$.

Figure 8 shows the initial algorithm of the minimum missing aggregation policy. The aggregation number of the feed that has maximum $EPPA_{i,j}$ increases by one (see lines 18–20, in Fig. 8) and this process is repeated for M times. $EPPA_{i,j}$ is set to be S_i when $TP_{i,j}$ is greater than S_i. Otherwise it is set to be $TP_{i,j}$ (see lines 11–16). Note that there is an assumption that new postings (as many as S_i) are generated as early as possible before aggregation times.

There are cases in which the newly generated postings are less than S_i when an RSS aggregator aggregates F_i. That is, if all $TP_{i,(j+1)}$ are 0 (which means there are no postings to aggregate at the current aggregation time) even though there are more aggregations to take place (i.e., $\sum_{i=1}^{n} m_i < M$), set all $TP_{i,(j+1)}$ to λ_i (see lines 6–10).

Example 3. Let RSS feed F_1, F_2, F_3, F_4 generate postings 30, 30, 10, 10 per day, and S_1, S_2, S_3, S_4 are 15, 10, 10, 5, respectively (see Fig. 7). Assume that their importance weight is of the same ($\omega_i = 1$) and the RSS aggregator can aggregate as many as 8 times.

In minimum missing aggregation policy, calculate $EPPA_{i,j}$ (see Table 2) and give an aggregation to the feed that has the maximum value of $EPPA_{i,j}$, and repeat this process for 8 times, because M is 8.

In practice, posting time may change dynamically. As a result, the aggregator may not aggregate postings as much as $EPPA_{i,j}$ in each aggregation.

For this, we present another algorithm for the minimum missing aggregation policy that periodically reschedules aggregations for each feed (for example, reschedule

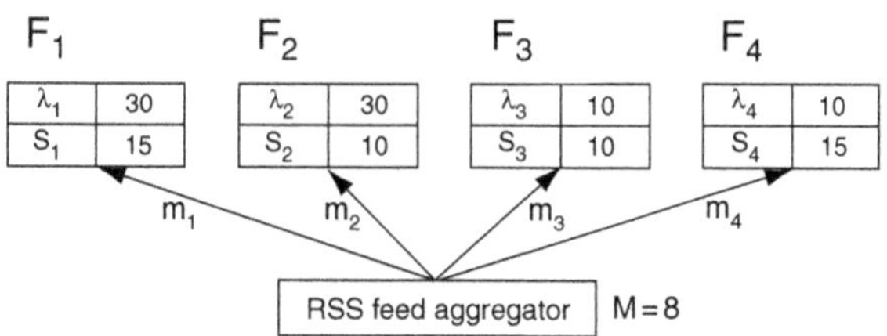

Fig. 7 Feeds, posting rates, storage capacity

Table 2 Example of allocating aggregations by calculating $EPPA_{i,j}$

	Computation to find the maximum $EPPA_{i,j}$								m_i			
	F_1		F_2		F_3		F_4					
M	$TP_{1,j}$	$EPPA$	$TP_{2,j}$	$EPPA$	$TP_{3,j}$	$EPPA$	$TP_{4,j}$	$EPPA$	m_1	m_2	m_3	m_4
1	30	15	30	10	10	10	10	5	1	0	0	0
2	15	15	30	10	10	10	10	5	2	0	0	0
3	0	0	30	10	10	10	10	5	2	1	0	0
4	0	0	20	10	10	10	10	5	2	2	0	0
5	0	0	10	10	10	10	10	5	2	3	0	0
6	0	0	0	0	10	10	10	5	2	3	1	0
7	0	0	0	0	0	0	10	5	2	3	1	1
8	0	0	0	0	0	0	5	5	2	3	1	2

```
Algorithm of minimum missing aggregation policy
Input : M,
        n,
        λi = {λ1,...,λn}
        Si = {S1,...,Sn}
Procedure
[1] for i ← 1 to n
[2]       mi = 0, TPi,1 = λi
[3] end for
[4] total_TP = Σ(i=1..n) TPi,1
[5] for total_m ← 1 to M
[6]       if ( total_TP = 0 ) then
[7]             for i ← 1 to n
[8]                   j = mi + 1
[9]                   TPi,j = λi + 1
[10]            end for
[11]      for i ← 1 to n
[12]            j = mi + 1
[13]            if ( TPi,j ≥ Si) then
[14]                  EPPAi,j = Si
[15]            else
[16]                  EPPAi,j = TPi,j
[17]      end for
[18]      Find the maximum value of EPPAi,j
          (where 1≤i≤n, j=mi+1)
[19]      Let indexes i and j of maximum EPPAi,j be maxI,
           maxJ, respectively
[20]      mmaxI = mmaxI + 1
[21]      TPmaxI(maxJ+1) = TPmaxI,maxJ - EPPAmaxI,maxJ
[22]      total_TP = Σ(i=1..n) TPi,1
[23] end for
```

- $TP_{i,(j+1)}$ (target postings): The number of total postings that can be aggregated after j^{th} aggregation in i^{th} RSS feed
- $EPPA_{i,j}$ (expected postings per aggregation): The number of postings that is expected to be aggregated at j^{th} aggregation in i^{th} RSS feed

Fig. 8 Algorithm of minimum missing aggregation policy

in every 24 h) and exploits the number of actually aggregated postings in previous aggregations.

We denote the number of postings that are actually aggregated at the jth aggregation in the ith RSS feed as $APPA_{i,j}$ (actual postings per aggregation). Note that the number of the total postings that can be aggregated after the jth aggregation in the ith RSS feed in the previous algorithm (see line 21 at Fig. 8) is defined as follows:

$$TP_{i,(j+1)} = TP_{i,j} - EPPA_{i,j}. \tag{9}$$

In this paper, we define the ratio of the number of actually aggregated postings during aggregations to the posting rate in a feed to be *aggregation rate*. For example, when the RSS feed F_1 that has aggregation rate 10 aggregate 7 postings, the aggregation rate for F_1 is 0.7.

During aggregation, we can expect many postings to be aggregated from a feed with high aggregation rate, while a small number of postings are likely to be aggregated from a feed with low aggregation rate. If extra aggregations were given to a feed with high aggregation rate, a large number of postings would be aggregated system-wide. On the same token, if extra aggregations were given to a feed with low aggregation rate, a small number of postings would be aggregated system-wide. In the second algorithm, we give extra aggregations to feeds with high aggregation rate, while decreasing aggregations from feeds with low aggregation rate, in order to minimize the missing postings during aggregations as many as possible. We implement the aforementioned approach by adjusting $TP_{i,j}$. Moreover, the second algorithm dynamically schedule aggregations by calculating $TP_{i,j}$ in every predefined interval, while $TP_{i,j}$ are initialized only once during the entire execution of the previous algorithm.

We call a feed that has the aggregation rate greater than 0.8 *hot feed*; we call a feed that has the aggregation rate less than 0.2 *cold feed*. We recalculate $TP_{i,j}$ to apply the aggregation rate of the previous aggregation. $TP_{i,j}$ of the hot feeds can be defined as:

$$TP_{i,j} = \lambda_i + \left(\lambda_i - \sum_{k=l}^{j-1} APPA_{i,k}\right). \tag{10}$$

In this formula, l stands for the latest time when the $TP_{i,j}$ was updated. $TP_{i,j}$ is updated to the addition of posting rate and the number of missing postings $(\lambda_i - \sum_{k=l}^{j-1} APPA_{i,k})$. Hot feeds that have many missing postings in the previous aggregation are likely to take extra aggregations. In case of the cold feeds, $TP_{i,j}$ can be calculated as

$$TP_{i,j} = \sum_{k=l}^{j-1} APPA_{i,k}. \tag{11}$$

$TP_{i,j}$ is updated to the number of postings actually aggregated (which is less than the posting rate), hence less aggregation are given in the current scheduling. $TP_{i,j}$ of the rest of the feeds are calculated as

$$TP_{i,j} = \lambda_i. \tag{12}$$

Note that in our new calculation of $TP_{i,j}$ that differently treats feeds based on the aggregation rate, hot feeds are likely to get the highest value of $TP_{i,j}$ (hence extra aggregations could take place).

Example 4. Let RSS feed F_1, F_2, F_3, F_4 has posting rates 35, 30, 15, and 10 per day, and S_1, S_2, S_3, S_4 are 15, 10, 10, and 7, respectively. Table 3 shows the distribution of the number of postings for each feed per hour. Note that the summation of posting

Table 3 Example of the distribution of the number of posting rate per hour

	Day 1				Day 2				Day 3			
F	F_1	F_2	F_3	F_4	F_1	F_2	F_3	F_4	F_1	F_2	F_3	F_4
λ_i	35	30	15	10	35	30	15	10	35	30	15	10
S	15	10	10	7	15	10	10	7	15	10	10	7
0~ 1	0	0	1	0	0	0	2	1	2	0	1	0
1~ 2	2	0	2	0	0	0	0	0	1	0	2	0
2~ 3	1	0	0	0	1	0	0	0	0	0	0	3
3~ 4	0	0	2	0	0	0	0	0	2	0	0	0
4~ 5	1	0	0	0	1	0	0	0	0	0	0	0
5~ 6	1	0	1	0	0	0	0	0	0	0	0	0
6~ 7	2	0	0	0	0	0	0	0	0	0	0	1
7~ 8	2	0	0	0	0	0	0	0	0	0	0	2
8~ 9	3	0	1	1	1	1	1	1	0	0	2	1
9~ 10	0	0	0	0	2	0	1	0	0	0	1	0
10~ 11	0	0	0	0	2	2	0	0	3	1	0	0
11~ 12	1	1	0	0	5	0	0	0	2	0	0	0
12~ 13	1	0	0	0	2	0	0	0	2	0	0	0
13~ 14	1	0	0	1	2	0	0	3	2	0	1	0
14~ 15	1	0	1	0	1	0	5	0	2	0	0	0
15~ 16	3	0	4	0	1	0	4	1	2	0	2	0
16~ 17	1	0	4	0	3	2	2	5	3	0	2	0
17~ 18	3	0	2	0	2	0	0	1	1	0	3	0
18~ 19	2	3	0	0	2	0	2	0	2	3	0	0
19~ 20	3	0	0	0	2	0	0	0	2	0	0	1
20~ 21	0	0	0	0	2	0	1	1	3	0	2	1
21~ 22	2	0	1	0	2	0	0	1	3	1	0	0
22~ 23	3	0	1	0	3	1	0	0	2	0	0	0
23~ 24	2	0	0	0	1	0	1	0	1	0	2	0

per day does not always match with given posting rate. Assume that their importance weight is of the same ($\omega_i = 1$) and the RSS aggregator can aggregate 8 times every day and the aggregations are rescheduled in every 24 h.

Table 4 shows the result of rescheduling aggregations. When M is one, $TP_{i,j}$ and $EPPA_{i,j}$ are initialized to λ_i and S_i, respectively. The feed that has the maximum value of $EPPA_{i,j}$ (which is F_1) is chosen. Then, m_1 (the number of aggregations for F_1) is increased to one and $TP_{1,j}$ is decreased to 20. Consider when M is 3, F_2 is chosen since it has the largest value of $EPPA_{i,j}$. After allocating aggregations for day 1 is finished (after repeating this process 8 times), $APPA_{i,k}$ represents the number of postings actually aggregated for each feed. Note that in this example, F_1 and F_3 aggregated many postings while F_2 and F_4 aggregated only few postings. The aggregation rate for feeds F_1, F_2, F_3, and F_4 are 0.97, 0.13, 0.67, and 0.2, respectively. Hence, F_1 is determined to be hot feed while F_2 and F_4 are cold feeds. Especially, the posting rate of F_2 is notably high but only few postings are newly aggregated.

In day 2 (when M is nine), $TP_{i,j}$ are recalculated for each case. $TP_{i,j}$ for F_1 is increased while F_2 and F_4 are decreased. The aggregations are given similarly.

Table 4 Allocation result for second approach of minimum missing aggregation policy

	Computation to find the maximum $EPPA_{i,j}$								m_i			
	F_1		F_2		F_3		F_4					
M	$TP_{1,j}$	$EPPA$	$TP_{2,j}$	$EPPA$	$TP_{3,j}$	$EPPA$	$TP_{4,j}$	$EPPA$	m_1	m_2	m_3	m_4
1	35	15	30	10	15	10	10	7	1	0	0	0
2	20	15	30	10	15	10	10	7	2	0	0	0
3	5	5	30	10	15	10	10	7	2	1	0	0
4	5	5	20	10	15	10	10	7	2	2	0	0
5	5	5	10	10	15	10	10	7	2	3	0	0
6	5	5	0	0	15	10	10	7	2	3	1	0
7	5	5	0	0	5	5	10	7	2	3	1	1
8	5	5	0	0	5	5	3	3	3	3	1	1
	$APPA_{1,k}$	34	$APPA_{2,k}$	4	$APPA_{3,k}$	10	$APPA_{4,k}$	2	3	3	1	1
	$TP_{1,j}$	$EPPA$	$TP_{2,j}$	$EPPA$	$TP_{3,j}$	$EPPA$	$TP_{4,j}$	$EPPA$	m_1	m_2	m_3	m_4
9	36	15	4	4	15	10	2	2	1	0	0	0
10	21	15	4	4	15	10	2	2	2	0	0	0
11	6	6	4	4	15	10	2	2	2	0	1	0
12	6	6	4	4	5	5	2	2	3	0	1	0
13	0	0	4	4	5	5	2	2	3	0	2	0
14	0	0	4	4	0	0	2	2	3	1	2	0
15	0	0	0	0	0	0	2	2	3	1	2	1
16	36	15	4	4	15	10	2	2	4	1	2	1
	$APPA_{1,k}$	35	$APPA_{2,k}$	6	$APPA_{3,k}$	14	$APPA_{4,k}$	7	4	1	2	1
	$TP_{1,j}$	$EPPA$	$TP_{2,j}$	$EPPA$	$TP_{3,j}$	$EPPA$	$TP_{4,j}$	$EPPA$	m_1	m_2	m_3	m_4
17	35	15	6	6	16	10	7	7	1	0	0	0
18	20	15	6	6	16	10	7	7	2	0	0	0
19	5	5	6	6	16	10	7	7	2	0	1	0
20	5	5	6	6	6	6	7	7	2	0	1	1
21	5	5	6	6	6	6	0	0	2	1	1	1
22	5	5	0	0	6	6	0	0	2	1	2	1
23	5	5	0	0	0	0	0	0	3	1	2	1
24	35	15	6	6	16	10	7	7	4	1	2	1
	$APPA_{1,k}$	35	$APPA_{2,k}$	5	$APPA_{3,k}$	16	$APPA_{4,k}$	7	4	1	2	1

Note that after iteration 15, all $TP_{i,j}$ became 0, therefore they are set to λ_i (see lines 6–10 of Fig. 8). After all, the number of aggregations in day 2 for F_1 and F_3 were increased, and decreased for F_2 in comparison with those of day 1. This is exactly what we would like to do about our policy; giving aggregations to feeds that would aggregate more postings than feeds that would not.

In this example, the aggregator can aggregate 171 postings out of 202 postings. In the previous approach of the minimum missing aggregation policy, 148 postings can be aggregated

The architecture of the RSS aggregator for our experiment is shown in Fig. 9. The URLs of RSS feeds are loaded into DB (Feed URL) by the Importer. URLs stored in DB are fetched into the Feed Queue by the Feed Fetcher. The Feed Reader gets URLs from the Feed Queue, read RSS feeds, parse elements, and store them

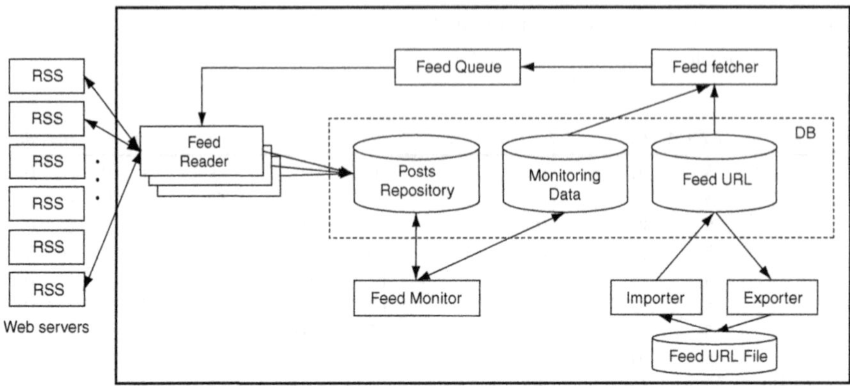

Fig. 9 Architecture of the RSS aggregator

into the Posts repository in DB. The Feed Monitor calculates λ_i and S_i and store them in Monitoring Data in DB.

We have randomly selected 1,000 RSS feeds from Allblog [1], which is a meta blog portal, for the experimental data. We have aggregated 57,096 postings for 11 weeks. To check for missing postings, each feed has been aggregated every 2 h and compared to see if duplicated postings are found. When duplicated postings are found, we know that new postings are not generated as much as S in the feed (i.e., there was no overflow in the feed). In this case, we know that no postings are being missed.

The number of daily postings in all RSS feeds is illustrated in Fig. 10. The average of daily postings is 687. The number of postings generated daily ranges from 442 to 917. The distribution of daily posting rate for total RSS feeds is shown in Fig. 11. Approximately 98% of total RSS feeds generate less than 10 postings per day.

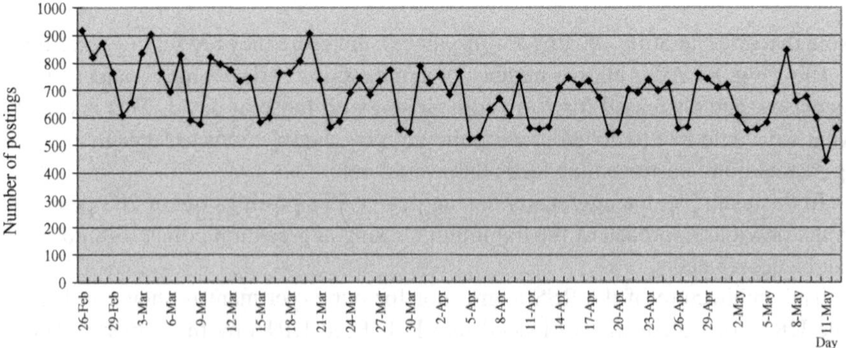

Fig. 10 The number of daily postings in all RSS feeds

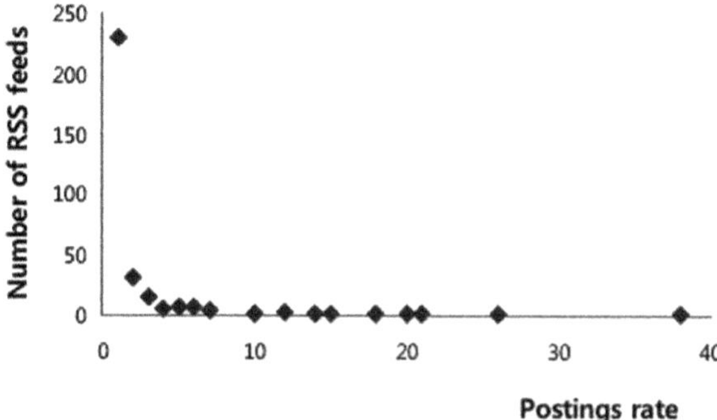

Fig. 11 The distribution of daily posting rate

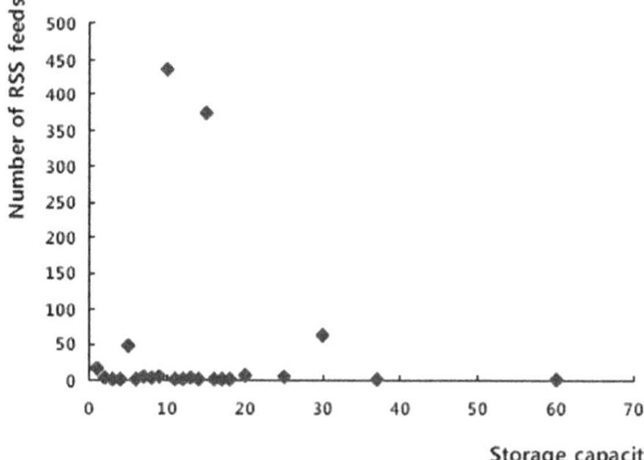

Fig. 12 The distribution of storage capacity

Figure 12 shows the distribution of the number of postings that can be stored at feeds. The storage capacity of the feeds is by no means uniform; feeds are different from each other in terms of storage capacity. Approximately 83% of the RSS feeds store 10–15 postings while the other RSS feeds store 1–60 postings. This observation implies that the consideration on the storage capacity of feeds pays off (cannot be negligible).

4 Results and Analysis

The objective of the experiments is to compare aggregation efficiency of the minimum delay aggregation policy, the two approaches of minimum missing policy in perspective of the number of missing postings. We assumed that all RSS feeds have the same importance weight ($\omega_i = 1$). For our experiment, the value of M, which is the maximum number of aggregation, is ranging from 1,000 to 30,000. λ_i and S_i were determined from the experimental data of the first 3 weeks, and used for the rest of 8 weeks of the experiments, in which the missing postings and aggregation delay were actually calculated.

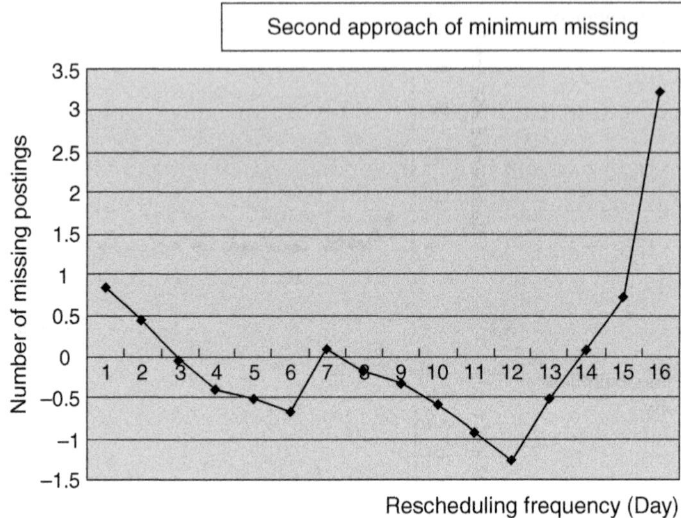

Fig. 13 z-score normalization of the number of missing postings

One concern we have in the second approach of our policy is how often we should set $TP_{i,j}$, in order to periodically reschedule aggregations. The normalization serves our purpose for this experiment, where we are not interested in the actual number of missing postings for each case. In fact, we are interested in the patterns of the number of missing postings under different rescheduling frequency in the second approach of the minimum missing aggregation policy. Let p_i denote the number of missing postings when the rescheduling period is i days. The normalized value for p_i is $\frac{p_i - average(P)}{stddev(P)}$.

In Fig. 13, axis x indicates the rescheduling frequency for the second approach of the minimum missing aggregation policy, while axis y indicates the normalized number of missing postings. Rescheduling period of 12 days shows the best performance. When the rescheduling period is less than 12 days, the number of missing postings increases, because the rescheduling period is not sufficient to judge which feed is hot and which one is cold. When the period is over 12 days, the number of missing postings also increases due to low updates.

In Fig. 14, we now compare the first approach of the minimum missing aggregation policy and the best case in the second approach. The average rate of the missing postings for the first approach of the minimum missing aggregation policy is 14% while the second approach is 12%. The second approach reduces 14% of the missing postings of the first approach.

There are two drawbacks in the first approach that possibly cause lower performance in comparison to the second approach. First, when allocating aggregations to each feed, it exploits the posting rate but does not consider the actual posting time and aggregation time. Second, it allocates all aggregations at once. However, the number of postings stored in each feed may change over time and it needs to be

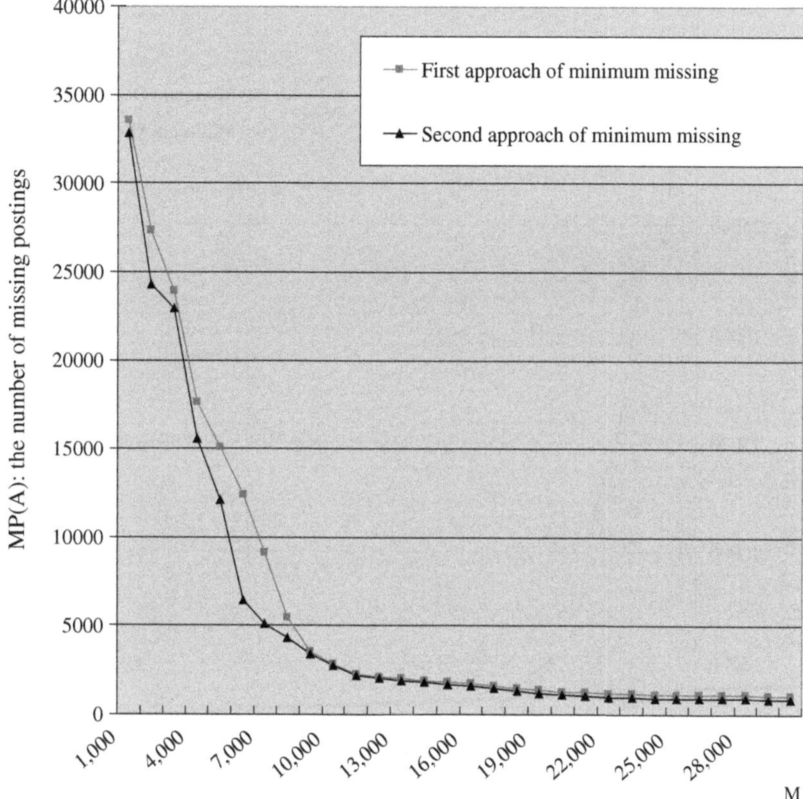

Fig. 14 Missing postings for 2 approaches of the minimum missing aggregation policy

updated. In this paper, we present the second approach as our proposed minimum missing aggregation policy.

Figure 15 illustrates the results for missing postings for the minimum delay aggregation policy and the minimum missing aggregation policy. As M increases, the number of missing postings decreases in both policies. When M is greater than 6,000, the minimum missing aggregation policy outperforms the minimum delay aggregation policy in terms of minimizing the number of missing postings. The average rate of missing postings for the minimum missing aggregation policy is 12% while the minimum delay aggregation policy is 18%. When M is 30,000, the rate of missing postings for the minimum missing aggregation policy is 2% which is acceptable and may decrease as M increases. The minimum missing aggregation policy can reduce approximately 29% of missing postings in the minimum delay aggregation policy.

It is worthwhile to consider why the minimum delay performed better than the minimum missing in the case that M is less than approximately 6,000. The reason for this is that M is far less than would-be-required numbers. For example, when M

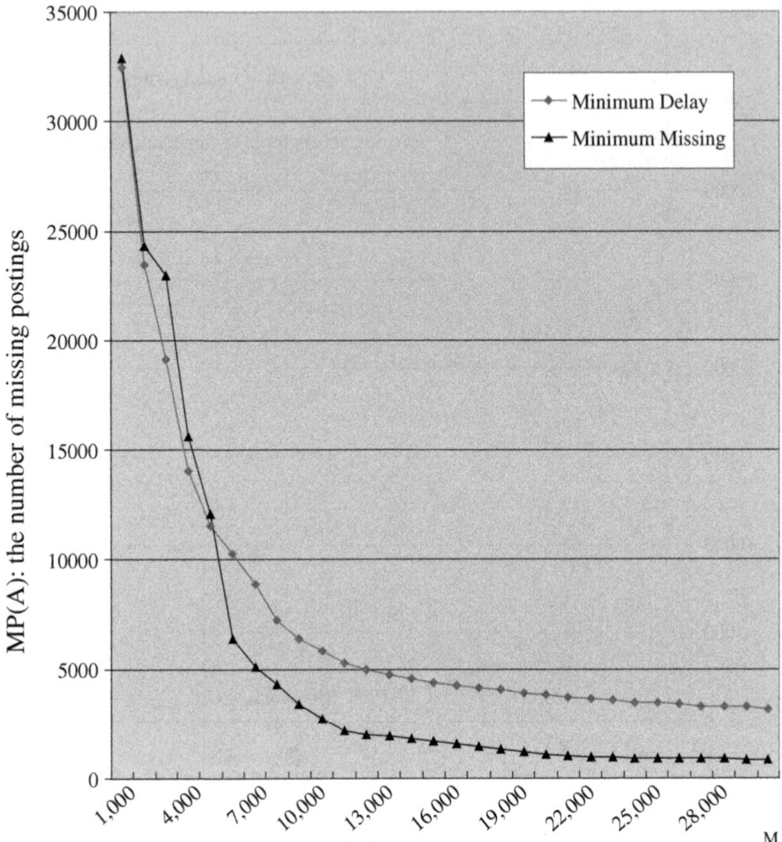

Fig. 15 The number of missing postings

is set to be 6,000, it implies that the total number of aggregations in a single day for 1,000 feeds becomes roughly 80, which is far less than the number of aggregations of visiting each feed only once in a single day.

Figure 16 shows the aggregation delays. When the value of M is greater than 3,000, the minimum delay aggregation policy performed better than the minimum missing aggregation policy in terms of aggregation delay. The minimum missing aggregation policy increased approximately 10% aggregation delay of the minimum delay aggregation policy.

In summary, in terms of missing postings, 71% of missing postings of the minimum delay aggregation policy are missed in the minimum missing aggregation policy. In terms of aggregation delay, 10% of aggregation of the minimum delay aggregation policy is additionally added to the minimum missing aggregation policy. In other words, the minimum missing aggregation policy can reduce approximately 29% of the missing postings in comparison with the minimum delay aggregation policy, while increasing only 10% of the aggregation delay. As such, we may conclude that our proposed aggregation policy can efficiently reduce missing postings.

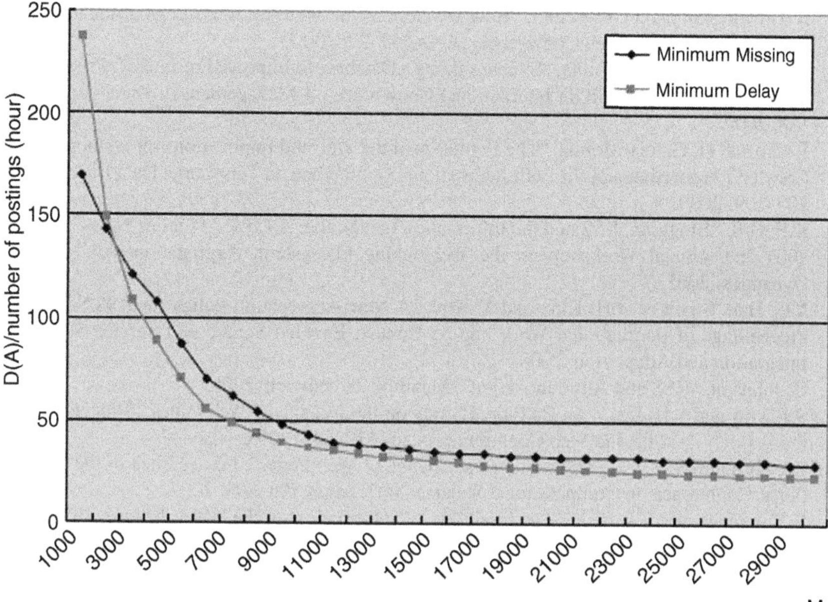

Fig. 16 The aggregation delay

5 Conclusion and Future Work

This paper presents the minimum missing aggregation policy that efficiently reduces missing postings. We proposed the minimum missing aggregation policy that reschedules aggregations for each feed periodically and exploiting the number of actual aggregated postings in previous aggregations. We have also conducted an experiment to show the performance of our algorithm and compared with other existing methods. We believe that our study help users choose an appropriate aggregation policy of RSS services for their particular computing environment.

As for the future work, we plan to explore the possibility of exploiting the general posting pattern of RSS feeds based on their past posting history to schedule aggregations. Knowledge on the posting patterns could help us aggregate RSS feeds in an efficient way (such as, predicting the posting times).

Acknowledgments This work was supported by the Korea Research Foundation Grant funded by the Korean Government (MOEHRD). (KRF-2006-005-J03803).

References

1. Allblog, http://www.allblog.net.
2. Bloglines, http://www.bloglines.com.

3. B. Brewington and G. Cybenko, "How Dynamic is the Web?", Proceedings of the 9th International World Wide Web Conference, pages 257–276, 2000.
4. J. Cho and H. Garcia-Molina, "Synchronizing a Database to Improve Freshness", Proceedings of the 2000 ACM SIGMOD International Conference on Management of Data, pages 117-128, 2000.
5. J. Cho and H. Garcia-Molina, "The Evolution of the Web and Implications for an Incremental Crawler", Proceedings of the 26th International Conference on Very Large Data Bases, pages 200–209, 2000.
6. K.E. Gill, "Blogging, RSS and the Information Landscape: A Look At Online News", WWW 2005 2nd Annual Workshop on the Weblogging Ecosystem: Aggregation, Analysis and Dynamics, 2005.
7. Y.G. Han, S.H. Lee, J.H. Kim, and Y. Kim, "A New Aggregation Policy for RSS Services", Proceedings of International Workshop on Context Enabled Source and Service Selection, Integration and Adaptation, 2008.
8. D. Johnson, "RSS and Atom in Action", Manning, Greenwich, 2006.
9. S.J. Kim and S.H. Lee, "An Empirical Study on the Change of Web Pages", Proceedings of the Seventh Asia-Pacific Web Conference, pages 632–642, 2005.
10. S.J. Kim and S.H. Lee, "Estimating the Change of Web Pages", Proceedings of the International Conference on Computational Science 2007, pages 798–805, 2007.
11. S. Lawrence and C.L. Giles, "Accessibility of Information on the Web", Nature, 400(6740), pages 107–109, 1999.
12. A. Ntoulas, J. Cho, and C. Olston, "What's New on the Web? The Evolution of the Web from a Search Engine Perspective", Proceedings of the 13th International World Wide Web Conference, pages 1–12, 2004.
13. Pew Internet and American Life, "The State of Blogging", http://www.pewinternet. org/pdfs/PIP_blogging_data.pdf.
14. M. Rosenblum and J.K. Ousterhout, "The Design and Implementation of a Log-Structured File System", ACM Transactions on Computer Systems, 10(1):26–52, February 1992.
15. RSS 2.0 Specification. http://blogs.law.harvard.edu/tech/rss.
16. K.C. Sia, J. Cho and H.K Cho, "Efficient Monitoring Algorithm for Fast News Alert", IEEE Transaction on Knowledge and Data Engineering, 19(7):950–961, July 2007.
17. K.C. Sia, J. Cho, K. Hino, Y. Chi, S. Zhu and B.L. Tseng, "Monitoring RSS Feeds Based on User Browsing Pattern", Proceedings of the International Conference on Weblogs and Social Media, 2007.
18. What is RSS?, http://www.xml.com/pub/a/2002/12/18/dive-into-xml.html.

Evolution of the Mobile Web

Rittwik Jana and Daniel Appelquist

Abstract The Mobile Web refers to accessing the World Wide Web from a mobile device. This chapter discusses the evolution of the mobile web from a perspective of the mobile web research community that has published at the WorldWideWeb conference satellite workshop series – MobEA. This workshop has been developed over a period of six years covering a wide range of topics. We summarize some of our findings and report on how the mobile Web has evolved over the past six years.

1 Introduction

There are several drivers that have motivated us to write this article. First, there are important technical questions such as "What technology will drive the next wave in the mobile web?" to more business and opportunity related questions such as "What are the most sustainable business models?" and "How do you capitalize on the mobile web?". Second, the research community is often inundated with a huge amount of information that ties some of the above drivers (e.g. technical, business, operational) together. We hope to bridge or make associations for some of these areas in due course and attempt to carve a picture that is hopefully coherent to a general research audience.

Just a few words about the workshop series before we get started. The MobEA series started in 2003 and has continued till date. This workshop has always been collocated with the World Wide Web conference series to draw a similar web community that is also interested in the "mobile" aspect of the Web [1]. The particular themes of the conference varied from year to year. Specifically, they can be enumerated as follows

---

R. Jana (✉)
AT&T Labs Research, Bldg 103, Rm B229, 180 Park Ave, Florham Park, NJ, 07932, USA
e-mail: rjana@research.att.com

I. King, R. Baeza-Yates (eds.), *Weaving Services and People on the World Wide Web*,
DOI 10.1007/978-3-642-00570-1_5,

MobEA 2003 - Emerging Applications for the Mobile Web [2]
MobEA 2004 - Multimedia and collaborative systems [3]
MobEA 2005 - Customer focused mobile services [4]
MobEA 2006 - Empowering the mobile Web [5]
MobEA 2007 - Mobile Web in the developing world [6]
MobEA 2008 - Personal rich social media [7]

These workshops have brought together people working in industry and academia, as well as government, non-governmental organizations and even religious groups to explore the convergence between the Web and Mobile universes. This convergence has been described as a culture clash. The MobEA workshops have been rare opportunities to bring members of both communities together. What has often emerged from the workshops have been new insights on both sides and opening up of new lines of communications.

2 [MobEA 2003] – Emerging Applications for the Mobile Web

This was the first year of the workshop. The focus was mainly on emerging and novel applications that will set the stage for next generation services. Application disciplines varied from real time end user services for example, a personalized voice call assistant [8], wireless mobile health system [9] to architectural and design related questions regarding flexible pagination for device independent authoring [10] and models for content-based billing using XML [11]. Interesting contributions were made particularly in the area of computing [12] and the business impact of future mobile applications [13].

Theo Kanter [12] points out that context aware computing has so far dealt mainly with *user* level context. However, there is much more to gain if *infrastructure* level context can also be used. For example, infrastructure level context represents what the infrastructure is trying to achieve in order to deliver the content appropriately to the mobile end user. In other words service delivery can be made context-aware, more specifically, directly related to infrastructure context and indirectly related to user level context. This aims to maximize the user attention for accomplishing his task at hand while the service delivery framework senses and manages to adapt to the user's computing and communications environment.

Arie Segev [13] raises an interesting question that is very relevant today. In particular, how should one evaluate the business value of mobile technology when requested to convert a business to go mobile (i.e. what are some of the broad concepts that companies should investigate before making mobile technology investment decisions?). This transformation process that is ongoing today to create the value of *mobile* business from an eBusiness model needs to be carefully evaluated. In particular, he argues that the primary focus on m-business enablement must be one that is "customer and process" oriented and should target the following properties:

1. Must have a context dependent workflow or process.
2. Must have an adaptive architecture that can sense and respond to management, people, process and technology needs.
3. Must be able to provide process continuity.
4. Must preserve the key properties of a process.

3 [MobEA 2004] – Multimedia and Collaborative Systems

This was clearly an important workshop theme slightly ahead of its time. Looking back it was never a far fetched idea then that multimedia would one day revolutionize the Internet in terms of the number of appealing applications and their usefulness. For example, YouTube [14], Flickr [15] and Facebook [16] completely changed the viewpoints of how users share content (more importantly multimedia content) for the purposes of social networking. This workshop focused on two sub themes namely, mobile multimedia systems and collaborative systems.

In particular, [17] set the stage with an impressive presentation on the next generation technology trends including prognosis on the future 4th generation (4G) broadband service suite depicted in Fig. 1. The concept of service convergence was also explained Fig. 2. Traditionally, separate service environments will become an all encapsulating merged and blended service environment. In particular, different access technologies (e.g. Ethernet, DSL, 3G wireless, 4G wireless) will converge in an all IP-network that will form the basis for future communications. In fact, this is today known more commonly as fixed-mobile convergence (FMC) and has paved the way for a new breed of applications namely seamless mobility and unified communications. The core infrastructure that has been attributed for enabling such a convergence is IP Multimedia Subsystem (IMS) [18], standardized by 3GPP [19].

One of the highlights of this workshop was a unique technique called content-based sampling analyzed by Gibbon et al. [20] that is used to provide personalized delivery of video information on mobile devices. Different multimedia processing techniques are used namely, audio processing that employs automatic speech recognition (ASR) and speaker segmentation algorithms, video segmentation that employs content-based sampling algorithms to extract "clips" of interest. The user interface is also a key component of the design for delivering a personalized look-and-feel. Making good use of the limited screen size and limited input capabilities allows users to easily jump across topics and segments using a highlight-and-click paradigm on a touch screen.

Another interesting paper was the design of a scalable alerting and notification service for mobile users that separates the design of the alert management platform and the alert dissemination platform [21]. The dissemination platform used multiple gateways or protocol adaptors to customize content on the fly to their destination devices. The alert management platform was designed to customize the business logic of how alerts are managed and reported back to the message initiator.

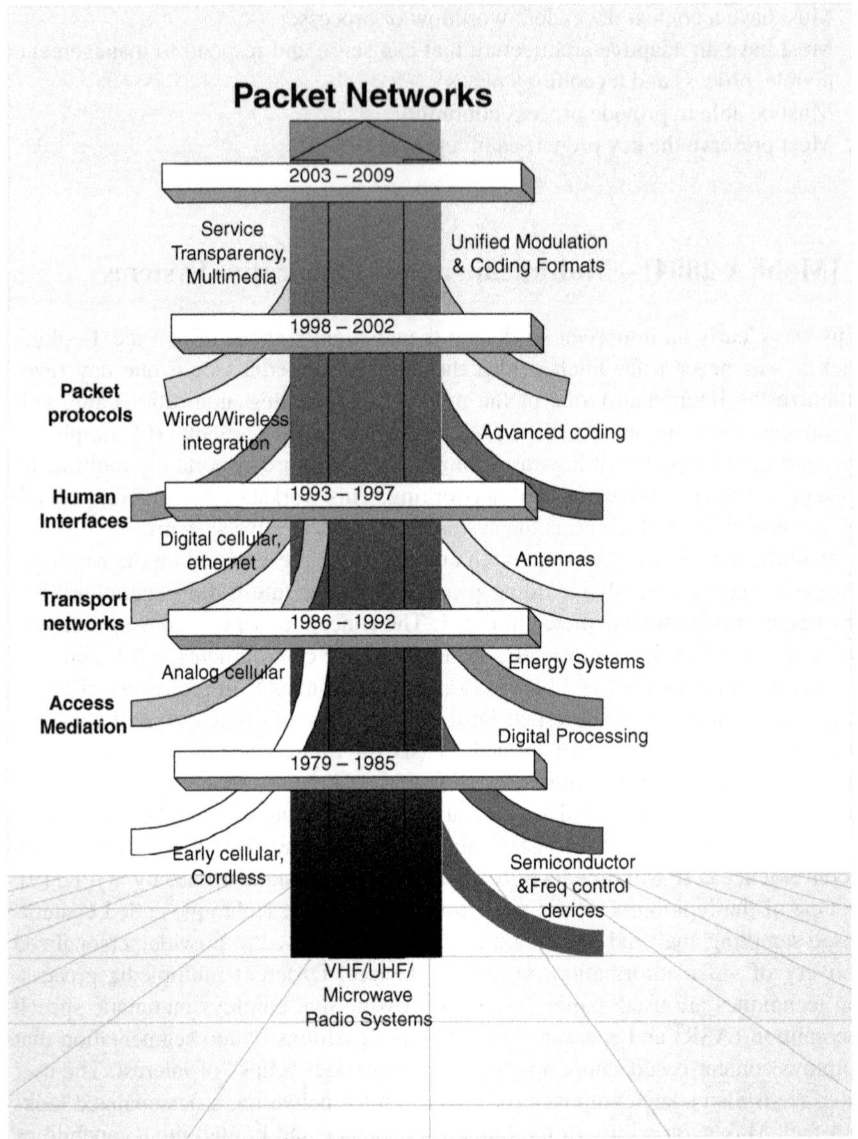

Fig. 1 Wireless technology evolution

Participatory sensing is only recently becoming a popular phenomenon with the advent of smart devices and embedded GPS. Muthukrishnan et al. [22] proposed an architecture for collecting data from wearable sensor devices. They study the use of on-person sensors for monitoring physiological, behavioral and health-related aspects.

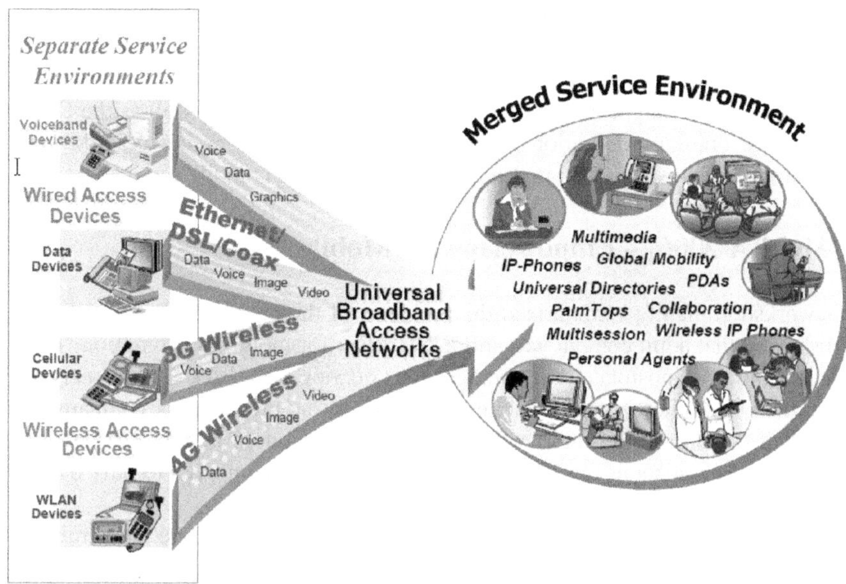

Fig. 2 Broadband narrowband service fusion

4 [MobEA 2005] – Customer Focused Mobile Services

This workshop was dedicated to the usability aspects of the mobile Web. Roto [23] addresses mobile browsing from various dimensions namely, device usability, browsing usability and site usability. All of these dimensions provide for a holistic experience to the end user. Device usability has a lot to do with the actual constructs of the mobile phone. In particular, the access keys, the size of the display, the style of the user interface are all important aspects that the device manufacturer needs to take into account.

The earlier browser experience has primarily been navigating WAP pages and decks. They were essentially text based with limited multimedia capability. Today the mobile browser experience is enhanced to be much more interactive using speech as an input rather than just point-and-click [24], faster page rendering with clever use of optimized content layout techniques, and frequent use of caching to eliminate repeated downloads especially over an impoverished access link.

Site usability has to do with content structure and relevance, one that is easy for the user to navigate to his information of interest with just a few clicks. Aesthetics and good content layout rules is of paramount importance. This brings us to an article presented by Appelquist [25] where he discusses that the semantic enrichment of content using metadata can be very helpful for downstream processors. Appelquist also gives an example where a list of links intended to be displayed as a navigation menu should be annotated using inline semantics. This annotation will later help content transcoders and browsers to render the menu differently than another type of list. He advocates that the adoption of Semantic Web across industries (tool vendors, platform vendors, content providers, handsets manufactures, browser vendors, network components, etc.) can bring down the cost of implementation. The Semantic Web activity has brought us the RDF model and XML syntax as well as the OWL language for ontology definition. Using standards developed by the W3C Mobile Web initiatives is instrumental in driving customer focused mobile services.

5 [MobEA 2006] – Empowering the Mobile Web

This workshop mainly summarized the problems of the mobile Web. Baluja et al. [26] showed that adult content was still a key driver for mobile consumption. They further went on to postulate that homogeneous queries are related to the emerging nature of the mobile content. Mobile content is not as prevalent as compared to the regular desktop in the Internet. There is less variation on mobile queries (e.g. top 1000 queries account for 20% of mobile browsing as compared to only 6% on desktop browsing).

Elina [27] highlighted the fact that the cost of mobile data traffic is restraining mobile browsing from becoming widespread. From a survey conducted across several countries it was observed the user perceived billing model did not equate to the actual bill that the user pays for. Carriers do not communicate clearly the cost for each transaction and this is believed to be a stumbling block in wider acceptance of mobile browsing. It was also highlighted that a flat fee-based subscription may not be suitable for developing countries. With dual mode phones, users are switching to alternate bearers like WiFi. There could be an opportunity for smart proxies (e.g. Opera) to make costs more transparent to the user.

Weiss [28] addressed the importance of doing usability testing by quoting examples from a media download experience study and presented some real customer insight studies showcasing user frustration with badly designed mobile user experience. There were lots of issues related to internationalization. The combination of the carrier portal offering the catalogue of songs to purchase, the vending machine the dispenses the media and the media rights owner all lack interoperability testing and create a confusing user experience. Some interesting facts on mobile browsing traits were also discussed.

1. People want the mobile Web because the thing they are looking for is not on the device as a stand alone application.
2. Urgency is also a key driver for mobile Web. Vital information like "I need to get this particular bus schedule now!"
3. Time killer: "Sitting on the bus, at a gas station filling up etc."
4. People use the mobile Web in very non-standard ways. The common (non-technical) user has a different way/perspective of using the Web.
5. The cost to develop a mobile Web site decreases with time. Upfront design and planning is critical to the success of a good Web site.

What emerged from MobEA 2005 and 2006 was a clear consensus that user experience is paramount in the world of the Mobile device. While advanced Web

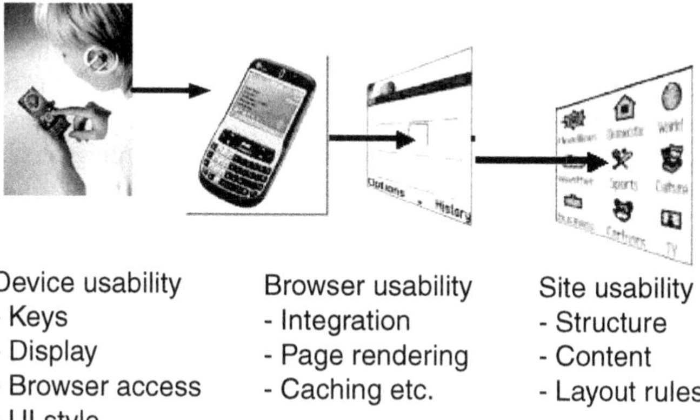

Fig. 3 Device, browser and site usability

technologies (such as the Semantic Web) can be brought to bear to greatly enhance user experience, good interaction design and human factors work by those designing mobile, and mobile Web, services and applications is requisite. Figure 3 illustrates the key usability design factors to keep in mind while designing mobile sites.

The 2006 event also coincided with the publication of the Mobile Web Best Practices "Basic Guidelines" document from the W3C Mobile Web Best Practices working group). These guidelines, which were discussed at the workshop, were published with the intention of making it easy for content providers to deliver better mobile Web user experience.

6 [MobEA 2007] – Mobile Web in the Developing World

We have come a long way from making the Web available and accessible to a vast majority of users in the Internet. However, there is still a significant portion of users in the world that do not have access to basic communications infrastructure. This workshop was devoted to understand the issues associated with the mobile Web in the developing world. The W3C has championed a lot of the standards related work in founding key enabling technologies that create the Web as we know of today. A particular mention is the Web Accessibility Initiative (WAI) working group and the Mobile Web Initiative (MWI) tasked to make the Web more accessible from mobile phones. Mobile phone service is fairly ubiquitous and has penetrated even in remote parts of the world. As a result a large number of services in the developing world is based on messaging (specifically SMS). However, SMS has its disadvantages. Its size limitation, text only and session-less behavior makes it difficult to develop complex applications. The Web on the other hand is a natural platform of choice on which to build such next generation services. There were some exceptional points driven in this forum.

Ramamritham [29] has developed a knowledge management service named aAQUA that allows rural people to ask questions and get relevant answers from subject matter experts. (e.g. "How does a farmer take care of his goats during heavy rainfall?"). The answers can be given in a context sensitive manner since the location of the user is known. The subject matter experts essentially "own" the answer and a collaborative environment is set up to facilitate the discussion. Answers (and supporting data) is also fed into the system using SMS. Multilingual support is a necessity for these kind of services. There is a viable business model. Kiosk owners charge 5–10 rupees for a page of answers. In rural areas this doesn't work, so they have supplemented with advertising. Company makes money through SMS. Some entrepreneurs have built businesses around it. He also noted that they did the right thing by not having a business model on day 1.

Esteve et al. [30] investigates the desirable characteristics for devices to access the mobile Web in a developing country. It was mentioned that out of the next two billion new mobile phone users, about 90% of them will be from the developing world. He outlined the basic characteristics to be considered in a device to be fit for the developing world, namely,

1. Price – Adoption of new features of mobile telephony has always been driven traditionally by the decrease in the cost of terminals including such a feature.
2. Usability – Ease of use will drive a quick service adoption rate. Summarized in Fig. 4 are the tradeoffs between having screen real estate and better input modalities. It is observed that the needs for mobile browsing falls somewhere in the middle where there is a need for above the baseline mobile phone and a reasonable input modality.
3. Power – Awareness has certainly changed dramatically in the past 6 years when taking energy consumption as a factor. Businesses and consumers are striving to conserve energy and create a green footprint in daily activities. Reliable mobile web services need to be delivered under the circumstances of intermittent power supply and impoverished access links.

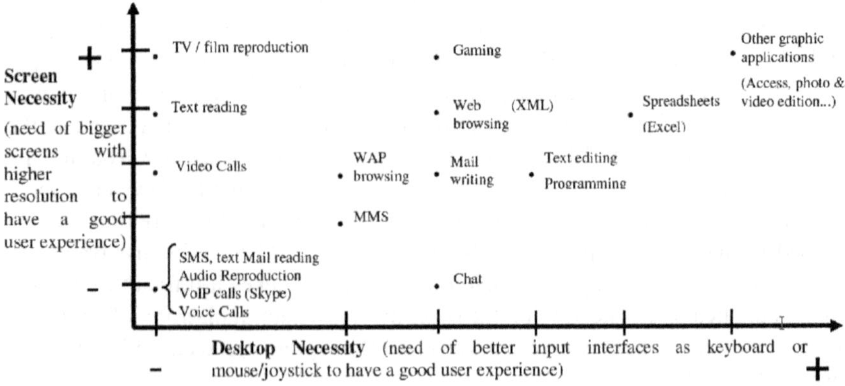

Fig. 4 Screen necessity vs. desktop necessity

4. Operating conditions – Generally speaking, the operating conditions are far harsher than a lab environment. Devices need to be tested under a ruggedized specifications.

There are also laptops that are starting to emerge for Internet access namely, One laptop per child [31]. Other alternatives are second hand market that sell mobile phones for less than $30 as positioned by the Emerging Market Handset of the GSM association [32]. Esteve et al. also mention that the best device that is available right now for the developing market is a PC with WiFi and satellite connectivity, however, this is not a scalable solution.

Ken Banks [33] presented material regarding the current state of mobile technology use in the developing world, exposing some interesting trends. In particular, his work on application of mobile phones in global conservation and development for social and environmental benefit is another reminder that the ultimate needs of the local people are not forgotten in our quest for better technology.

7 [MobEA 2008] – Personal Rich Social Media

This was the most recent workshop and its theme was devoted to applications for mobile users with a focus in rich social media. This included topics of the emergence of social networking trends on the mobile and immersive services like connecting virtual worlds to the real world. We kicked off by an interesting keynote from Lee [34] on Mobile Web 2.0. Jeon et al. [35] also highlighted the differences of Mobile Web 1.0 and Mobile Web 2.0. Figure 5 shows some of the concept differences and notes that the basis for Mobile Web 2.0 is that it is a platform that allows integration and creation of various services and applications. The general conclusion was that awareness for mobile Web 2.0 has grown, however, there still lacks innovations that can tie all these different "concepts" together. There are many application possibilities of machine learning and data mining technologies for use in mobile web technologies.

Affective computing where clothes change color with mood are slowly emerging – T-shirts that will transmit touch information. Context aware computing leverages on a network of sensors that are able to sense and capture environment conditions/context. All these point to the fact that social networking and participatory sensing will be a driving factor in defining the mobile Web 2.0 space. Technology trends of the mobile Web point to the following categories [35]:

1. Full browsing capability
2. Mobile web standardization
3. Mobile AJAX and Widgets
4. Search & Advertising – Future of mobile search – use in real life [augmented reality view]
5. Mobile Mashups & Open APIs
6. Mobile RFID & 2D barcode [Use of RFID-based phones in Germany]

	Mobile Web 1.0	Mobile Web 2.0
Network	Low speed (<0.5MB)	High speed (>0.5MB) – HSXPA, WiBro
Protocol	WAP protocol-based WAP browsing	(w)TCP/IP-based full browsing
Contents	HTML and WML-based contents	XML and XHTML-based contents
Business Model	Walled garden, backyard	Open business model and wired/wireless integrated model
Technical Model	Closed, proprietary	Open and standard based (MobileOK)
Browsing Method	Browsing of WAP sites	Ubiquitous browsing linked to RFID and LBS, real-world tagging and RSS reader function
Terminal	Connection through the mobile phone	Connection through various mobile devices
Service	Only hyperlink supported	REST-, SOAP-, and WSDL-based Mobile Web service
Authentication	Centralized authentication	Distributed authentication and identity management
Connection	Input the Entry URL	Automatic connection (WINC, mobile RFID, 2D barcode, etc.)
UI	One hand/Both hands/ Hands-free	Multi-modal/Ubiquitous Web access technology (voice, gesture, RFID, etc.)
API Interface	One service, some API	Mashups, Open APIs
Fee	Measured rate system (very expensive)	Flat rate system (normal)
Advertising	No advertising	New business model based on mobile advertising
Characteristics	Dedicated to browsing	Mobile Web as a platform

Fig. 5 Comparison of mobile web 1.0 and 2.0

7. Mobile Social Networks
8. Mobile User Generated Content – The mobile user is becoming the information creator, not just the information consumer.

Work presented by Yahoo! labs [36] regarding the automatic determination of "importance" of content on a Web page in order to ensure the display of this content is prioritized in a small-screen environment. Again, there was a focus at this workshop on Web technologies that enable better user experience in the mobile Web, underscoring the importance of user experience in mobile.

8 The Mobile Web Initiative

Last but not least, we want to say a few words about the Mobile Web Initiative (MWI) championed by the W3C [37]. MWI's goal is to make browsing the Web from mobile devices a reality. MWI has several working groups as listed below. Some work items are completed and some are still in progress.

1. Mobile Web Best Practices Working Group [38]
   The Best Practices Working Group develops a set of technical best practices and associated materials in support of development of web sites that provide an appropriate user experience on mobile devices. Figure 6 illustrates the mobile web best practices recommendations [34]. To date, this group has produced the Mobile Web Best Practices "Basic Guidelines" and MobileOK tests and checker which tests conformance of content to the best practices. The group is currently working on Mobile Web Applications Best Practices, guidelines for proxy-based content transformation, and documents detailing the relationship between Mobile Web Best Practices and W3C's Web Content Accessibility Guidelines.
2. Device Description Working Group [39]
   The Device Description Working Group develops an API and a set of properties to enable the development of globally accessible, sustainable data and services that provide device description information applicable to content adaptation. The Device Descriptions working group has completed its work and has delivered a core vocabulary for device descriptions as well as a universal API for device capability detection.
3. Test Suites Working Group [40]
   The Test Suites Working Group helps create a strong foundation for the mobile Web through the development of a set of test suites targeted at browsers. The

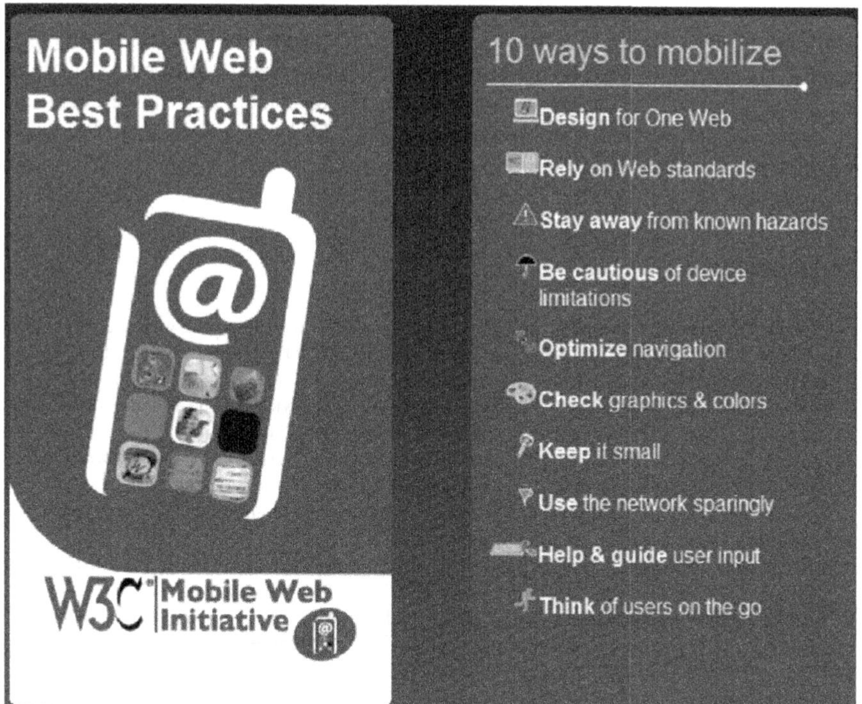

Fig. 6 Mobile Web best practices recommendations

test suites working group has delivered, among other things, a Web Compatibility Test for Mobile Browsers which tests for compliant implementation of a number of key Web technologies key to delivering consistent mobile Web user experience.

4. Mobile Web for Social Development Interest Group [41]
   The MW4D Interest Group explores how to use the potential of Information and Communication Technologies (ICTs) on Mobile phones as a solution to bridge the Digital Divide and provide minimal services (health, education, governance, business, ...) to rural communities and under-privileged populations of Developing Countries. This Interest group recently ran a workshop in Sao Paolo Brazil, supported by the World Bank and the UN development fund.

This year, the work of the W3C Mobile Web Initiative continues into a new phase, including more developer outreach, work on mobile widgets and rich mobile web applications, and further development of the work on the mobile Web in the developing world.

9 Conclusion

We have highlighted the progression of mobile Web from the standpoint of research contributions made in a series of workshops for the past six years. Activities ranged from simple applications that make the web more accessible in the developing world to sophisticated page layout schemes and content-based sampling techniques that make the mobile web more personalized. We also identified standardization activities conducted within the framework of W3C. Mobile Web has seen phenomenal growth globally and will continue to evolve in the coming years.

References

1. "International world wide web conferences steering committee," http://www.iw3c2.org/.
2. Charles Petrie and Rittwik Jana, "Emerging applications for the mobile web," in *MobEA*, 2003, http://www.research.att.com/~rjana/mobea.htm.
3. Rittwik Jana and Robin Chen, "Emerging applications for wireless and mobile access," in *MobEA II*, 2004, http://www.research.att.com/~rjana/mobea2004.htm.
4. Rittwik Jana, Bin Wei, and Johan Hjelm, "Customer focused mobile services," in *MobEA III*, 2005, http://www.research.att.com/~rjana/mobea2005.htm.
5. Rittwik Jana, Daniel Appelquist, and Bin Wei, "Empowering the mobile web," in *MobEA IV*, 2006, http://www.research.att.com/~rjana/mobea2006.htm.
6. Rittwik Jana and Daniel Appelquist, "Mobile web in the developing world," in *MobEA V*, 2007, http://www.research.att.com/~rjana/mobea2007.htm.
7. Rittwik Jana, Daniel Appelquist, Galit Zadok, and Bin Wei, "Personal rich social media," in *MobEA VI*, 2008, http://www.research.att.com/~rjana/mobea2008.htm.
8. Florian Wegscheider, Michael Pucher, and J. Tertyshnaya, "Personal voice call assistant: Voicexml and sip in a distributed environment," in *MobEA*, 2003.
9. Jaime Delgado and Ramon Mart, "Security in a wireless mobile health care system," in *MobEA*, 2003.

10. Gabriel Dermler, Michael Wasmund, Guido Grassel, Axel Spriestersbach, and Thomas Ziegert, "Flexible pagination and layouting for device independent authoring," in *MobEA*, 2003.
11. Reinhardt A. Botha and Peter J. De Villiers, "An architecture for selling xml content," in *MobEA*, 2003.
12. Theo Kanter, "Cooperative mobile ambient awareness," in *MobEA*, 2003.
13. Arie Segev, "Assessing the business value of mobile applications," in *MobEA*, 2003.
14. "Youtube," http://youtube.com.
15. "Flickr," http://www.flickr.com.
16. "Facebook," http://www.facebook.com.
17. Robert Miller, "4g – technology, tele-trends, and tele-prognosis," in *MobEA*, 2004.
18. "Ims – ip multimedia subsystem," http://en.wikipedia.org/wiki/IP_Multimedia_Subsystem.
19. "3gpp," http://en.wikipedia.org/wiki/3gpp.
20. David Gibbon, Zhu Liu, Behzad Shahraray, Lee Bageja, and Bernard Renger, "Multimedia processing for enhanced information delivery on mobile devices," in *MobEA*, 2004.
21. Bin Wei, Yih Farn Chen, Huale Huang, and Rittwik Jana, "A multimedia alerting and notification service for mobile users," in *MobEA*, 2004.
22. Su Chen, Amit Gaur, S. Muthukrishnan, and D. Rosenbluth, "Wireless in loco sensor data collection and applications," in *MobEA*, 2004.
23. Virpi Roto, "Browsing on mobile phones," in *MobEA*, 2005.
24. "Yellowpages.com," http://www.yellowpages.com/.
25. Daniel Appelquist, "Enabling the mobile web through semantically-driven user experiences," in *MobEA*, 2005.
26. Shumeet Baluja and Maryam Kamvar, "A large scale study of wireless search behavior: Google mobile search," in *Conference on Human Factors in Computing Systems*. 2006, ACM.
27. Virpi Roto, Roland Geisler, Anne Kaikkonen, Andrei Popescu, and Elina Vartiaine, "Data traffic costs and mobile browsing user experience," in *MobEA*, 2006.
28. Scott Weiss, "Mobile media purchases are difficult," in *MobEA*, 2006.
29. Kirthi Ramamritham, "Information access through mobiles: Opportunities and challenges," in *MobEA*, 2007.
30. Guillermo Esteve and Angel Machin, "Devices to access internet in developing countries," in *MobEA*, 2007.
31. "One laptop per child," http://wiki.laptop.org/go/The_OLPC_Wiki.
32. "Gsm world," http://www.gsmworld.com/index.shtml.
33. Ken Banks, "Mobile web in the developing world," in *MobEA*, 2007.
34. Seungyun Lee, "Mobile web goes 2.0," in *MobEA*, 2008.
35. Seungyun Lee and Jonathan Jeon, "Integrating mobile services and content with the internet," in *MobEA*, 2006.
36. Amit Madaan, Srinivasan Sengamedu, and Rupesh Mehta, "Web page layout optimization using section importance," in *MobEA*, 2008.
37. "Mobile web initiative," http://www.w3.org/Mobile/.
38. "Mobile web best practices," http://www.w3.org/2005/MWI/BPWG/Group/.
39. "Device description working group," http://www.w3.org/2005/MWI/DDWG/.
40. "Test suites working group," http://www.w3.org/2005/MWI/Tests/.
41. "Social development interest group," http://www.w3.org/2008/MW4D/.

Personalized Service Creation and Provision for the Mobile Web

Quan Z. Sheng, Jian Yu, José M. del Álamo and Paolo Falcarin

Abstract The convergence of telecom networks and the Internet is fostering the emergence of environments where Web services are available to mobile users. The variability in computing resources, display terminal, and communication channel require intelligent support on personalized delivery of relevant data and services to mobile users. Personalized service provisioning presents several research challenges on context information management, service creation, and inherent limitations of mobile devices. In this chapter, we describe a novel framework that supports weaving context information and services for personalized service creation and execution. By leveraging technologies on Web services, agents, and publish/subscribe systems, our framework enables an effective, user-centric access of integrated services over the mobile Web environments. This chapter overviews the design, architecture, and implementation of the framework.

1 Introduction

The advances of telecom and mobile technologies are changing the way services are delivered to end users. With the convergence of telecom networks and an all-Internet Protocol (IP) based core network—on the one hand—typical telecom services like voice call and Short Message Service (SMS) become accessible to Internet users—on the other hand—mobile users are also granted the opportunity to enjoy versatile Internet services from anywhere and at anytime [4, 9, 31]. In this sense from the end user point of view, mobile Web means using mobile devices to access both telecom and Internet services in a homogeneous way. Services become more accessible to end users. In addition, location- and presence-based service personalization is destined to provide richer and finer user experiences [5, 21].

Q.Z. Sheng (✉)
School of Computer Science, The University of Adelaide, Australia
e-mail: qsheng@cs.adelaide.edu.au

I. King, R. Baeza-Yates (eds.), *Weaving Services and People on the World Wide Web*,
DOI 10.1007/978-3-642-00570-1_6, © Springer-Verlag Berlin Heidelberg 2009

Recently, a new paradigm has emerged allowing non-skilled end users to easily generate their own content and services from the mashup of existing information services and data sources [7]. Web 2.0 [29] is the name given to this paradigm, which includes new communication channels like blogs or wikis. They support end users to communicate following a many-to-many scheme. This scheme is usually represented by a virtual community, where people with common interests create and share their own content. The Web 2.0 paradigm and virtual communities provide the basis to enhance the existing communications model with people, thus supporting weaving data, services and people over the Web. Recognizing this trend, telecom communities have realized that they can add a new ingredient: location to Web 2.0. Location, as any kind of context information, is a feature that allows a new generation of active communications services supported by rich service personalization and enhanced end user experience. These services are able to properly react according to end user, device or service context information [4, 5]. However, end user location information is usually difficult (if not impossible) to obtain on the Web. The extension of the Web to mobile devices, or so called *mobile Web*, is a must in order to succeed in this direction [21].

In order to create and provide/deliver personalized services for the mobile Web, we need to answer several key research questions in the first place. How to retrieve and manage context information from various context providers is at the very core of these issues. Secondly, apart from rendering rich and intuitive graphical service creation environment, non-expert users need considerable help in making a sound composite service. Some inherent complexity of programming should be shielded from these users. Last but not the least, we need to handle the short-of-resource feature of mobile devices. Mobile devices posses, to a certain extent, limited resources (e.g., battery power and input capabilities). Therefore, mobile devices should better act as passive listeners (e.g., receiving the results) than as active tools for service invocation, so that the computational power and battery life of the devices can be extended.

In this chapter, we introduce an innovative framework that supports weaving distributed data, context information, and communication services to allow personalized service creation and provision for mobile users. In this multi-agent based framework, user context is acquired by integrating presence and location service enablers provided by the underlying telecommunications network. A template-based service creation environment allows end users to build personalized integrated services by simply configuring a process template with personal information. Finally, publish/-subscribe techniques are used to ensure the passiveness of client devices. It is worth noting that agent technology help greatly in improving the adaptability of this framework.

The structure of this chapter is organized as follows. In Sect. 2, we briefly introduce the trends of how the World Wide Web is moving towards the mobile Web, together with a motivating example. In Sect. 3, we discuss the design principles of our framework, including our ideas on how to retrieve context information, the service creation approach, and the service provision approach. The whole system architecture of the framework is described in Sect. 4. Section 5 reports the implementation status and the initial evaluation. Section 6 overviews the related work and finally Sect. 6 concludes the chapter.

2 Towards the Mobile Web

During the last few years, there has been a convergence process in the telecommunications area, driven by three main axes: device convergence, multimedia convergence and network convergence. Devices have converged in the sense that now we can use a single device to do the things that we needed different devices in the past such as television, computer, and telephone. Multimedia has converged in a way that we can have voice, data and video in a single service.

Telecom network architectures have evolved from the original Public Switched Telephone Network (PSTN). Nowadays several access and core networks coexist both in wireless and wired-line domains. The evolution process has been characterized first by the introduction of mobile technologies in the early 1990s, and the generalized access to the Internet later. As a result of this process several access networks have been deployed. Just to mention a few, there are fixed networks such as the aforementioned PSTN and the Integrated Services Digital Network (ISDN), several radio networks such as the Global System for Mobile communications (GSM), the General Packet Radio Service (GPRS), the Universal Mobile Telecommunications System (UMTS) and the CDMA2000 networks (Code Division Multiple Access - CDMA), other wireless technologies such as WiFi and WiMax. Core networks have also evolved from the original circuit switched networks to the packet switched networks. At the beginning each network developed its own protocols with the aim of enhancing the previous ones. However, that means the coexistence of several network protocols that should communicate with each other, which produces both technological and business problems. Besides, each network followed a vertical approach where access entities, control systems and services were tightly coupled.

2.1 Expanding the World Wide Web to the Mobile Web

The convergence process for all the different networks began in 1998 when leading regional telecommunication standard bodies agreed on creating two 3rd Generation Partnership Projects (3GPP[1] and 3GPP2[2]), aiming at evolving the circuit and voice based mobile networks into 3rd Generation (3G) multimedia packet-based mobile networks. The main result of these projects was the specification of the IP Multimedia Subsystem (IMS) [9].

IMS is an architectural framework for delivering IP multimedia services to end users. It was originally focused on evolving mobile networks beyond GSM and thus

---

[1] http://www.3gpp.org

[2] http://www.3gpp2.org

its initial formulation represented an approach to delivering Internet services over GPRS. This initial approach was subsequently updated by 3GPP itself, 3GPP2, the Telecommunication and Internet converged Services and Protocols for Advanced Networking (TISPAN) and the Alliance for Telecommunication Industry Solutions (ATIS) by providing requirements for support of packet-based networks other than GPRS such as Wireless Local Access Networks (WLAN), CDMA2000 and fixed line. Finally, due to concerns on possible overlaps, delays, and incompatibilities among future standards, the International Telecommunication Union – Telecommunication Standardization Sector (ITU-T)[3] has coordinated the standardization process.

As a result, nowadays there is a common IP core network with multiple IP-based access networks. Next Generation Network (NGN) is the term used to refer to these new IP-based network architectures. The ITU-T has defined an NGN as "a packet-based network able to provide telecommunication services and able to make use of multiple broadband, Quality of Service (QoS)-enabled transport technologies and in which service-related functions are independent from underlying transport-related technologies. It enables unfettered access for users to networks and to competing service providers and/or services of their choice. It supports generalized mobility which will allow consistent and ubiquitous provision of services to users".

NGN architectures allow for having services that were previously precluded to mobile networks due to signaling delays and latencies, low throughput, etc. End users now can have personal broadband mobile services at any time and any place and can begin to expect the flexibility, scope, and service variety they have experienced through the Web: therefore the raise of the mobile Web.

This new IP, multimedia-based mobile Web has blurred the border between the Internet and Telecommunications domains. Moreover, as regulation has required Telecommunications operators to open up their networks to third parties development, this has allowed new competition to be introduced into the telecom service provision business, and nowadays it is possible for third parties outside the network operator domain to develop new services for the Web enhanced with mobile features.

2.2 Opening Up the Mobile Web for Development

The efforts to open up Telecommunications networks can be initially dated as early as the 1980s with the standardization of Intelligent Networks (IN) [16]. IN is an architecture by which customized service logic programs can be created by a service provider for enhanced features on calls in the PSTN.

IN introduced a set of functional entities comprising the distributed functions that need to interact during call origination and call termination in the provision of IN call-related services, thus decoupling the service development from the network

[3] http://www.itu.int/ITU-T

infrastructure. From that, the IN infrastructure has evolved to support some of the new features and requirements of the evolving networks. For instance CAMEL, which is the technology used in GSM networks to enable services such as roaming and international pre-paid, is based on IN [42].

However, IN is not able to fulfill some of the requirements that new converged networks impose such as shorter time to market of new services and the development of value-added, network independent services. To cover this gap IP-based NGN architectures such as the IMS have been specified. Initiatives such as the Open Service Architecture (OSA), Parlay, the Open Mobile Alliance (OMA)[4], and the JAIN Service Logic Execution Environment (JAIN SLEE or JSLEE) [26] have also been developed in different context.

The specification of the OSA/Parlay is a joint effort between ETSI, 3GPP and the Parlay Group.[5] It is an open Application Programming Interface (API) for application access to telecoms network resources. OSA/Parlay technology integrates telecom network capabilities with IT applications via a secure, measured, and billable interface. The APIs are network independent, and applications can be hosted within the telecom network operator's own environment, or by external third party service providers.

A Web services API is also available, known as Parlay X.[6] This is also standardized jointly by ETSI, Parlay and the 3GPP. Parlay X is a simplified Web services interface to telecom network functionality. It may be used in conjunction with the base OSA/Parlay APIs, or on its own. Within the mobile domain, OMA is the focal point for the development of service enabler specifications. OMA does not deliver platform implementations, but provides specifications of service enabling functionalities such as location, instant messaging, and device management. It is left to others to implement the platforms and functionalities that they describe, specially using Web services technologies.

JSLEE [26] defines a component model for structuring application logic of communications applications as a collection of reusable object-orientated components, and for composing these components into higher level, richer services. The specification also defines the contract between these components and the container that will host these components at runtime. JSLEE provides support asynchronous applications based on an event model. Application components receive events from event channels that are established at runtime. Network resource adapters create representations of calls and pass events generated by the calls to the JSLEE. Application components are in turn invoked by the JSLEE to process these events in a transactional context.

---

[4] http://www.openmobilealliance.org

[5] http://www.parlay.org

[6] http://www.parlayx.com/

2.3 A Motivating Scenario

Let's assume a university student, Donatella, wants to use her PDA as an advanced campus assistant to help organize her daily life efficiently. The following describes some most significant items extracted from her wish list.

First of all, although an engineering student, she is also interested in history and arts, especially art history and any paintings, sculpture and architecture from ancient time. She hopes that her PDA could notify her whenever a lecture of interest is posted on the university's website. Furthermore, she hopes that how the PDA gives notifications could base on her presence: when attending a class, she would like to be informed only after class; when riding a bicycle or driving a car, she would like the PDA give her a voice message; and at any other situations, she is pleased if the notification arrives as a piece of short message. She hopes that her presence could be changed intelligently based on her calendar and location parameters. In other words, at anytime when her calendar is marked as a lecture and she is within one of the campus buildings, her presence will be set to `Attending Lecture`. Whenever she is moving at an average speed higher than 35 km/h, her presence will be set to `Driving`. Of course she can manually override the automatic settings.

During the lecture, she wants to submit her questions via the PDA. She browses the questions asked by other students and decides to either vote for a posted question (if a similar question has been already asked), or post her question (if no one has asked yet). She may ask several questions during the lecture. After the class, a consultation booking might be requested and a feedback on the lecture is provided by her.

3 Design Principles

In this section, we describe the main design principles adopted in creating an personalized service creation and provision architecture. These design principles target the major challenges in the mobile Web field we mentioned at the beginning of this chapter.

3.1 Service Provision Approach

Our approach aims at identifying the main abstractions and mechanisms that support service provisioning in the mobile Web. We believe that leveraging Web services and software agents in combination with publish/subscribe systems provides the foundation to enable effective access to integrated services in mobile Web environments.

Web Services. Web services provide the pillars for evolving the Internet into a service-oriented integration platform of unprecedented scale and agility. The foundation of this platform lies in the modularization and virtualization of system functions and resources as services that: (i) can be described, advertized and discovered using (XML-based) standard languages, and (ii) interact through standard Internet protocols. More specifically, Web service technology is characterized by two aspects that are relevant to accessing heterogeneous resources and applications. The first is that from a technology perspective, all interacting entities are represented as services, whether they providing or requesting services. This allows uniformity that is needed for the interaction among heterogeneous applications and resources such as mobile devices. Web services can bring about the convergence of wired and wireless applications and services. Since Web services are described and interacted in a standardized manner, the task of developing complex applications by composing other services is considerably simplified [30, 40]. This allows for the aggregation of resources and applications for completing a specific complicated task.

Agents. Agents are software entities that exhibit certain autonomy when interacting with other entities [41]. Agents use their internal policies and knowledge to decide when to take actions that are needed to realize a specific goal. Internal policies can use context information (e.g., user preferences, device characteristics, and user location) to enable agents to adapt to different computing and user activities. Agents can also be used to pro-actively perform actions in dynamic environments. In fact, the combination of services and agents, will provide a self-managing infrastructure. Agents extend services by embedding extensible knowledge and capabilities (e.g., context aware execution and exception handling policies) making them capable of providing personalized and adaptive service provisioning in dynamic environments.

Publish/Subscribe System. The publish/subscribe paradigm offers a communication infrastructure where senders and receivers of messages interact by producing and consuming messages via designated shared spaces [11]. The communication is *asynchronous* in the sense that it completely decouples the senders and receivers in both space and time. This enables mobile users to disconnect at any time—either voluntarily to save e.g., communication cost and battery power, or involuntarily due to breakdowns of connections—and re-synchronize with the underlying infrastructure upon reconnection. This form of decoupling is of paramount importance in mobile Web environments, where the entities (e.g., mobile users) involved in communication change frequently due to their movement or connectivity patterns. This communication paradigm caters for loosely coupled interactions among service agents, which has been identified as an ideal platform for a variety of Internet applications, especially in wireless environments.

A widely recognized effort is the *tuple space model* that has its origins in the Linda language [2] for distributed programming. Tuple spaces have the advantage of providing direct support for *pull-based asynchronous interactions* in which the "sender" (e.g. the client device) and the "receiver" (e.g. a component service) are separated in both space and time. This enables mobile users to disconnect at any time, and re-synchronize with the underlying infrastructure upon reconnection. Tuple spaces also support multi-channel interactions, since a given user can interact with a tuple space from multiple computing resources (e.g. place a tuple from a device, then disconnect, and then reconnect and get a tuple from another device).

3.2 Context Information Retrieval

In order to personalize the service creation and provision processes some context information is needed. This information can be categorized, within the scope of this work, into three major sets: *user context*, *device context*, and *service context*.

User Context. User context refers to the information related to a user such as preferences, calendar or location. This information is also referred to in the literature as *Personal Identifiable Information* (PII). PII is any piece of information that—related both digital and real identities—that can potentially be used to uniquely identify, contact, or locate a single person [10, 37].

Telecom operators have gathered loads of information about their customers over the years, thus creating rich users' profiles. They are also able to retrieve dynamic personal information such as customers' location or presence status. Therefore, we leverage on the underlying telecom infrastructure to get user context information. This information is exposed by means of Web services interfaces, which are standardized as OMA enablers.

Device Context. The device context information includes hardware and software characteristics of the user's devices, which could be used to drive the service execution or tailor the contents that a service will present to the user.

The World Wide Web Consortium (W3C) has created the Composite Capability/Preference Profiles (CC/PP) Recommendation [22], which allows defining capabilities and preferences of users' mobile devices. OMA has specified the *User Agent Profile* (UAProf) [38], capturing capabilities and preference information for wireless devices. UAProf allows describing device and user agent capabilities as an XML description, and is fully compatible with CC/PP. Moreover, OMA has also specified the Mobile Client Environment enabler, which is specifically chartered to be responsible for base content types, with the intention of enabling the creation and use of data services on mobile hand held devices, including mobile telephones.

Service Context. The service context includes information related to a service. Examples of service context include: (i) service location, (ii) service status (e.g., available, busy), and (iii) Quality of Service (QoS) attributes (e.g., price, availability). The service context information can be obtained via a monitoring application that oversees the execution status of the service (e.g., exceptions). For example, if the value of a monitored item (e.g., CPU usage) is beyond a critical point (e.g., 85%), the workload of the service will be set as `heavy`.

Context Privacy and Security. The Internet experience has demonstrated that personal data (i.e., user context information) is a valuable asset that can be used incorrectly or fraudulently, and thereafter is prone to be abused and misused. Fortunately, in most countries there are laws that require companies to ensure security and privacy when using, storing or revealing personal information about a customer [17].

In the technical plane, Identity Management (IM) is the discipline that tries to address all these issues: it refers to the processes involved with management and selective disclosure of PII within an institution or between several of them, while preserving and enforcing privacy and security needs. If different companies have established trust relationships between themselves the process does not require a common root authority and is called *Federated Identity Management*. Each company maintains its own customer list and some identity attributes or PII, but they can securely exchange them while preserving users' privacy. IM is related to network security, service provisioning, customer management, Single Sign On (SSO), Single Logout (SLO) and the means to share identity information [39].

A federated approach for IM in a Web Services environment is supported by various standards and frameworks, among which the most important ones are Security Assertion Markup Language (SAML),[7] Liberty Alliance,[8] and WS-Federation [27]. While all of them support similar features, Liberty Alliance specifications have got greater acceptance within the telecom domain.

3.3 Service Creation Approach

In a world where technology complexity is growing, one of the big and constant challenges is to keep the technology reachable by users while increasing the amount of features available. This is even more critical in recent trends of Web development, where the buzzword "Web 2.0" [29] represents, along with a new rich set of Web technologies, the goal of bringing a user from a passive role to an active role in the system, both as a content producer and as a service creator. Sites as Wikipedia, Flickr, YouTube, or the blog phenomenon show how the user is now assuming the content producer role too, providing expert knowledge and information, images, and video clips.

One step more is needed to allow users to create not only static content, but applications and services. The success of this trend is proved by the increasing popularity of mashups (i.e., little applications that combine information from many web sites) and the birth of various environments for the intuitive non-expert creation of Web based information services, driven by the biggest and most successful companies of the IT world, such as Yahoo! Pipes.[9] or Microsoft Popfly[10]. These environments present graphical tools based on drag-and-drop interfaces that allow a user to create Web-based applications even without any computing knowledge.

In the same direction, the OPUCE (Open Platform for User-centric Service Creation and Execution) platform[11] aims at bridging advances in networking, communication and information technologies towards a unique converged service creation environment, where personalized IT-telecom services can be created by end users. Another related approach is provided by the SPICE service creation environ-

---

[7] http://docs.oasis-open.org/security/saml/v2.0
[8] http://www.projectliberty.org
[9] http://pipes.yahoo.com
[10] http://www.popfly.ms
[11] http://www.opuce.eu

ment [4], where natural-language goals are interpreted by an Automatic Composition Engine (ACE) in order to obtain a set of suitable compositions of semantic-annotated services [34]. Such compositions can be evaluated and possibly deployed by a service designer and its GUI is intuitive enough to be used by an end user.

The challenge for all these research initiatives is to put a non-expert in the center of a Service Creation Environment (SCE). Some approaches based on rules (like ECA rules) [24] or policy languages [23] have been used in telecom world for personalization of value-added services from the service developer's viewpoint, as long as the usage of scripting languages, and domain-specific SCEs [25].

Our personalized service creation approach is centered on the concept of *process templates*. Users specify their needs by reusing and adjusting existing process templates, rather than building their own services from scratch.

Process Templates. Process templates are reusable business process skeletons that are devised to reach particular goals such as arrangement of a trip. Each process template has one or more tasks and each task is associated with a service operation. Process templates are modeled using process definition languages such as statecharts [18] and BPEL4WS [3].

In a process template, each task has a set of input and output parameters. The value of a task's input parameter may be: (i) requested from user during task execution, (ii) obtained from the user's profile, or (iii) obtained as an output of another task. For the second and third cases, the value of an input parameter is obtained via queries. Queries vary from simple to complex, depending on the application domain and users' needs. Queries can be expressed using languages like XPath [13].

In our approach, values that users supply as input parameters are handled differently from the values obtained from user profiles. Indeed, because mobile devices are resource-constrained, values that can be obtained from user profiles should not be requested from users. Users only supply the values for data items that are labeled *compulsory*. However, in a process template specification, the template provider only indicates which input parameters users have to supply a value. It is the responsibility of the user to specify, during the configuration phase, if the value will be provided manually or derived from her profile.

Similarly, the value of a task's output parameter may be: (i) sent to other tasks as input parameters, and/or (ii) sent to a user in case she wants to know the execution result of the task. Note that the value of an output parameter can be submitted to multiple places (e.g., to a task and the user as well). Again, due to low bandwidth and limited presentation capabilities of certain mobile devices, results of tasks are progressively delivered to users. Similar to input parameters, the provider of a process template does not decide which output parameters need to be returned.

Configuring Process Templates. Personalization implies making adjustment according to user preferences. Three kinds of user preferences are associated for each process template's task:

- *execution constraints* can be divided into *temporal* and *spatial* constraints, which respectively indicate *when* and *where* the user would like to see a task executed,

- *data supply and delivery preferences* are related to supplying values to the input parameters and delivering values of output parameters of the task, and
- *execution policies* are related to the preferences on service selection (for communities) and service migration during the execution of a task.

Generally, a temporal constraint involves current time, ct, comparison operator, co (e.g., =, $\leq$, and `between`), and a user-specified time, ut, which is either an absolute time, a relative time (e.g., termination time of a task), or a time interval. A temporal constraint means that a task can be triggered only if the condition $ct\ co\ ut$ is evaluated to true. Similarly, a spatial constraint involves current location, cl and a user-specified location, ul. A spatial constraint means that a task can be fired only when the condition $cl = ul$ is evaluated to true. A location is considered the same as another location if the distance between two locations does not exceed a certain value (e.g., 2 m). It should be noted that the temporal and spatial constraints can be empty, meaning that the corresponding task can be executed at anytime and at anywhere.

As stated before, the values of some input parameters of a task can be obtained from a user's profile. The user proceeds in two steps: (i) identify which input parameter values can be derived from her profile, and (ii) supply the location of the profile and the corresponding attribute names. Similarly, for the output parameters of a task, a user may specify which parameter values need to be delivered to her.

The execution policies include the *service selection policy* and the *service migration policy*. For a specific task, users can specify how to select a service for this task. The service can be a fixed one (the task always uses this service), or can be selected from a specific service community [6] or a public directory (e.g., UDDI) based on certain criteria (e.g., location of the mobile user). Furthermore, users can specify whether to migrate the services to their mobile devices (e.g., if mobile devices have enough computing resources) or to the sites near the users current location for the execution. Policies can be specified using policy languages like Houdini [19] and Ponder [28].

4 System Architecture

In this section, we introduce the architecture of our context-aware service creation and execution framework. As shown in Fig. 1, the framework is separated into several logical layers, namely the *agent layer*, the *service layer*, and the *network layer*.

4.1 Agent Layer

The agent layer consists of a set of agents that collaborates among each other for the robust and context-aware creation and execution of composite services in the mobile Web environments.

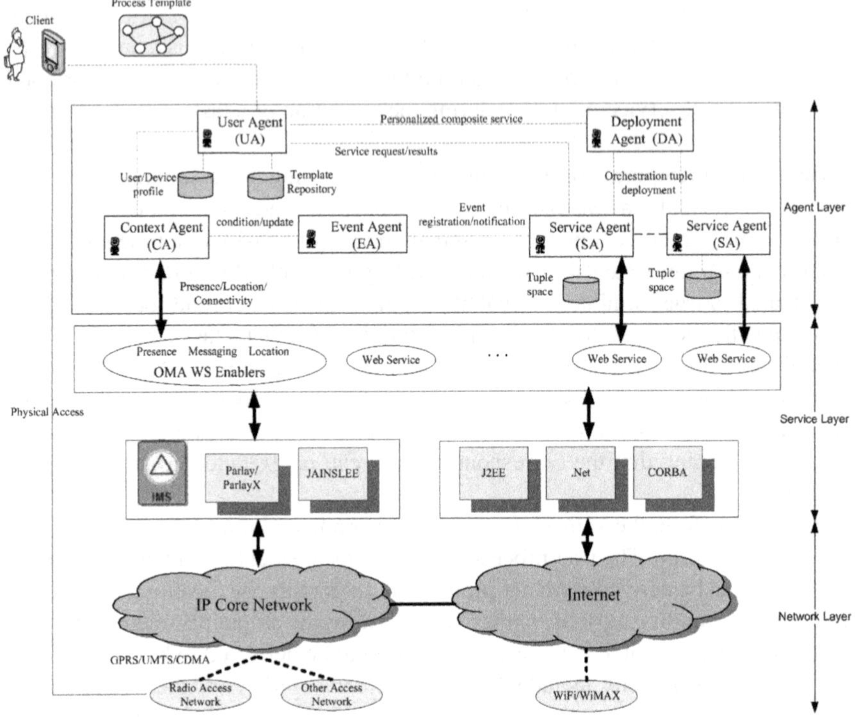

Fig. 1 System architecture

User Agent. Mobile users access our service provisioning environment through two main components, namely the *client* and the *user agent*. The client is an application that can be downloaded and runs on mobile devices. It provides users with an interface for (i) specifying user activities, and (ii) interacting with the user agent.

Users' activities (e.g., travel planning) are usually complex. The fulfillment of an activity may call for multiple services executed in a specific chronology. It is too tedious to specify activities from scratch through small devices like PDA, which have limited input capabilities. To ease the activity specification process, we introduce the notion of *process templates*. We specify process templates with statecharts [18]. Succinctly, a statechart is made up of states and transitions. States can be basic or compound. A basic state (also called task) corresponds to the execution of a Web service. Compound states enclose one or several statecharts within them.

The client allows users to define their activities by specifying *personal preferences* (e.g., temporal/spatial constraints, data supply/delivery preferences) over the tasks of process templates, thereby defining *personalized composite services*. A user can specify *temporal* and *spatial* constraints for each task, which respectively indicate *when* and *where* the user wants to have a task executed. For example, Donatella, the university student in our motivating example (see Sect. 2.3), can specify that the question asking services (e.g., `Question Vote` service) can be executed only during the lecture time and when she is in the classroom. Meanwhile, data supply and delivery preferences are related to supplying values to the input parameters and delivering the values of output parameters of a task. Donatella can specify that the value of a task's input parameter should be obtained from her profile so that she does not have to provide the value manually. Similarly, she can also specify that the value of a task's output parameter should be sent to her user agent in case she wants to know the results.

A user agent (UA) acts on behalf of a specific mobile user. The UA maintains profile information including the user's contact information, personal preferences, and mobile device characteristics. Based on the profile, the UA can identify data formats and interaction protocols for communicating with the client that runs on the mobile device. The UA subscribes to the template repository where all the process templates are stored, which in turn notifies the UA about the availability of each new process template. Upon receiving the notification, the UA prepares a short description outlining the functionalities and potential charges of the process template and sends it to the user in the notification message (e.g., SMS). If the user is interested in the process template, the UA will contact the template repository to deliver an XML document of this process template, which is going to be stored in the user's mobile device upon reception for later configuration.

The client submits a configured process template (i.e., user's personalized composite service) to the UA, which is responsible for executing the service, collecting service results, and delivering results to the user. The UA accomplishes this by interacting with other agents in the architecture, which is described in the following.

Context Agent. The context agent (CA) is responsible for retrieving the context information and disseminating it to other agent in order to personalize the service creation and provision processes. As we have previously described, the CA maintains three kinds of contexts, namely user context, device context, and service context. The CA collects the context information from context providers and since there are three kinds of contexts there are also three kinds of context providers. Since it is quite straightforward to provide device context (e.g., UAProf) and service context (e.g., service monitoring application), we will focus on user context providers.

User context providers are asked for PII regarding the users. Three different entities are possible in the role of user context provider: the telecom operator, third parties and the users themselves. Telecom operators provide dynamic user information related to the mobility such as the user location and the presence status. It can also provide more advanced data such as billing information or even charging information (micro-payments) which are closely related to the (financial) identity of the user. Following a similar model, third parties can participate in providing the CA with some specialized PII such as contact agenda or list of friends. Finally, end users can also provide static information such as their preferences at registration time.

The CA consists of a set of configurable context collectors. Each context collector handles one type of context information and encapsulates the details of interactions with the context provider for that information (e.g. the context collector pulls the context information periodically from the context provider).

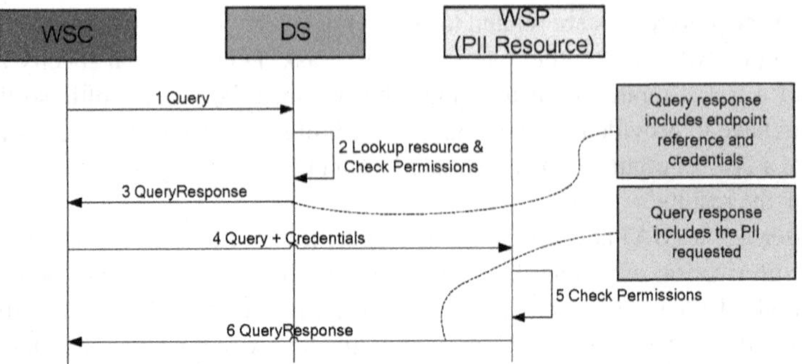

Fig. 2 Liberty Identity Web Services Framework

Liberty Identity Web Services Framework (ID-WSF) [35] provides a means to communicate between context providers and context collectors. Moreover, ID-WSF architecture allows for a greater degree of abstraction supporting dynamic discovery and binding of context providers. ID-WSF basically defines three entities that participate in an identity transaction as shown in Fig. 2: a Web service identity provider (WSP) that offers PII, a Web service identity consumer (WSC) that consumes the PII, and a Discovery Service (DS) that plays the role of a broker putting both in contact. Whenever a WSC needs a type of PII, it asks the DS about a WSP storing the requested information. The DS checks whether the WSC is allowed to access the information and if so, provides it with the address of the WSP and some credentials to access the information requested. Eventually, the WSC directly requests the WSP for the PII, showing the credentials delivered by the DS.

ID-WSF also provides some other advanced features such as an Interaction Service that is able to prompt the user for permission whenever it is needed: if the WSP is not sure about whether it should allow the WSC to retrieve the PII, it asks the user to explicitly grant access. Therefore, it provides a high degree of protection when it comes to the management of users' PII.

Orchestration Agents. The orchestration agents include a set of agents, facilitating the asynchronous, distributed, and context-aware execution of composite services. These agents are *deployment agent*, *event agent*, and *service agent*. The deployment agent (DA) generates orchestration tuples, which will be described later, from the specification of personalized composite services that are submitted from the user agent (UA). The DA then deploys (uploads) these orchestration tuples into the *tuple spaces* of the corresponding services.

Service agents (SAs) act as proxies for Web services, monitoring and coordinating service executions. The knowledge required by an SA is a set of orchestration tuples, stored in a tuple space associated with the SA. The orchestration tuples are generated and deployed by the DA. There is one SA per service. For each Web service in the service layer, the service administrator needs to download and install SA, together with a tuple space.

The event agent (EA) is responsible for disseminating events. The EA maintains the information of events supported by the platform, i.e., for a specific event, what context attributes are relevant to this event and what condition should be satisfied to fire the event. For example, event `failed(s)` indicates that an execution failure of service s has occurred. The related context of this event is `executionStatus` and the condition, `executionStatus="failed"`, should be satisfied in order to fire the event.

Orchestration Tuples. The orchestration of a composite service is encoded in the form of *orchestration tuples*. Orchestration tuples are expressed as event-condition-action (`E[C]/A`) rules specifying the actions that must be performed when specific events occur and when the conditions hold. We introduce three types of orchestration tuples to coordinate the execution of personalized composite services:

- *Precondition tuples* specify the conditions that need to be satisfied before the execution of a service,
- *Postprocessing tuples* specify the actions that need to be performed after the execution of a service, and
- *Exception handling tuples* specify the instructions that dynamically react to runtime exceptions (e.g., mobile device disconnection and services failures).

For example, `unpresentable(r,d)[true]/transform(r,TS,d)` is an exception handling tuple that indicates that if the service result r cannot be displayed in the user's current device d, the result will be sent to TS, a transformation service, for adaptation.

The orchestration tuples of a composite service are statically derived by analyzing the information encoded in the statechart of the service (e.g., control flow and data dependencies, exception handling policies, and personal preferences).

Orchestration Interactions. Figure 3(a) is a sequence diagram showing the process of the orchestration of personalized composite services. Firstly, the DA takes as input the specification of a personalized composite service from the UA, generates orchestration tuples for each task of the personalized composite service, and injects these orchestration tuples into the tuple spaces of the corresponding SAs. Then, SAs parse the orchestration tuples and retrieve relevant information (e.g., events, conditions, and actions). The events (e.g., `lowBattery`) are registered to the EA, which in turn subscribes relevant conditions (e.g., `batteryRemaining < 15%`) to the context agent (CA). The EA fires and distributes events if the corresponding conditions are matched (e.g., when the current battery capacity of the device is less than 15% of its full battery power). Upon receiving the notifications (i.e., the occurrence of the events) from the EA, the SAs extract the corresponding orchestration tuples from the associated tuple spaces, evaluate the conditions, and perform the proper actions (e.g., service invocation in the diagram).

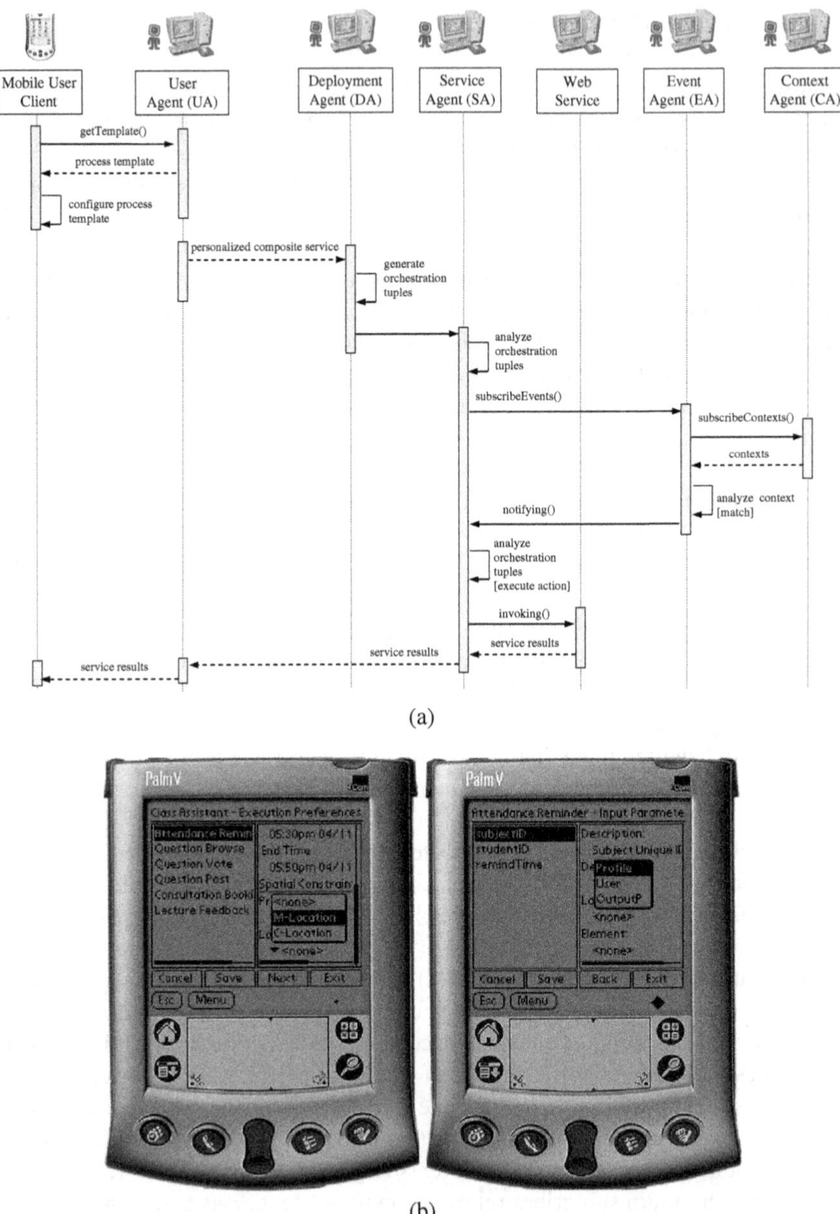

Fig. 3 (**a**) Sequence diagram of personal service orchestration (**b**) Screenshots of process template configuration

4.2 Service and Network Layer

The service layer hosts both the actual service implementation and the exposed Web service interfaces. On top of the convergent telecom IP core network, standardized middleware like IMS, Parlay/ParlayX and JSLEE provide advanced network control functionalities to bearer capabilities, call/session, and applications/services, and open up network resources by means of reusable telecom service enablers.

IMS can host three kinds of application services: the SIP application server, OSA application server, and the Camel service environment. These servers interact with the serving call session-control function (S-CSCF), home subscriber server (HSS), and multimedia resource function control (MRFC) with SIP protocol [21]. OSA/Parlay is a set of open APIs for easy access to core network capabilities from outside of the network. ParlayX evolves the OSA APIs into simplified Web service interfaces. As we have described in the previous paragraph, the OSA application server can also reside on top of the IMS control layer and becomes a part of the IMS architecture. JSLEE is the Java component and container specification for the event-driven, high-performance service logic execution environment (SLEE). It is worth noting that JSLEE can be used for both IMS SIP application servers and OSA application servers.

In the service interface sub-layer, ParlayX evolves the OSA APIs into simplified Web service interfaces, and OMA defines specifications of service enabling functionalities such as presence, instant messaging and location. From the Internet side, services are hosted and executed in different kinds of application servers such as J2EE, .NET and CORBA.

The network layer provides physical communication infrastructure. As we can see from Fig. 1, hand-held devices of end users can physically access services through radio access networks (e.g., GPRS, MTS, and CDMA), or wireless Internet protocols (e.g., WiFi and WiMAX). It is clear that although we have services from both the telecom network and the Internet, at the service interface layer, they are converged under a unified Web service technology umbrella.

5 Implementation and Evaluation

To test the applicability of our architecture, we implemented a prototype system. We developed a process template builder, which assists template providers or mobile users in defining and editing process templates. The template builder offers a visual editor (an extension of [33]) for describing statechart diagrams of templates. It also provides means to locate services in the registry. The client was implemented using J2ME Wireless Toolkit 2.[12] kXML 2[13] is used to parse XML documents on mobile

[12] `http://java.sun.com/products/sjwtoolkit`

[13] `http://kxml.enhydra.org`

devices and kSOAP 2.0[14] is used by the client to handle SOAP messages. Figure 3 (b) shows the screenshots of process template configuration.

Currently, the functionalities of agents are realized by a set of pre-built Java classes. In particular, the class *deployAgent* (for the deployment agent) provides method called `deploy()` that is responsible for generating orchestration tuples from composite services. The input is a personalized composite service described as an XML document, while the outputs are orchestration tuples formatted as XML documents as well. The orchestration tuples are then uploaded into the tuple spaces of the corresponding service agents. IBM's TSpaces[15] is used for the implementation of tuple spaces. IBM TSpaces is a network communication buffer with database capabilities (see Fig. 4). Orchestration agents communicate asynchronously through the shared spaces by writing, reading, and taking control tuples. Each tuple is implemented as a vector of Java objects.

To validate our design of the system architecture, we conducted a usability study. We presented our system to 18 people, all from different educational backgrounds (8 undergraduate students, 2 masters students, and 8 PhD students) and computer literate. The presentation includes a powerpoint show of the architecture overview, a demonstration of the usage of the system, and `classAssistant`, the prototype

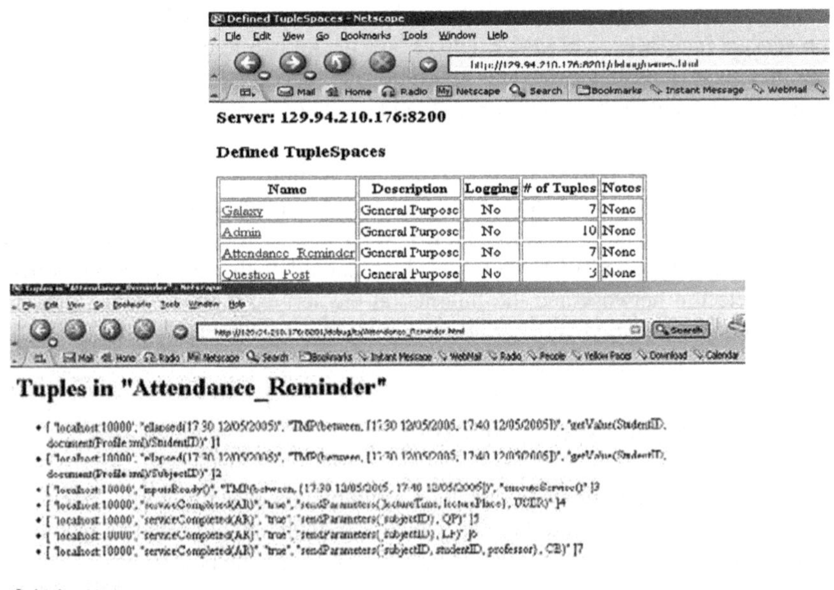

Name	Description	Logging	# of Tuples	Notes
Galaxy	General Purpose	No	7	None
Admin	General Purpose	No	10	None
Attendance_Reminder	General Purpose	No	7	None
Question_Post	General Purpose	No	3	None

Fig. 4 Control tuples implemented using IBM TSpaces

[14] `http://ksoap.objectweb.org`
[15] `http://www.alphaworks.ibm.com/tech/tspaces`

Table 1 Evaluation results of system design principles

Questions	Responses A	B	C
Suppose you are invoking a remote service using a PDA and the invocation will take some time, which action you prefer to take: (A) wait with the handheld on till receive the result; (B) turn off the handheld and catch the results in another time	6	12	N/A
Suppose you are invoking a service using a PDA and the service needs some inputs, which strategy is your favorite to supply values for the service inputs: (A) manually input using stylus; (B) automatically collect the data (e.g., from user profile) (C) does not matter	1	15	2
Suppose you are receiving the results of a service using a PDA, you would like to receive: (A) all of them; (B) only important and necessary ones (C) does not matter	6	11	1

application built on top of the architecture. The participants were then asked to use the system and given a questionnaire to report their experience in using the system.

Table 1 shows some of the questions from the questionnaire and the participants' responses. The responses actually validate and highlight some important design principles of the architecture: (i) users should avoid data entry as much as possible, (ii) the interactions during service execution should be asynchronous, and (iii) the bandwidth consumption should be minimized. It should be noted that this usability study was conducted in a relatively small scale environment. Currently, we are planning a larger scale usability study of the system. More experimental results (e.g., performance study) are not reported here due to space reasons. Readers are referred to [32] for a detailed description of the system evaluation.

6 Related Work

Service personalization has recently become a very promising research area because it paves the way to a more widespread usage, creation, and customization of services. Its goal is to bring users from a passive role (i.e., content and service consumer) to an active role (i.e., content producer and service creator). Service creation technology is the key criterion which represents how user interacts with the system to create or compose a new service. Since ease-of-use is a key success factor of a service creation approach, we group different service creation approaches in increasing order of ease-of-use, namely: (i) script-based, (ii) rule-based, (iii) choreography-based, (iv) template-based, and (v) natural-language based.

Service personalization performed by means of domain-specific scripting languages [25] is generally hard to use for developers. Rule-based approaches based on ECA rules [24] or policy languages [23] have been used in telecom world for personalization of value-added services. While rules are easy to set, it is quite difficult for end users to foresee possible undesired side effects due to rules conflicts. Choreography-based approaches are gaining their momentum in the end-user service creation world, as proved by the increasing popularity of mashups and the birth of various environments for the intuitive non-expert creation of Web based information services, driven by the big companies, such as Yahoo! Pipes or Microsoft Popfly. These environments present graphical tools based on drag-and-drop interfaces which allow the user to create this little web-based applications even without any computing knowledge.

The natural language approach aims at deriving the formal specification for a service composition starting from an informal request expressed in natural language. Such formal, machine-understandable specification can then be used as input for providing the composite service through automated reasoning, like backward-chaining [8]. The core idea behind this approach resides in matching textual tokens within the natural language request to a semantic properties embedded in the service description, usually represented with labels annotated on the service interface: an implementation of this idea in the telecom domain was provided by the SPICE service creation environment [4], where natural-language goals are interpreted by an Automatic Composition Engine (ACE) in order to obtain a set of suitable compositions of semantic-annotated services [34]. Unfortunately, natural-language based techniques such as [14] are still limited to the predefined vocabularies and ontology concepts, scalability, and the intrinsic difficulties in handling the ambiguities of natural languages.

Our process templates approach aims at simplifying choreography approach, offering different common templates to be completed by user's data, thus providing a easier-to-use interface. Users can select a process template which can be seen as a pre-defined standard workflow (i.e. service composition). Related works like [36] proposes that choreographies and orchestrations (internal implementations) are described using a particular form of Petri Nets. Also the approach in [1] is considered as a choreography approach, where end-to-end web services composition methodology is realized by putting together semantically-annotated web service components in a BPEL flow.

In fact, very little work is being done on Web services orchestration for the benefit of mobile users. A middleware named Colomba [5] handles the dynamic binding for mobile applications. This middleware addresses multiple issues such as frequent disconnection, limited supply of battery power and absence of network coverage. A personal process-oriented system for mobile users is presented in [20], which investigates the specification and querying of processes that involve personal tasks and data. The objective of these works is to support simple applications for mobile users, rather than providing personalized specifications and adaptive orchestrations of composite services, fulfilling complex user requirements.

PerCollab [12] is a middleware system that integrates multiple communication devices with workflow systems. Relying on a centralized BPEL engine (which could lead to bottlenecks) and a context service, tasks can be proactively pushed to users. However, PerCollab does not consider the personalized specification of business processes, nor distributed orchestration of the processes.

The emerging semantic Web efforts such as OWL-S[16] and WSMF (Web Service Modeling Framework) [15], promote the use of ontologies as a means for reconciling semantic heterogeneity between Web resources. Such efforts focus on designing rich and machine understandable representations of service properties, capabilities, and behavior, as well as reasoning mechanisms to select and aggregate services. The issues addressed in this area are complementary to those addressed in our work.

Finally, we also note that some industrial efforts in mobile Web services such as IBM's Web Service Toolkit for Mobile Devices[17] and Microsoft and Vodafone's Mobile Web Service initiative.[18] The former provides tools for developing Web services on mobile devices while the latter plans to create new standards to integrate IT and mobile worlds through Web services.

7 Conclusion

While much of the work on Web services has focused on low-level standards for publishing, discovering, and provisioning Web services in wired environments and for the benefit of stationary users, we deemed appropriate to put forward novel solutions and alternatives for the benefit of mobile users. In this chapter, we have presented the design and implementation of a layered, multi-agent framework that enables personalized composition and adaptive provisioning of Web services. Our system builds upon the building blocks of Web services, agents, and publish/subscribe systems and provides a platform through which services can be offered to mobile users. One possible extension to our current system is a mechanism for seamlessly accessing services among multiple computing devices. Indeed, during the invocation of a Web service, especially one having long running business activities or with complex tasks (e.g., composite services), users are more likely to be switching from device to device (e.g., from office PC to PDA). Applications can not be allowed to terminate and start again simply because users change devices and users should not experience a break during the service invocation while they are moving. This is extremely important for the people in time critical working environments (e.g., doctors in hospitals). A second possible extension is to support team work so that multiple (mobile) users can virtually collaborate with each other in the same business processes. Finally, we plan to extend the architecture to support large-scale environments, and building more mobile applications on top of the architecture to further study its performance.

---

[16] http://www.daml.org/services/owl-s

[17] http://www.alphaworks.ibm.com/tech/wstkmd

[18] http://www.microsoft.com/serviceproviders/mobilewebservices/mws_tech_roadmap.asp

References

1. Vikas Agarwal, Koustuv Dasgupta, Neeran Karnik, Arun Kumar, Ashish Kundu, Sumit Mittal, and Biplav Srivastava. A Service Creation Environment Based on End to End Composition of Web Services. In *Proc. of the 14th International Conference on World Wide Web (WWW'05)*, pages 128–137, Chiba, Japan, May 2005.
2. Sudhir Ahuja, Nicholas Carriero, and David Gelernter. Linda and Friends. *IEEE Computer*, 19(8):26–34, August 1986.
3. Tony Andrews et.al. Business Process Execution Language for Web Services 1.1. `http://www-106.ibm.com/developerworks/library/ws-bpel`.
4. Mariano Belaunde and Paolo Falcarin. Realizing an MDA and SOA Marriage for the Development of Mobile Services. In *Proc. of the 4th European Conference on Model Driven Architecture (ECMDA08)*, Berlin, Germany, June 2008.
5. Paolo Bellavista, Antonio Corradi, Rebecca Montanari, and Cesare Stefanelli. Dynamic Binding in Mobile Applications: A Middleware Approach. *IEEE Internet Computing*, 7(2):34–42, March/April 2003.
6. Boualem Benatallah, Quan Z. Sheng, and Marlon Dumas. The Self-Serv Environment for Web Services Composition. *IEEE Internet Computing*, 7(1):40–48, January/February 2003.
7. Djamal Benslimane, Schahram Dustdar, and Amit P. Sheth. Service Mashups. *IEEE Internet Computing*, 12(5), September/October 2008, to appear.
8. Alessio Bosca, Giuseppe Valetto, Roberta Maglione, and Fulvio Corno. Specifying Web Service Compositions on the Basis of Natural Language Requests. In *Proc. of the 3rd International Conference on Service Oriented Computing*, Amsterdam, The Netherlands, December 2005.
9. Gonzalo Camarillo and Miguel-Angel García-Martín. *The 3G IP Multimedia Subsystem (IMS): Merging the Internet and the Cellular Worlds*. 2nd Edition, John Wiley & Sons Ltd., New York, 2006.
10. L. Jean Camp. Digital Identity. *IEEE Technology and Society Magazine*, 23(3):34–41, 2004.
11. Mauro Caporuscio, Amtorio Carzaniga, and Alexander L. Wolf. Design and Evaluation of a Support Service for Mobile, Wireless Publish/Subscribe Applications. *IEEE Transactions on Software Engineering*, 29(12):1059–1071, December 2003.
12. Dipanjan Chakraborty and Hui Lei. Extending the Reach of Business Processes. *IEEE Computer*, 37(4):78–80, April 2004.
13. James Clark and Steve DeRose. XML Path Language (XPATH) Version 1.0. http://www.w3.org/TR/xpath, November 1999.
14. Kurt Englmeier, Javier Pereira, and Josiane Mothe. Choreography of Web Services Based on Natural Language Storybooks. In *Proc. of the 8th International Conference on Electronic Commerce (ICEC'06)*, Fredericton, New Brunswick, Canada, August 2006.
15. Dieter Fensel and Christoph Bussler. The Web Service Modeling Framework WSMF. *Electronic Commerce Research and Applications*, 1(2):113–137, 2002.
16. James J. Garraham et al. Intelligent Network Overview. *IEEE Communications Magazine*, 31(3):30–36, March 1993.
17. Marit Hansen, Ari Schwartz, and Alissa Cooper. Privacy and Identity Management. *IEEE Security and Privacy*, 6(2):38–45, 2008.
18. David Harel and Amnon Naamad. The STATEMATE Semantics of Statecharts. *ACM Transactions on Software Engineering and Methodology*, 5(4):293–333, October 1996.
19. Richard Hull, Bharat Kumar, and Daniel Lieuwen. Towards Federated Policy Management. In *Proc. of the 4th International Workshop on Policies for Distributed Systems and Networks (POLICY'03)*, Lake Como, Italy, June 2003.
20. San-Yih Hwang and Ya-Fan Chen. Personal Workflows: Modeling and Management. In *Proc. of the 4th International Conference on Mobile Data Management (MDM'03)*, Melbourne, Australia, January 2003.
21. Hechmi Khlifi and Jean-Charles Grégoire. IMS Application Servers: Roles, Requirements, and Implementation Technologies. *IEEE Internet Computing*, 12(3):40–51, May/June 2008.

22. Graham Klyne et al. Composite Capability/Preference Profiles (CC/PP): Structure and Vocabularies 1.0. http://www.w3.org/TR/CCPP-struct-vocab, visited on 24 June 2008.
23. Patricia Lago. A Policy-Based Approach to Personalization of Communication Over Converged Networks. In *Proc. of the 3rd International Workshop on Policies for Distributed Systems and Networks (POLICY'02)*, Monterey, California, USA, June 2002.
24. Carlo A. Licciardi, Gianni Canal, Alessandra Andreetto, and Patricia Lago. An Architecture for IN-Internet Hybrid Services. *Computer Networks*, 35(5):537–549, April 2001.
25. Carlo A. Licciardi and Paolo Falcarin. Analysis of NGN Service Creation Technologies. *IEC Annual Review of Communications*, 56:537–551, November 2003.
26. Swee B. Lim and David Ferry. JAIN SLEE 1.0 Specification. http://jcp.org/en/jsr/detail?id=22, visited on 20 June 2008.
27. Hal Lockhart et al. Web Services Federation Language (WS-Federation). http://www.ibm.com/developerworks/library/specification/ws-fed/, visited on 24 June 2008.
28. Rebecca Montanari, Emil Lupu, and Cesare Stefanelli. Policy-Based Dynamic Reconfiguration of Mobile-Code Applications. *IEEE Computer*, 37(7):73–80, 2004.
29. Tim O'Reilly. What is Web 2.0. http://www.oreillynet.com/pub/a/oreilly/tim/news/2005/09/30/what-is-web-20.html, visited on 27 June 2008.
30. Michael P. Papazoglou, Paolo Traverso, Schahram Dustdar, and Frank Leymann. Service-Oriented Computing: State of the Art and Research Challenges. *IEEE Computer*, 40(11):38–45, 2007.
31. Mike P. Papazoglou and Willem-Jan van den Heuvel. Service Oriented Architectures: Approaches, Technologies and Research Issues. *The VLDB Journal*, 16(3):389–415, 2007.
32. Quan Z. Sheng. *Composite Web Services Provisioning in Dynamic Environments*. PhD thesis, The University of New South Wales, Sydney, NSW, Australia, 2006.
33. Quan Z. Sheng, Boualem Benatallah, Marlon Dumas, and Eileen Mak. SELF-SERV: A Platform for Rapid Composition of Web Services in a Peer-to-Peer Environment. In *Proc. of the 28th International Conference on Very Large Databases (VLDB'02)*, Hong Kong, China, August 2002.
34. Mazen Shiaa, Paolo Falcarin, Alain Pastor, Freddy Lécué, Eduardo Silva, and Luis F. Pires. Towards the Automation of the Service Composition Process: Case Study and Prototype Implementations. In *Proc. of the ICT Mobile and Wireless Communications Summit*, Stockholm, Sweden, June 2008.
35. Jonathan Tourzan and Yuzo Koga, Ed. Liberty ID-WSF Web Services Framework Overview. http://www.projectliberty.org/liberty/content/download/1307/8286/file/liberty-idwsf-overview-v1.1.pdf, visited on 24 June 2008.
36. Wil M. P. van der Aalst and Mathias Weske. The P2P Approach to Interorganizational Workflows. In *Proc. of the 13th International Conference on Advanced Information Systems Engineering (CAiSE'01)*, Interlaken, Switzerland, June 2001.
37. Phil Windley. *Digital Identity*. O'Reilly Media Inc., Sebastopol, 2005.
38. Wireless Application Forum. Wireless Application Protocol User Agent Profile Specification. http://www.openmobilealliance.org/tech/affiliates/wap/wap-248-uaprof-20011020-a.pdf, visited on 27 June 2008.
39. Juan C. Yelmo, José M. Del Álamo, and Rubén Trapero. Privacy and Data Protection in a User-Centric Business Model for Telecommunications Services. In *Proc. of the IFIP International Federation for Information Processing: The Future of Identity in the Information Society*, Karlstad University, Sweden, June 2008.
40. Qi Yu, Athman Bouguettaya, and Brahim Medjahed. Deploying and Managing Web Services: Issues, Solutions, and Directions. *The VLDB Journal*, 17(3):537–572, 2008.
41. Franco Zambonelli, Nicholas R. Jennings, and Michael Wooldridge. Developing Multiagent Systems: The Gaia Methodology. *ACM Transactions on Software Engineering and Methodology*, 12(3):317–370, July 2003.
42. Johan Zuidweg. *Implementing Value-Added Telecom Services*. Artech House Inc., 2006.

Selecting the Best Mobile Information Service with Natural Language User Input

Qiangze Feng, Hongwei Qi and Toshikazu Fukushima

Abstract Information services accessed via mobile phones provide information directly relevant to subscribers' daily lives and are an area of dynamic market growth worldwide. Although many information services are currently offered by mobile operators, many of the existing solutions require a unique gateway for each service, and it is inconvenient for users to have to remember a large number of such gateways. Furthermore, the Short Message Service (SMS) is very popular in China and Chinese users would prefer to access these services in natural language via SMS. This chapter describes a Natural Language Based Service Selection System (NL3S) for use with a large number of mobile information services. The system can accept user queries in natural language and navigate it to the required service. Since it is difficult for existing methods to achieve high accuracy and high coverage and anticipate which other services a user might want to query, the NL3S is developed based on a Multi-service Ontology (MO) and Multi-service Query Language (MQL). The MO and MQL provide semantic and linguistic knowledge, respectively, to facilitate service selection for a user query and to provide adaptive service recommendations. Experiments show that the NL3S can achieve 75–95% accuracies and 85–95% satisfactions for processing various styles of natural language queries. A trial involving navigation of 30 different mobile services shows that the NL3S can provide a viable commercial solution for mobile operators.

1 Introduction

With the proliferation of mobile communication networks and currently 3.3 billion mobile subscribers worldwide (520 million in China), provision of information services directly relevant to subscribers' daily lives via mobile phones is becoming a large market [14]. Eyeing this potential market, mobile operators are offering an

Q. Feng (✉)
NEC Laboratories, China, 14/F, Bldg. A, Innovation Plaza, Tsinghua Science Park, Beijing 100084, China
e-mail: fengqiangze@research.nec.com.cn

I. King, R. Baeza-Yates (eds.), *Weaving Services and People on the World Wide Web*,
DOI 10.1007/978-3-642-00570-1_7, © Springer-Verlag Berlin Heidelberg 2009

ever increasing menu of information services to their subscribers [13], including route services, congestion services, weather services, and flight services. These services usually come from different service providers, and they usually have different service parameters, so that mobile operators have to provide a unique gateway for each service. It becomes very inconvenient for users if they have to remember a large number of different gateways for the services they wish to access. In order to maximize subscriber take-up, there is a considerable need for a service selection system which will allow users to interrogate dozens of services via a single gateway in a uniform way.

There are three models for service selection in current use.

1. Users call the human operator to make a query, and the human operator searches for the answer from dozens of services. One such example is 114 Best Tone [1].
2. Users find a relevant service using service directories or search engines, and then navigate to that service to input a query directly to the service. For example, Google Mobile [7] and Yahoo Mobile [19] offer such search engines.
3. Users send a query directly, and the query is forwarded to the relevant service. For example, AskMeNow [3] and mInfo [12] can provide such solutions.

In the first model, the query can be formatted in any natural language, but a large number of human operators are needed. In the second model, the query format is particular to each service, and users have to execute two operations (first find a relevant service, and then input the query to that service) in order to obtain an answer. In the third model, the query format ideally should be a general one expressed in a natural language, and users simply need to input the query to obtain an answer.

Of these three models, the third is both the most economical for mobile operators and the most convenient for users. Furthermore, in China almost all users have experience of sending short messages (SMS) and 1.1 billion messages are sent every day [11]. Since subscribers are accustomed to writing short messages in natural language, we chose to develop a natural language based service selection system in order to improve the efficiency of the third model outlined above. For example, when a user queries "How about the weather in Beijing?", the query is automatically forwarded to a weather service, which then returns the answer.

Generally, a typical natural language based service selection system consists of a query parsing step, a service type and parameter identification step, and a service execution step. Currently, the keyword based matching method is commonly used by both the query parsing step and the service type and parameter identification step. However, it suffers from the following two problems:

Firstly, it is difficult for current systems to achieve high accuracy and coverage in processing a variety of styles of natural language queries. If the user inputs a simple query, high coverage but low accuracy usually result. Conversely, if the user inputs a complicated query, high accuracy but low coverage are usually obtained.

Secondly, it is difficult for current systems to anticipate which other services a user might want to query. Since at least some users have such requirements, anticipation of their wishes can improve the efficiency of the system (and increase revenue). For example, when a user queries "How to get to Shining Plaza from Silver Plaza?", the user can receive an answer from not only a route service but also a traffic congestion service. Existing recommendation methods can suggest related services [9], but these services are not necessarily what a user wants to query.

In this chapter, we propose a Natural Language Based Service Selection System (NL3S) based on Multi-service Ontology (MO) and Multi-service Query Language (MQL) in order to provide an effective solution to the above two problems.

In order to tackle the first problem, Multi-service Ontology (MO), Multi-service Query Language (MQL), and a Service Selection Engine based on them have been developed. MO provides accurate semantic knowledge, by defining a group of Service Ontologies which conceptualize each service and a Mapping Ontology to connect the Service Ontologies together organically. MQL provides accurate linguistic knowledge, by defining a group of Service Query Languages which cover various natural language query forms for each service. By employing both MO and MQL, the Service Selection Engine can achieve high accuracy in processing various styles of natural language queries. High coverage is achieved by three-level service selection methods which try to find relevant services even if a query can't be understood perfectly.

In order to tackle the second problem, Service Selection Engine also provides an Adaptive Service Recommendation method based on a Service Correlation Base which is defined by MQL. The Service Correlation Base records the query correlations between different services, and it is used by the Adaptive Service Recommendation method to anticipate which other service or services a user might want to query.

Our Natural Language Based Service Selection System (NL3S) involves a combination of these methods. The NL3S aims to provide mobile operators with a solution which can not only navigate various styles of natural language queries to the corresponding service with high accuracy and high coverage, but can also anticipate which other services a user might want to query. A trial involving navigation of 30 commonly used services of a mobile operator in China shows that the NL3S can provide a viable commercial solution for mobile operators.

The remainder of this chapter is organized as follows: Sect. 2 introduces the related work, Sect. 3 describes the architecture of the NL3S, Sect. 4 describes the Multi-service Ontology (MO), Sect. 5 explains the Multi-service Query Language (MQL), Sect. 6 presents the Service Selection Engine, Sect. 7 outlines the implementation and evaluation of the NL3S and Sect. 8 offers our conclusions.

2 Related Work

Many efforts have been made in system development for mobile information services.

114 Best Tone [1] is a service provided by China Mobile, China's largest mobile phone company. To better serve the company's large number of subscribers, 114 Best Tone provides dozens of information services, such as directions, weather, flight and hotel reservations, yellow pages, etc. 114 Best Tone uses a live operator

to conduct the information searches. All a user has to do is simply dial 114 and tell the operator what information they are looking for. The operator will conduct the search and provide the information. For example, a user can ask the operator "How do I get to Shining Plaza from Silver Plaza?" and the operator will tell the user the best route. 114 Best Tone processes a wide variety of natural language queries with a high degree of accuracy, although this requires a large number of operators.

Google Mobile [7] and Yahoo Mobile [19] offer search engines and service directories for mobile phone users. Users can find a relevant service using service directories or search engines, and then navigate to that service to input a query directly to the service. For example, a user can select a flight service from a service directory, and then input the point of origin and the destination in order to receive an answer regarding the available flights. However, this is inconvenient for users because they have to execute multiple operations in order to obtain an answer.

There are also some natural-language-based mobile search engines, such as AskMeNow [3], mInfo [12], and Any Question Answered [2], among others. These provide a more user-friendly interface. Users simply need to input a natural language query to obtain an answer.

AskMeNow gives users the option of searching for information using an SMS short code or a mobile application, and it allows users to ask an English natural language query and receive an answer within minutes. AskMeNow delivers 411 listings of search content, such as weather, movie times, sports scores, directions, horoscopes, flight information, etc. AskMeNow uses a combination of computer-automated searching and human-operated searching to come up with answers to short queries. Depending on their clarity and simplicity, some types of queries can be automatically answered in seconds, but many queries have to be answered by human beings.

mInfo is a mobile search service provider in China, offering mobile search services via SMS, WAP, and embedded client systems, with support for natural language queries in Chinese and English. mInfo delivers over 30 categories of search content, and its services are available at no cost nationwide for both China Mobile and China Unicom customers. mInfo uses computer-automated searching.

Any Question Answered (AQA) is a premium-rate SMS information and entertainment service, and mobile phone users can text AQA with any query and get an answer within minutes for a fee. AQA uses a combination of computer-automated searching and human-operated searching, while most of the queries need to be answered by human beings.

In looking at the existing natural language-based mobile search engines, we find it is difficult to achieve high accuracy and coverage in processing flexible natural language queries, without the help of human beings. The reasons are as follows.

Firstly, most of them do not have enough semantic knowledge. They often gather many terms but generate limited semantic relations among terms. Therefore it is difficult for them to understand some complex queries, and irrelevant answers or no answers are often provided to the user.

Secondly, most of them do not have enough linguistic knowledge. Many of them only use general lexical and syntactical features, and even if some of them consider linguistic features, semantic features are seldom considered. Therefore they often support limited natural language query forms. Moreover, most of them do not have accurate service correlation knowledge that can be used to anticipate which other services a user might want to query.

3 Architecture of the NL3S

The NL3S (shown in Fig. 1) has been designed to provide a gateway for navigating various styles of natural language queries to the appropriate service. The NL3S also incorporates the ability to recommend other services that the user might want to query, as described in the previous section.

The lower panel in Fig. 1 contains the Multi-service Ontology (MO) and the Multi-service Query Language (MQL) components which, respectively, provide accurate semantic knowledge and linguistic knowledge for both processing various styles of natural language queries, and anticipating which other services the user might want to query.

The MO provides the semantic knowledge necessary for processing various styles of natural language queries and for anticipating which other services the user might want to query. The MO incorporates semantic knowledge accumulated from a variety of services. Furthermore, there are some semantic relevancies between

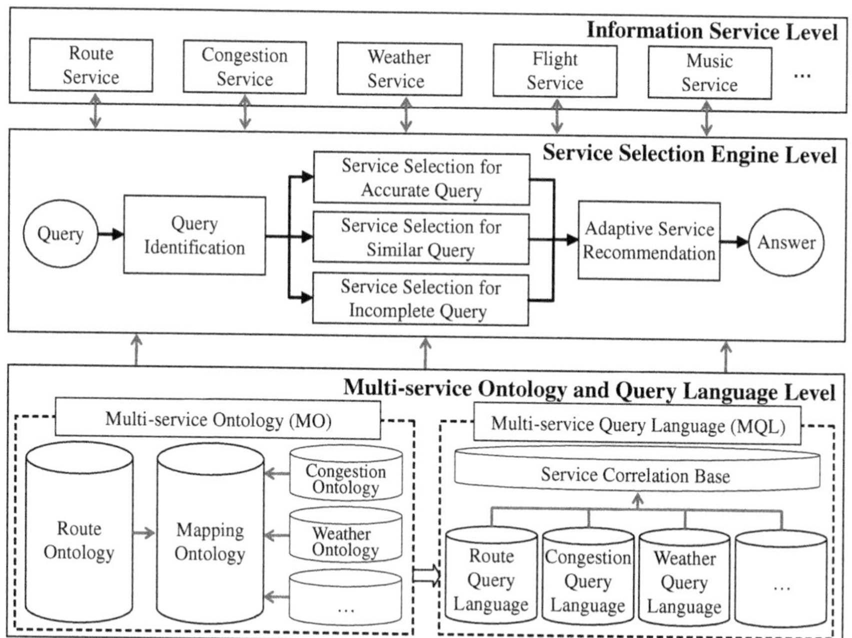

Fig. 1 Architecture of the natural language based service selection system (NL3S)

different services, and the MO is needed in order to map them together and provide more effective semantic knowledge. Therefore the MO is structured as a combination of a group of Service Ontologies, which represent the knowledge of various services, and a Mapping Ontology which represents the relevancies between these Service Ontologies.

The MQL is necessary both in order to process the various styles of natural language queries, and to anticipate which other services the user might want to query. Users often employ different query formats for different services. Furthermore, there are some strong query correlations between different services which show that after querying a given service, users often query a second service. Thus MQL is structured as a group of Service Query Languages which summarize the various query forms for each service and a Service Correlation Base which summarizes the query correlations between different services.

The central panel in Fig. 1 contains the Service Selection Engine, which has been developed based on MO and MQL. Generally speaking, the MQL is hard to cover all styles of natural language queries, and we classify user queries into the following three types:

1. Accurate Query. This type of query can be covered by MQL accurately.
2. Similar Query. This type of query cannot be covered by MQL accurately, but MQL contains similar syntax to it.
3. Incomplete Query. This type of query lacks the essential words that are required by MQL, but the complete format of the query can be covered by MQL.

Thus the Service Selection Engine incorporates a Query Identification module to identify the type of user query, a Service Selection for Accurate Query module to process Accurate Queries, a Service Selection for Similar Query module to process Similar Queries, and a Service Selection for Incomplete Query module to process Incomplete Queries. Furthermore, the Service Selection Engine also contains an Adaptive Service Recommendation module to suggest other services that the user may want to query.

The top panel in Fig. 1 describes various services available to mobile users. Using the Service Selection Engine in the central panel, the various services-such as a Route Service, a Congestion Service, a Weather Service, a Flight Service, and a Music Service-offered by mobile operators can be provided more conveniently to users.

4 Multi-Service Ontology

4.1 Background

Generally, an ontology is an explicit specification of conceptualization [8], and is fundamental in sharing knowledge among different agents and across different applications [4]. So we have utilized an ontology to conceptualize each service.

In order to process the various styles of natural language queries and to recommend other services the user may want to query, a Multi-service Ontology (MO) is needed to represent semantic knowledge accumulated from a variety of services. However, in the development of an MO, the following two problems are encountered:

Firstly, it is difficult to model an MO. There are some semantic relevancies between different services. Different services may use different terms to represent the same meaning. Moreover, many mobile information services are location-related, and there are some geospatial relations between different services. In order to provide more effective semantic knowledge, the relevancies between different services need to be mapped together.

Secondly, it is difficult to create an MO. Manual ontology building is a highly cost- and time-consuming task, especially in instance generation. A service's concepts and relations may number around a hundred. However, the instances of a service may amount to such a large number that it is not possible for the MO to be manually created.

In order to tackle the first problem, the MO is designed as a combination of a group of Service Ontologies and a Mapping Ontology. The Service Ontologies represent the knowledge of various services. The Mapping Ontology represents the relevancies between these Service Ontologies, and expression mapping and geospatial mapping are considered.

In order to tackle the second problem, the Service Ontologies are created semi-automatically, and the Mapping Ontology is created automatically.

4.2 MO Representation

4.2.1 Definition of MO

As noted above, the MO consists of a group of Service Ontologies and a Mapping Ontology. Generally, an ontology is composed of a set of concepts that are connected by relations. In other words, each concept is described by attributes and by its relations with other concepts.

Definition 1. *Formally, a concept C is a set of slot-value pairs. The slots are divided into two groups: attributes and conceptual relations. Therefore, we can also say a concept is a set of attribute-value pairs and relation-concept pairs,*

$$C = def\{< a_1, v_1 >, < a_2, v_2 >, \ldots, < a_i, v_i >\} \; U \; \{< r_1, C_1 >, < r_2, C_2 >, \ldots, < r_j, C_j >\}$$

where $a_1, a_2, \ldots, a_i$ are called the attributes of C, and $v_1, v_2, \ldots, v_i$ are the values of these attributes. The attributes and their values represent the properties of the concept C. $C_1, C_2, \ldots, C_j$ are concepts. $r_1, r_2, \ldots, r_j$ are relations from C to $C_1, C_2, \ldots, C_j$.

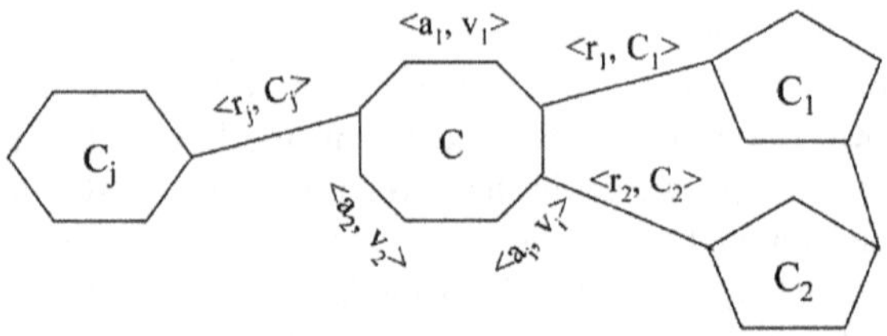

Fig. 2 Schematic of concepts and their relations

In Definition 1, each attribute a_i or relation r_j defines a perspective of a concept, and several attributes and relations describe an integrated view of the concept. Figure 2 is a schematic showing the meaning of the definition above.

Based on Definition 1, we consider two aspects: concepts and relations. Concepts can be further divided into classes and instances. Axioms should also be considered in order to constrain the interpretation of classes and their relations. To describe the four aspects above, we designed a frame-oriented ontology (see Fig. 3) that consists of the following components:

1. Classes. Each class describes a category of a domain.
2. Attributes and relations. Each attribute or relation defines a perspective of a class, and several attributes and relations describe an integrated view of the class. Each attribute or relation has several facets. For example, ": type" indicates the type of values an attribute or a relation takes, and ": lang" indicates the language type of an attribute or a relation.
3. Instances. Each instance is an actually existing thing. An instance is minimally introduced by declaring it to be a member of a class.
4. Axioms. Axioms are described by horn rules [5], and they can also be used to make some inferences.

```
DefClass <ClassName>
{
  Attribute: <AttributeName>
               : type <String|Numeric|Array|...>
               : lang <English|Chinese|Japanese|...>
  Relation: <RelationName>
               : type <(ClassName1, ClassName2, ...)>
               : lang <English|Chinese|Japanese|...>
  Axiom: <RelationName1(...)> & <RelationName2(...) & ... ->
            <RelationNameN(...)>
}

DefInstance <InstanceName>: <ClassName>
{
  <AttributeName>: <AttributeValue>
  <RelationName(InstanceName1, InstanceName2, ...)>
}
```

Fig. 3 Frame-oriented ontology

4.2.2 Service Ontology

An individual Service Ontology is created for each service, so that for example a Route Ontology and a Congestion Ontology are separately constructed for the Route Service and the Congestion Service, respectively.

Examples of Route Ontology and Congestion Ontology are illustrated in Fig. 4. Route Ontology contains all bridges (e.g. Baofusi Bridge), point-of-interests (e.g. Silver Plaza), roads (e.g. North Fourth Ring Road) and their geospatial relations (e.g. "Between (Baofusi Bridge, Xueyuan Bridge, Jianxiang Bridge)" means Baofusi Bridge is located between Xueyuan Bridge and Jianxiang Bridge). For the axiom "Between(Z, X, Y) → Between(Z, Y, X)", it can be deduced that Between(Baofusi Bridge, Jianxiang Bridge, Xueyuan Bridge) if Between(Baofusi Bridge, Xueyuan Bridge, Jianxiang Bridge).

Similarly, Congestion Ontology includes all congestion locations (e.g. Baofusi Bridge), directions (e.g. West to East) and traffic status descriptions (e.g. Jammed).

4.2.3 Mapping Ontology

Different services often contain some duplicated or related data. Thus the Mapping Ontology, which contains information about the relations between Service

```
DefClass Bridge
{
  Relation: Point-of
    : type (Bridge, Road)
  Relation: Between
    : type (Bridge, Bridge, Bridge)
  Axiom: Between(Z, X, Y)→Between(Z, Y, X)
}
DefClass Point-of-Interest
{
  Attribute: Address
    : type String
}
DefClass Road
{
  Relation: SectionOf
    : type (Road, Road)
}
DefInstance Baofusi Bridge: Bridge
{
  Between(Baofusi Bridge, Xueyuan Bridge,
          Jianxiang Bridge)
}
DefInstance Silver Plaza: Point-of-Interest
{
  Address: No.9, North Fourth Ring West Road
}
DefClass North Fourth Ring Road: Road
{
  SectionOf(North Fourth Ring Road,
            Fourth Ring Road)
}
```

```
DefClass CongestionLocation
{
  Attribute: RushHour
    : type String
}
DefClass Direction
{
  Relation: PartOf
    : type (Direction, Direction)
}
DefClass TrafficStatus
{
  ...
}
DefInstance Baofusi Bridge: CongestionLocation
{
  RushHour: 7:30~8:30, 17:30~18:30
}
DefInstance West to East: Direction
{
  PartOf(West to East, East-West)
}
DefInstance Jammed: TrafficStatus
{
  ...
}
```

Fig. 4 Examples of service ontology

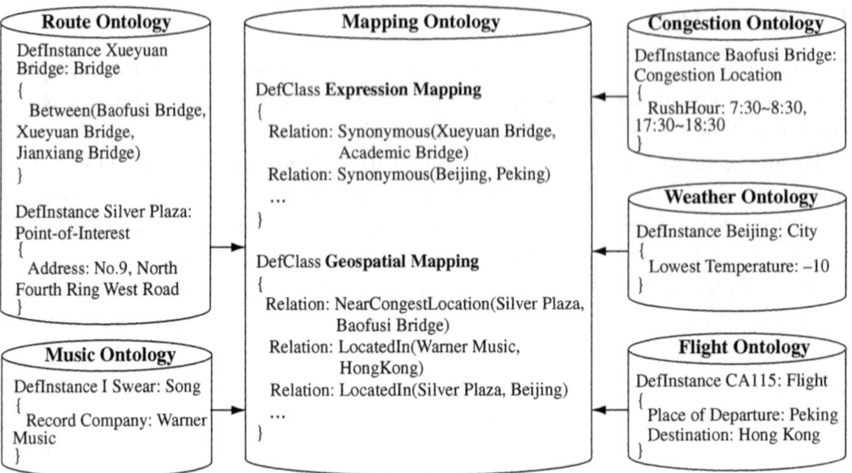

Fig. 5 Example of mapping ontology

Ontologies, is used to integrate the set of Service Ontologies. As shown in Fig. 5, two kinds of relations are used in making the mapping:

1. Expression Mapping. This type of mapping involves synonymous or abbreviated words. For example, "Xueyuan Bridge" and "Academic Bridge" are mapped because they are synonymous.
2. Geospatial Mapping. This type of mapping involves geospatially related words. For example, "Silver Plaza" and "Baofusi Bridge" are mapped because the congestion location "Baofusi Bridge" is spatially very near to the point-of-interest "Silver Plaza".

4.3 MO Creation

A Service Ontology is created semi-automatically from the service data. For each service, the Service Ontology is created as follows: (1) Automatic extraction of the classes, instances and relations from the service data; (2) Manual validation and modification of the extracted results; (3) Manual definition of the axioms.

For example, a Route Ontology can be created from an electronic map based on the functions of a Geographic Information System (GIS) [6, 10, 18]. For example, the GIS function corresponding to the relation "Point-of (x, y)" in Fig. 4 in SuperMap [18] is "soDatasetVector.QueryEx(objGeometry As soGeometry, scsCommonPoint, "") as soRecordset", which is used to query the point (Bridge) on a line (Road) in the electronic map. Axioms are defined manually based on the extracted relations.

The Mapping Ontology is created automatically. Firstly, we build the following data libraries to be used for the creation of the Mapping Ontology: (1) Synonymy Dictionary. This includes the set of words from each service and corresponding synonymous expressions; (2) Abbreviation Rules. These are necessary because relatively long words often have abbreviated forms. The Mapping Ontology is then created automatically based on the above data libraries in two steps as follows: (1) Expression Mapping is performed based on the Synonymy Dictionary and Abbreviation Rules; (2) Geospatial Mapping is performed based on the GIS functions, and the mapping among geospatially-related words is built automatically.

For example, "Beijing" and "Peking" are found to be synonymous by searching the synonymy dictionary, "NEC Laboratories, China" and "NEC Labs, China" are synonymous according to the abbreviation rule "Abbreviate (Laboratories, Labs)", and "Silver Plaza" and "Baofusi Bridge" are geospatially mapped because the distance between them in the electronic map is very short.

5 Multi-Service Query Language

5.1 MQL Representation

The Multi-service Query Language (MQL) is used to provide the linguistic knowledge necessary for processing the various styles of natural language queries. The MQL is also used to provide linguistic knowledge to assist in recommending other services the user may want to query. The MQL consists of a group of Service Query Languages and a Service Correlation Base. The Service Query Languages summarize the natural language query forms for each service, and the Service Correlation Base records the query correlations between different services. The Service Query Language and Service Correlation Base will be explained in detail.

5.1.1 Service Query Language

A separate Service Query Language is designed for each specific service, such as Route Query Language, Congestion Query Language, and Weather Query Language. The Service Query Language is defined based on the corresponding Service Ontology.

The Service Query Language consists of the following components:

1. Syntax attempts to record all possible natural language query forms. There are several components in the syntax, and each component has its own symbol definitions:

    a. <X>means X is a constant, and <?X>means X is a variable.
    b. <?X(Constraint)>means X should satisfy the constraint "Constraint", which is a set of classes that can be found in the corresponding Service Ontology. That means X can only be replaced with the instances that belong to any one of the above classes.
    c. "|" means "or" logic operator. "[ ]" means the string between "[" and "]" is optional.

<table>
<tr><th>Syntax</th><th>Service Type</th><th>Service Parameters</th></tr>
<tr><td>1) [<How to>]<get to><?X2(Bridge|Point-of-Interest)><from><?X1(Bridge| Point-of-Interest)>
2) [<What|Which>]<bus>[<go>]<from><?X1(Bridge| Point-of-Interest)><to><?X2(Bridge|Point-of-Interest)></td><td>Route</td><td>From=X1
To=X2</td></tr>
<tr><td>1) <traffic><from><?X1(CongestionLocation)><to> <?X2(CongestionLocation)>
2) <traffic><?X1(CongestionLocation)></td><td>Congestion</td><td>Start=X1
End=X2</td></tr>
<tr><td>1) [<What>]<weather><?X(City)>
2) [<How>]<cold|warm|hot><?X(City)></td><td>Weather</td><td>City=X</td></tr>
<tr><td>1) [<How to>]<get to><?X2(City)><from><?X1 (City)><by><air|plane>
2) [<What|Which>]<airline|flight>[<fly|go>]<from> <?X1 (City)><to><?X2(City)></td><td>Flight</td><td>Depart=X1
Land=X2</td></tr>
</table>

Fig. 6 Examples of service query language

2. Service type describes the corresponding service name when the query conforms to the above syntax.
3. Service parameters describe the parameters that are required by the above service.

Figure 6 gives examples of Route Query Language, Congestion Query Language, Weather Query Language and Flight Query Language. If the query conforms to the syntax of the Route Service, then that service is selected and the required parameters are "From" and "To". Similarly, if the query conforms to the syntax of the Congestion Service, then that service is selected and the required parameters are "Start" and "End".

From Fig. 6, we can find that many Service Query Languages have the common query features. A common query language can be summarized to extract the common query features of various services. It can be then inherited by various Service Query Languages. Such a hierarchical style can reduce repeated definitions through the inherit strategy. The inherit strategy is implemented by instantiating appropriate parameters.

As an example, we can extract the common query language from Fig. 6. The common query features of "Route" and "Flight" in Fig. 6 are summarized as "Common1" in Fig. 7. Then, the syntax of Route Query Language can be redefined as

<table>
<tr><th>Syntax</th><th>Service Type</th><th>Service Parameters</th></tr>
<tr><td>1) [<How to>]<get to><?X2(?para1)><from><?X1 (?para1)><?para2>
2) [<What|Which>]<?para3>[<go>]<from><?X1(?para1)><to><?X2(?para1)></td><td>Common1</td><td></td></tr>
</table>

Fig. 7 Example of common query language

"inherit Common1(?para1=Bridge|Point-of-Interest, ?para3=bus)", and the syntax of Flight Query Language can be redefined as "inherit Common1(?para1=City, ?para2=<by><air|plane>, ?para3=airline|flight)".

5.1.2 Service Correlation Base

Different services may have a strong or weak correlation. Examples of strong correlations are that users tend to query the traffic conditions after querying the route between two points, and users also tend to query the weather of the destination city after querying flights between two cities. The Service Correlation Base is used to record the correlations between services.

As shown in Table 1, in order to analyze both a given user's personal interests and all users' common interests, the Service Correlation Base contains two types of service correlation data:

1. Individual Service Correlation. This records the correlation between two services for a given user, and can be used to analyze that user's personal interests. For example, user "Tom" has a correlation between "Route" and "Congestion" of 0.9, whilst user "Bob" has a correlation of 0.4.
2. Common Service Correlation. This records the correlation between two services for all users, and can be used to analyze users' common interests. For example, users have an overall correlation between "Route" and "Congestion" of 0.65.

Table 1 Example of a service correlation base

User Name	Service 1	Service 2	Correlation
Tom	Route	Congestion	0.9
Bob	Route	Congestion	0.4
Tom	Flight	Weather	0.7
Bob	Flight	Weather	0.5
All Users	Route	Congestion	0.65
All Users	Flight	Weather	0.6

It should be noted that the service correlation is asymmetric. For example, the correlation between "Route" and "Congestion" is high, but the correlation between "Congestion" and "Route" is low. This is because few users tend to query the route after querying the traffic condition between two points.

5.2 *MQL Creation*

The Service Query Languages were mostly constructed manually. Firstly, we gather the actual natural language queries for each service from mobile users. Secondly, we define the syntax for each service by analyzing its query features. Thirdly, we enter the service type and service parameters for each service. Finally, the common query features of various Service Query Languages are extracted automatically, and then the corresponding Service Query Languages are redefined.

The Service Correlation Base is created automatically based on the Service Selection History, which stores a history of the use of selected services by all users as well as by individual users. The correlation between service X and service Y for a user is given by the probability of the user querying service Y after querying service X. The correlation between service X and service Y for all users is calculated by the average of the correlation between service X and service Y for each user. It should be noted that the Service Correlation Base is adjustable, since the time period over which the Service Selection History is analyzed can be varied.

6 Service Selection Engine

The Service Selection Engine has been developed based on MO and MQL, and is used to navigate the various styles of natural language queries to the corresponding service. The Service Selection Engine can not only process the various styles of natural language queries with high accuracy and coverage, but can also recommend which other services the user may want to query.

As previously shown in Fig. 1, the Service Selection Engine consists of five parts. The functions of these parts are discussed in detail in the following sections.

6.1 Query Identification

Query Identification is used to identify the type of user query, based on the MO and MQL. Firstly, the query is matched using MO and MQL in order to find the candidate syntax with the maximum number of matching words. Secondly, the type of query is determined based on the following criteria:

1. If the query contains all the variables and non-optional constants of the candidate syntax, then the query is assigned as an Accurate Query, otherwise;
2. If the query contains all the variables but not all the non-optional constants of the candidate syntax, then the query is assigned as a Similar Query, otherwise;
3. If the query does not contain all the variables of the candidate syntax, then the query is assigned as an Incomplete Query.

For example, the user query "How to get to Shining Plaza from Silver Plaza?" is an Accurate Query, because it contains all variables and non-optional constants of the syntax $[< How\ to >] < get\ to ><?X2(Bridge|Point-of-Interest) >< from ><?X1(Bridge|Point-of-Interest) >$. The user query "How to arrive Shining Plaza from Silver Plaza?" is a Similar Query, because it contains all the variables of the above syntax but does not contain the non-optional constant "get to". The user query "How to get to Shining Plaza?" is an Incomplete Query, because it does not contain the variable "X1" of the above syntax.

6.2 Service Selection for Accurate Query

Service Selection for Accurate Query is used to process an Accurate Query and access the corresponding service [15, 16]. Service Selection for Accurate Query is based on the MO and MQL, and consists of the following steps:

Firstly, the Semantic Parser module parses the query based on the MO and MQL, and then outputs the semantically tagged result containing the category of each instance in the query.

Secondly, the Syntax Matching and Service Selection module matches the semantically tagged result with MQL syntax by a relaxed keyword matching method. The method can transform any query keywords that do not satisfy the constraints of the matched syntax based on the Expression Mapping and Geospatial Mapping in the Mapping Ontology of MO. After matching, the module selects the service type and service parameters corresponding to the matched syntax.

For example, if a user queries "How to get to Shining Plaza from Silver Plaza?", parsing of the query based on the MO and MQL gives the semantically tagged result "How to, get to, Shining Plaza (Point-of-Interest), from, Silver Plaza (Point-of-Interest)". Secondly, matching the above tagged result with MQL syntax gives the matched syntax $[< How\ to >] < get\ to ><?X2(Bridge|Point-of-Interest) >< from ><?X1(Bridge|Point-of-Interest) >$ (as shown in Fig. 6). Finally, the query is assigned to the corresponding service type "Route" with the service parameters "From=Silver Plaza, To=Shining Plaza".

Using both the MO and MQL, high accuracies can be achieved in navigation of Accurate Queries to the corresponding service. However, the Service Selection for Accurate Query is unsuitable for processing Similar Queries and Incomplete Queries, because they often cannot be fully analyzed by MO and MQL. Thus additional Service Selection for Similar Query and Service Selection for Incomplete Query steps are necessary.

6.3 Service Selection for Similar Query

Service Selection for Similar Query is used to process Similar Queries and access the corresponding service. The Service Selection for Similar Query method is based on the MO and MQL and consists of the following steps:

Firstly, the Semantic Parser module parses the query based on the MO and MQL and outputs the semantically tagged result.

Secondly, the Similar Syntax Finding module finds those syntaxes that are similar to the tagged result of the query from the MQL, using the following criteria: (1) the tagged result should contain all the variables of the similar syntax; (2) the syntax similarity, in other words the similarity between the tagged result and the similar syntax, should be greater than a specified threshold (e.g. 0.9). The syntax similarity can be calculated by means of the weighted average of all word similarities, where the word similarity is calculated by existing semantic similarity assessment methods [17], and the weight of each word is calculated on the basis of the tagged result, part-of-speech and word frequency, e.g. an instance has higher weight than a syntax word, a noun has higher weight than an adjective, and a word with lower frequency has higher weight.

Thirdly, the Service Interaction module takes all candidate service types and service parameters corresponding to these similar syntaxes, sends the service parameters to all candidate services, receives the results from the candidate services, and finally selects the best service according to the following criteria: (1) if only one service returns a result, then it is selected as the best service; (2) if multiple services return results, then the service with the highest syntax similarity is selected.

Finally, the Syntax Adaptation module updates the MQL syntax of the best service, by adding the syntax corresponding to the semantically tagged result of the query.

For example, if a user queries “How to arrive Shining Plaza from Silver Plaza?”, this cannot be analyzed by MQL. Firstly, parsing the query based on the MO and MQL gives the semantically tagged result “How to, arrive, Shining Plaza (Point-of-Interest), from, Silver Plaza (Point-of-Interest)”. Secondly, a similar syntax $[< How\ to >] < get\ to >< ?X2(Bridge|Point-of-Interest) >< from >< ?X1(Bridge|Point-of-Interest) >$ is found. Thirdly, a candidate service “Route” is identified, which is then sent the corresponding service parameters “From=Silver Plaza, To=Shining Plaza”. Since the Route Service returns a result, “Route” is selected as the best service. Finally, the new syntax $< How\ to >< arrive >< ?X2(Bridge|Point-of-Interest) >< from >< ?X1(Bridge|Point-of-Interest) >$ is added to the Route Query Language.

Service Selection for Similar Query can navigate Similar Queries to the corresponding service with high accuracy, and furthermore, it makes the system self-adjustable by virtue of it learning the new syntax corresponding to a Similar Query automatically. However the Service Selection for Similar Query still cannot process Incomplete Queries.

6.4 Service Selection for Incomplete Query

Service Selection for Incomplete Query is used to process an Incomplete Query and access the corresponding service. Users may submit an Incomplete Query, if they omit some words when they formulate a query.

Generally, there are two categories of Incomplete Query:

1. The first kind involves incomplete concepts. For example, “How to get to Shining from Silver Plaza?” has an incomplete concept “Shining” and the corresponding complete concept should be “Shining Plaza”.
2. The second kind lacks essential concepts that are required by the corresponding service. For example, “How to get to Shining Plaza?” lacks an essential concept viz. the starting point of the Route Service.

Service Selection for Incomplete Query has been developed based on the MO and MQL in order to process both of the above kinds of Incomplete Queries.

The first kind of Incomplete Query is processed by means of the following steps. Firstly, the Incompleteness Checking module ascertains whether or not the query involves incomplete concepts and finds all candidate concepts that contain any incomplete concept, by searching the MO and MQL. Secondly, the Query Complementation and Service Selection module selects the best concept from the candidate concepts by ascertaining whether or not the concept satisfies the corresponding constraint that is defined in the syntax of MQL. The corresponding service type and service parameters are then assigned.

For example, if a user queries "How to get to Shining from Silver Plaza?", an initial search by MO and MQL ascertains that there is an incomplete concept "Shining" and finds all candidate complete concepts ("Shining Wind", "Shining Plaza", "Shining Friends", etc.). Secondly, because MQL contains the syntax $[< How\ to >] < get\ to >< ?X2(Bridge|Point{-}of{-}Interest) >< from ><$ $?X1(Bridge|Point{-}of{-}Interest) >$ and MO contains the relations "isa(Shining Wind, Game)", "isa(Shining Plaza, Point-of-Interest)", and "isa (Shining Friends, Song)", "Shining Plaza" is selected as the best concept.

The second kind of Incomplete Query is processed by means of the following steps. Firstly, the Incompleteness Checking module finds the syntax corresponding to the query from MQL, and then identifies the missing service parameters from the query. Secondly, the Query Complementation and Service Selection module finds the user's latest query from the user query log, and then extracts the missing parameters from the user's latest query.

For example, if a user queries "How to get to Shining Plaza?", an initial search by MQL finds the syntax of Route Service is involved in the query and decides that the missing parameter of the query is "From". Secondly, assuming it finds the user's latest query from the user query log was "Is there a bus station near Silver Plaza?", it allocates "Silver Plaza" as the value of "From".

By means of the Service Selection for Accurate Query, Service Selection for Similar Query and Service Selection for Incomplete Query, Accurate Queries, Similar Queries and Incomplete Queries can be processed with high accuracy. The quality of service will be further enhanced, however, if it is possible to recommend other services the user may want to query.

6.5 Adaptive Service Recommendation

The Adaptive Service Recommendation method is used to recommend other services the user may want to query. It is expected that users may require other information in addition to that sought in their first request. The Adaptive Service Recommendation method consists of the following steps.

Firstly, the Relevant Service Type Finding module finds all relevant service types for the current service by retrieving the Service Correlation Base of MQL (if the module cannot find the corresponding individual service correlation data, then retrieve the common service correlation data), and then selects the m relevant services with the highest correlations. Secondly, the Relevant Service Parameter

Acquisition module transforms the parameters of the query into words that satisfy the syntax constraints required by each relevant service, by retrieving MO and MQL. Thirdly, the Service Correlation Adaptation module adjusts the Service Correlation Base automatically according to the user's response.

For example, the user "Bob" queries "How to get to Shining Plaza from Silver Plaza?", and the corresponding service is "Route". Firstly, the system finds a relevant service "Congestion" by searching from the Service Correlation Base of MQL. Secondly, the point-of-interests "Shining Plaza" and "Silver Plaza" are transformed into the congestion locations "Academic Bridge" and "Baofusi Bridge" respectively, based on the Mapping Ontology. This generates the congestion service parameters "Start=Baofusi Bridge, End=Academic Bridge". Finally, if it is found that even after recommending the Congestion Service, the user "Bob" still does not query this service, then correlation between "Route" and "Congestion" for this user is reduced accordingly.

By recommending other services the user may want to query, the Adaptive Service Recommendation method can significantly increase user uptake of the various services.

7 Implementation and Evaluation

7.1 Implementation

As shown in Fig. 8, implementation of the NL3S consists of four components:

1. Service Providers, who provide various mobile information services, such as a Route Service, a Congestion Service, a Weather Service and a Flight Service.
2. Mobile Users, who query information via SMS.
3. Mobile Operators such as China Mobile and China Unicom. They transmit queries and system responses between Mobile Users and the Service Selection System.
4. Service Selection System, which is the key component of the NL3S. It connects Service Providers and Mobile Operators.

In this study, we used the NL3S to navigate 30 commonly-used services of a mobile operator in China. In order to do this, we have developed:

1. A Multi-service Ontology (MO), which covers 30 Service Ontologies—a Route Ontology, Congestion Ontology, Weather Ontology, Flight Ontology, Music Ontology, Game Ontology, TV Ontology, Lottery Ontology, Stock Ontology, Location Ontology, Ringtone Ontology, Multimedia Ringtone Ontology, Voice Mail Ontology, Mobile Mail Box Ontology, Personal Mail Box Ontology, Fee Notification Ontology, Handset Manager Ontology, Handset News Ontology, Handset Navigation Ontology, Wireless Music Ontology, Music Ranks Ontology, Music Search Ontology, Music Download Ontology, SMS Filter-

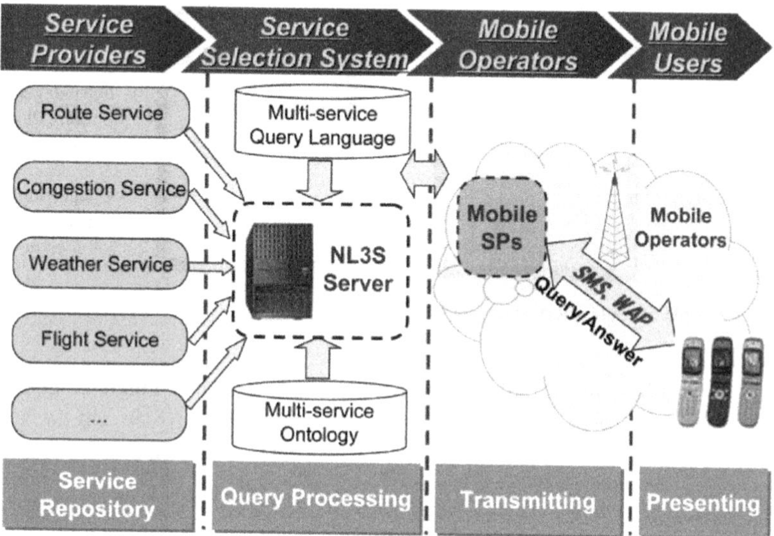

Fig. 8 Implementation architecture of the NL3S

ing Ontology, SMS Transfer Ontology, Phone Changing Notification Ontology, Phone Number Display Ontology, Call Reminder Ontology, School Communication Ontology, and Speech-based Music Search Ontology—and includes about 860 classes, 930 attributes and relations, 260 axioms, and 3 million instances.

2. A Multi-service Query Language (MQL), which contains more than 2800 syntaxes that are mostly built manually by analyzing the query features of the 30 mobile information services whose ontologies are listed in 1.
3. A Service Selection Engine for navigating the 30 mobile information services whose ontologies are listed in 1.

Figure 9 shows some examples of Chinese natural language queries and their English translations.

Chinese Query Example	English Translation
从银谷大厦到世宁大厦怎么走？	How can I get to Shining Plaza from Silver Plaza?
联想桥到四通桥之间拥堵吗？	How is the traffic congestion between Lianxiang Bridge and Sitong Bridge?
今天北京天气如何？	What's the weather like today in Beijing?
北京到香港的航班有哪些？	What flights are there from Beijing to Hong Kong?

Fig. 9 Examples of Chinese natural language queries

Fig. 10 Example of route query and answer

Figure 10 shows an example for navigating Chinese natural language queries to the corresponding service. A user submits a route query via SMS, and the system provides replies from both the Route Service and the Congestion Service.

7.2 Experiment 1: Accuracy Evaluation

In order to evaluate the performance of the following methods,

1. Method 1: Service Selection for Accurate Query
2. Method 2: Service Selection for Similar Query
3. Method 3: Service Selection for Incomplete Query
4. Method 4: Adaptive Service Recommendation

we defined their corresponding accuracies as follows:

1. Accuracy of Method 1 = (Number of accurate queries whose service type and service parameters are extracted correctly) / (Number of accurate queries)
2. Accuracy of Method 2 = (Number of similar queries whose service type and service parameters are extracted and selected correctly) / (Number of similar queries)
3. Accuracy of Method 3 = (Number of incomplete queries whose service type and service parameters are extracted and complemented correctly) / (Number of incomplete queries)
4. Accuracy of Method 4 = (Number of satisfied recommendations) / (Number of all recommendations)

In above definitions, the service type and service parameters are defined in Fig. 6. In the above four kinds of evaluation, we asked 20 users to judge if the service type and the service parameters were extracted correctly or not for each query of Method 1, 2, 3, and if the recommendation satisfied the user or not for each query of Method 4. Then the final judgment for each query was determined by the majority of 20 users' judgment results.

We used a test set of 3,000 Chinese language queries (1,000 Accurate Queries, 1,000 Similar Queries and 1,000 Incomplete Queries) collected for 30 services from mobile users. These 3,000 queries were made up of the 100 most commonly used queries for each of the 30 services. Given the limitations of SMS in China, almost all these queries contained less than 70 Chinese characters.

We then constructed 6 groups of different sizes from the set of 30 services made up of 5, 10, 15, 20, 25 and all 30 services. We used the tests described above to evaluate the four types of accuracies for each of the 6 groups. In this way, we can evaluate how the performance of Service Selection for Accurate Query, Service Selection for Similar Query, Service Selection for Incomplete Query and Adaptive Service Recommendation varies with the increase in number of the services.

The accuracy evaluation results, given in Fig. 11, indicate that:

1. High degrees of accuracy were obtained for processing Accurate Queries, Similar Queries and Incomplete Queries and for recommending other services the user may subsequently want to query.
2. The accuracy decreased slowly as the number of services was increased, and the system can meet the demands of navigating 30 or more services.

By careful examination of those queries that were not processed correctly, two types of errors were identified:

1. User errors (25%). This means errors generated in the query by the users themselves, such as semantic errors or spelling errors. For example, a semantic error is generated in the query "Is Baofusi Bridge on the West Second Ring Road jammed?" where Baofusi Bridge is in fact on the North Fourth Ring Road and not the West Second Ring Road. In another example, a spelling error is generated in the query "Where is Sivor Plaza?" where "Sivor" should be "Silver".
2. System errors (75%). This means that although a user's query was correct, the system could not process it appropriately, for reasons such as an unrecognized word or unrecognized syntax being present. For example, the query "Where is WhiteJade Restaurant?" could not be processed because the MO did not include the point-of-interest "WhiteJade Restaurant". In another example, the query

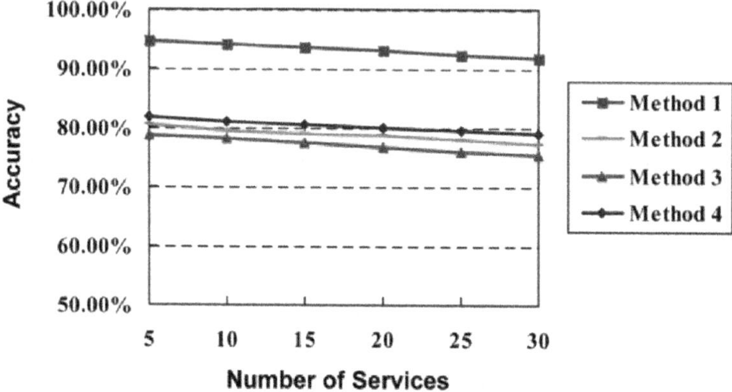

Fig. 11 Results of accuracy evaluation

"How many traffic lights are there from Baofusi Bridge to Xueyuan Bridge?" could not be processed because the MQL did not include the syntax for querying traffic lights.

7.3 Experiment 2: Satisfaction Evaluation

The second experiment involved an evaluation of users' satisfaction for the whole NL3S, by combining the four methods:

1. Method 1: Service Selection for Accurate Query
2. Method 2: Service Selection for Similar Query
3. Method 3: Service Selection for Incomplete Query
4. Method 4: Adaptive Service Recommendation.

We used the NL3S to navigate 30 mobile services of a mobile operator in China, using the following four sets of solutions: (a) Method 1, (b) Method 1 + Method 2, (c) Method 1 + Method 2 + Method 3, and (d) Method 1 + Method 2 + Method 3 + Method 4. We asked 20 users to query freely the 30 mobile services. After a user received the answer to his or her query, the NL3S asked them to rate the answer on a satisfaction score of Excellent (1.0), Good (0.7), Average (0.5), Poor (0.3), or Useless (0). In this way we accumulated the satisfaction scores for about 2,000 queries and could evaluate the combined performance of the four methods.

We defined the satisfaction rating as follows:

Satisfaction=(The sum of satisfaction scores that are given by user) / (Number of all queries)

Table 2 shows the satisfaction evaluation results for the above four solutions.

The 87.5% satisfaction rating for the Service Selection for Accurate Query alone was enhanced by 1.8% by adding the Service Selection for Similar Query, by a further 2.4% by adding the Service Selection for Incomplete Query, and by a further 1.5% by including the Adaptive Service Recommendation, giving a combined satisfaction rating for the four methods of over 93%. The satisfaction rate was increased by only 5.7% between Method 1 and all four methods, because most queries are accurate queries.

Table 2 Results of satisfaction evaluation

System	Method 1	Method 1+2	Method 1+2+3	Method 1+2+3+4
NL3S	87.5%	89.3%	91.7%	93.2%

7.4 Experiment 3: Performance Evaluation

The third experiment examined the overall performance of the NL3S, by including all four methods and 30 trial services. We deployed the NL3S on an HP DL580 server.

Table 3 Results of performance evaluation

Number of services	Scalability (Queries/Second)	Response time (Milliseconds/Query)
5	10 * 15 (thread)	100
10	9.2 * 15 (thread)	116
15	8.6 * 15 (thread)	125
20	8.2 * 15 (thread)	134
25	7.6 * 15 (thread)	147
30	7.2 * 15 (thread)	158

We used the same test set as that used in Experiment 1, composed of 3,000 Chinese queries collected for 30 services. Because of the limited number of queries, each query was repeated 10 times. The performance of the system in navigating different numbers of services was evaluated.

The scalability and response time evaluations are shown in Table 3, where scalability represents the number of threads which can be started by the NL3S simultaneously and the number of queries which can be processed by each thread on average in a given time interval, and the response time measures the delay between a query and its answer.

The results showed that both the scalability and response time decreased slowly as the number of services increased, and the system is capable of meeting the demands of navigating at least 30, and probably more, services.

8 Conclusion

A Natural Language Based Service Selection System (NL3S) for a large number of mobile information services, based on a Multi-service Ontology (MO) and Multi-service Query Language (MQL) has been devised. The MO and MQL provide semantic and linguistic knowledge, respectively, for service selection of user queries and Adaptive Service Recommendation in the NL3S. By deploying both MO and MQL, the NL3S can not only navigate various styles of natural language user queries to the required service with high accuracy and coverage, but can also recommend other services the user may want to query. Trial experiments with 30 mobile services show that the NL3S can provide an effective commercial solution for mobile operators.

References

1. 114 Best Tone: Website. http://www.chinatelecom.com.cn/products/01/02/. Cited 5 Nov 2008
2. Any Question Answered: Website. http://www.issuebits.com/. Cited 5 Nov 2008
3. AskMeNow: Website. http://www.askmenow.com/. Cited 5 Nov 2008
4. Cao, C.; Feng, Q.; et al.: Progress in the Development of National Knowledge Infrastructure. Journal of Computer Science and Technology, 17(5), 523–534 (2002)
5. Chandra, A., and Harel, D.: Horn Clause Queries and Generalizations. Journal of Logic Programming. 2(1), 1–15 (1985)

6. ESRI.: *Understanding GIS: The ARC/INFO Method*, ESRI, Redlands (1998) p 608
7. Google Mobile: Website. http://www.google.com/intl/zh-EN/mobile/. Cited 5 Nov 2008
8. Gruber, T.R.: A Translation Approach to Portable Ontology Specification. Knowledge Acquisition, 5(2), 199–220 (1993)
9. Hughes, E., McCormack, D.; et al.: Service Recommendation Using SLP, IEEE International Conference on Telecommunications 2001, Bucharest (2001)
10. Ian J.: *Understanding MapInfo: A Structured Guide*. Published by the Archaeological Computing Laboratory, University of Sydney (1996) p 300
11. iResearch Co. Ltd.: Market Size of China SMS Market 2003-2008. 2005 China WVAS Market Research Report (2006)
12. mInfo: Website. http://www.minfo.com/. Cited 5 Nov 2008
13. Paulson, L.D.: Search Technology Goes Mobile. IEEE Computer, 38(8), 19–22 (2005)
14. Portio Research Ltd.: *Worldwide Mobile Market Forecasts 2006-2011: Global Analysis and Forecasts of Mobile Markets, Technology and Subscriber Growth* Portio Research Ltd, Chippenham (2006) p 480
15. Qi, H., Liu Y., et al.: A Map Ontology Driven Approach to Natural Language Traffic Information Processing and Services. First Asian Semantic Web Conference, Beijing, China, September 2006. Lecture Notes in Computer Science, vol 4185 (Springer, Berlin Heidelberg New York 2006) pp 696–710
16. Qi, H., Feng, Q., et al.: Ontology-Based Mobile Information Service Platform. 10th Asia-Pacific Web Conference, Shenyang, China, April 2008. Lecture Notes in Computer Science, vol 4976 (Springer, Berlin Heidelberg New York 2008) pp 239–250
17. Seco, N.: Computational Models of Similarity in Lexical Ontologies. MSc Thesis, University College Dublin (2005)
18. SuperMap GIS Technologies, Inc.: Understanding SuperMap GIS. Beijing (2003)
19. Yahoo Mobile: Website. http://mobile.yahoo.com/search. Cited 5 Nov 2008

Location Concepts for the Web

Martin Kofahl and Erik Wilde

Abstract The concept of location has become very popular in many applications on the Web, in particular for those which aim at connecting the real world with resources on the Web. However, the Web as it is today has no overall location concept, which means that applications have to introduce their own location concepts and have done so in incompatible ways. On the other hand, there are a number of interfaces and techniques that make location information available to networked devices. By turning the Web into a location-aware Web location-oriented applications get better support for their location concepts on the Web, and the Web becomes an information system where location-related information can be more easily shared across different applications and application areas. This chapter describes a location concept for the Web supporting different location types and its embedding into some of the Web's core technologies.

1 Introduction

The Web as the most successful information system ever built supports applications with very diverse data models and interface requirements. The reason for the Web's versatility is that it provides a universally accepted language for describing documents (which as dynamic documents often serve as interfaces to information repositories), and an architecture which scales well and is based on declarative languages and simple operations. Specifically, the concept of *Representational State Transfer (REST)* [12], the principle underlying the *Hypertext Transfer Protocol (HTTP)* [11], allows the Web to evolve by introducing new resource types (by introducing new representations for resources), without any change in the basic infrastructure. The most important organizations who contributed to the success of the World Wide Web are also involved in the establishment of geoinformation on the Web. Their and other players' line of action is presented in Sect. 2.

M. Kofahl (✉)
University Rostock, Geodesy and Geoinformatics, Germany
e-mail: m.kofahl@gmx.de

I. King, R. Baeza-Yates (eds.), *Weaving Services and People on the World Wide Web*,
DOI 10.1007/978-3-642-00570-1_8,

Existing proposals for the use of location data on the Web either use it for specific application areas, or define a single location scheme. In order to avoid competing methods, the community has to discuss the question of how the Web can be turned into a location-aware information system. In this chapter you will find existing drafts merged into a single location concept which can be used for several areas on the Web and refer to this new location-aware Web as the *Locative Web*. The motivation for this is the observation that "location" has become an important concept in a wide variety of application areas, some of these areas are described in Sect. 3. Current capabilities of positioning for networked devices are summarized in Sect. 4.

Some application areas require a much more sophisticated model of locations than what the Web could possibly support, these areas are the ones which typically use some sort of *Geographic Information System (GIS)*. GIS provide very sophisticated spatial data models and excel at managing spatial data, but most GIS have Web-based user interfaces, but do not integrate their data into the Web. But even for areas with sophisticated location models, it makes sense to provide a limited perspective of their internal data models in a Web-friendly way, so that some of their services can easily be integrated into Web scenarios [41]. Section 5 describes the location concept for the Web that we are proposing, and Sect. 6 takes these concepts and describes how they are embedded into different components of Web architecture.

Sections 7 and 8 describe two implementations that use these concepts and their representation in Web technologies. They shall provides a valuable starting point for a discussion about how to realize the locative Web and should not be referred to a global realization.

2 Standardization Bodies

Owing to the distributed evolution of the Web and its standards, there are a number of organizations and individual activists working towards further development of the Web. Originally, the use of geospatial data was treated as an application feature which might use web services, but with no particular integration with the Web's core technologies. Thus, beside the groups of the Internet Engineering Task Force (IETF) and the World Wide Web Consortium (W3C) there is also the Open Geospatial Consortium (OGC) to be considered among the major bodies regarding the standardization of geospatial data on the Web, where location is part of the data or the application. Additionally, there are several boards and companies who work on adjoining technologies or individually further the evolution of the locative Web.

The Geographic Location/Privacy Working Group at IETF bundles activities in relation to privacy and security of location information about resources or entities on the Internet. The main applications are management and emergency services and other location-based services. Some of the following standards and drafts released by this working group may be important for the further evolution of the locative Web. A draft introducing geographical hyperlinks [26] addresses the hyperlink as one of the Web's core elements. Two drafts address spatial metadata at a basic level in HTML documents [9] and HTTP transactions [10] in order to reference with a real world position. When more detailed location information is required, an object format for different representations of locations might be valuable. It is already published as RFC [31] and may influence the design of upcoming interfaces. In addition, the Dublin Core Metadata specification [40], published under the banner of the IETF, is a widely accepted way for referencing web resources in time and space.

The top objective of the Geolocation Working Group hosted at the W3C is to define an interface for Web browsers in order to access client-side location information. The first Candidate Recommendation Track of an interface specification is scheduled for 2009. Since *Google* is a member of this working group, it is likely that the new Gears Geolocation API [13] may be considered a preview of the interface [33] to be expected.

The most important enabler of geospatial web services is the OGC. It has released a number of specifications which are used as the base of various mapping services and the like. Although the OGC did not strive for an integration of geospatial information in existing protocols or markup languages, there are fundamental rule types that are already adopted by others such as the Geography Markup Language [21].

A successful technology introduced by individuals is the *ICBM* metadata tag for HTML [35]. It overlaps with other methods for geotagging Web resources developed under the auspices of the IETF, but has at least the same prevalence. Another successful example of standards worked out by the community is *GeoRSS* [29]. It is a popular extension for expressing location information in RSS feeds is GeoRSS. Due to the support by most applications it may be seen as defacto standard for referencing real-world locations in feeds. While the NTT DoCoMo Inc. made the first attempt at adding a client's geographical position to hyperlinks [19] by bundling this technology with the company's hardware, this concept was neither adopted by other manufacturers nor by the above mentioned groups.

3 Application Areas

Sections 3.1 through 3.4 describe some application areas where the locative Web provides better support for implementing services and applications than the current Web (this overview does not claim to be complete and should only demonstrate that there are many potential application domains for a locative Web). Section 3.5 concludes this brief overview of application areas with a scenario that spans multiple areas of utilization and demonstrates how the concept of location is percolating through all interactions described in the scenario. By using a consistent location concept across all fields of the application, it is possible to obtain network effects which are impossible to attain without a location-aware infrastructure.

3.1 Location-Based Services

Location-Based Services (LBS) are based on the assumption that many services for (mostly mobile) clients can be enhanced by customizing the service based on the client's location. The idea originated with the widespread availability of data services for mobile phones, providing proprietary services which work best in semi-closed architectures such as the *Wireless Application Protocol (WAP)* [39], but which are hard to extend to mobile clients with full Internet connectivity and standard browsers.

Mobile phone carriers are selling the current location of their customers to service providers, and therefore it is hard to determine a client's location by independent providers. For a more open approach and for privacy reasons, a client should state the current (or assumed) location by itself in an appropriate way. Positioning sources may be the *Global Positioning System (GPS)* or local network services (Sect. 7 describes an implementation using HTTP for transmitting location information, Sect. 8.2 describes a similar implementation of a proxy server).

Location information not only can be very useful for providing services, it is also very sensitive information that should only be disclosed with the consent of the user. Privacy policies for location information and mobile devices and LBS still have to be developed, but there are many scenarios where LBS on mobile devices can provide better services than without location information.

3.2 Web of Things

Pervasive [16] and ubiquitous [14] computing are fusing networked computer technology with many aspects of our daily lives. To a large extent, these fields have been concerned so far with how to take things which are more embedded into the physical world than the usual computer hardware, and make them available in ways which enable new classes of applications beyond the traditional networking scenarios. Many of the questions in these areas currently revolve around networking capabilities, such as ad-hoc networking algorithms, and the integration of computing infrastructure into the physical world.

The *Web of Things* is a vision which takes the *Internet of Things* (a common term in the pervasive and ubiquitous computing communities) one step further, so that physical objects are not only networked through ad-hoc setup of Internet connections, but instead are made available as resources on the Web, and can be used in standard Web interactions. Since physical resources always have a location, this scenario very often requires support for location-aware interactions, and thus could greatly benefit from a location-aware infrastructure.

3.3 Resource-Object Associations

The scenario presented in Sect. 3.2 is based on the assumption that networked computer technology is embedded into everyday objects and augments the physical world. However, there also is a large set of applications which are not augmenting the real world, but still are interested to associate Web resources with it. Examples for this are all *field sciences*, which often create Web artifacts (such as images, documents, or video/audio recordings) and want to associate these with location information.

In many cases, these scenarios have layered levels of complexity. In archaeology, for example, if some ancient artifact is found, this is a physical resource which may be moved to a different location such as an archive or a museum, but it also is related to the location where it has been found, and this again can have different levels of descriptions, such as the coordinates in some grid used for an excavation project, or symbolic names for certain areas in the excavation area. Whatever the exact information model that is used for a specific project will be, it will contain a substantial number of location-related concepts, because this information is of great significance for future interactions with the artifact.

3.4 Social Networking

Social networking (which often is perceived to be one of the central aspects of Web 2.0) has become an important driver for Web applications and Web content. Since social networking is yet another area where Web applications aim to represent something in the real world, location concepts often play an important role in these applications. For social networking, the question of where users are can become an important driver of making these services more valuable and more interesting, because this enables those services to match users spatially.

Many social networking sites provide some location concepts, but these in most cases are closed concepts and only useful with one particular service. In addition, an increasing number of services are implementing some social networking by providing a platform for managing information that is intended to be shared across users. Popular examples are photo sharing sites such as *Flickr* and *Panoramio*, which use geotagging of pictures to make them available in as many ways as possible (for example, both services provide interfaces where it is possible to explore pictures using a map-based interface). Currently, there are two major trends in the social networking landscape:

- Big services such as *Facebook* attempt to become the one place on the Web where social networking happens. These services typically open up a little bit by providing an API to integrate other services, but the main goal still is to be the main hub for social networking. The main motivation for this movement is the underlying business model of targeted advertising.
- A large number of new providers implement services which often are not sufficient as stand-alone social networking services, but are valuable as add-ons. These services must be able to be integrated into other services. This integration not only requires technical alignment, it also requires a data model which can be easily reused in an integration platform.

Both developments are currently active, but it is likely that the big aggregators will not last very long. The important observation is that in both scenarios, social networking happens as service aggregation, which means that shared underlying models (of all the data that should be aggregated, location being an important type among those) are essential. So far, location is not treated in great detail, though. For example, *Open Social*, Google's attempt to publish an API for social networking platforms to counter Facebook's dominance, does have location as part of an information about a person, but allows a coordinate-based position as the only way to represent location.

3.5 Scenario

The following scenario combines different aspects of a locative Web, which benefits from a standardized way of addressing locative issues. In the following different applications will be referenced which can be hosted in a single Web browser on a mobile device, however. A Web browsers' ability of processing positions better links between different Web sites and applications.

A calendar of events distributed as GeoRSS feed may persuade someone to jaunt a nearby (by the help of spatial filtering) museum. The feed provides a locative hyperlink which either point to the civic or to the geographical address of the museum and makes the Web browser calling a routing Web site with preset destination. Because of the browser-accessible geolocation of the device, the Web site acts as a navigator. When arrived, the mobile client can access a local wireless network, allowing extensive access to museum resources. Since GPS is not working inside buildings, a proxy takes over network-based positioning which may even use a local frame of reference. Thus, the Web-based visitor guide can use accurate location data inserted by the proxy to each request and thereby provide appropriate content and functions for controlling exhibits via a Web interface. Live-linked geotagged images from community sites such as *Flickr* establish a relationship to the real world where an exhibit originated.

4 Network-Based Positioning Techniques

Some capabilities of the locative Web rely on the assumption that a client is aware of its current location. Modern devices have integrated GPS and attain a sufficient level of location availability. Since clients exploring the locative Web are inherently networked, one could also take advantage of already existing networked-based methods and interfaces. As presented subsequently, the combination of different positioning technologies can ensure the constant availability of location information and therefore greatly support the development of the locative Web.

The simplest way of supplying a client with basic location information are additional data in the Dynamic Host Configuration Protocol (DHCP). If configured, a client — mobile and stationary likewise — can query the GeoConf option [32] and obtain a geographic coordinate pair together with its precision. The position will usually represent a larger region the network covers. Because topological and geographical areas are not necessarily the same this methods leaves the risk of receiving wrong location information. A client can nevertheless profit from this basic and easily obtainable information. Particularly devices in geographically small-sized networks can further benefit from the DHCP Option for Civic Addresses Configuration Information [36] which can be configured sufficiently precise in this case.

Some web services offer more sophisticated positioning interfaces. Depending on which positioning technique is used [6] they usually provide more detailed and more precise location information. Potential interfaces are specified in various protocols working independent of the network and positioning technology: the HTTP Enabled Location Delivery (HELD) [3], the *Mobile Location Protocol (MLP)* [2] and the OGC *Open Location Services (OpenLS)* [25] modeled after the MLP. The Location Information Server used for HELD will be discoverable by common protocols [37] while access servers for MLP and OpenLS have to be known by the client.

Google's Network Location Provider Protocol [18] can be used to geocode other location types. A well-known type is the base station id in cellular networks. In rare cases, the position of each antenna mast is even published unencrypted as a cellular broadcast message. Such a measurement can be enhanced by evaluating the signal strength and its change.

Taking the number of possible positioning interfaces into account, each network device should have the chance of retrieving its current location. But to achieve this, at least one interface must be offered globally which is currently, and in the foreseeable future, not the case. However, with the variety of complex positioning methods and interfaces available, it may be preferable for a device to contain an all-embracing *Location Finder* which can access many different sources.

5 Location on the Web

For the Web to evolve into the locative Web, a location-aware information system, the most fundamental issue is that there must be shared semantics for location concepts, and ideally there also should be guidelines for location syntax, so that these semantics are represented in compatible ways (if possible).

There are two dimensions to this problem. The first dimension is what the location concepts are that the Web should support. Obviously, location concepts used in applications vary widely based on the requirements of the application. The second dimension is the question of where these concepts should be embedded into the Web's architecture, so that they can be used in standard scenarios of Web-based interactions. In the following sections, we describe the location concepts that we identified as being the core concepts for location across a wide variety of applications. The question of how these should be embedded into Web architecture is then discussed in Sect. 6, which also discusses the syntax issues that arise because of the different environments into which the concepts should be embedded.

5.1 Coordinates

An objective way of talking about locations is to measure coordinates. These coordinates have to refer to some well-defined coordinate system, and the *World Geodetic*

System (WGS84) [27] is the coordinate system that is most widely used and supported today. It is the coordinate system that is natively used by the popular *Global Positioning System (GPS)*, which allows satellite-based measurements of locations anywhere on earth. Of course, not all devices that might want to position themselves have GPS receivers, and there exist a number of well-known techniques for positioning in mobile phone networks and ad-hoc networks. These position types can then be mapped to WGS84 coordinates, with varying degrees of accuracy. However, regardless of what method a device uses to evaluate its position, a coordinate-based position can always be represented in an interoperable way.

Elevation is an optional part of coordinates, which might be necessary for specific applications. Since local elevations might refer to different references, the *Earth Gravity Model (EGM96)* [24] geoid must be used to map elevations to a single reference system, such as *Mean Sea Level (MSL)*.

5.2 Countries

Apart from coordinates as discussed in the previous section, there are few location features which are universally used, and where some vocabulary is maintained in a well-defined and open way. One example might be continents, another one is countries. While countries are not very stable over time, at any point in time there is a consensus on which countries exist and where they are.[1] *ISO Country Codes* [20] are standardized codes for countries as well as for country subdivisions, and many other standards (such as the Internet's DNS top-level domain names) use these codes and simply rely on ISO to determine what countries exist at any given time.

ISO defines three different codes for countries, *alpha-2* (two-letter codes, for example `us`), *alpha-3* (three-letter codes, for example `USA`), and *digit-3* (three-digit codes). Furthermore, ISO also defines codes for country subdivisions. However, only the alpha-2 codes are available free of charge, the other codes (although widely-used and referenced) must be purchased from ISO. Figure 1 shows the current country codes of ISO 3166, and as can be seen, the code space is sufficiently big to accommodate many more countries than currently exist.

Since only alpha-2 codes can be obtained free of charge, this should be the only way of identifying countries as a location. Countries are a pretty broad way of localization, but for example on the current Web there exist many applications where one of the first interactions is to choose the country from which one is accessing the site, which often is done for legal reasons or to present country-specific variants of a Web site which display a localized set of branches and/or products.

For more fine-grained localization, it often is necessary to rely on other place names, but these have to be managed and used in a way which requires an agreement

[1] This is not entirely true since countries for political reasons sometimes take different stances than the majority of the world, and because borders are sometimes contentious, but for most locations of the earth's land surface, the attribution to a country can be done reliably.

Map of ISO 3166-1 alpha-2 codes

AA	AB	AC	AD	AE	AF	AG	AH	AI	AJ	AK	AL	AM	AN	AO	AP	AQ	AR	AS	AT	AU	AV	AW	AX	AY	AZ
BA	BB	BC	BD	BE	BF	BG	BH	BI	BJ	BK	BL	BM	BN	BO	BP	BQ	BR	BS	BT	BU	BV	BW	BX	BY	BZ
CA	CB	CC	CD	CE	CF	CG	CH	CI	CJ	CK	CL	CM	CN	CO	CP	CQ	CR	CS	CT	CU	CV	CW	CX	CY	CZ
DA	DB	DC	DD	DE	DF	DG	DH	DI	DJ	DK	DL	DM	DN	DO	DP	DQ	DR	DS	DT	DU	DV	DW	DX	DY	DZ
EA	EB	EC	ED	EE	EF	EG	EH	EI	EJ	EK	EL	EM	EN	EO	EP	EQ	ER	ES	ET	EU	EV	EW	EX	EY	EZ
FA	FB	FC	FD	FE	FF	FG	FH	FI	FJ	FK	FL	FM	FN	FO	FP	FQ	FR	FS	FT	FU	FV	FW	FX	FY	FZ
GA	GB	GC	GD	GE	GF	GG	GH	GI	GJ	GK	GL	GM	GN	GO	GP	GQ	GR	GS	GT	GU	GV	GW	GX	GY	GZ
HA	HB	HC	HD	HE	HF	HG	HH	HI	HJ	HK	HL	HM	HN	HO	HP	HQ	HR	HS	HT	HU	HV	HW	HX	HY	HZ
IA	IB	IC	ID	IE	IF	IG	IH	II	IJ	IK	IL	IM	IN	IO	IP	IQ	IR	IS	IT	IU	IV	IW	IX	IY	IZ
JA	JB	JC	JD	JE	JF	JG	JH	JI	JJ	JK	JL	JM	JN	JO	JP	JQ	JR	JS	JT	JU	JV	JW	JX	JY	JZ
KA	KB	KC	KD	KE	KF	KG	KH	KI	KJ	KK	KL	KM	KN	KO	KP	KQ	KR	KS	KT	KU	KV	KW	KX	KY	KZ
LA	LB	LC	LD	LE	LF	LG	LH	LI	LJ	LK	LL	LM	LN	LO	LP	LQ	LR	LS	LT	LU	LV	LW	LX	LY	LZ
MA	MB	MC	MD	ME	MF	MG	MH	MI	MJ	MK	ML	MM	MN	MO	MP	MQ	MR	MS	MT	MU	MV	MW	MX	MY	MZ
NA	NB	NC	ND	NE	NF	NG	NH	NI	NJ	NK	NL	NM	NN	NO	NP	NQ	NR	NS	NT	NU	NV	NW	NX	NY	NZ
OA	OB	OC	OD	OE	OF	OG	OH	OI	OJ	OK	OL	OM	ON	OO	OP	OQ	OR	OS	OT	OU	OV	OW	OX	OY	OZ
PA	PB	PC	PD	PE	PF	PG	PH	PI	PJ	PK	PL	PM	PN	PO	PP	PQ	PR	PS	PT	PU	PV	PW	PX	PY	PZ
QA	QB	QC	QD	QE	QF	QG	QH	QI	QJ	QK	QL	QM	QN	QO	QP	QQ	QR	QS	QT	QU	QV	QW	QX	QY	QZ
RA	RB	RC	RD	RE	RF	RG	RH	RI	RJ	RK	RL	RM	RN	RO	RP	RQ	RR	RS	RT	RU	RV	RW	RX	RY	RZ
SA	SB	SC	SD	SE	SF	SG	SH	SI	SJ	SK	SL	SM	SN	SO	SP	SQ	SR	SS	ST	SU	SV	SW	SX	SY	SZ
TA	TB	TC	TD	TE	TF	TG	TH	TI	TJ	TK	TL	TM	TN	TO	TP	TQ	TR	TS	TT	TU	TV	TW	TX	TY	TZ
UA	UB	UC	UD	UE	UF	UG	UH	UI	UJ	UK	UL	UM	UN	UO	UP	UQ	UR	US	UT	UU	UV	UW	UX	UY	UZ
VA	VB	VC	VD	VE	VF	VG	VH	VI	VJ	VK	VL	VM	VN	VO	VP	VQ	VR	VS	VT	VU	VV	VW	VX	VY	VZ
WA	WB	WC	WD	WE	WF	WG	WH	WI	WJ	WK	WL	WM	WN	WO	WP	WQ	WR	WS	WT	WU	WV	WW	WX	WY	WZ
XA	XB	XC	XD	XE	XF	XG	XH	XI	XJ	XK	XL	XM	XN	XO	XP	XQ	XR	XS	XT	XU	XV	XW	XX	XY	XZ
YA	YB	YC	YD	YE	YF	YG	YH	YI	YJ	YK	YL	YM	YN	YO	YP	YQ	YR	YS	YT	YU	YV	YW	YX	YY	YZ
ZA	ZB	ZC	ZD	ZE	ZF	ZG	ZH	ZI	ZJ	ZK	ZL	ZM	ZN	ZO	ZP	ZQ	ZR	ZS	ZT	ZU	ZV	ZW	ZX	ZY	ZZ

Color legend

Officially assigned: code element of a country or territory
User-assigned: code element that can be assigned by users
Exceptionally reserved: code element reserved on request for restricted use
Transitionally reserved: code element deleted from ISO 3166-1
Indeterminately reserved: code element used in other coding systems associated with ISO 3166-1
Not used at present stage: code element currently not used in ISO 3166-1
Un-assigned: code element free for assignment by ISO 3166/MA only

Fig. 1 Currently registered/reserved and not used ISO 3166-1 alpha-2 Codes

of the place names being used. One example could be the list of US state names, which could be defined and managed by a variety of entities. Section 5.3 describes place names and identification and definition of place name vocabularies in greater detail.

5.3 Places

While coordinates (Sect. 5.1) and countries (Sect. 5.2) refer to well-defined and geographically identifiable concepts of locations, there often are more loosely defined location concepts, with two typical examples being the following scenarios:

- *Centrally Controlled Vocabularies:* Frequently, place names are used in a context where it is clear how such a name should be interpreted. Examples include state names, zip codes, or city names within a certain geographic region (in the latter case, city names may need disambiguation if there are cities with the same name).

In all these cases, there is some controlled vocabulary of these place names, and any name used in this context essentially is a reference into this vocabulary.

- *User-Defined Vocabularies:* For smaller user groups, it might make more sense to use a customized vocabulary with a more limited extent. For example, for social networking applications, users might only want to disclose their location in broad concepts such as "at work," "at home," "at school," or "on vacation." These concepts might or might not be associated with a concrete geographical region, but in either case they serve as a place name which might be useful for matchmaking between users of the social network.

When talking about vocabularies, the two main questions are how to *identify* them, and how to *define* them. Our approach is to provide a standardized way of identifying vocabularies, but no standardized way for defining them. For identification, we use the standard Web abstraction for that, which is the *Uniform Resource Identifier (URI)* [5]. This strategy is the same as for XML, which also supports the identification of *XML Namespaces* [7] by using URIs, but does not mandate any specific format for a namespace description, or for an XML vocabulary. Similarly, when using a place name for location identification, there must be an identifier for the vocabulary, either explicitly or implicitly through the context in which the place name occurs.

In the same way as it is good practice to use URIs for XML namespaces which somehow describe the vocabulary, our recommendation is that a URI for a place name vocabulary should identify a Web resource which serves as a description and possibly definition of the vocabulary. We do not anticipate, however, that a single language will be universally used to define place name vocabularies, because requirements for these vocabularies will differ substantially, based on the requirements of the applications for which these vocabularies are developed. As one possibility, Sect. 8.1 presents the *Place Markup Language (PlaceML)*, which is a simple XML-based language for defining place names.

Depending on the application area, there can be very large place name vocabularies, such as the *Getty Thesaurus of Geographic Names (TGN)*[2] or *GeoNames*[3], or very small place name vocabularies, such as customized place name vocabularies for use by individuals in social networks. Sometimes it might make sense to be able to exchange the complete vocabulary as part of a Web interaction, whereas for large place name vocabularies this is not practical. So exchanging vocabularies is an option (and can be covered by agreeing on some representation), but probably will not be the norm. Referring to the vocabulary to which a place name belongs, however, is essential for being able to interpret that name in the correct context.

Place name vocabularies need a well-defined policy on updates. The maintainer of a place name vocabulary should explicitly state their policy with respect to changes in the place names defined in that place name vocabulary. Otherwise, it is impossible to determine how an update policy for a local copy of the vocabulary should be implemented.

[2] The thesaurus currently contains more than 1.1 million place names.

[3] A free database with over 8 million geographical names.

6 Location Web Architecture

To use the location concepts presented in Sect. 5 and put them into use on the Web, they must be supported in different parts of *Web Architecture* [22]. The Web supports certain concepts natively (such as language identification and negotiation for content and transfer), and in order to implement the locative Web, the location concepts must become part of this native support as well.

The most important concepts on the Web are *identification*, *transfer*, and *content*. The main Web technologies in these areas are URIs for identification, HTTP for transfer, and HTML and XML for content. Sections 6.1 through 6.3 look at these Web technologies and describe how our location concepts are embedded into these components of Web architecture.

6.1 Location Resources

The *Uniform Resource Identifier (URI)* [5] is the Web's way of identifying resources. Identification can be a useful function in its own right, as demonstrated by *XML Namespaces* [7]. As another example, the `tag` URI scheme [23] is only intended as an identification mechanism, it does not define resolution or access methods. The proposed `geoloc` URI scheme (as well as the `geo` scheme [26]) also is only defined for identification and has no resolution or access methods. However, there are semantics associated with it according to the location concepts described in Sect. 5.

`geoloc` URIs can be used with or without a vocabulary identifier (a URI). Any URI reserved characters in names must be escaped.[4] The identifier can be omitted if there is a context of the URI which establishes the vocabulary. Otherwise we expect decimal WGS84 coordinates being the default context. Thus, the following first two examples shown in Fig. 2 are synonymous. The third example specifies an US zip code, the last one the US as a country.

```
geoloc:27.988056,86.925278

geoloc:27.988056,86.925278;http%3A%2F%2Fwww.                         \
                         opengis.net%2Fgml%2Fsrs%2Fepsg.xml%234326

geoloc:94720;http%3A%2F%2Fusps.gov%2Fns%2Fzip

geoloc:us;http%3A%2F%2Fiso.org%2Fns%2Fiso3166-1
```

Fig. 2 Distinction between different location types enables expansion options for the future

[4] It would be legal for place name vocabularies, however, to define and encode hierarchic place names, in which case they should use URI syntax for hierarchies. `geoloc:Berlin/Berlin/Tempelhof` could for example use a province, city, borough hierarchy for place names in Germany and identify the *Tempelhof* borough in *Berlin* (which is located in the province of *Berlin*).

6.2 HTTP Location Metadata

The *Hypertext Transfer Protocol (HTTP)* [11] defines a number of header fields which are used for various purposes, they are broadly classified into *general*, *entity*, *request*, and *response* headers. Location information could be transferred by the client (indicating the location of the client), and the server (indicating the location of the server), and since it does not apply to the entity being transferred, a new `geoloc` header field is being defined as a general header field. It uses the same syntax as the URI described in Sect. 6.1, but allows whitespace around separators and does not require escaping of characters.

As an additional functionality apart from merely embedding location information, *content negotiation* for location concepts (as described in Sects. 5 and 6.1) could become part of HTTP. An `Accept-Geoloc` header could specify a server's capabilities in terms of supported location concepts using corresponding URIs. Content negotiation would work in the same way as for content types (`Accept`), languages (`Accept-Language`), content encodings (`Accept-Encoding`), and character sets (`Accept-Charset`).

HTTP content negotiation is defined sufficiently open so that a new header field could be introduced and could then be legally used as information for location-based content negotiation. HTTP's concept of *transparent negotiation* would nicely map to the scenarios described in Sect. 8, where a cache can map location concepts based on its knowledge of the location concepts used by the client, and the location concepts supported by the server.

6.3 Resource Location Metadata

The location concepts described in Section 5 should be supported as concepts that can be used in content. The main content format on the Web is *HTML* [34] and increasingly its XML-variant *XHTML* [30], but there are also many *XML* [8] formats, which should be able to embed this information. One example for this is the *Atom* [28] format, which is a popular format for feeds.

Most previous attempts at adding location information to the Web look at specific content formats only, *GeoRSS* [29] only considers feed formats (and has been updated to cover Atom as well), and another proposal [9] only looks at HTML and XHTML. Another question is how embedding should be specified, for HTML alone there exist three main approaches, one being a custom syntax (microformats often use this approach), the second being adding *RDF/XML* [4], and the third being *RDFa* [1]. For XML, there also are various ways how reusable vocabularies can be defined, often differing substantially in their usage of elements, attributes, and namespaces.

Conciliating HTML and XML metadata standards is not as easy as it may seem at first sight, because HTML markup is often created manually and has its focus on simplicity and ease of use and robustness, whereas XML markup often is machine-generated and the focus is more on modularity and clean design and extensibility.

The two most important approaches for representing location within resources is Daviel's format [9] for HTML (which is limited to making statements about the complete Web site), and *GeoRSS* [29] (which supports rather complex GML expressions) for feeds. Both are based on different location concepts and thus are hard to use together consistently.

We propose to use RDFa-compliant syntax for HTML, and an attribute-based form for integration into XML-based resources. While so far we have not created concrete schemas for embedding our location concepts into resources, we believe that it is essential that there are formats for HTML and XML which are aligned with the location concepts used in other parts of the Web architecture.

6.4 Locative Hyperlinks

The locative Web must also support a method for hyperlinks pointing to real-world locations. This is a basic requirement in order to put the Web of things into practice, because location is a universal way of identifying objects on earth. The previously (in Sect. 6.1) presented `geoloc` URI scheme can be used for this purpose. Thus, contrary to other recommendations [15, 19] about spatial data in hyperlinks, we do not suggest adding location information to existing schemes but to directly reference the location. The usage of the `geoloc` URI scheme in browsers is identical to the usage in HTTP. The simplest form of such a hyperlink is thus `<a href="geoloc:27.988,86.925">text</a>` with WGS84 coordinate being the default location type. A more complex style will include the vocabulary identifier, e.g. `geoloc:94720;http%3A%2F%2Fusps.gov%2Fns%2Fzip`.

This structure is similar to other non-HTTP URI schemes such as `mailto` [17]. There is no need to describe a uniform behavior of this URI used in hyperlinks in this case. The action initiated by these links is highly device-, context- and application-dependent; and has therefore to be defined by the user or by the user agent. On the one hand, a hyperlink pointing to a concrete civic address (such as for navigation purposes) has to behave differently than one pointing to a country (where an encyclopedia might better satisfy the users' interest). On the other hand, a mobile device is likely to be used as a navigation unit and has to implement other strategies than a regular Web browser. Criteria for the differentiation of locative hyperlinks in Web browsers are the device type, the current location, the hyperlink's location type and its spatial precision. Figure 3 shows a feasible decision model which a URI handler might use in order to choose a proper action.

6.5 Scripting Interfaces

A standardized interface for retrieving a client's location information would be a valuable extension for Web 2.0 applications providing location dependent content. The W3C, with substantial participation from Google, Inc., are currently promoting this topic (see Sect. 2) and will release a Geolocation API specification. The current

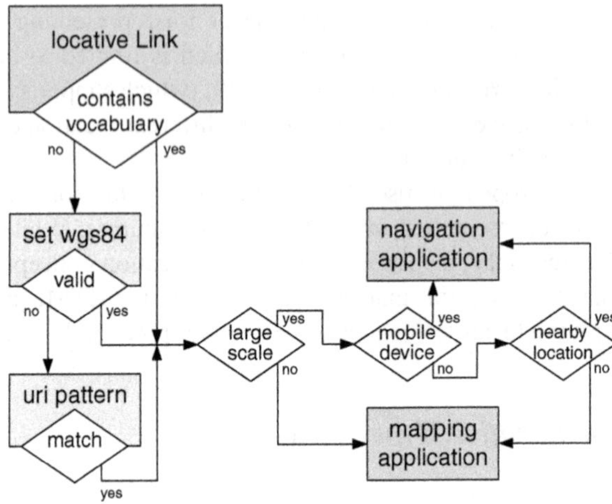

Fig. 3 A decision model for proper actions of locative hyperlinks

draft [33] requires any implementation to provide latitude and longitude coordinates together with an accuracy value and to define a desired accuracy level. Furthermore, they must support the last known position without requiring extra positioning as well as one-time and continuous position requests being agnostic to the positioning engine. Civic address information is optional and will be derived by reverse geocoding.

The specification draft currently is not open to other location types since location providers might offer locations that can not be converted into common types by

```
interface Geolocation {
  readonly attribute Location lastPosition;
  boolean supportsType(in string locationType);
  (...)
};

interface PositionOptions {
  attribute string locationType;
  (...)
};

interface Location {
  readonly attribute string locationType;
};

interface GeographicalPosition : Location {
  readonly attribute string locationType = "...";
  readonly attribute double latitude;
  (...)
};
```

Fig. 4 Proposal of an adapted geolocation interface [33] supporting multiple location types

the client. The vocabulary identifier introduced in Sect. 6.1 can be used to identify returned location objects and to request a concrete location type when required. Based on the Geolocation API Specification Draft [33], an interface supporting any location types should support additional methods as presented in Fig. 4.

7 Geo-Enabled Browser

In order to design and test locative Web applications, we implemented a few capabilities turning a regular user agent into a geo-enabled browser. In particular, we focused on the negotiation of different location concepts. An *IE Mobile* running on *Windows Mobile 6* is used as a testbed. A vendor-specific extension using common browser APIs contains improvements to the underlying system.

The ability to retrieve location based information from the Web is basically established by querying a local location finder before modifying requests made to the Web. Currently, we use GPS, DHCP's *GeoConf* [32], and GSM Cell ID for positioning and thus only support location types provided by these techniques. Web services for geocoding and reverse geocoding (such as Google's *Gears* or *GeoNames.org* will help to retrieve the desired location type in the future, e.g. zip code instead of geographical coordinates.

The process of retrieving localized content follows the concept described in Sect. 6.2, illustrated in Fig. 5. As long as there are no predefined rules, the browser acts as usual. However, the browser analyzes possible `Accept-Geoloc` headers sent by the Web server. The resulting list of supported location types (each identified by an URI as described in Sect. 6.2) has to be compared to general privacy rules or user settings for this specific Web site. In order to apply one of the remaining location types, the available position drivers mentioned above are queried. Subsequent HTTP requests will contain the desired `geoloc` header.

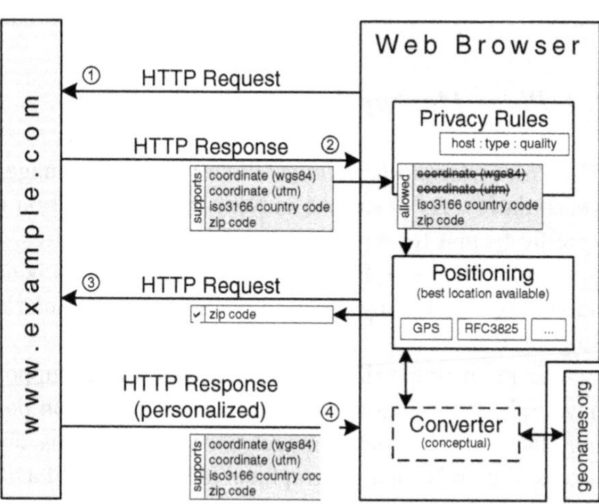

Fig. 5 Prototype architecture for a geo-enabled web browser with privacy rules and a spanned positioning engine being the main components

An experimental feature further enhancing the locative Web is to make location data available to scripts. Mobile devices (for example Web 2.0 city guides) can benefit from permanently available position information.

8 LocProxy

Even though mobile phone carriers often have high-quality location information for individual phones (which in the US for example is mandated by E911 [38]), they usually do not make that information openly available. This means that even though mobile phones often could be located precisely (by the carrier or by GPS-enabled phones as described in Sect. 7), in practice this does not happen, and HTTP requests from mobile phones do not carry any location information.

While the approach described in Sect. 7 is more elegant because it directly updates the mobile device's Web client to be location-aware, this requires an update to the device's software, and also requires some sort of position information (such as a GPS position) that can be accessed by the updated software.

An alternative approach is described in this section. The approach is based on the idea to implement the location support in a Web intermediary, which then acts as the location-aware component in the HTTP request/response chain. This approach is independent from any specific client and aims at solving the chicken-and-egg problem of location-based services. While the proxy architecture described here is not feasible as a large-scale and long-term solution, it is ideally suited for prototype services. Our main goal thus is to provide an environment where location-based services can be developed without the need to update all clients. Instead, all clients use the *Location Proxy (LocProxy)*, which augments the plain HTTP requests sent by clients with location information.

One of the most important parts of the LocProxy concept is to keep the concept of locations as flexible as possible. To achieve this goal, we have developed a format for representing place name vocabularies, which is used by the LocProxy and allows users to easily define and configure a place name vocabulary.

8.1 Place Markup Language (PlaceML)

The *Place Markup Language (PlaceML)* is a language for representing place name vocabularies. As described in Sect. 5.3, our location concept does not mandate a specific format for defining place name vocabularies, all that is required is a URI-based identification. However, in many cases it is beneficial to have some agreed-upon language for representing place name vocabularies, and PlaceML is one such language.

The main properties of PlaceML are that it supports place hierarchies (which have to be acyclic graphs), inclusion and exclusion polygons and circles for defining places, aliases, place images, place descriptions, and internationalization. Since places often rely on a geographical identification of a place, we support import from KML, which is a format for representing map-related data. Figure 6 shows an exam-

Fig. 6 Google Maps interface for defining places

ple of a very simple place name vocabulary created in Google Maps, which consists of few places, all of them identified by polygons using Google Maps "My Maps."

When exported as KML, it can be mapped to PlaceML in the way shown in Fig. 7, which demonstrates some of the core features of PlaceML (the only part edited by hand is that "South Hall" is part of the "Main Campus").

```
<placeml xml:lang="en">
 <name>UC Berkeley Campuses</name>
 <place id="MainCampus">
  <name>Main Campus</name>
  <description>The main campus has ...</description>
  <location>
   <polygon type="include">...</polygon>
  </location>
 </place>
 <place id="SouthHall">
  <name>South Hall</name>
  <parent ref="MainCampus"/>
  <description>South Hall is ...</description>
  <location>
   <polygon type="include">...</polygon>
  </location>
 </place>
</placeml>
```

Fig. 7 PlaceML example

KML and PlaceML are not perfect matches, which means that a transformation in either way most likely will be lossy. KML supports more geographic constructs (such as lines), while PlaceML allows richer descriptions (aliases, internationalization), the association of places (hierarchies), and places without geographic definitions. However, KML is popular and useful for visualization in many different applications (e.g., Google Maps and Google Earth), so we also support transformations from PlaceML to KML.

8.2 HTTP Proxy

PlaceML is a markup language for defining a vocabulary of place names. We use this markup language as the configuration for an experimental HTTP proxy which is used to "simulate" location-aware clients. The basic idea is that users use a simple interface for selecting their current location, and this interface is driven by PlaceML. Figure 8 shows this as the first step of interacting with the LocProxy. After configuring the location, the proxy knows a user's identity and the associated location, which is based on a PlaceML definition.

LocProxy users then have to configure LocProxy as their HTTP proxy. LocProxy uses HTTP *proxy authentication* to identify users, which means that each request going through the proxy has to carry a `Proxy-Authorization` header field. This proxy authorization information allows the proxy to identify and authenticate users. It also allows the proxy to look up the associated location information in the database (which contains information about users, their locations, and the supported place name vocabularies), and include it as a HTTP `geoloc` header field in the request that is forwarded along the HTTP chain.

The current version of LocProxy simply inserts the user's configured location information into the user's HTTP request before forwarding the request to the server. This works well for a prototype and limited deployment, because the location infor-

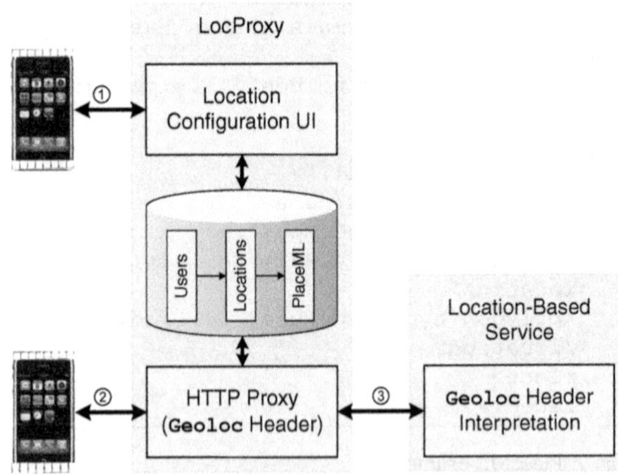

Fig. 8 LocProxy architecture

mation is based on a PlaceML definition (a place name vocabulary as described in Sect. 5.3), and all participants in the scenario support this specific vocabulary.

However, more generally, a location proxy could also negotiate and even map between different location notations or place name vocabularies. There are three basic scenarios:

- *Name to Coordinate:* If the place name used for configuring a location is unknown to the service being contacted, the most useful approach would be to map it to coordinates. If the PlaceML contains geolocation information for places, place names can be mapped to, for example, the geometric center of the place's geolocation.
- *Coordinate to Name:* If the device itself supports geolocation (Sect. 7 describes such a device), but the service expects a place name, the coordinates determined by the device's location service can be mapped to the service's places. This again requires the PlaceML to contain geolocation information.
- *Name to Name:* If the user uses a certain PlaceML to configure locations, but the service expects a different place name vocabulary to be used, there can be some mapping between place names, which can either be based on conceptual knowledge,[5] or on mapping from a place name to coordinates using the first PlaceML, and mapping coordinates to a place name using the second PlaceML.

While the limited functionality of the current LocProxy does not support these scenarios, we believe that this scenario of negotiating between different location concepts (see discussion of HTTP content negotiation in Sect. 6.2) will become an important component of handling locations.

9 Future Work

In order to push the development of the locative Web, a number of issues have to be discussed. The main tasks pertain the domains of location metadata in the Web's resources (see Sect. 6.3) and in its communication (see Sect. 6.2). A consistent way about how to embed location information into HTML and XML has to be defined. The concept and the syntax of HTTP-included location data has to be discussed, and in particular how to ensure user privacy. HTTP content negotiation may help by using different forms of location. But in order to support interoperability, it is necessary to define commonly used location types (see Sect. 5) which every client or server should support.

Manufactures of end-user devices might quickly close the gap between integrated positioning units and "Web 2.0" applications. To ensure a uniform evolution of the Web, a scriptable *geolocation* object as referenced in Sect. 6.5 must be finalized before proprietary interfaces come up.

---

[5] For example, mapping cities to states, or city districts to cities.

10 Conclusions

The *Locative Web* is a Web which supports location as a Web-level concept. This paper describes a location concept which is based on different ways of how locations can be expressed, e.g. as coordinates, as country names, or as other place names. Locations must be qualified by identifying a vocabulary. We follow the idea of XML namespaces and require the vocabulary to be identified by a URI, but do not mandate a format for a description of the vocabulary or the vocabulary itself.

The location concepts are mapped to various components of Web architecture, specifically URIs, HTTP, and resources. For URIs and HTTP we present a concrete syntax, whereas for resources we only have requirements for markup which should make location information within resources easy to use and embed.

Finally, we describe two prototype implementations. The first one is a geo-enabled browser, which uses locally available location information to add location information to HTTP requests. This allows location-based Web services to deliver localized content. The other prototype uses a different approach to support location-based services on the Web. It uses an HTTP proxy where users can configure their location, which will then be added to all requests which are sent through the proxy. This has the disadvantage that the users need to manually change the location information, but the advantage that no special software is required on the client side. Both prototypes aim at providing environments within which it is possible to provide and experiment with location-based services. The novelty of supporting different location types produces advantages in compatibility and privacy but may also exclude user groups from Web services due to rejected location types.

References

1. Ben Adida, Mark Birbeck, Shane McCarron, and Steven Pemberton. RDFa in XHTML: Syntax and Processing — A Collection of Attributes and Processing Rules for Extending XHTML to Support RDF. World Wide Web Consortium, Recommendation REC-rdfa-syntax-20081014, October 2008.
2. Open Mobile Alliance, editor. *Mobile Location Protocol*. Open Mobile Alliance, 6 2008.
3. Mary Barnes, James Winterbottom, Martin Thomson, and Barbara Stark. HTTP Enabled Location Delivery (HELD). Internet Draft draft-ietf-geopriv-http-location-delivery-10, October 2008.
4. Dave Beckett. RDF/XML Syntax Specification (Revised). World Wide Web Consortium, Recommendation REC-rdf-syntax-grammar-20040210, February 2004.
5. Tim Berners-Lee, Roy Thomas Fielding, and Larry Masinter. Uniform Resource Identifier (URI): Generic Syntax. Internet RFC 3986, January 2005.
6. Ralf Bill, Clemens Cap, Martin Kofahl, and Thomas Mundt. Indoor and Outdoor Positioning in Mobile Environments – A Review and Some Investigations on WLAN-Positioning. *Geographic Information Sciences*, 10(2):91–98, 2004.
7. Tim Bray, Dave Hollander, Andrew Layman, and Richard Tobin. Namespaces in XML 1.0 (Second Edition). World Wide Web Consortium, Recommendation REC-xml-names-20060816, August 2006.
8. Tim Bray, Jean Paoli, C. Michael Sperberg-McQueen, Eve Maler, and François Yergeau. Extensible Markup Language (XML) 1.0 (Fourth Edition). World Wide Web Consortium, Recommendation REC-xml-20060816, August 2006.

9. Andrew Daviel and Felix A. Kägi. Geographic Registration of HTML Documents. Internet Draft draft-daviel-html-geo-tag-08, October 2007.
10. Andrew Daviel, Felix A. Kägi, and Martin Kofahl. Geographic Extensions for HTTP Transactions. Internet Draft draft-daviel-http-geo-header-05, December 2007.
11. Roy Thomas Fielding, Jim Gettys, Jeffrey C. Mogul, Henrik Frystyk Nielsen, Larry Masinter, Paul J. Leach, and Tim Berners-Lee. Hypertext Transfer Protocol — HTTP/1.1. Internet RFC 2616, June 1999.
12. Roy Thomas Fielding and Richard N. Taylor. Principled Design of the Modern Web Architecture. *ACM Transactions on Internet Technology*, 2(2):115–150, May 2002.
13. Inc. Google. Gears Geolocation API, July 2008.
14. Adam Greenfield. *Everyware: The Dawning Age of Ubiquitous Computing*. New Riders, Indianapolis, Indiana, March 2006.
15. Amir Haghighat, Cristina Videira Lopes, Tony Givargis, and Atri Mandal. Location-Aware Web System. In *Proceedings of the Workshop on Building Software for Pervasive Computing at OOPSLA'04*, Vancouver, Canada, October 2004.
16. Uwe Hansmann, Lothar Merk, Martin S. Nicklous, and Thomas Stober. *Pervasive Computing: The Mobile World*. Springer-Verlag, Berlin, Germany, 2nd edition, August 2003.
17. Paul E. Hoffman, Larry Masinter, and Jamie Zawinski. The mailto URL scheme. Internet RFC 2368, June 1998.
18. Google Inc. Gears GeolocationAPI, August 2008.
19. NTT DoCoMo Inc. Information on i-mode Technical Topics – GPS, November 2007.
20. International Organization for Standardization. Codes for the Representation of Names of Countries and their Subdivisions. ISO 3166, November 2001.
21. ISO. Geographic information – Spatial Schema. ISO Standard 19107, May 2003.
22. Ian Jacobs and Norman Walsh. Architecture of the World Wide Web, Volume One. World Wide Web Consortium, Recommendation REC-webarch-20041215, December 2004.
23. Tim Kindberg and Sandro Hawke. The 'tag' URI Scheme. Internet RFC 4151, October 2005.
24. Frank G. Lemoine, Steve C. Kenyon, John K. Factor, Ronald G. Trimmer, Nikolaos K. Pavlis, Douglas S. Chinn, Christopher M. Cox, Steven M. Klosko, Scott B. Luthcke, Mark H. Torrence, Yan Ming Wang, Ronald G. Williamson, Erricos C. Pavlis, Richard H. Rapp, T. Rob Olson. The Development of the Joint NASA GSFC and the NIMA Geopotential Model EGM96. NASA/TP-1998-206861, July 1998.
25. Marwa Mabrouk. *OpenGIS Location Services (OpenLS): Core Services*. Open Geospatial Consortium Inc., 05 2005.
26. Alexander Mayrhofer and Christian Spanring. A Uniform Resource Identifier for Geographic Locations ('geo' URI). Internet Draft draft-mayrhofer-geopriv-geo-uri-00, May 2008.
27. National Imagery and Mapping Agency. Department of Defense World Geodetic System 1984. NIMA TR8350.2, Third Edition, January 2000.
28. Mark Nottingham and Robert Sayre. The Atom Syndication Format. Internet RFC 4287, December 2005.
29. Open Geospatial Consortium. An Introduction to GeoRSS: A Standards Based Approach for Geo-enabling RSS feeds. OGC 06-050r3, July 2006.
30. Steven Pemberton. XHTML 1.0: The Extensible HyperText Markup Language (Second Edition). World Wide Web Consortium, Recommendation REC-xhtml1-20020801, August 2002.
31. Jon Peterson. A Presence-Based GEOPRIV Location Object Format. Internet RFC 4119, December 2005.
32. James M. Polk, John Schnizlein, and Marc Linsner. Dynamic Host Configuration Protocol Option for Coordinate-Based Location Configuration Information. Internet RFC 3825, July 2004.
33. Andrei Popescu. Geolocation API Specification (Draft), June 2008.
34. Dave Raggett, Arnaud Le Hors, and Ian Jacobs. HTML 4.01 Specification. World Wide Web Consortium, Recommendation REC-html401-19991224, December 1999.
35. Joshua Schachter and Ask Bjœrn Hansen. The GeoURL ICBM Address Server.

36. H. Schulzrinne. Dynamic Host Configuration Protocol (DHCPv4 and DHCPv6) Option for Civic Addresses Configuration Information, November 2006.
37. Martin Thomson and James Winterbottom. Discovering the Local Location Information Server (LIS). Internet Draft draft-ietf-geopriv-lis-discovery-04, October 2008.
38. United States Code. Wireless Communications and Public Safety Act of 1999 (911 Act). Pub. L. No. 106-81, 113 Stat. 1286, October 1999.
39. WAP Forum. Wireless Application Protocol — Architecture Specification. WAP-210-WAPArch-20010712, July 2001.
40. Stuart L. Weibel, John A. Kunze, Carl Lagoze, and Misha Wolf. Dublin Core Metadata for Resource Discovery. Internet RFC 2413, September 1998.
41. Erik Wilde. The Plain Web. In *Proceedings of the First International Workshop on Understanding Web Evolution (WebEvolve2008)*, pages 79–83, Beijing, China, April 2008.

Ad Hoc Determination of Geographic Regions for Concept@Location Queries

Andreas Henrich and Volker Lüdecke

Abstract Textual geographic queries to search engines usually consist of the desired concept and also of one or more terms describing a location, which is often the name of a city, which in turn can usually be grounded with the help of a gazetteer. On other occasions, though, the location refers to a (vague) geographic region and may also be a vernacular expression for that region, so that this location specification cannot be found in a gazetteer.

In this chapter we describe an approach to determine the boundaries for such locations and how to integrate this approach into the query process. The key features of our approach are that a geographic search engine is able to handle any textual description of a geographic region at query time and that this computation can be done completely automatically. In our approach we derive a representation for a region from the toponyms found in the top web documents resulting from a query using the terms describing the location.

In addition to that, we introduce two other uses of this approach: first, this method can be used for answering where-is queries (where only a query location, but no query concept is given), and second, we can determine geographic representations for arbitrary terms that are not genuine geographic regions. In that case, the geographic representation provides a visual impression of the geographic correlation of those terms.

1 Introduction

In Geographic Information Retrieval, textual user queries in the format concept@ location are quite common. While the concept-part usually refers to a real-world object, the location-part mostly consists of a certain place or a region, which defines a geographic constraint of the query. Examples are *hotels in Bamberg* or *jobs in*

A. Henrich (✉)
University of Bamberg, Germany
e-mail: andreas.henrich@uni-bamberg.de

I. King, R. Baeza-Yates (eds.), *Weaving Services and People on the World Wide Web*,
DOI 10.1007/978-3-642-00570-1_9,

southern Germany. A geographic search engine processing such a query therefore has to be able to know the position or the boundary of the given location, which is usually done by looking it up in a gazetteer-like database [12]. Places not contained in there thus cannot be found that way.

Gazetteers usually contain information about cities, locations or regions with distinct boundaries, like administrative regions. In everyday language you can find many more region names, many of which are only vaguely or ambiguously defined and do not have strict borders.

In this chapter we elaborate an approach, which was first published by us in a preliminary version [10][1] that uses knowledge from the World Wide Web to automatically determine any location that is not yet in the database of a search engine at query time, so that any user query in the above format could be answered. While the location-part of a query is usually considered to be geographic in nature, it does not necessarily have to be, which is the second proposition we make in this chapter: a geographic reference in a query must not be restricted to a place or a (vernacular) region, but may be any concept, for which the search engine then has to find out an appropriate corresponding geographic extension. Examples of such queries are *camping ground near theme park* or maybe *cycle path near brewery*.

The chapter is structured as follows: Our approach is explained in Sect. 2, while the usage of arbitrary terms as location-identifier is covered separately in Sect. 3.1. Section 3.2 deals with the application of this approach for answering where-is queries. In Sect. 4 we give an evaluation of the quality and performance of the system, which also shows the influences of some of the parameters involved in the process. Section 5 covers related work. Finally, Sect. 6 concludes the chapter and discusses future work.

2 Our Approach

The situation we are concerned with can be described as follows: We are given a set of terms T_{loc} describing the location part of a concept@location-query.[2] We want to derive a geographical footprint of query region R_{query} (or more precisely $R_{query}(T_{loc})$) representing that location.

In this section we outline a system architecture and its components for a search engine that is able to automatically compute geographic representations for arbitrary terms at query time. Since we want to focus on delimiting geographic regions while processing a geographic query and not on standard text search engines, we assume the following whenever we refer to a geographic search engine:

---

[1] This chapter extends the preliminary version considering additional potential application scenarios (where-is queries) and extending the experimental results (e. g. considering additional parameter settings and quality measures).

[2] With the query *camping ground near golf course* we get T_{loc} = *golf course* and with the query *hiking in Franconia* we get T_{loc} = *Franconia*.

- This search engine has indexed a good-sized part of the world wide web, as every major search engine has, since we need the WWW-knowledge for determining geographic regions.
- This search engine is able to handle standard textual queries and to provide relevance rankings.
- Users can enter textual queries in the format concept@location. Whether this is done by two separate textfields or by a more sophisticated analysis of the queries does not matter for our purposes.

We will provide the necessary details on how we actually handle this for our experiments in the corresponding passages.

2.1 Aims

Since we want to delimit the query-region R_{query} at query time, the system must be able to do that very fast. So we aimed at a response time of less than one second (using a standard desktop PC). Secondly, we want to provide a geographic representation for any set of terms entered by the user and not just for terms describing a geographic region. Finally, the whole process must work completely automatically without user interaction.

Our prototype system is restricted to text in German language and to locations in Germany. While there are certain differences concerning phrases and patterns for example, the methods are applicable to any language and location data.

2.2 System Architecture

Figure 1 shows the relevant system components of our proposed geographic search engine and how they are related to each other.

Gazetteer A gazetteer provides the location data of known places (and regions) to the search engine.

Region-Engine The Region-Engine comprises all specific methods for delimiting vague or unknown regions. If a location from a concept@location-query is not contained in the gazetteer, the Region-Engine uses location information from the gazetteer for determining the boundaries of the unknown location. We will cover it later in this section in detail.

Geographic Search Engine The ranking process of the geographic search engine has to use distances of geographic coordinates and regions rather than ontological connections between places for the ranking process. The geographical similarity is thus computed by degree of overlap or a distance measure between the query region and the geographic footprint of the document.

Fig. 1 Proposed system architecture

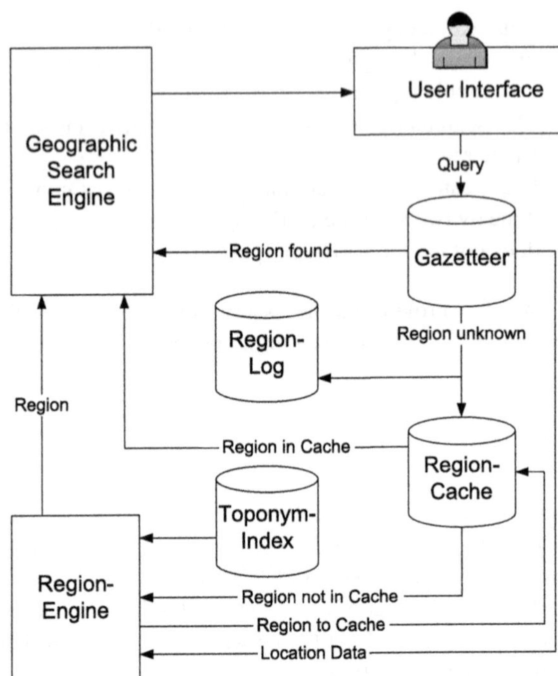

Region-Cache Caching will improve the performance of the system, but has no other specific function.

Toponym-Index This contains information about the toponyms contained in a document. It is used for improving the performance of our approach.

Region-Log It certainly makes sense to log the location terms entered by users of a live system. Frequently used regions should probably be manually revised and added to the database / gazetteer of the system.

User-Interface In addition to any existing user interface, we recommend giving the user feedback as to what was actually considered his query-location. Ways of providing some kind of relevance feedback are not discussed here, though.

2.3 Region-Engine

The Region-Engine is the main focus of our work. It will take one or more terms T_{loc} and try to determine a corresponding geographic region, whenever that region is used in a query and cannot be found in the gazetteer used by the system or in the cache of previously delimited regions.

The first step is to retrieve documents $D_{retrieved}$ relevant to T_{loc}, describing the query-region R_{Query}. Since our prototype system does not have indexed enough web documents yet, we used the Google-API to get the first 500 results (html-pages only) for each region description T_{loc} and archived them locally (T_{loc} was used as Google-query without further modifications). We used the first k of these documents as $D_{retrieved}$, while k is a design parameter. That way we can better evaluate the total performance of our approach, since a working geographic search engine would simply use its own (local) data.

The subsequent steps are to extract toponyms contained in $D_{retrieved}$ and to determine their geographic coordinates (which can be done at index time). Finally, we compute a two-dimensional (region) representation based on all coordinates found.

2.3.1 Toponyms

A time consuming process step is to detect and disambiguate toponyms in the documents $D_{retrieved}$. We used the GeoNames gazetteer as well as the OpenGeoDB, but found the former to lead to slightly better results, since it is more comprehensive. We then parsed a German dictionary to remove all location names that were also common German words, but if a location had a population of more than 30.000 people, we did not remove that location name. These decisions are the result of manual experiments and may not be optimal for all kinds of queries or documents. That way we had a list of about 70.000 toponyms in Germany.

All potential toponyms were extracted from the retrieved documents $D_{retrieved}$. If a toponym had more than one corresponding location, we used a simple disambiguation mechanism that chose those toponyms that resulted in the smallest bounding region over all toponyms in the document.

For a better performance at query time, we built a toponym index that contains a list of toponyms contained in $D_{retrieved}$ with their document-weights for each document. Since the toponym extraction should be made at index time, the time spent on retrieving the toponyms of a document at query time is reduced to an index lookup. For a geographic search engine to work, toponym extraction is usually done anyway for determining the geographic footprint of a document. For this step, performance is certainly an issue, but out of the focus of this paper. Obviously, toponym extraction at index time is not possible if $D_{retrieved}$ is derived via the GoogleAPI at query time, but it would be possible and straightforward if $D_{retrieved}$ is taken from the geographic search engine, so for further considerations we assume that our methods are to be used in a geographic search engine that has an index of its own and that does toponym extraction at index time.

2.3.2 Density Surfaces

Having determined all toponyms contained in $D_{retrieved}$, we create a two-dimensional representation based on the aggregation of the geographic coordinates of these toponyms. For this, we used density surfaces, as did Purves et al. [22], using a kernel density estimation with a standard Gaussian function as kernel. That means that we determine the location(s) for each toponym found and weight them by their document and term frequency. As a consequence, each location has an *area of influence* with a peak at the exact location and a decreasing influence according to the kernel function. Then we sum up all areas of influence. For a faster computation, we discretize this step. That way, the whole target area (which is Germany in our case) is divided into tiles, and we determine the total value V_i for the center of each tile i. We chose a tile size of about one square kilometer per tile, but the ideal tile size depends on the intended application. For a Germany-wide search engine, a maximum resolution of 1 km seems about right, since most regions are larger than a few kilometers and all methods involved are afflicted with a considerable level of uncertainty.

The density surface may be used in two different ways for a relevance ranking by location or distance respectively.

First, all tiles with a value greater than a threshold value T_{min} may be considered to be part of the region, while all others are not. The resulting 2D-area may then be stored in a quadtree or any other representation the search engine uses for storing geographic footprints of documents or query footprints. The geographic similarity between the query footprint and each document footprint can then be computed by region overlap or any other distance measure, which is not the focus of this chapter.

Secondly, depending on the similarity measure used, the density surface representation provides additional information about the area. The higher the values of some tiles, the more likely it is that these tiles lie near the core of the query-region R_{Query}: although in the first instance these high values result from a number of locations that are often mentioned in documents relevant to the query-region and have no immediate causal connection to the core region, experiments show that more often than not the core of the target region indeed lies near the maximum of the density function.

While the kernel density estimation is usually computed on a cell-by-cell basis, this is very time consuming, since there are usually a lot of tiles with values only slightly above zero. We therefore took a different approach and iterated over all location names found in the documents. For each location we computed the corresponding fraction of the total density function for only a number of tiles, as long as the contributing value was above a (low) threshold and added it to the result matrix. If, for example, *Berlin* was the only toponym found in all $D_{retrieved}$, the resulting density surface would have a single peak value in the tile where Berlin is located, falling off to all sides. We would compute the value of this peak as well as the values of a number of neighbouring tiles, leaving out the rest of Germany. When multiple toponyms are found, we compute a fraction for each of them and the resulting sum over all tiles is the result. This is more than 100 times faster than a computation cell-by-cell, as you will see in the evaluation section.

In order to get a satisfying result area A_{result}, it is necessary to determine a threshold value T_{min} for the density surface, with all tiles with a smaller value not being part of A_{result}. Experiments showed that the best threshold-value heavily depends on the query-region R_{query}. In the following we describe a way how to determine a good threshold-value automatically.

2.3.3 Training Data

For evaluating the quality of an automatically computed region representation (A_{result}) we need a correct representation for comparison. For that reason, two persons diligently researched various sources of information to find out the commonly accepted borders of about 120 regions R_{user} of various sizes in Germany. When both persons agreed to a certain border of a region, a polygon shape was drawn in GoogleMaps and later imported by GoogleEarth to get the coordinates of the polygon. Since the borders of most of the regions are vague, the resulting polygons must be seen as an approximation, but are well suited for our purposes, because all regions were created by using the same criteria and judgements. An exemplary region can be seen in Fig. 2, showing the *Havelland* in its geographic representation, while Havelland is also an administrative unit, which has a slightly different border.

Even with a given 'correct' region, it is not easy to define the best threshold-value T_{min}, as there is a trade-off between coverage of the targeted region and a too large,

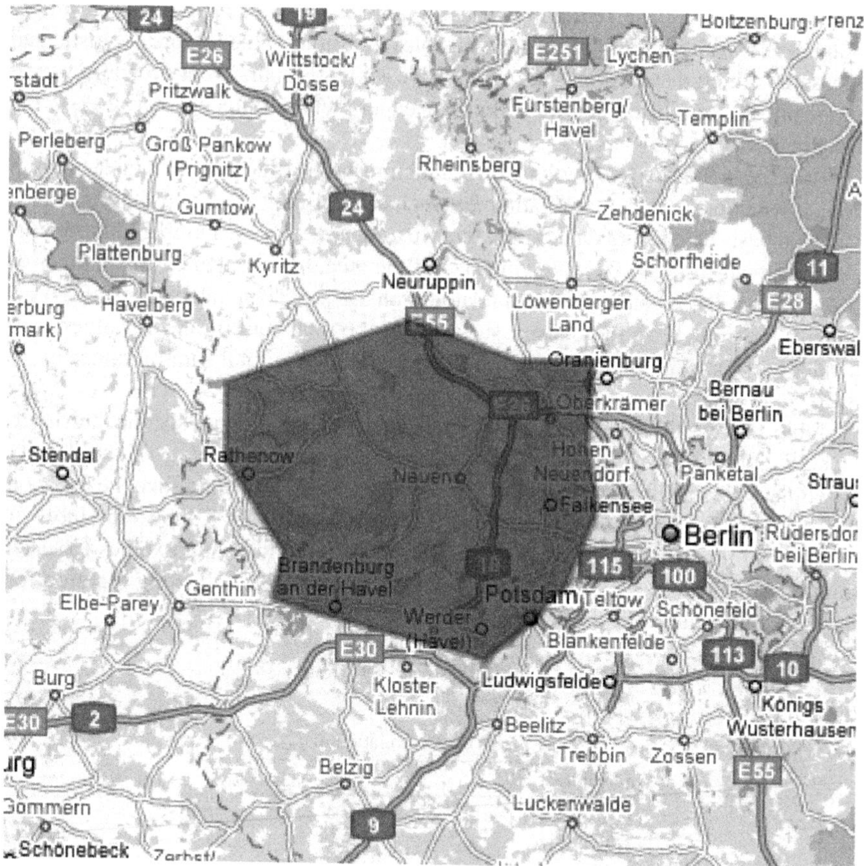

Fig. 2 Polygon representation of *Havelland* (Background ©2008 Google – Map data ©2008 PPWK, Tele Atlas)

faulty shape. Therefore, we implemented two simple measures to automatically find the best threshold-values for 39 regions. One measure takes the absolute values of the density function / the tiles into account, while the other simply counts the number of tiles. Which measure makes more sense thus depends on whether or not the actual values are used in the later ranking process or not. Let *sim* be the similarity between a given user-created region R_{user} and the density surface with a given threshold value T, n the number of tiles being part of R_{user}, m the number of tiles outside the region R_{user} and V_x the value of tile x (n and m depend on the threshold-value, of course.) The measures are:

$$sim_{bin} = 2 * n - m \tag{1}$$

$$sim_{val} = 2 * \sum_{i=1}^{n} V_i - \sum_{j=1}^{m} V_j \tag{2}$$

For determining the optimal threshold-value T_{min} for each region, we simply maximized *sim* by iterating over all (sensible) threshold-values. More sophisticated measures taking distance into account are possible, of course, but probably would not result in very different values. Further experiments in this chapter refer to the usage of sim_{val}.

To derive a function to predict the optimal threshold-value T_{min} for a query-region R_{query}, we computed the correlation between several indicators and the threshold-value on basis of learning data. Indicators we used were: (1) the number of toponyms per document from $D_{retrieved}$, (2) the size of the area, represented by the number of tiles with a value greater than the threshold-value T_{min}, (3) the maximum value V_{max} of all tile values V_i in the density surface, (4) the total sum of all tile values with a value greater than the threshold-value T_{min}, and (5) the total sum of values of all tiles.

Table 1 shows the resulting pairwise correlation values. Obviously, the threshold-value T_{min} correlates quite strongly with the maximum value V_{max} of the density function, which is often greater than one, because we did not normalize the function to the number of toponyms to get a better distinction. Figure 3 shows the individual optimal threshold-values T_{min} in dependency on the maximum values for each training region R_{user}. A simple linear regression lead to the following function for the threshold value:

$$T_{predicted} = max\,(0.2, 0.91 * V_{max} - 0.79) \tag{3}$$

Table 1 Pairwise correlation to T_{min}

Indicator	Correlation to T_{min}
(1) Toponyms per doc	0.604
(2) Area size	−0.369
(3) Maximum Value	0.923
(4) Sum above threshold	−0.177
(5) Total sum	−0.312

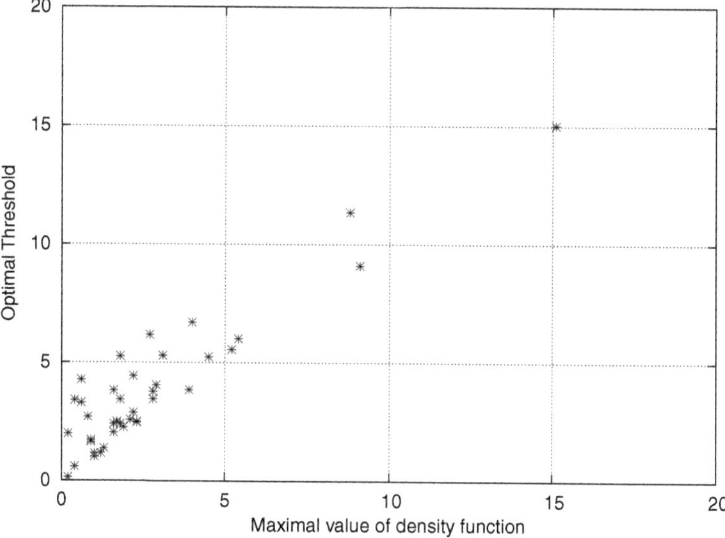

Fig. 3 Correlation between V_{max} and T_{min}

The number of documents k used for delimiting a geographic region influences the performance both in quality and computation speed, of course. A comparison of the influence of k on the results is done in the evaluation section.

3 Application Scenarios

3.1 Arbitrary Terms as Regions

There are certainly geographic information needs which result in queries that do not use toponyms as location reference. For example, a user might want to find a camping ground near a theme park or a cycle path near some breweries. In these cases, *theme park* and *brewery* would be used in much the same way as any toponym as location reference.

If a search engine was able to deal with arbitrary terms as regions using the same automated mechanism to delimit these *region-like references*, it could answer a lot more information needs. The prerequisite for that is that this approach is indeed applicable to any non-toponym terms and that the quality of the results is sufficiently high. With that, *where-is*-like queries can also be answered.

Another application of this approach is to find out whether certain terms have a significant geographic correlation. That may be region specific expressions for things (e.g. bread rolls have completely different names in several parts of Germany) or other things that are typical only for a certain region.

We applied all the mechanisms described in the preceding section to arbitrary terms.

3.2 Where-is-like Queries

Our approach can also be used to answer where-is queries, where no concept-part is given and where the answer to a query is either a geographic region or a location. The region engine as described above provides answers to the former by default, only that in this case the region representation does not have to be integrated further in the ranking process. An evaluation for that is given in the following section. For the latter, where basically a single point is requested, the approach has to be adapted slightly.

For a simple evaluation, we considered the (first) tile with the highest value of the density estimation V_{max} to be the answer. The resolution of that is therefore about 1 km^2. For the scope of a germany-wide tool, this seems to be reasonable enough, but of course this approach as is has an important drawback for this application: There is only one coordinate per city, even for cities which are larger than 1 km^2.

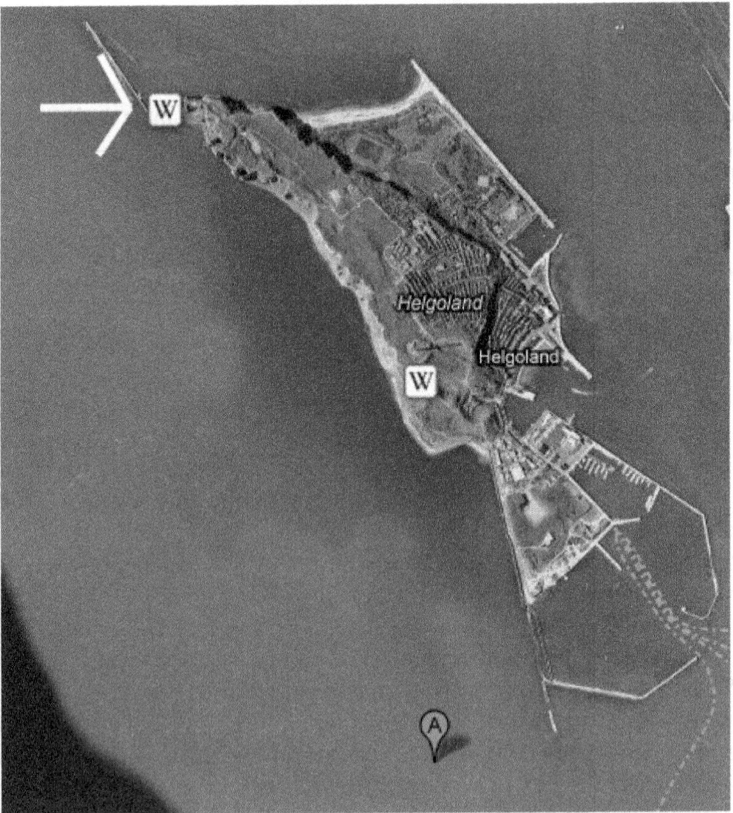

Fig. 4 Result of *where-is Lange Anna* (marked with *A*) and the actual position of it (wikipedia-link, marked by the *arrow*) (Background ©2008 Google – Map data ©2008 PPWK, Tele Atlas)

In [27] the authors show that the general method of this approach can also be used with other data sources, which can provide a finer resolution.

For this evaluation we used our system to determine the location of 27 randomly chosen showplaces in Germany and reviewed the results manually. We measured the distance from the center of the resulting tile to the correct position of the showplaces. Figure 4 shows the answer to *where-is Lange Anna* (which is a famous rock on the island of Helgoland, marked with the arrow). This also shows that other data sources can provide a more fine grained result, as indicates the geocoded wikipedia-article that is linked into the map by Google. Table 2 summarizes the quality of the where-is results. While the results are not bad, a distance of up to 5 km might not be good enough for some applications.

Table 2 Quality of results for where-is queries for single locations

	Up to 5 km	Up to 10 km	Up to 20 km	Completely wrong	Total
Number of results	18	7	1	1	27

4 Evaluation

In this section we want to evaluate three aspects of our approach: (1) Performance and applicability of our system for delimiting regions at query time, (2) Quality of representations for geographic regions and (3) Use of *geographizing* arbitrary terms.

4.1 Performance

As we already mentioned, the performance of the system is very important and mainly depends on the number of documents used for delimiting each region as well as the resolution of the density surface (the number of tiles used). The costs of looking up a region in a gazetteer or in the region cache thereafter are negligible, as is the cost of looking the toponyms up in the toponym index.

For performance evaluation, we computed 20 region representations and measured the time effort for each region. In Fig. 5 you can see the performance of building the density surface incrementally in comparison to computing it on a cell-by-cell basis, each once for $k = 20$ and once for $k = 100$ web documents $D_{retrieved}$ per query-region R_{query}. We used a tile resolution of about one square kilometer and a resolution of about four square kilometers per tile, both of which should be sufficient for the context of (not too small) regions within a Germany-wide search engine. It is clearly visible that the modification of computing the density surface improves the performance by a factor of more than 100. Both versions of the kernel density estimation show the same trend. The reason for that is that both computations depend on the absolute number of locations found, which is identical for both approaches.

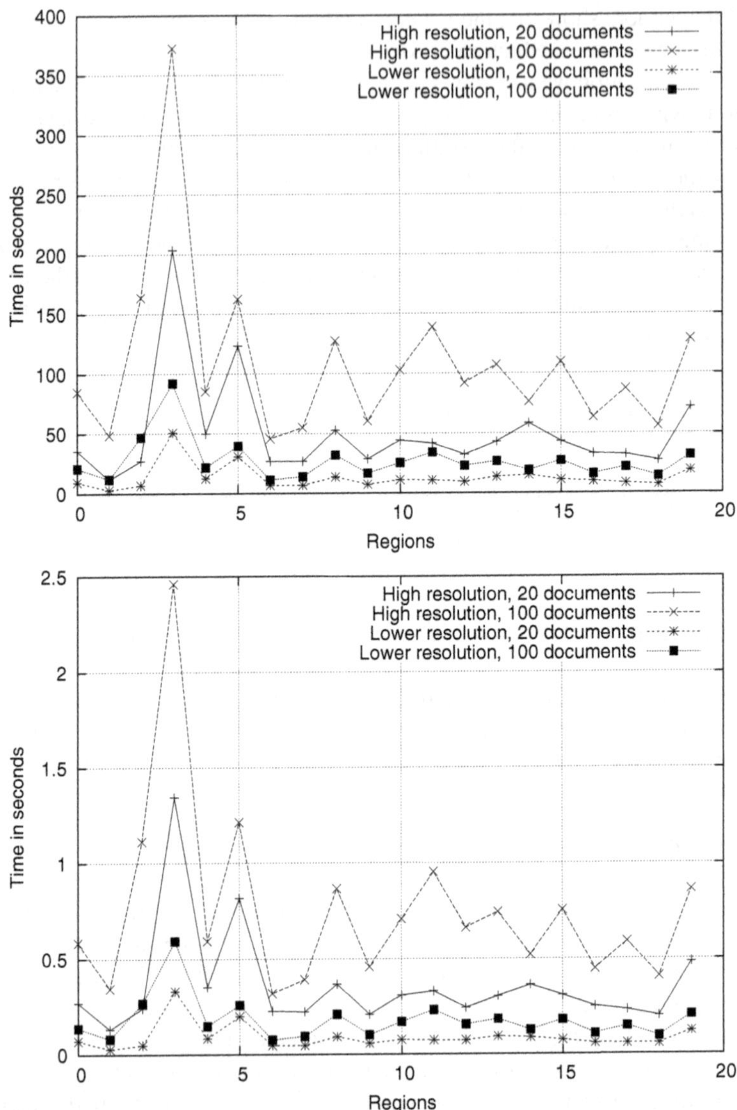

Fig. 5 Performance of standard kernel density estimation (*top*) vs. tuned kernel density estimation (*bottom*) with varying resolution and number of documents k

Overall, the performance of our system seems to make it possible to use our approach at query time, since it usually needs considerably less than one second per query representation (standard desktop PC).

4.2 Quality of Region Representations

There are two aspects to consider for evaluating the quality of the region representations: First, the computation of the predicted optimal threshold value $T_{predicted}$ for the density surface in comparison to the optimal threshold value for each region T_{min}, which leads to a relative evaluation. Second, an absolute evaluation of the region representation by comparing it to the target region. We will evaluate both aspects in the following.

We tested formula (3) by comparing the predicted threshold values for 39 regions R_{user} not contained in the training set to their corresponding computed T_{min}, so we could see how good the regression function works for further regions. Figure 6 shows the results of this comparison. Obviously, the predicted values come close to the optimum.

Measuring the absolute quality of the representations is difficult for several reasons. Since most of the regions are no crisp regions, but have a vague border, which might also be seen differently by different persons, there is no exact ground truth. As we pointed out earlier, the polygons R_{user} seem to be a good approximation of a ground truth, though. Second, there are several possible points of view regarding similarity between regions. A common baseline approach measures regions of overlap between approximated and correct areas and regions of non-overlap between them. This is a simple point of view that assumes that there are only two states: either a point is within the correct region or not. Distances do not matter therefore, because each point outside the correct region is equally worthless, and each one inside is equally good. This is a very strict semantic, but in some scenarios it is important that an approximation of a geographic region is strictly within the borders of the original region. For example, a query might refer to a law that is only valid inside a region delimited by a border (like a US state). Even a small crossing of that border makes the geographic position worthless.

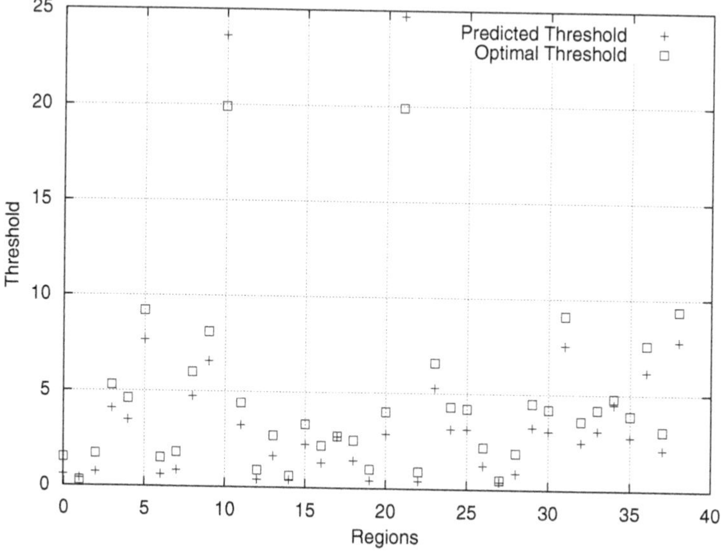

Fig. 6 Predicted threshold value in comparison to optimal threshold value T_{min}

The simplicity of these measures makes them suitable for a rough comparison of absolute result quality, though. One example of those measures can be found in [11, 19]. $A(R)$ is the surface area of a region R, R_{query} is the approximation of the query region, and R_{user} is the correct region:

$$sim_{prec} = \frac{2 * A\left(R_{query} \cap R_{user}\right)}{A\left(R_{query}\right) + A\left(R_{user}\right)} \quad (4)$$

We used this measure to calculate values for the absolute result quality for 75 geographic regions, none of them being part of the training data. Figure 7 shows the corresponding values for $k = 20$.

To get a better understanding of what the similarity numbers actually mean, we will give three examples for them. Figure 8 shows the best result, *Niederbayern*, with a similarity value of 0.84.

The worst result, *Spessart*, has a similarity value of 0, which is because *Spessart* refers to a geographic region as well as an administrative district, which seems to be slightly more popular in the first 20 results, so that the threshold value $T_{predicted}$ for that regions causes the geographic region *Spessart* to vanish. Although the administrative district can be seen as a geographic region, the corresponding R_{user} only refers to the genuine geographic region. The representation for *Ammerland* has a similarity score of 0.06. You can see in Fig. 9 that this region is very small and the formula for $T_{predicted}$ did not work very well here. Increasing the threshold value slightly improves the result a lot. It is probably possible to use heuristics and other

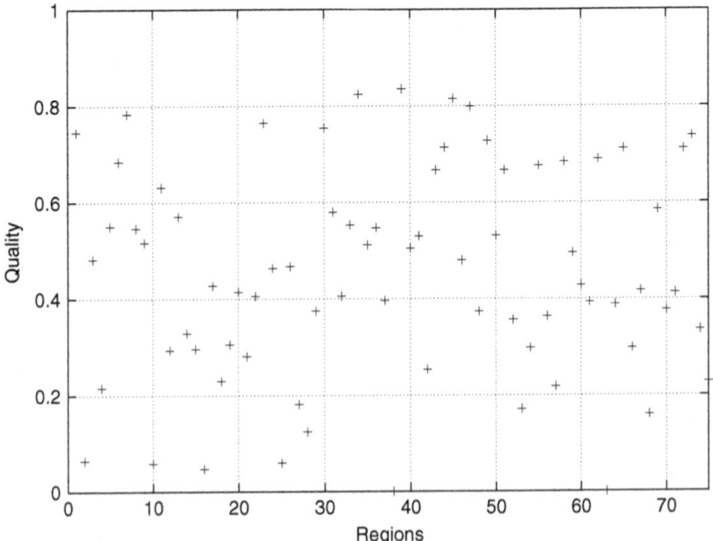

Fig. 7 Absolute quality of automatically determined region representations, $k = 20$

Fig. 8 Comparison of R_{user} and computed region representation for region *Niederbayern* with sim_{prec} = 0,84. The R_{user} is the polygonal area

more sophisticated methods than the pure linear function for $T_{predicted}$. The same holds true for the region *Sauerland*, which can be seen in Fig. 10.

We found that the shape of a region did not change much between $k = 20$, 100 and 500 documents. Figure 11 shows these effects by the example of the region *Harz*. The main difference between the resulting density surfaces is that the peaks get softer. For arbitrary concepts, such as *mining*, instead of real geographic regions, the number of documents seemed a lot more important, since they are not well defined and as such, a more comprehensive coverage of documents makes more sense.

We used the measure sim_{prec} given in formula (4) to analyse the effect of k on the result quality. Therefore we calculated the quality for the same 75 geographic regions we used above and set k to 20, 50, 100 and 200. Figure 12 shows the resulting graphs. For this figure we sorted the data for each graph separately by

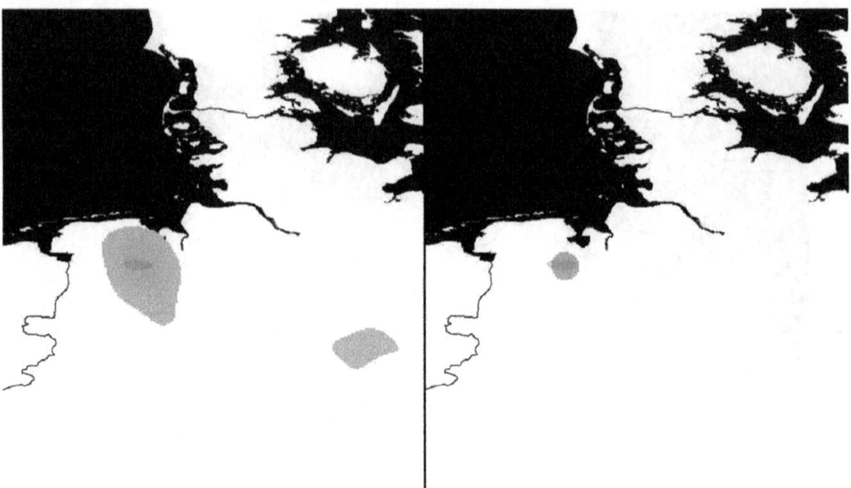

Fig. 9 Comparison of R_{user} and computed region representation for region *Ammerland* with $sim_{prec} = 0.06$ (**left**) and resulting region with a higher threshold T_{min} (**right**). The R_{user} is the polygonal area

result quality (descending) to better visualize the effects. Therefore, one point on the x-axis (e.g. 10) does not stand for a certain region, but for the 10th highest quality. In addition, we calculated the average quality as well as the number of regions where a certain k lead to the best result per region (e.g. for 17 of 75 regions, $k = 20$ lead to

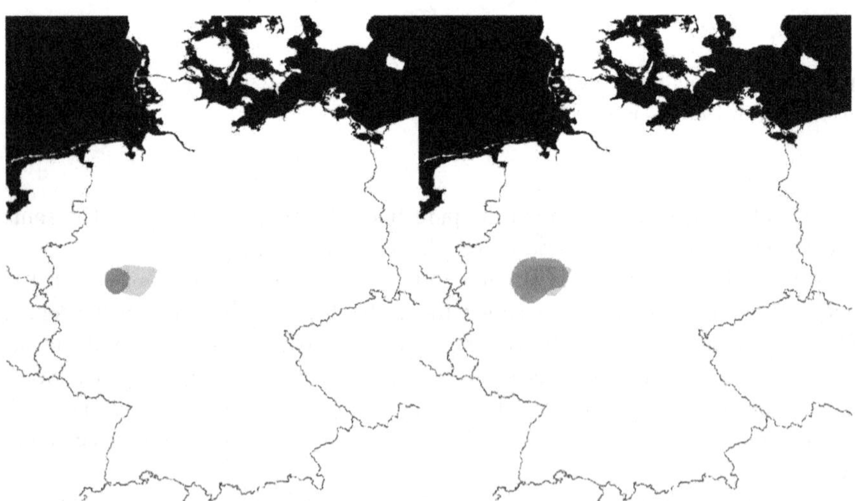

Fig. 10 Comparison of R_{user} and computed region representation for region *Sauerland* with $sim_{prec} = 0.43$ (*left*) and resulting region with a higher threshold T_{min} (*right*). The R_{user} is the solid area

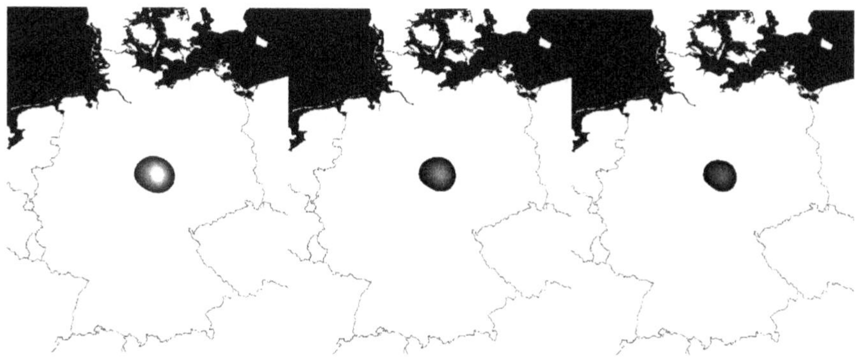

Fig. 11 Region *Harz* with 20, 100 and 500 documents used

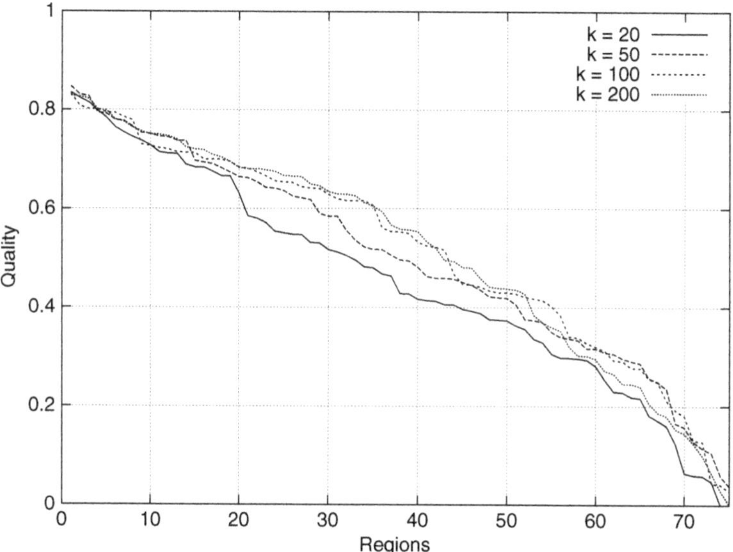

Fig. 12 Comparison of the effects of k, the number of documents $D_{retrieved}$ considered, on the result quality

Table 3 Effects of k on result quality

k	No. of regions with best qual.	Ø quality
20	17	0.45221
50	19	0.49902
100	11	0.51527
200	28	0.51278

the best quality). This data can be found in Table 3. It seems like the quality of the results improves by raising k to about 100, but this data is only an indication for that, since there are many parameters involved. Future work will be to further analyse the effects of k, to adapt the regression function used for determining $T_{predicted}$, and to use further heuristics to improve result quality.

Another important factor in this respect might be the (Google-)rank of a document. We therefore made a simple analysis of considering the rank of a document as a weight in the kernel density estimation. Obviously, the top ranked documents $D_{retrieved}$ should be more valuable than lower ranked documents. On the other hand, the ranks of documents (should) reflect the similarity between the query terms and the content of the documents. For this application, though, we are interested in the geographic correlation of the document's content to the geographic concept named by the query, which might not correlate to the result rank.

For this experiment, we compared four weighting functions for the toponym locations for the kernel density estimation, one of them being the none-weighted standard case used in the rest of this chapter ($w = 1.0$). Two of them were simple linear functions, one decreasing ($w = 1.0 - rank * 0.01$) and one increasing ($w = 1.0 + rank * 0.01$) (and as such weighting lower ranks higher than top ranks), and the fourth is a logarithmic function ($w = 1/rank$).

Figures 13 and 14 show the results for $k = 20$ and $k = 100$, while Table 4 summarizes these results, which indicate that there is no strong correlation between the rank of a result and its impact on result quality. With $k = 100$ the weights for the low ranked documents become very small for logarithmic and linear (decreasing) weighting, so that the regression function (3) does not work very well here. We therefore normalized the weights:

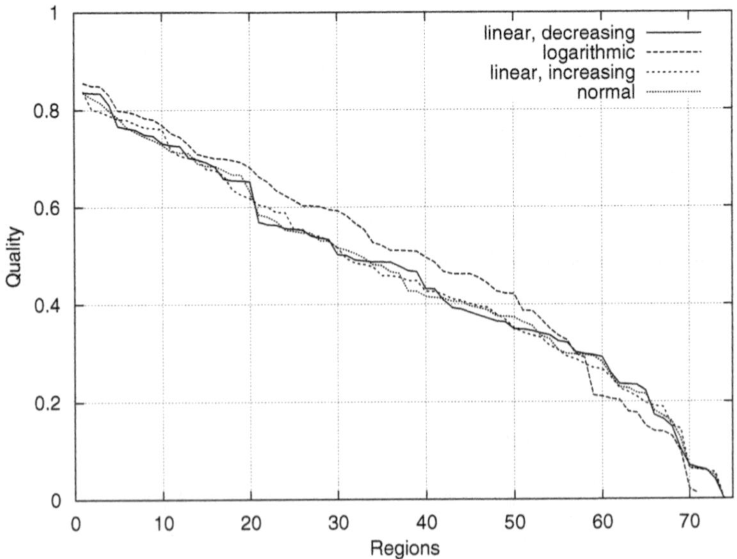

Fig. 13 Effects of weighting the Google result rank with $k = 20$

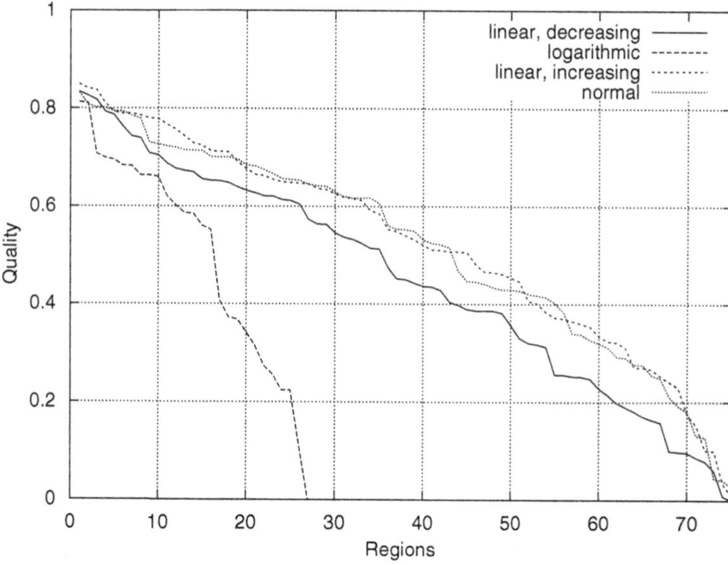

Fig. 14 Effects of weighting in the Google result rank with $k = 100$

$$w_{i,normalized} = w_i * \frac{k}{\sum_{j=1}^{k} w_j} \tag{5}$$

The results achieved with these normalized weights for $k = 100$ are given in the last columns of Table 4.

The presented results suggest that a weighting of the rank of a document does not significantly improve the quality of the geographic representations. The reason seems to be that the first 100 documents $D_{retrieved}$ (with often more than two million result documents overall) are more or less equally good. Future work will be to consider additional parameters, since these results might change slightly with adapted regression functions for T_{min}.

Table 4 Effects of weighting in the Google result rank on result quality

		Without normalization		With normalization	
k	Weighting	No. of regions with best qual.	Ø qual.	No. of regions with best qual.	Ø qual.
20	None	0	0.45221	–	–
20	Linear, decreasing	15	0.45312	–	–
20	Logarithmic	41	0.47757	–	–
20	Linear, increasing	19	0.45091	–	–
100	None	18	0.51527	18	0.51527
100	Linear, decreasing	15	0.44874	17	0.49913
100	Logarithmic	8	0.17963	26	0.43884
100	Linear, increasing	34	0.52264	14	0.49859

4.3 Geographizing Arbitrary Concepts

Evaluating the geographic representations for arbitrary terms is much more difficult, since there is usually no correct result to compare it to. We will discuss the applicability of our approach on the basis of some examples.

Weisswurst (Bavarian veal sausage) is especially popular in the south of Germany. It is often said that the border for this is the Main River, which is therefore often called the *Weisswurstaequator*, the equator of veal sausage. Geographic references like *south of the Weisswurstaequator* are commonly used in German language.

Fig. 15 Visualization of the concept *Weisswurstaequator*, a common word for the Main River (highlighted for comparison)

Figure 15 shows the result of representing it by means of our approach. It is a bit wide, but otherwise represents the term quite correctly. Since this is more or less a geographic region, it is one of the easier examples.

We found a map on the cultivation of sugar beets in Germany (see Fig. 16)[3]. We used the heading of that map as query-region. The resulting area of that query can be seen in Fig. 17, which is by no means exact, but the general idea is correct, anyway.

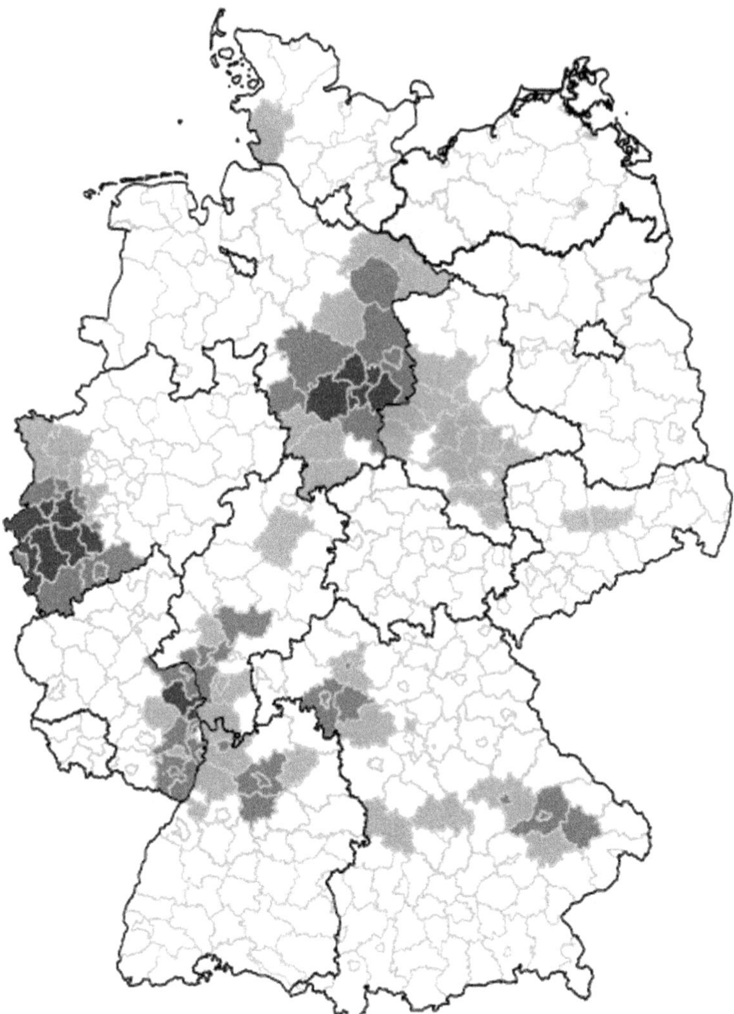

Fig. 16 Cultivation of sugar beets in Germany, source: i.m.a – information.medien.agrar e.V

[3] http://www.ima-agrar.de/_redesign/Dateien/Zuckerrueben anbau_.pdf, February 1, 2008

Fig. 17 Cultivation of sugar beets in Germany as result area A_{result}

We discovered a project run by linguists, who manually created maps about the region-specific use of language [7]. Figure 18 (right) shows the regional distribution of various terms used for *bumper cars*. The circle highlights the region where the very uncommon word *Knuppautos* is used for that. Our automatically created representation for *Knuppautos* can be seen in Fig. 18 (left).

While there were a lot of interesting and promising results, there were of course also many terms, for which we could not find a suitable geographic representation, while suitable refers to what we *expected*, since there does not seem to be a correct result to compare against, so we do not provide a numerical evaluation of the overall quality of this kind of representation. Nevertheless, we think that applying this approach to arbitrary concepts will be of some use for geographic search engines as well as standalone applications.

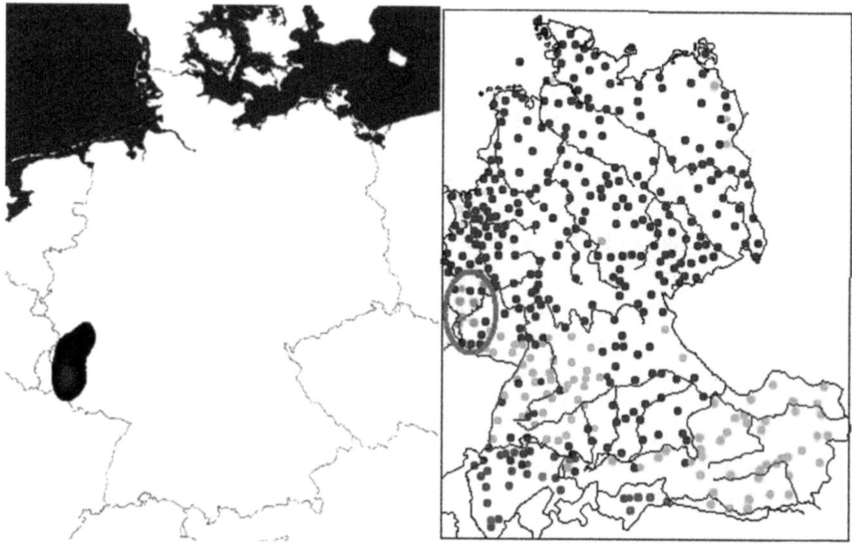

Fig. 18 Geographic representation for *Knuppauto* (*left*) and geographic extension of the language use of *Knuppauto* (*right*)

5 Related Work

Gazetteers or geo-ontologies form the geographical database of most geographic search engines [15]. They usually contain a place-name, the type of place, and a geographic footprint representing its location or its geographical extent [12]. This data is used for query disambiguation, query term expansion, relevance ranking or simply toponym detection in text [14]. A review of these functions is given by Jones et al. [13].

Unfortunately, not all geographic references used in queries can be found in those gazetteers, so that terms used for a geographic constraint cannot be matched to a certain region. The boundaries of these regions are also often only vaguely defined [4, 8]. Apparently, there is a need for identifying the boundaries of vague regions.

Several different formalisms have been proposed as an appropriate representation for vague regions, including supervaluation semantics [3, 4, 17], pairs of non-fuzzy sets [5, 6] and fuzzy footprints [9, 22, 25].

Alani et al. [1] approximate regions based on Voronoi diagrams which are constructed by a set of points known to be inside the target region and another one with points outside the region, but they do not deal with the source of the information about the sets. Vögele et al. [28] present a similar approach, where regions are represented by indeterminate boundaries with an upper and a lower approximation, which is also based on given sets with points and regions inside/outside the target region.

Methods for (semi-)automatically creating representations for vague regions usually mine the knowledge contained in the world wide web. The following approaches use documents retrieved from the www with certain queries or phrases containing the targeted region. Toponyms contained in these documents are extracted and disambiguated [18, 20] and provide the data for the algorithms.

Purves et al. [22] use kernel density surfaces for the representation of the imprecise regions. The authors elaborate their approach in Jones et al. [16], describing alternative web harvesting techniques for mining location information for geographic regions from the web. Reinbacher et al. [23] present two approaches to compute representations of regions, based on evidence of points that are likely to lie inside or outside this region. Arampatzis et al. [2] present methods to obtain locations inside the target region and locations outside from the www and use trigger phrases and patterns for the document retrieval to improve precision. They then approximate regions based on Voronoi diagrams. Schockaert et al. [25] also make use of regular expressions to acquire place names by a web search. They present a method for automatically determining vague footprints, represented as fuzzy sets.

A side aspect of Schöning et al. [26] deals with visualizations of geotagged Wikipedia articles.

Some approaches focus on small regions or domain specific regions. Schockaert et al. [24] present a technique to construct representations of the spatial extent of neighbourhoods. Pasley et al. [21] deal with the usefulness of different information resources depending on the size of the region.

While the basic principles of our approach are quite similar to some of the approaches above, we focus on integrating these mechanisms into the query process. Automation and performance are big issues therefore. While using phrases and additional concepts for retrieving $D_{retrieved}$ seems to lead to promising results for pure geographic regions like in Jones et al. [16] or Schockaert et al. [25], we try to evaluate the application of these methods to any given term. Thus, we want to be able to provide a representation or a map for arbitrary terms, which might be a geographic region or something completely different, like *mining* or *walking*, in which case the result should be a geographic representation of locations associated with that particular term.

6 Conclusion and Future Work

In this chapter we described an approach how to integrate a mechanism for delimiting geographic regions efficiently into a geographic search engine and showed that the performance of our system is good enough to provide such a feature at query time and that the quality of the representations were also appropriate for that application.

In addition to that we applied this approach to arbitrary terms instead of geographic regions only and showed that it produced reasonable results, leading to interesting further applications.

Future work will certainly be to further optimize the results for geographic regions as well as for arbitrary concepts. An interesting piece of work is how to best mine the information provided by the density surface for the ranking process. It may be also important to use other sources of data to get a finer resolution for small areas or single places.

References

1. H. Alani, C. B. Jones, and D. Tudhope. Voronoi-based region approximation for geographical information retrieval with gazetteers. *International Journal of Geographical Information Science*, 15(4):287–306, 2001.
2. A. Arampatzis, M. J. van Kreveld, I. Reinbacher, C. B. Jones, S. Vaid, P. Clough, H. Joho, and M. Sanderson. Web-based delineation of imprecise regions. *Computers, Environment and Urban Systems*, 30(4):436–459, 2006.
3. B. Bennett. Application of supervaluation semantics to vaguely defined spatial concepts. In *COSIT 2001*, pages 108–123, London, UK, 2001. Springer-Verlag.
4. B. Bennett. What is a forest? On the vagueness of certain geographic concepts. *Topoi*, 20(2):189–201, 2001.
5. T. Bittner and J. G. Stell. Vagueness and rough location. *Geoinformatica*, 6(2):99–121, 2002.
6. E. Clementini and P. D. Felice. Approximate topological relations. *International Journal of Approximate Reasoning*, 16(2):173–204, 1997.
7. S. Elspaß. Variation and change in colloquial (standard) german – The Atlas zur deutschen Alltagssprache (AdA) Project. *Standard, Variation und Sprachwandel in germanischen Sprachen/ Standard, Variation and Language Change in the Germanic Languages*, 41:201–216, 2007.
8. M. Erwig and M. Schneider. Vague regions. In *SSD '97: Proc. of the 5th Intl. Symposium on Advances in Spatial Databases*, pages 298–320, London, UK, 1997. Springer-Verlag.
9. M. F. Goodchild, D. R. Montello, P. Fohl, and J. Gottsegen. Fuzzy spatial queries in digital spatial data libraries. In *Fuzzy Systems Proc.*, volume 1, pages 205–210, Anchorage, AK, USA, 1998.
10. A. Henrich and V. Lüdecke. Determining geographic representations for arbitrary concepts at query time. In *LOCWEB '08: Proc. of the First Intl. Workshop on Location and the Web*, pages 17–24, New York, NY, USA, 2008. ACM.
11. L. L. Hill. *Access to Geographic Concepts in Online Bibliographic Files: Effectiveness of Current Practices and the Potential of a Graphic Interface*. PhD thesis, University of Pittsburgh, 1990.
12. L. L. Hill. Core elements of digital gazetteers: Placenames, categories, and footprints. In *ECDL '00*, pages 280–290, London, UK, 2000. Springer-Verlag.
13. C. B. Jones, A. I. Abdelmoty, and G. Fu. Maintaining ontologies for geographical information retrieval on the web. In *CoopIS/DOA/ODBASE*, pages 934–951, 2003.
14. C. B. Jones, H. Alani, and D. Tudhope. Geographical information retrieval with ontologies of place. In *COSIT 2001*, pages 322–335, London, UK, 2001. Springer-Verlag.
15. C. B. Jones, R. Purves, A. Ruas, M. Sanderson, M. Sester, M. van Kreveld, and R. Weibel. Spatial information retrieval and geographical ontologies an overview of the spirit project. In *SIGIR '02*, pages 387–388, New York, NY, USA, 2002. ACM.
16. C. B. Jones, R. S. Purves, P. D. Clough, and H. Joho. Modelling vague places with knowledge from the web. *International Journal of Geographical Information Science*, 22(10):1045–1065, 2008.
17. L. Kulik. A geometric theory of vague boundaries based on supervaluation. In *COSIT 2001*, pages 44–59, London, UK, 2001. Springer-Verlag.
18. R. Larson. Geographic information retrieval and spatial browsing. In L. Smith and M. Gluck, editors, *Geographic Information Systems and Libraries: Patronsand Mapsand and Spatial Information*, pages 81–124, 1996.

19. R. R. Larson and P. Frontiera. Spatial ranking methods for geographic information retrieval (gir) in digital libraries. In R. Heery and L. Lyon, editors, *Research and Advanced Technology for Digital Libraries: 8th European Conf., ECDL 2004*, LNCS 3232, pages 45–57. Springer-Verlag, 2004.
20. J. L. Leidner. Toponym resolution in text (abstract only): "which sheffield is it?". In *SIGIR '04*, pages 602–602, New York, NY, USA, 2004. ACM.
21. R. C. Pasley, P. D. Clough, and M. Sanderson. Geo-tagging for imprecise regions of different sizes. In *GIR '07: Proc. of the 4th ACM Workshop on Geographical Information Retrieval*, pages 77–82, New York, NY, USA, 2007. ACM.
22. R. Purves, P. Clough, and H. Joho. Identifying imprecise regions for geographic information retrieval using the web. In *Proc. of GIS RESEARCH UK 13th Annual Conf.*, pages 313–318, Glasgow, UK, 2005.
23. I. Reinbacher, M. Benkert, M. J. van Kreveld, J. S. B. Mitchell, and A. Wolff. Delineating boundaries for imprecise regions. In G. S. Brodal and S. Leonardi, editors, *ESA*, volume 3669 of *LNCS*, pages 143–154. Springer, 2005.
24. S. Schockaert and M. D. Cock. Neighborhood restrictions in geographic ir. In *SIGIR '07*, pages 167–174, New York, NY, USA, 2007. ACM.
25. S. Schockaert, M. D. Cock, and E. E. Kerre. Automatic acquisition of fuzzy footprints. In R. M. et al., editor, *OTM Workshops*, volume 3762 of *LNCS*, pages 1077–1086. Springer, 2005.
26. J. Schöning, B. Hecht, M. Raubal, A. Krüger, M. Marsh, and M. Rohs. Improving interaction with virtual globes through spatial thinking: Helping users ask "why?". In *Proc. of the Intl. Conf. on Intelligent User Interfaces (IUI)*, 2008.
27. F. Twaroch, C. Jones, and A. Abdelmoty. Acquisition of a vernacular gazetteer from web sources. In *LOCWEB '08: Proc. of the First Intl. Workshop on Location and the Web*, pages 61–64, New York, NY, USA, 2008. ACM.
28. T. J. Vögele, C. Schlieder, and U. Visser. Intuitive modelling of place name regions for spatial information retrieval. In *COSIT*, pages 239–252, 2003.

Acquisition of Vernacular Place Names from Web Sources

Florian A. Twaroch, Christopher B. Jones and Alia I. Abdelmoty

Abstract Vernacular place names are names that are commonly in use to refer to geographical places. For purposes of effective information retrieval, the spatial extent associated with these names should reflect peoples perception of the place, even though this may differ sometimes from the administrative definition of the same place name. Due to their informal nature, vernacular place names are hard to capture, but methods to acquire and define vernacular place names are of great benefit to search engines and all kinds of information services that deal with geographic data. This paper discusses the acquisition of vernacular use of place names from web sources and their representation as surface models derived by kernel density estimators. We show that various web sources containing user created geographic information and business data can be used to represent neighbourhoods in Cardiff, UK. The resulting representations can differ in their spatial extent from administrative definitions. The chapter closes with an outlook on future research questions.

1 Introduction

Place names play a key role in formulating queries for geographical information retrieval on the Web. A typical generic structure for explicit enquiries about geographical information takes the form of triples of *<subject>* *<relation>* *<somewhere>*, in which the subject specifies the thematic aspect of the search, the somewhere is the name of a place and the relation stipulates a spatial relationship to the named place such as in, near or north of. Processing a query in this form usually entails transforming the place name and its qualifying spatial relation to a query footprint that represents a region of space to which the query is assumed to refer. Generation of a query footprint requires that the place name itself is represented by a footprint which is then modified according to the spatial relation. For the purposes

F.A. Twaroch (✉)
Cardiff University, UK
e-mail: f.a.twaroch@cs.cf.ac.uk

I. King, R. Baeza-Yates (eds.), *Weaving Services and People on the World Wide Web*,
DOI 10.1007/978-3-642-00570-1_10,

of most geographical web search facilities, gazetteers provide the main source of knowledge of the footprint associated with place names. Place footprints are frequently just a single point, but they may also be a bounding box (lower left and upper right coordinate of a rectangle) or a polygon. The majority of gazetteers are derived from the content of topographic maps produced by national mapping agencies, and as such they represent a relatively official or administrative view of geography. This causes a problem for geo-information services that use these gazetteers, because people often use vernacular place names that are not recorded in the gazetteers and hence result in failure to process a query that contains such a name.

Vernacular place names are names that are commonly in use to refer to geographical places and the spatial extent associated with them reflects the common perception. In many cases, as indicated above, the name may not correspond to an officially designated region or place. Examples would be the "South of France", the "English Midlands" and the "American Midwest". Many vernacular names, such as these, are vague in spatial extent. Thus there may be locations (possibly corresponding to other named places) that most people would agree are part of the vernacular place and others that are borderline without uniform agreement. Sometimes a vernacular name may be the same as an official name, but the common understanding of its spatial extent may not match exactly with the official interpretation. For public access information systems the objective is to understand what a user is referring to and so it is the vernacular interpretation of a place that is required in order to meet users needs.

Consequently, we are faced with the challenge to acquire knowledge of the intended spatial interpretation of vernacular place names. There have been several earlier descriptions (summarised in the next section) of techniques for acquiring vernacular place name knowledge that are relatively labour intensive. More recently it has become apparent that the Web itself is a valuable source of such knowledge. It has been observed that web pages that include a vernacular place name often include the names of other places that are inside or in the vicinity of the vernacular place [24]. Maps of the extent of vernacular places can be generated from locations of the most frequent co-occurring names. Here we exploit just a few individual web resources that contain numerous geo-referenced place names that relate to business entities and to other private or community services and facilities. One of these sources, Google Maps, enables retrieval of the coordinates of businesses, georeferenced by their address, and other user created entities with vernacular place names. Another source, the Gumtree web site, has been screen scraped to acquire georeferences of advertised services for which a place name has been provided.

In what follows we review briefly previous efforts to acquire knowledge of vernacular places before describing how georeferences of vernacular names are extracted from selected web sites. We then present methods for visualising and modelling the spatial extent of the extracted point clouds that are associated with individual place names. We discuss the relative merits of the different sources that we employ and analyse sources with different bias. The chapter concludes with proposals for future work.

2 Representation of Place

The perception and cognition of place varies among people. Even for the same person a place might be differently perceived given two different contexts. In this section we review literature to represent place formally. Formal representations of place may help to improve the interfaces of information and decision support systems. Our aim is to use automated methods to build representations of vernacular place name geography on a nationwide scale. A method to represent vernacular place names such as "downtown" has been based on human subject tests and interviews (cf. [20]), but turns out to be too labour intensive for the definition of vernacular place names for a whole country.

Automated definition of "city centres" in the UK has been based on census and socioeconomic data. The latter served to derive indices for property, economy, diversity, and visitor attractions. Each index has been modelled as a density surface model and combined with map overlay operations to yield a surface model of "town centeredness" [30]. A comparison of how the derived representation matches peoples cognition of city centres was not provided.

A web based method that considers the cognition of place has been implemented by Evans and Waters [7]. The authors utilized a spray can tool to define "high crime regions" in "Leeds". A spray can allows users to define vague regions through drawing clouds of different point density on a map and label the sprayed contents accordingly. The tool also allows one to define crisp boundary features by spraying hard edges, and to distinguish between locations that are better examples for a certain place than others by spraying more in certain locations of a map than at others. This is in accordance with the typicality concept in cognitive science [25], stating that some locations might be better examples for a certain region than others. However, the regions captured with such a tool are biased by the maps used and Evans and Waters [7] did not report tests on a wide scale.

The neighbourhood project is another example for a web based tool to capture vernacular geography (`http://hood.theory.org`). It is a mashup of Craig's List and Google Maps. People are asked to provide a postcode and a place name. The postcodes are converted into coordinates utilising a postcode database. The resulting point clouds are analysed using a metaball algorithm to define clusters, i.e. neighbourhoods [10]. As this method is not statistically grounded, two problems appear: (1) multiple dense points cause the algorithm to overemphasize the spatial extent of neighbourhoods and (2) the method can not deal well with outliers.

Recently a considerable number of researchers have used search engines to query the Web as a source from which to extract information to model vernacular place names [16, 24, 26]. In these approaches, web pages are parsed automatically for references to places. Some of these places can be found in gazetteer services like the Alexandria Digital Library [14] or the Getty Thesaurus of Geographic Names [13]. Using the gazetteer services, these places can be grounded, i.e. georeferenced with a set of coordinates. Borges et al. [5] carried out experiments to evaluate the presence and incidence of urban addresses in web pages to discover geographic locations. A set of web pages is collected using e.g. a web crawler. In a geoparsing step, potential geographic entities are identified such as postcodes, telephone numbers, and other address information, and converted into structured addresses to feed a geocoding process, i.e. looking the address up in a gazetteer. The authors tested 4 million pages and found that, in 15% of the web pages, addresses could be found. Furthermore, they concluded that postal codes were superior over other address information as a geocoding resource.

Fuzzy footprints have been defined utilizing trigger phrases and other web queries to search for places that lie within a region under consideration, regions that include the region under investigation, and regions that are neighbouring the investigated region [27]. The derived place names have been grounded with the Alexandria Digital Library gazetteer. The study was carried out on political regions in order to validate the achieved results. Schockaert and Cock state in a later paper [26] that the perception of administrative boundaries often deviates from the official definition.

Other work by Schockaert et al. [28] addresses the detection of place names for the region of "Cardiff, UK". The authors use a focused crawler to extract relevant web pages, similar to Borges et al. [5], and interpret addresses found on web pages. Heuristics based on rules and document frequencies serve to define filters. With the filtered list of place names spatial relationships are extracted, and their consistency is tested with further queries to the Web and fuzzy spatial reasoning. Pasley, Clough, and Sanderson [23] investigate the definition of imprecise regions of different sizes using web queries and a geo-tagging algorithm. The study reveals that regions as big as several counties have to be treated differently from vernacular place names in city environments, as the source of error in geo-tagging changes with the scale and the used resources. Whether or not vague phenomena can be described at all by a crisp boundary polygon is currently an open question [7]. A number of qualitative representation methods have been proposed in recent literature [4, 17, 31].

A simple way to describe a region utilizing a set of points, labelled as belonging to a specific region has been summarized by [9]. Alani et al. [1] and Arampatzis et al. [2] describe methods based on Voronoi diagrams and Delaunay triangulations to determine approximate boundaries of regions represented by sets of points.

A representation of a vernacular place should maintain the uncertainty of the definition. Different people have different beliefs about how to define the extent of a certain place. Methods based on fuzzy regions [26, 27] consider that fact in providing models of spatial regions carrying a varying degree of membership.

Our work is similar to previous methods found in the literature [16, 24]. The delineation of the spatial extent of vernacular place names is based on kernel density estimation methods. Thresholds of these models at different levels yield footprints of certain confidence values, expressing degrees of familiarity with the modelled region. See also Chapt. 9 of this volume on the determination of geographic representations for arbitrary concepts at query time.

3 Extracting Vernacular Knowledge from Web Sources

One measure of usability of current web systems is in the extent to which users can express queries using place names that reflect vernacular geography, and then gain access to the relevant resources effectively and efficiently. Progress towards this goal may be achieved by complementing the traditional gazetteer services with gazetteers of vernacular place names, populated from web resources.

Multiple sources of vernacular place names are emerging on the Web. In this paper, we focus on social web applications as a potentially rich source for collating this information. Web sites such as Flickr and Geograph are facilitating the geotagging of personal resources, allowing people to annotate photo collections. Other sites such as Gumtree allow local sourcing of products and services in an informal way; Wikipedia is a user maintained web-based encyclopaedia with extensive geographic coverage [22]; Placeopedia is a project to geocode Wikipedia articles. In summary, a plethora of volunteered geographic information exists on the Web and the amount of available data is growing every day [11].

Place vocabularies used on volunteered geographic sites include place names and relationships to place names. For this study, we focus mainly on studying absolute references to places and their location in web resources, in that the vernacular names are accompanied by an explicit geographic reference such as a postcode. This is in contrast to earlier work, such as that of Purves et al. [24] or Jones et al. [16], in which the extent of vernacular regions is found indirectly in terms of the georeferences of places that are assumed to lie inside the vernacular place. The current approach makes the process of acquiring vernacular names data much simpler and eliminates errors introduced during the extraction (and grounding) of geo-references.

Another category of web systems offering structured place information are yellow pages and other business directories. Specific examples from both types of resources are used here to illustrate the study.

We have queried these latter sites using a web mining method (explained in Sect. 3.1), applying two different strategies to mine data for the representation of vernacular regions. Firstly, we utilize businesses addresses to delineate the spatial extent of vernacular regions (Sect. 3.2). Then we query sources of user created geographic information, such as social web pages and community directories, to gain access to user generated content (Sect. 3.3). For illustration purposes, the paper focuses on regions within the broader geographic region of "Cardiff, UK". The authors are familiar with the study area and can identify gross errors in the retrieved vernacular data.

3.1 Mining the Web

Search engines are a good source of data since their aim is to index any web page that might be of interest to some audience. Search engines rely on software agents to discover pages automatically by following links in known pages. They do so by processing an initial seed list of Uniform Resource Identifiers (URIs) and crawling the URIs recursively from there. Pages discovered are stored in an index which can be searched using a user interface. The search engines generally also expose search services in developer friendly ways that allow the data to be collected (e.g. through an Application Programming Interface, or API).

A large part of the Web is not indexed and search engines themselves introduce biases of unknown nature. Secret ranking algorithms rate and interpret the content of web pages. The Web which exists but is not indexed by search engines, can be termed the Hidden Web [15]. Often it contains databases that can be accessed via web pages. A technique to collect data from this set of pages is called web scraping. Web scraping can be utilized whenever no public API is available. A web scraping program issues automatically created URIs to query the database behind web pages. The program can automate tasks such as filling in forms. A crawler cannot find such pages as it always seeks for links but does not interact with a web page. For example to query an imaginary web page the following URI might be used `http://www.example.com?q=cardiff\&page=3`. In this hypothetical case the third page about "Cardiff" would be returned. Since this would be returned in a format designed to be rendered by a browser, further processing would then be needed to extract information as required. This would normally use pattern matching or Natural Language Processing (NLP). It can be seen that this requires knowledge about the structure of the URI and the markup format of the web pages. Whenever the provider of the site changes structure or contents, the scraping tool needs to be adapted.

Data sets mined with web scraping tools can be considerably different from data sets retrieved via the exposed query APIs. APIs are often restricted in their content and do not allow to extract all the relevant information [19]. Therefore a web scraping tool has been implemented that creates URIs to query Google Maps. The required parameters are documented on Wiki pages for the Google Maps API [18]. The most important parameters are listed below:

- *q*: a query string
- *near*: a place name that the returned point will be related to
- *start*: an integer. The results returned will be those found after ignoring this many results.
- *num*: return at most this number of matches
- *mrt*: a parameter that speficies the search type
  - *mrt=loc*: specifies a location search.
  - *mrt=yp*: searches for businesses, yp stands for yellow pages.
  - *mrt=kmlkmz*: data indexed as user contributed contents

Queries were submitted with URIs containing "city centre" or "Roath" (a community in "Cardiff") in the q term and "Cardiff" in the near term. Spaces and special characters have to be escaped in the URIs. The number of matches is by default set to ten (num=10). In order to receive the next 10 results, a new query had to be formulated with the start value incremented by 10. We generated queries until the start value reached 200. One series of queries issued collected just business data (e.g. `http://maps.google.co.uk/?q=city%20centre\&near=cardiff\&mrt=yp`) another series just user contributed contents (e.g. `http://maps.google.co.uk/?q=city%20centre\&near=cardiff\&mrt=kmlkmz`). Using the various parameters described, a set of web pages was collected. Placenames and coordinates were retrieved from the pages using natural language processing techniques.

3.2 Geo-References from Business Directories

Google Maps offers a free service called Local Business Center where businesses can register their location with some descriptive contents and are in turn indexed by Googles search engine, showing up on Googles map service. In the spirit of [32] we assumed that place names can occur as part of business names, such as those registered with Google. We sent queries of place names found in Gumtree to Googles map search engine (see Sect. 3.1) and mined the results retrieved through these queries.

The postcode of each business can be looked up in a postcode database and facilitates geocoding. Each business can then be associated with coordinates and visualized on a map (Fig. 1). This step was not necessary as the coordinates for each business could be directly found in the mined web pages. Figure 1 illustrates the results mined for the administrative area "Splott", a ward and community in "Cardiff". The mined data points are scattered over more areas than just the one labelled as "Splott". The reason for that is partly due to the methodology used.

Businesses such as real estate agents that are actually not located in the ward "Splott", but refer to it, are currently not filtered out. The scattered data mined through Google business maps suggests that businesses can carry place names, as part of the business name, relating to places that are far away from the location of the business. Future versions of the present mining algorithm will have to consider spatial relationships mentioned on business web pages and consider if the mined places are located near, around, etc. the region of interest.

3.3 Geo-References from a Social Website

The social web site Gumtree serves a user-community to trade items and properties as well as offer a virtual place to meet and arrange meetings in real space. A free ad can be posted on the web site. Users can associate the ad with a postcode which can then be published by Gumtree using a Google map service to display the location of the ad. Place name data on this site have been mined to find vernacular regions in the "city of Cardiff" with the aim of finding clusters of points labelled with place names. Figure 2 shows an example of a map of a point cluster located in the ward "Splott" in "Cardiff".

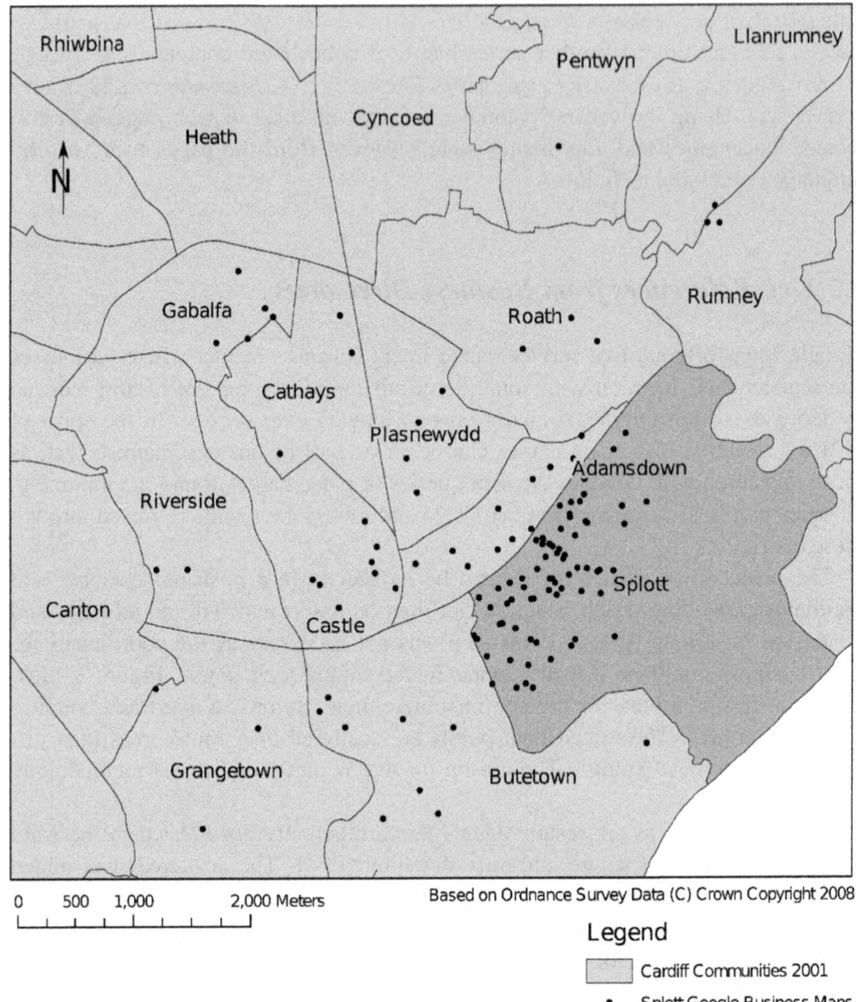

Fig. 1 Points mined from Googles Business Directories associated with "Splott" (a ward and community in "Cardiff")

The density of the mined data points is dependent on the availability of current ads related to specific regions. In some regions, only a few labelled points could be mined from Gumtree. Hence, mining over a longer period of time is needed to increase the density of the data collected.

The different symbols in Fig. 2 represent data from two different periods of time associated with the label "Splott". Each point/triangle represents an ad in Gumtree. Figure 2 shows that the majority of mined data points lie within or near "Splott", suggesting that data mined through the social web site are more suitable for direct geocoding than data coded through business addresses (Sect. 3.2).

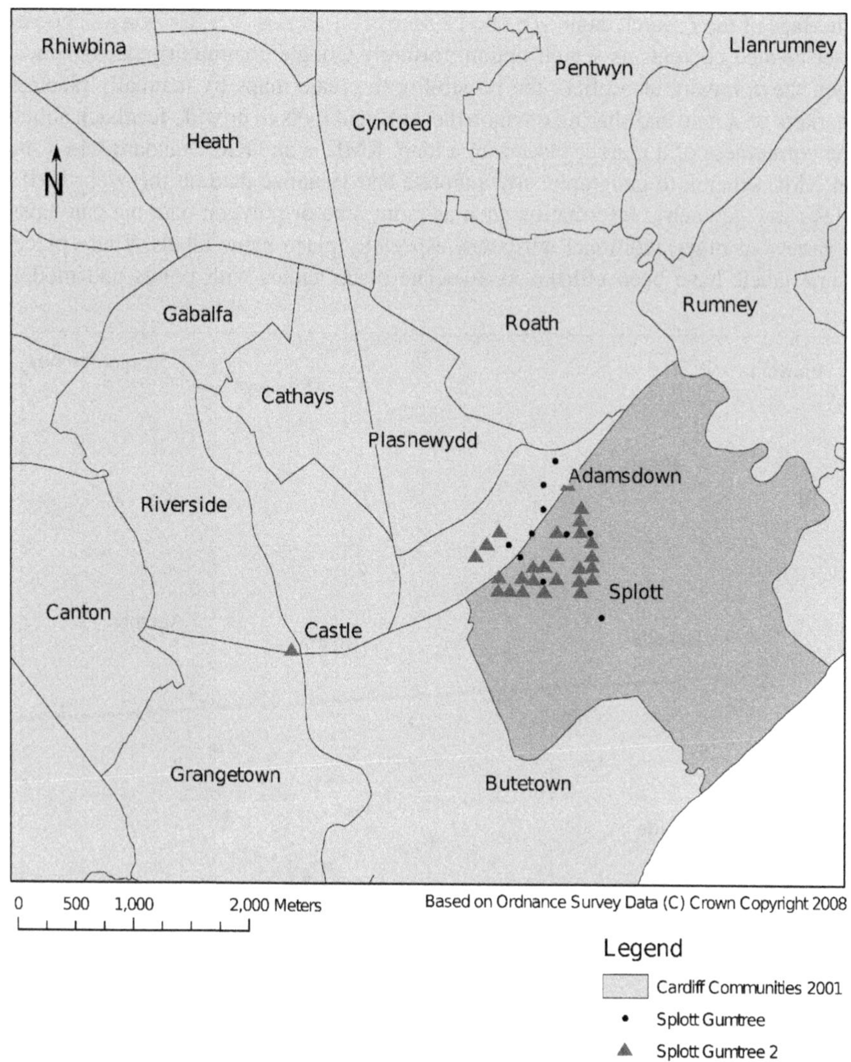

Fig. 2 Points mined at two different timepoints from Gumtree associated with "Splott"

3.4 Geo-References from Google User Created Geographic Information Sources

In order to increase the point density for regions, other sources of volunteered geographic information [11] have to be queried. This would require writing a number of web scraping tools for each of the sources. Instead, we utilized a single web scraping tool via Googles search engine. Recently, Google indexed a number of user created geographic information sources e.g. KML files of GPS tracks of hiking and cycling tours, geotagged photos, etc. and made them available through the web interface of their search engine (`http://maps.google.co.uk/maps` choose user created contents as search option, formerly Google community maps). Since then the company also offers the possibility to create maps by manually placing markers on a map and sharing them on the web, and tools to provide feedback about the correctness of a marker placed on a map. KML is an OGC Standard based on an XML schema to geographically annotate and visualize data on the Web. KML files carry geometric information such as point, line or polygon data but can have a variety of other additional attributes, especially place name labels. These place name labels have been utilized to associate place names with points and model

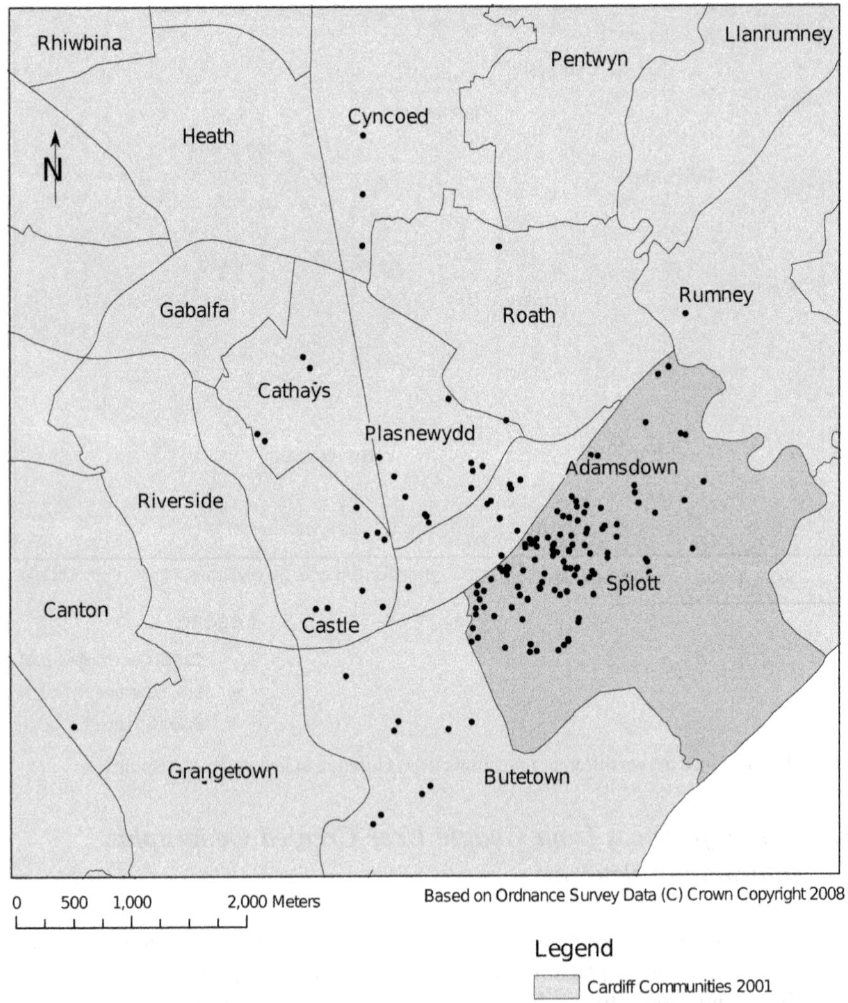

Fig. 3 Data points for the ward "Splott" mined from different sources that were indexed by Google as user created contents

the regions of "Cardiff". A number of items found through this interface actually referred to business related items again.

Figure 3 shows that the majority of points mined from data sources that Google describes as user created content coincide with the region of interest. Mining more of these sources, i.e. Google user created contents, introduces more noise. A number of points, similar to the result for data points mined from business directories, are found to lie outside and far away from the actual region. Future work will have to address the development of quality measures to judge the accuracy of different Google user created web sources.

4 Determination of the Spatial Extent of Vernacular Place Names

The described mining methods facilitate retrieval of a huge amount of point data for place names. We can then apply methods from spatial statistics, specifically kernel density estimation [29], to represent the spatial extent of place names. In the following two subsections, we briefly describe how outliers that can skew the data have been identified and introduce the kernel density estimation method.

4.1 Outlier Identification

We constrained the mined point data to a certain geographic region and can therefore eliminate coordinates that are not located within the boundary polygon of the superior region of the place names under investigation, i.e. the "city of Cardiff". Multiple postings of a place name by a single person can falsify the result by skewing the data to a single point.

We apply simple heuristics to get rid of multiple postings: Markers placed by hand or positioned by GPS differ from the multiple posting data in that they exceed a certain measurement error. We can therefore delete points within an epsilon region of the measurement error and hence remove duplicate data mined from Google before applying the kernel density estimation.

4.2 Kernel Density Estimation

Kernel density estimation has been applied in the literature [16, 30] to represent vernacular place name geography. The principle of KDE is based on determining a weighted average of data points within a moving window centred on a grid of points p. KDE turns a vector into a field representation. Different kernel functions can be applied, but it has been previously found [21] that the choice of the kernel function is less important than the choice of the bandwidth parameter. This parameter controls the influence of the kernel functions on the summed local intensity values. As we investigate regions within a city environment, we set the parameter to 300 m (cf. Thurstain-Goodwin and Unwin [30]). We are aware that at this point we will have to improve our method by investigating adaptive methods such as those proposed by Brunsdon [6], that allow automatic defining and adapting of the bandwidth of the kernel based on the underlying data. The kernel function used in this chapter is a Gaussian kernel.

4.3 Current Results

In our approach we use coordinates derived from geotags. Three different sources are available and thus each region of "Cardiff" can be modelled three times using the data points from the three different sources. We compare the different results by visual inspection and evaluate them using local expert knowledge. Based on this evaluation, three types of place names could be classified: (1) place names whose commonly perceived extent coincides with the administrative definition of the same name, (2) place names whose extent does not coincide with the correspondingly named administrative definition and (3) place names that exist in peoples minds but not in the administrative geography.

4.3.1 Administrative Places Names

Part of our experimental work was to find out if peoples description of certain places coincides with administrative definitions. For a number of wards we found that data points mined and models derived approximate the spatial extent of the investigated region as defined by the available administrative boundary datasets.

Figure 4 shows an example where the derived region coincides with the administrative geography. Almost all points derived from Google user created contents are within the boundary of the administrative definition, suggesting that peoples use of the place name coincides with its administrative definition. The name "Plasnewydd" does not seem very popular as neither of the other data sources, i.e. Gumtree and Google business queries, yield enough data points to derive further representations.

4.3.2 Semi-Vernacular Place Names

Peoples perception of the spatial extent of a place can significantly deviate from the administrative definition. When mining data from the three different sources for the region "Roath", which neighbours "Plasnewydd" in the administrative geography, we found that the majority of points were actually not located in the community labelled as "Roath" (Fig. 5). Data from Gumtree even suggests that the former place "Plasnewydd" is overridden by the definition of "Roath" in peoples mind. Data points from Gumtree that should be labelled as "Plasnewydd" were consistently labelled as "Roath".

A possible explanation for this result is that the region "Roath" is a popular area where students and families with children are living. A number of web documents that promote real estate would therefore refer more often to "Roath" than to less popular adjacent areas. Future research will uncover such effects by mining and analysing further data from the web sources, such as the authors identity, the intention of the description, the age of the data source, and others.

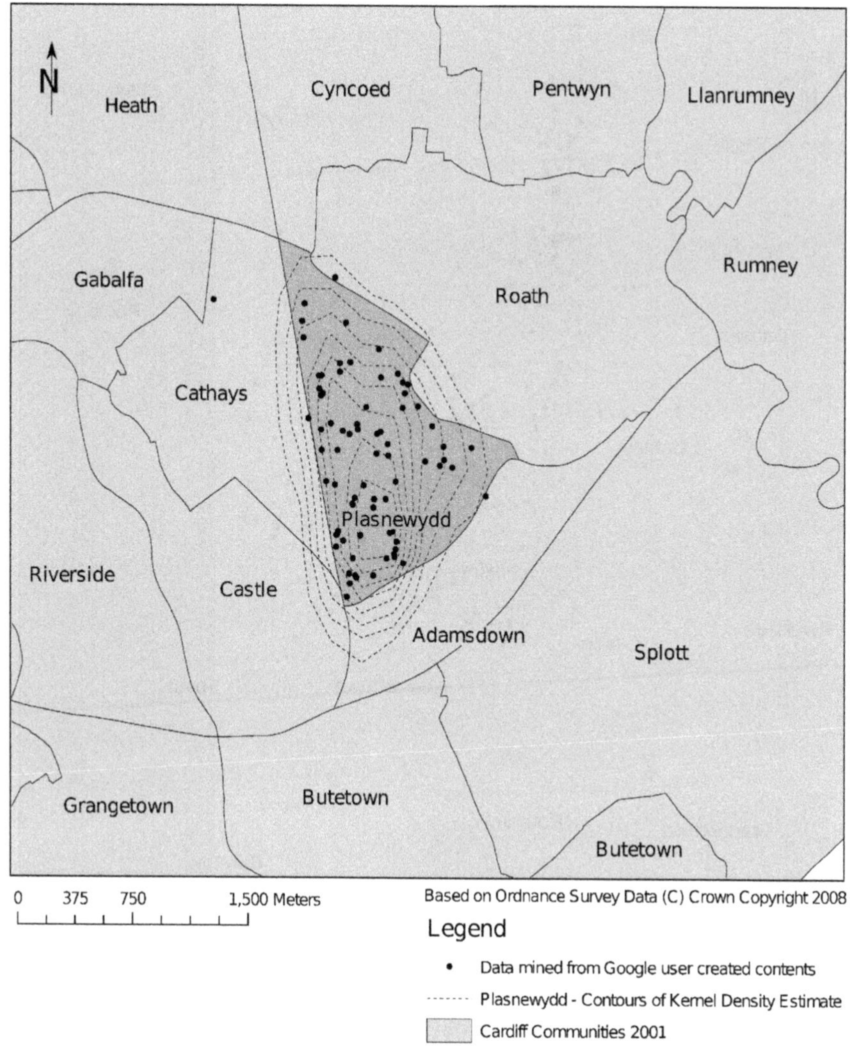

Fig. 4 Vernacular and administrative definition coincide ("Plasnewydd" ward in "Cardiff")

4.3.3 Vernacular Place Names

Some place names like city centre do not exist in administrative geography. A new development area in "Cardiff" is called "Cardiff Bay", and its spatial extent has not been defined in administrative boundary data sets. We used the three different data sources to create a model of "Cardiff Bay" (Fig. 6).

According to the results obtained, "Cardiff Bay" is a region that overlaps with the areas that have been administratively labelled as "Grangetown" and "Butetown". The dashed lines in Fig. 6 represent three different kernel density estimations. The dashed contours are the one that result from points mined from Gumtree, while

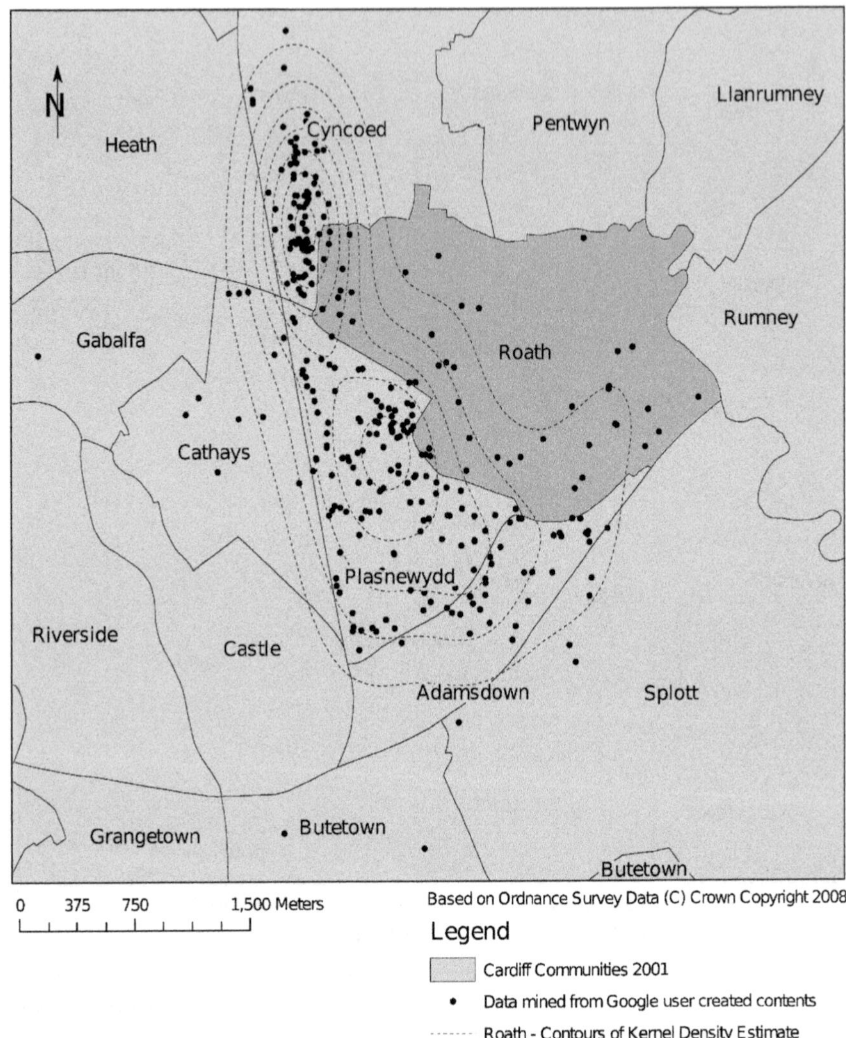

Fig. 5 Vernacular and administrative definition do not coincide

the solid contour lines are derived from points mined from Googles user created contents. The dotted contour lines stretch all over the area and are the result of delineating "Cardiff Bay" using the postcodes of businesses that carry "Cardiff Bay" in their business name.

With the latter representation based on business addresses, we find the most general definition of the spatial extent of "Cardiff Bay". The regions investigated during this study and represented by business data differed considerably in size compared to regions derived solely from community driven data (Gumtree, Google user created contents). Note, however, that the core of all three data sources (Gumtree, Google user created contents, and business addresses) describe an area of similar spatial extent.

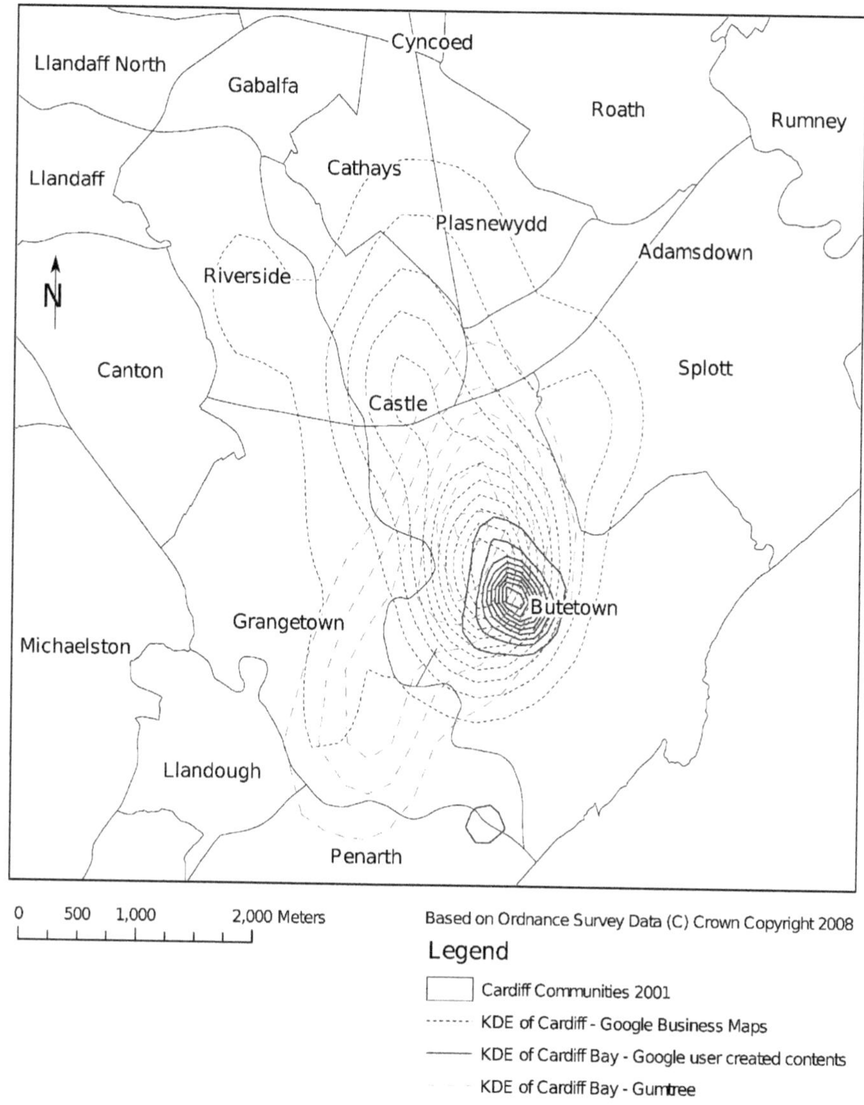

Fig. 6 Three different kernel density estimates for an area known as "Cardiff Bay". See text for explanation of line symbols

Place names that exist in common usage but not in administrative geography, like the case of "Cardiff Bay", leave a number of open questions. Currently, we lack methods to validate the acquired results. Comparing models derived from different data sources is a first important step towards a representation of vernacular regions.

4.3.4 Popular Locations

A problem not discussed so far is the popularity of regions. Popular locations can skew the definition of a region towards single points (as described in Sect. 4.1) or to a number of densely located points. An example is given in the figure below for the "St. Fagans" region in "Cardiff", which is known for its museum. Most data points mined from the web cluster around the museum, while the rest of the region shows a very sparse point distribution. This can cause spurious peaks in the resulting kernel density estimation, as illustrated in Fig. 7. Jones, Purves et al. [16] observed the same effect when mining data from the web for the "Highlands", a region in "Scotland, UK".

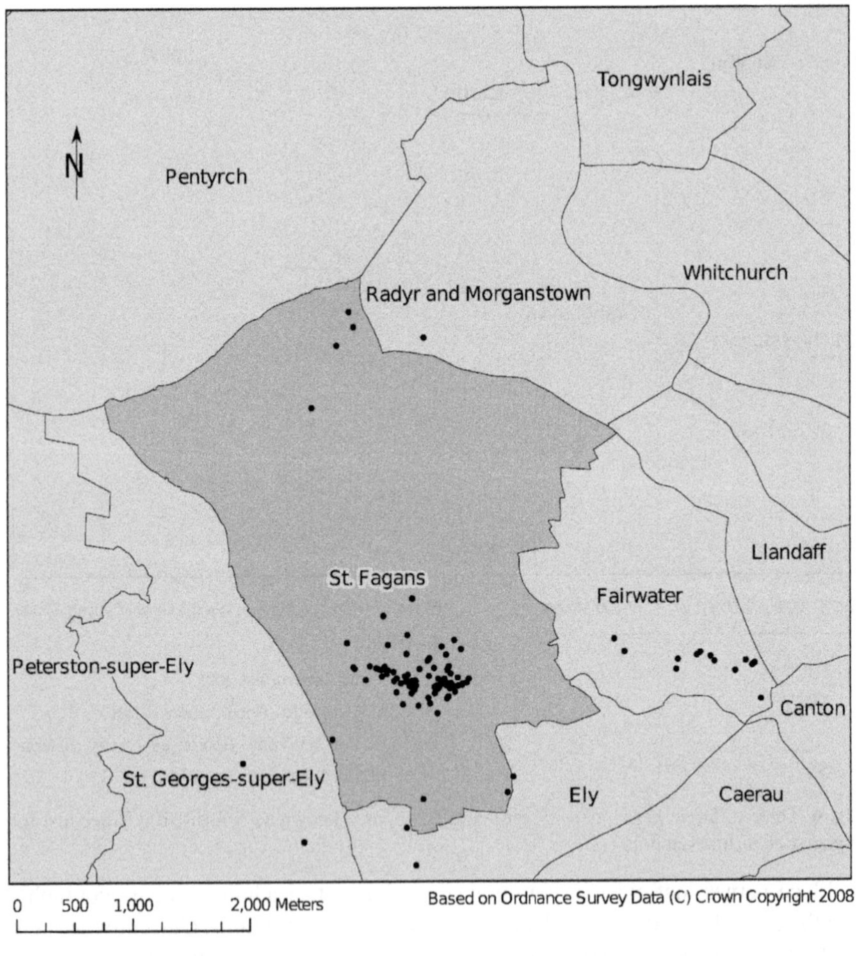

Fig. 7 Points clustering at a popular region

To overcome this problem, another approach must be taken to calculate the kernel density estimates. Brunsdon [6] suggests an adaptive kernel bandwidth that varies with the density of the point data. While this strategy usually smooths the kernel density surface too much, it seems to be a viable method to model popular regions with only sparse point data in the surroundings. Criteria are needed to decide when an adaptive kernel density estimation is to be favoured vs. a non parametric kernel method. Future research will address this problem.

4.3.5 Evaluation of the Results

In the literature, administrative regions have been used to evaluate the mined data set or to train methods to detect geographic regions [12, 27]. This approach is not suitable for vernacular regions, as no authority exists that defines such a region. Especially in the UK, the use of administrative definitions is open to question as a number of different definitions exist and traditionally these definitions change over time [3, 8]. For example, ward definitions can differ from community definitions with the same name. In "Cardiff", the ward "Cathays" is split into two communities called "Cathays" and "Castle", and depending on the context, people will sometimes use the community name and sometimes the ward name. Another example is that the community "Roath" has the same spatial extent as the ward "Penylan". The evaluation of our method leaves a number of unsolved open research questions.

5 Conclusions and Future Work

The proposed method of mining user created geographic information from the Web enables the representation of the spatial extent of vernacular place names. The spatial extent of a number of places in our study region have coincided with the same named administrative boundaries. However, we have shown that this is not the case for all neighbourhoods in "Cardiff". A number of resulting representations have differed significantly from the equivalently named administrative geography.

Three different web sources have been employed to model the regions: Gumtree, business addresses, and a variety of user created geographic information sources exposed through Googles (map) search engine. A simple geocoding procedure has been utilized, extracting coordinates from web pages directly by pattern matching.

All three sources have contributed to approximating the spatial extent of vernacular place names. Representations based on user created geographic information have tended to scatter less in space than representations derived from business addresses. For all of the sources, no filtering step has been carried out. The core of the representations of the three different sources has been similar for a number of investigated regions. For some regions we could not mine enough data points from a single source.

A priority for future work is the validation of the results. Here we want to address the combination of data from different (web) sources and investigate the influence of scale. This includes experiments with different parameters for the kernel density models like determining the optimal bandwidth or a robust method to threshold the representations. We plan to carry out a web questionnaire on a large scale to gain access to an independent data source and training data for our representation method. The identification of vernacular place names within a query is a problem in itself that has not been addressed in the present paper. It requires identifying a term as being a place and a method to measure the degree of vernacularity. Not all place names can be described by polygons or fields: the Tour de France is an event with a spatial extent that changes every year. At the same time, it is the name of a place people would look for in a search engine query. The temporal aspect of a place will have to be considered in future representations of vernacular place names.

We are especially interested in cognitive models for the representation of vernacular regions. The complexity of the problem and the variety of factors that influence human cognition of place constitute a significant challenge to future work. The results can be expected to contribute to the improvement of geographic information retrieval systems and a better understanding of peoples definition of place.

Acknowledgments We would like to thank Ordnance Survey for funding our research on representation of place for geographic information retrieval. This work has also been partly funded by the EC FP6-IST 045335 TRIPOD project.

References

1. Alani, H., Jones, C.B., Tudhope, D.: Voronoi-based region approximation for geographical information retrieval with gazetteers. International Journal of Geographic Information Systems **15**, 287–306 (2001)
2. Arampatzis, A., van Kreveld, M., Reinbacher, I., Jones, C.B., Vaid, S., Clough, P., Joho, H., Sanderson, M.: Web based delineation of imprecise regions. Computers, Environment and Urban Systems **30**(4), 436–459 (2006)
3. Association of British Counties: The problem of 'county confusion' – and how to resolve it. online – retrieved 17.09.2008 (2007). URL `http://www.abcounties.co.uk/counties/confusion.htm`
4. Bennett, B.: Application of supervaluation semantics to vaguely defined spatial concepts. In: COSIT'01, *Lecture Notes in Computer Science*, vol. 2205, pp. 108–123 (2001)
5. Borges, K., Laender, A.H.F., Medeiros, C., Davies Jr., C.A.: Discovering geographic locations in web pages using urban addresses. In: GIR, pp. 31–36. ACM, Lisbon, Portugal (2007)
6. Brunsdon, C.: Estimating probability surfaces for geographical point data: An adaptive kernel algorithm. Computers & Geosciences **21**(7), 877–894 (1995). DOI: http://dx.doi.org/10.1016/0098-3004(95)00020-9
7. Evans, A.J., Waters, T.: Mapping vernacular geography: Web-based GIS tools for capturing 'fuzzy' or 'vague' entities. International Journal of Technology, Policy and Management **7**(2), 134–150 (2007)
8. Fairlie, J.: Administrative regions in Great Britain. The American Political Science Review **31**(5), 937–941 (1937)
9. Galton, A., Duckham, M.: What is the region occupied by a set of points? In: 4th International Conference, GIScience 2006, *Lecture Notes in Computer Science*, vol. 4197, pp. 81–98 (2006)
10. Geiss, R.: Metaballs. online, retrieved 17.09.2008 (2000). URL `http://www.geisswerks.com/ryan/BLOBS/blobs.html`

11. Goodchild, M.: Citizens as sensors: The world of volunteered geography. GeoJournal **69**(4), 211–221 (2007)
12. Grothe, C., Schaab, J.: An evaluation of kernel density estimation and support vector machines for automated generation of footprints for imprecise regions from geotags. In: International Workshop of Computational Models of Place (PLACE'08). Park City, Utah, USA (2008)
13. Harpring, P.: Proper words in proper places: The thesaurus of geographical names. MDA Information 2/3. Museum Documentation Association (1997)
14. Hill, L., Frew, J., Zheng, Q.: Geographic names. The implementation of a gazetteer in a georeferenced digital library. Digital Library (1999). URL `www.dlib.org/dlib/january99/hill/01hill.html`
15. Ipeirotis, P., Jain, P., Gravano, L.: To search or to crawl? Towards a query optimizer for text-centric tasks. In: SIGMOD '06: ACM International Conference on Management of Data, pp. 265–276. ACM Press, New York, NY, USA (2006)
16. Jones, C.B., Purves, R.S., Clough, P.D., Joho, H.: Modelling vague places with knowledge from the Web. International Journal of Geographic Information Systems **22**(10), 1045–1065 (2008)
17. Kulik, L.: A geometric theory of vague boundaries based on supervaluation. In: D.R. Montello (ed.) Spatial Information Theory. Foundations of Geographic Information Science : International Conference, COSIT 2001 Morro Bay, CA, USA, September 19-23, *Lecture Notes in Computer Science*, vol. 2205, pp. 44–59 (2001)
18. Mapki: Google map parameters. online - retrieved 17.09.2008 (2008). URL `http://mapli.com/wiki/Google_Map_Parameters`
19. McCown, F., Nelson, M.L.: Agreeing to disagree: Search engines and their public interfaces. In: 7th ACM/IEEE-CS joint conference on Digital Libraries, pp. 309–318. ACM New York, Vancouver (2007)
20. Montello, D.R., Goodchild, M.F., Gottsegen, J., Fohl, P.: Where's downtown?: Behavioral methods for determining referents of vague spatial queries. Spatial Cognition and Computation **3**, 185–204 (2003)
21. O'Sullivan, D., Unwin, D.: Geographic Information Analysis. Wiley Hoboken, NJ (2002)
22. Overell, S.E., Rüger, S.: Geographic co-occurence as a tool for GIR. In: 4th ACM Workshop on Geographical Information Retrieval – GIR'07 (2007)
23. Pasley, R., Clough, P., Sanderson, M.: Geo-tagging for imprecise regions of different sizes. In: Proceedings of Workshop on Geographic Information Retrieval GIR'07 (2007)
24. Purves, R., Clough, P., Joho, H.: Identifying imprecise regions for geographic information retrieval using the web. In: GIS Research UK 13th Annual Conference, pp. 313–318 (2005)
25. Rosch, E.: Cognition and categorization, chap. Principles of Categorization, pp. 27–48. Lawrence Erlbaum Publishers Hillsdale, NJ (1978)
26. Schockaert, S., Cock, M.D.: Neighborhood restrictions in geographic IR. In: SIGIR '07: Proceedings of the 30th annual international ACM SIGIR conference on Research and development in information retrieval, pp. 167–174. ACM Press, New York, NY, USA (2007). DOI: http://doi.acm.org/10.1145/1277741.1277772
27. Schockaert, S., Cock, M.D., Kerre, E.E.: Automatic acquisition of fuzzy footprints. In: On the Move to Meaningful Internet Systems 2005: OTM 2005 Workshops, OTM Confederated International Workshops and Posters (SeBGIS 2005), *LNCS*, vol. 3762, pp. 1077–1086 (2005)
28. Schockaert, S., Smart, P.D., Abdelmoty, A.I., Jones, C.B.: Mining topological relations from the Web. In: DEXA Workshops 2008, pp. 652–656. Los Alamitos, CA, USA (2008). DOI: http://doi.ieeecomputersociety.org/10.1109/DEXA.2008.15
29. Silverman, B.: Density Estimation: For Statistics and Data Analysis. Chapman and Hall, London (1986)
30. Thurstain-Goodwin, M., Unwin, D.: Defining and delineating the central areas of towns for statistical monitoring using continuous surface representations. Transactions in GIS **4**(4), 305–317 (2000)

31. Vögele, T., Schlieder, C., Visser, U.: Intuitive modelling of place name regions for spatial information retrieval. In: W. Kuhn, M.F. Worboys, S. Timpf (eds.) Spatial information theory: foundations of geographic information science International Conference, COSIT 2003, Kartause Ittingen, Switzerland, Sept. 24-28, *Lecture Notes in Computer Science*, vol. 2825, pp. 239–252. Springer Verlag, Berlin (2003)
32. Zelinsky, W.: North America's vernacular regions. Annals of the Association of American Geographers **70**(1), 1–16 (1980)

Part II
Social Computing

Social Web and Knowledge Management

Peter Dolog, Markus Krötzsch, Sebastian Schaffert and Denny Vrandečić

Abstract Knowledge Management is the study and practice of representing, communicating, organizing, and applying knowledge in organizations. Moreover, being used by organizations, it is inherently social. The Web, as a medium, enables new forms of communications and interactions and requires new ways to represent knowledge assets. It is therefore obvious that the Web will influence and change Knowledge Management, but it is very unclear what the impact of these changes will be. This chapter raises questions and discusses visions in the area that connects the Social Web and Knowledge Management – an area of research that is only just emerging. The World Wide Web conference 2008 in Beijing hosted a workshop on that question, bringing together researchers and practitioners to gain first insights toward answering questions of that area.

1 Introduction

The social web, the most interesting part of the Web 2.0, aims at bringing people together and facilitating richer interaction among them. It is characterized by a strong focus on communities where people share experiences, information and knowledge, meet and discuss, or do business together.

Knowledge management systems focus on knowledge and experience sharing. They enhance organizational capabilities by externalizing knowledge of its employees and combine them in novel forms. Therefore, there is a common interest in social structures as well as social computing in both fields. The social web can be the common underlying platform for novel and web-based knowledge management systems. It breaks up rigid processes and enables much richer interaction possibilities and creativity. As a research question, it requires experts in social web technologies, semantic systems, and knowledge management, leading to a study of

---

P. Dolog (✉)
Aalborg University, Computer Science Department, Selma Lagerlöfs Vej 300 DK-9220 Aalborg, Denmark
e-mail: dolog@cs.aau.dk

I. King, R. Baeza-Yates (eds.), *Weaving Services and People on the World Wide Web*, DOI 10.1007/978-3-642-00570-1_11, © Springer-Verlag Berlin Heidelberg 2009

synergies between social computing, social web, semantic systems, and knowledge management.

This chapter raises questions and discusses visions in the area that connects the Social Web and Knowledge Management (SWKM2008) – an area of research that is only just emerging. The World Wide Web conference 2008 in Beijing hosted a workshop on that question, bringing together researchers and practitioners to gain first insights toward answering questions of that area.

The chapter is structured as follows. Section 2 raises questions on direct applicability of social web tools in enterprise knowledge management and puts in contrast the advantage the social web tools have on the web as opposed to the closer enterprise context. Section 3 discusses the questions in the context of the SWKM2008 workshop papers. Section 4 identifies fallacy of assumptions recent knowledge management 2.0 attempts have. Section 5 drafts a technical research agenda for the area of social web and knowledge management gained from analysis performed in two large companies. Section 6 puts the drafted research agenda into the context of two ongoing EU research projects. Finally, Section 7 summarizes the chapter.

2 The Advantage of the Web

Recent years saw the first time that commonly available web-based systems advanced in functionality and ease of use beyond internal enterprise knowledge management solutions. The free encyclopedia Wikipedia[1] or social networking sites like Facebook[2] are often cited as examples for successful web-based systems that aggregate and organize huge amounts of knowledge, whereas at the same time many intranet solutions fail to achieve a comparable success. Inspired by their public counterparts, companies both huge and small set up similar systems, just to find, more often than not, that they did not meet the high expectations put into them.

Furthermore, the mere existence of better solutions on the web will make even good systems appear much worse than they are. Users will criticize a *Companypedia* as a cheap copy that no one wants to edit. They will compare access and edit counts with the few well known and successful Web 2.0 sites they know – which is an unfair comparison. Most Web 2.0 sites are failures. People hardly remember pages like Nupedia, BBC's h2g2, or other projects that aimed at creating a free web-based encyclopedia. There are numerous Web 2.0 sites that aimed at creating communities or photo-sharing sites, but ultimately failed. And even the sites that are regarded as major success stories often were so by accident: Wikipedia was started as a side project to help evolve the failing Nupedia project, flickr was a part of a massive multiplayer online game that became far more successful than the game itself.

Companies can not exercise the same freedom as the Web. No company can afford to start a few hundred Web 2.0 inspired internal sites, knowing that only 1%

---

[1] http://www.wikipedia.org

[2] http://www.facebook.com

of them will survive the test of time. Internal knowledge management projects can hardly be repurposed in the same way that flickr changed. Also, whereas the Web is big enough to let systems where far less than 2% of the users do almost all the work voluntarily, companies are rarely big enough to achieve reasonably sized volunteer communities.

How can it be that I can find information on my company's health care plan easier with Google than with our internal enterprise search application? How is it that every SourceForge open source project has a mailing list archive that is easier accessible than the one used for our own department mailing list (if any)? How comes that Wikipedia knows more about my competitors than my own document repository? And maybe Wikipedia has even more succinct information about my own company than it is available to the company itself? For many of these question we even know (or think to know) the answer, but a solution to the given problem is still often missing.

The Web is the showcase of the most creative minds in the world. The best AJAX hackers and CSS gurus mingle in order to create numerous astonishing sites and offer them to a market that will quickly select the best among these. Not many companies can create viable competitors for them. Computing is more and more becoming a utility [3], and services will become outsourced. But many companies will refuse to regard Knowledge Management solutions as utilities that can be outsourced to third parties, thus putting their most valuable assets in the hands of external entities.

We expect the following few years to provide interesting challenges to Knowledge Management as it is today.

3 The Direction of the Workshop

We were surprised by the submissions for the SWKM 2008 workshop [4]. Knowledge Management is traditionally defined as managing the knowledge within an organization. But all the accepted papers dealt with data and questions on the open web: for example, both Boulain et al. [2] and Ronzano et al. [8] used data from Wikipedia in their research. Yeung et al. used del.icio.us in order to evaluate their approach towards folksonomy-based profile generation [1], and Hong and Shen based their work on data acquired from Facebook [7]. The workshop naturally would hold a view biased towards the Web, since it was a workshop at the World Wide Web conference – but nevertheless it was surprising that none of the papers dealt with classical, intranet Knowledge Management.

Besides the bias, this may have several reasons:

- Data is much easier available on the Web. Systems like Wikipedia, flickr, del.icio.us offer numerous APIs and download possibilities to gather the data from their sites. Intranet solutions rarely offer such an easy access to their data.
- Legal issues, privacy considerations or other pragmatic aspects may often restrict the usage of data for mining and classification tasks within enterprises.

- Due to the fear of giving too much information to competitors, companies may prefer not to disclose data to external parties if they are not sure what the data could mean.
- Analyzing open online communities is often more rewarding than analyzing company networks. Such work will stir interest in the communities themselves, thus leading to a heightened readership of the article, and also researchers may be part of such a community, thus leading to possible advantages during the peer review process[3]

This reasons will lead to more research being diverted to the open web, which in turn may lead to enterprise Knowledge Management solutions to further fall back with regards to open web systems. Whereas previously there was no option to evaluate findings in Knowledge Management but to go to a company and experiment and measure the application of novel solutions there, the web now offers readily a multitude of data sources to be evaluated, often much bigger than any enterprise could provide.

The results and insights gained from such data have the potential of being valuable and important. They will help us to understand open collaborative systems better, and eventually enable us to engineer such systems with predictable outcomes. Hopefully we will begin to understand the economic and social impact of such platforms. But the next section shows why we will hardly ever learn something for enterprise knowledge management.

4 The Fallacy of Knowledge Management 2.0

The assumption that insights gained from analyzing the Blogosphere or mining social networks in MySpace can be readily applied to Knowledge Management is always a far stretch and often wrong. Incentive structures for creating and organizing photo albums in flickr can not be assumed for organizing technical deliverables in a project. The fact that Wikipedia works does not lead to the conclusion that an internal knowledge management wiki will work the same way.

Blogs, tagging sites, wikis, and other Web 2.0 sites are often offered to the public, and barely advertised. Users find such sites, tell other users, and start using them voluntarily. It may take years for such pages to get wide recognition eventually, and most never get there. Companies cannot use the same approach. Instead they engineer such a system, usually without adequate expertise, and then advertise it heavily to their potential users. Sometimes users may even be required to use such system. They often are not allowed to discover them by themselves, but are pushed towards using them. There are also other examples, like Bluepedia which was started

[3] Though this may backfire if the authors do this on purpose and without properly understanding the analyzed community, since a member of such a community will be able to quickly discern serious involvement from calculated actions.

as a grass root effort within IBM [5]. This requires an environment that mimics the open nature of the web, i.e. that allows such systems to be started by employees without central control, and where such systems may grow or fail. A study done at a local company with about 800 employees revealed 32 wikis, most of them having been barely edited – but others thriving [10].

This does not mean that research on Web systems is not usable for Knowledge Management. The results that will be found on the open Web will be interesting and bring insights, this is not the question. But we must be very careful not to naïvely transfer these results and insights to closed enterprise Knowledge Management systems. This requires the diligent study of Web 2.0 inspired enterprise Knowledge Management systems, and discussion about such work was started during the Social Web and Knowledge Management workshop. Three selected papers of this workshop are part of this book, and can give a brief view at the current state of the art in this research.

5 Research Directions in Social Web and Knowledge Management

Let us look at the knowledge management issues in connection to social web more closely. While there is no obvious way to apply successful cases from open web into the enterprise environment, there have still been some positive cases reported from that area. In general one should always distinguish between two kinds of enterprises: *social web aware* and already practicing some social web tools and *social web not aware* companies where there are some knowledge management practices ongoing but they rather rely on strict workflows. The first kind of enterprises is usually represented by those performing mostly some kind of engineering tasks such as software development. Blogs and wikis seem to work there already especially due to the easiness of editing and contributing with own view on tasks, activities and knowledge needed to perform them. Sun Microsystems is one example of an enterprise where blogs and wikis are used to a larger extend [6]. The later case of companies are usually workflow based administrative companies where either traditional rigid knowledge management approaches apply or no knowledge management strategy is available.

5.1 Social Web Aware Enterprises

Even in the companies like Sun Microsystems, it is usually difficult to find a common knowledge sharing platform or wiki. Each team, group of people, or specialized area usually has its own solution, own wiki, or own blog. Let us have a closer look at what you can find on the Sun Microsystems NetBeans Web as one branch of the company. Figure 1 depicts some of the knowledge sharing web platforms such as wiki, issue tracking tools and similar.

NetBeans uses for example an independent platform to store and manage ideas and information related to user interface of their product. Similarly, usability issues

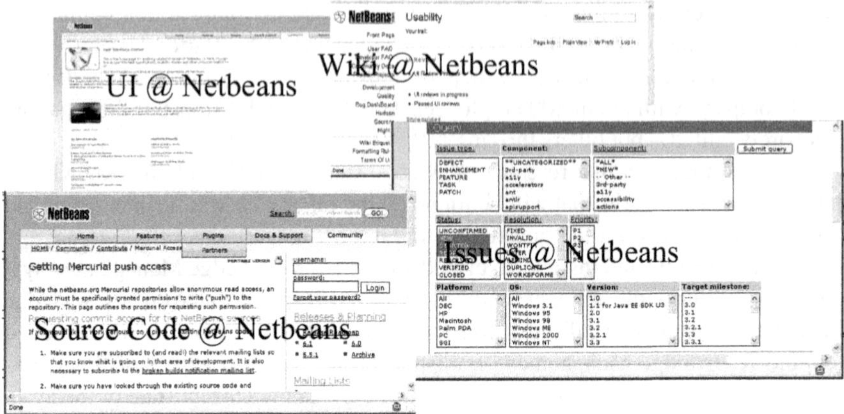

Fig. 1 A fragment of Sun Microsystems platforms at NetBeans

are maintained at a separate wiki. Issues and bugs are managed in an issue tracker system separately from the other systems mentioned above. Source code and associated knowledge is managed also without a connection to the other systems. Thus, even though Sun Microsystems already has good experiences with social web platforms, also very likely because of the open source strategy and community building policy around its products, it now faces another problem, i.e. how to access and link information and knowledge which is made explicit at various separated systems and furthermore how to link it to a concrete person or a team who contributed with such an information.

Integration. Integration seems to be therefore the first step to support this challenge. There are various ways how to deal with this situation ranging from traditional component based integration approaches through service based approaches. Also, important decision is whether to introduce a new system which will serve as a social portal connecting people as well as machines or whether to connect existing social web platforms in peer-to-peer way. One particularly interesting way of integration is ad-hoc configuration according to the needs. Especially recent advances in service mash-ups allow for easier integration of existing applications without reprogramming their user interfaces. The only requirement is to provide a RESTful API. However, there are still too few reports and approaches on how to do it inside systems like wikis and blogs.

Knowledge Annotations. Different systems used for partial knowledge management can be seen as knowledge islands with particular vocabularies, ways of annotating the knowledge, describing issues and so on. Particular issue here is how to actually push knowledge coming from other islands to people who have in fact different style of annotating and different vocabulary. Semantic web research try to answer this question by studying ontologies, ontology management and their use in information and knowledge annotations. Furthermore, once there is a formal representation of annotations, the knowledge push approach across communities with different vocabularies may be one day sufficiently supported by mapping, transformation, and integration of annotations.

Another issue is actually how to support annotations. We have seen a success of tagging on the open web as one promising approach also for the enterprises. In some enterprises the tagging has gained a considerable attention and for example delicious is used as a shared platform to share bookmarks pointing to interesting information. Tags, however, are very simple means to express semantics of content or information usually not preserving any semantic relationships. Therefore, a question on how to support more complex annotations which would be of an advantage for example for automated reasoning supporting more complex tasks remains open.

Incentives to Contribute vs. Automatic Extraction. Another issue connected to the knowledge annotations is how to motivate people to contribute. We have seen various incentive mechanisms applied to motivate people to contribute with articles, pages, documents, and explicated experiences as well as annotations on them ranging from personal standing and visibility in the community through monetary values. In general, however, incentives of people differ very much and as pointed above, it is usually much more difficult to catch this in enterprises than on the web. Therefore, different social, economical, and other models need to be studied further in this context.

Another way to attract the problem of missing annotations is to apply natural language processing for (semi-) automatic extraction of them. However, here it is especially difficult to mine the tacit knowledge on intentions the authors of particular articles or documents have had in mind when writing it. It is only possible to assume what is written inside the document which is sometimes even not linked to the other documentation. Further processing and reasoning is therefore required to relate those information or knowledge items in the documents. Some of the relations might be impossible to discover even if advanced processing and algorithm exist due to the missing knowledge.

Machine Processing, Automated Reasoning, and Personalization. Once there is a formally defined annotation, new possibilities for improving knowledge practices become available. The machine processing and automated reasoning might help in clarifying inconsistencies, conflicts between documents and annotations made by different people and raise an awareness to solve them. Reason maintenance and belief revision is a promising approach here to be studied.

Query evaluation seem to be another area of interest. In general, a combination of structured, semi-structured, and unstructured data is present in knowledge management systems including those with semantics such as semantic wikis. Combination of information retrieval, keyword based search and structured query languages is unsolved issue both on the open as well as enterprise web.

Another area where automated reasoning can be applied is personalization. Once the all information islands represented by various platforms used for knowledge sharing are connected, the amount of information actually causes an information overload. In a dynamic business environment, therefore, one needs to be supported by facilities which would select, filter out or push relevant information to a user based on a task context, a user profile, preferences, background, or help other ways in planning, composing teams and so on.

5.2 Enterprises Not Aware of Social Web Solutions

There are plenty of enterprises where an average employee is not aware of social web platforms such as wikis and sometimes nor about traditional knowledge management solutions which could help in his task. In this case, the challenge is rather of a social character and learning of advantages the social web solutions can have. But at the end, the culture of the enterprise might be the main obstacle in adopting such solutions. Various sources report on different possibilities how to approach this problem ranging from top management commitment and continuous support through organizational and culture changes.

Editing and Integration. A success of the social web solutions rely usually on integration with the tools which are already used in these companies such as for example office automation tools. Microsoft products are usually those which are used with different templates for different tasks. The problem is therefore how to connect them or how to simulate them on top of the wiki and blog systems.

Another problem is how to deal with semantics and annotations. Information extraction here is even more difficult than in the companies where the social web tools are used. It is mostly due to the fact of different information formats and tools used for writing documents. Similarly, those tools are not prepared for a semantic annotation task and even hard to effectively integrate. Social web tools therefore can bring in the tagging, semantic annotations, and other services which would wrap around an integrated office automation system with editing, calculation sheets, planning and a like.

Linking Between Various Systems. Linking between various pieces of information in word documents, excel sheets, and databases is difficult. However, here, semantic social web environments such as wikis could serve as mediators with ontology, annotations, linking and reasoning capabilities. Those tools can be instantiated as containers within the wiki and wiki will serve as a connector between them as well as a context which re-invokes those applications whenever a user is coming back.

Other Features. Once the knowledge sources are integrated and annotated, and a barrier in using social web tools diminished, the aforementioned challenges of enterprises aware of social tools will apply: machine processing, reasoning, extraction, mapping, personalization.

6 Directions in Active and KIWI

Two research projects funded by the European Commission are currently investigating the topic of enterprise knowledge management with (Semantic) Web and Web 2.0 approaches. Whereas KiWi (Knowledge in a Wiki) is focussing on the application of Semantic Wiki technology on enterprise knowledge management, the ACTIVE project takes a broader stance, aiming to integrate various knowledge management tools by means of Semantic Web technologies. We briefly introduce the objectives of the two projects in the following.

6.1 KiWi

The vision of the KiWi project [9] is that the wiki philosophy, supported by advanced semantic technologies, can change the way knowledge is managed in enterprises and support the user in sharing knowledge without restricting her unnecessarily. It is based on the conviction that traditional knowledge management is too formal, but current social software systems do not provide sufficient support for enterprise users.

Traditional approaches to knowledge management are usually very formal and driven by the conviction that all the knowledge that employees have should be made explicit, e.g. for making the "knowledge" readily available to other employees and for being able to more easily hand over tasks of one employee to another in case of someone being ill or leaving the company. Following the mantra "knowledge is power", such knowledge management is also often considered part of the company's quality management activity. However, this kind of knowledge management is usually not very well accepted by employees, as it requires significant effort, encumbers creativity by enforcing certain processes, and raises fears of being made redundant.

Instead, modern knowledge management rather follows the idea of "sharing is power". Modern knowledge management follows the constructivist view, where rather than seeing knowledge as something that can and should be made explicit, knowledge is conceived to be something that every individual constructs for herself by social interaction. In such a setting, knowledge management is thus a social process where technology, instead of enforcing a certain process, is seen as an enabler to better communication and information sharing.

KiWi follows this "sharing is power" approach to knowledge management. It does so by combining the wiki philosophy that is underlying many social software systems with technologies from the Semantic Web. Whereas the wiki philosophy gives the freedom to be creative and share knowledge as appropriate to the context, wikis by themselves are insufficient in an enterprise context: there are less people contributing (no critical mass, no "gardeners"), there are different incentives for participation (policy rather than intrinsic motivation), there are different people working on the content. The combination of wiki philosophy with Semantic Web technologies has the potential to support users in knowledge sharing: by making it easier to share (reducing barriers), by making it easier to find (improving benefit), by providing incentives for participation, and by adapting to the specific needs of each user. A very important aspect of Semantic Web technologies is that they can be considered "semi-structured" in that they are rather flexible compared to database driven applications because schemas are not strictly enforced and the user has the option to diverge from them if he deems necessary.

The outcome of KiWi will be a knowledge management system that gives flexibility to the user like a wiki but also provides support to the user by employing advanced Semantic Web technologies. Specifically, KiWi will make improvements in the areas of user interface and personalisation, reasoning, reason maintenance, and information extraction. In a sense, this "KiWi System" can be seen as a next generation social software platform that integrates the content and functionalities of to-date separate applications.

6.2 ACTIVE

Knowledge workers are central to an organisation's success — yet the tools they must use often stand in the way of maximising their productivity. ACTIVE addresses the need for greater knowledge worker productivity with three integrated research themes: easier sharing of information through a combination of formal techniques based on ontologies and informal techniques based on user tags — so-called folksonomies; sharing and reusing informal knowledge processes — by learning those knowledge processes from the user's behaviour; and understanding the user's context — so as to tailor the information presented to the user to fit the current task. The results of ACTIVE are being validated in the domains of consultancy, telecommunications and engineering. We will discuss the first theme more closely.

Enterprises understand the need for knowledge workers to share knowledge. The problem is that the systems they provide are frequently time-consuming and cumbersome to use, typically employing formal schemas. Yet outside the enterprise, consumers are often with great success using informal techniques such as tagging to share metadata about documents and media objects. The advantage of such informal techniques are that they are easy to use; the disadvantage is that the resulting knowledge representation schemas lack the richness of the formal approach, and do not allow logical reasoning, e.g. to enable semantic search. ACTIVE seeks to combine the formal and informal approach, in particular by using machine intelligence to learn ontological structures from informal tags and the way they are used. Linked to this work, the project will be investigating the costs and benefits of the ACTIVE approach to knowledge sharing; and seeking to understand how knowledge workers can be encouraged to truly share knowledge.

7 Conclusions

This paper studies and discusses relations between social web and knowledge management. It raises several questions on direct applicability of findings from open social web systems such as wikipedia or delicious to the enterprise knowledge management. It discusses it also on the findings presented and discussed at the WWW 2008 workshop on social web and knowledge management (SWKM2008) with studies mostly on open social web knowledge management systems. In spite of many open issues, it seems that there are synergies. These synergies are pointed out in this chapter as well and discussed on examples from two kinds of enterprises: social web aware and social web not aware. The chapter drafts a vision on which technologies seem to be important to research in the context of applications of social web in knowledge management. This chapter also points out that such a research is already ongoing in the two EU projects: ACTIVE and KIWI.

Acknowledgments This work is supported by the European Union under the IST projects ACTIVE (http://www.active-project.eu) and KiWi (http://www.kiwi-project.eu).

References

1. Ching man Au Yeung, Nicholas Gibbins, and Nigel Shadbolt. A study of user profile generation from folksonomies. In Dolog et al. [4].
2. Philip Boulain, Nigel Shadbolt, and Nicholas Gibbins. Hyperstructure maintenance costs in large-scale wikis. In Dolog et al. [4].
3. Nicholas G. Carr. *The big switch: rewiring the world, from Edison to Google*. W.W. Norton & Co., New York, NY, 2008.
4. Peter Dolog, Markus Krötzsch, Sebastian Schaffert, and Denny Vrandečić, editors. *Proceedings of the WWW 2008 Workshop on Social Web and Knowledge Management, Beijing, China, April 22, 2008*, volume 356 of *CEUR Workshop Proceedings*. CEUR-WS.org, 2008.
5. Gunter Dueck. Bluepedia. *Informatik-Spektrum*, 31(3):262–269, 2008.
6. Wolf Hilzensauer and Sandra Schaffert. Wikis und weblogs bei sun microsystems. In Andrea Back, Norbert Gronau, and Klaus Tochtermann, editors, *Web 2.0 in der Unternehmenspraxis*, pages 210–220. Oldenbourg, München, 2008.
7. Dan Hong and Vincent Y. Shen. Setting access permission through transitive relationship in web-based social networks. In Dolog et al. [4].
8. Francesco Ronzano, Andrea Marchetti, and Maurizio Tesconi. Tagpedia: a semantic reference to describe and search for web resources. In Dolog et al. [4].
9. Sebastian Schaffert, François Bry, Peter Dolog, Julia Eder, Szaby Grünwald, Jana Herwig, Josef Holý, Peter-Axel Nielsen, and Pavel Smrž. The kiwi vision: Collaborative knowledge management, powered by the semantic web. Technical report, August 2008. FP7 ICT STREP KiWi project Deliverable D8.5.
10. Josef Wagner. Realisierung eines semantischen Wikis in Microsoft Office SharePoint Services. Master's thesis, Universität Karlsruhe (TH), 2008.

References

Setting Access Permission through Transitive Relationship in Web-based Social Networks

Dan Hong and Vincent Y. Shen

Abstract The rising popularity of various social networking websites has created a huge problem on Internet privacy. Although it is easy to post photos, comments, opinions on some events, etc. on the Web, some of these data (such as a person's location at a particular time, criticisms of a politician, etc.) are private and should not be accessed by unauthorized users. Although social networks facilitate sharing, the fear of sending sensitive data to a third party without knowledge or permission of the data owners discourages people from taking full advantage of some social networking applications. We exploit the existing relationships on social networks and build a "trust network" with transitive relationship to allow controlled data sharing so that the privacy and preferences of data owners are respected. The trust network linking private data owners, private data requesters, and intermediary users is a directed weighted graph. The permission value for each private data requester can be automatically assigned in this network based on the transitive relationship. Experiments were conducted to confirm the feasibility of constructing the trust network from existing social networks, and to assess the validity of permission value assignments in the query process. Since the data owners only need to define the access rights of their closest contacts once, this privacy scheme can make private data sharing easily manageable by social network participants.

1 Introduction

With the increasing popularity of social networking websites, more and more users post their articles, pictures, comments, etc. on the Web through blogs, forums or other Web applications. Based on the "State of the Blogosphere" report [22], 120,000 new weblogs are being created around the world each day. There are now

D. Hong (✉)
Department of Computer Science and Engineering, Hong Kong University of Science and Technology, Hong Kong
e-mail: csdhong@cse.ust.hk

I. King, R. Baeza-Yates (eds.), *Weaving Services and People on the World Wide Web*, DOI 10.1007/978-3-642-00570-1_12,

numerous online communities where users are connected through common interests. Each person can be members of several different communities depending on how they mark their "common interest" pages, and private data (e.g. identification, financial record, location, calendar, Web content) are shared along community connections. However, these data sharing activities through Web-based social networking bring serious privacy concerns since users do not have control over who can access their personal data.

Nowadays, many users use a Web-based calendar, such as Google Calendar [10], to arrange their appointment schedules. It is possible to provide a feature to let users define activity categories, such as "family activity", "work activity", "church activity", etc. Figure 1(a) shows such a calendar which has several different categories. When a visitor of the website clicks on an item of the calendar, detailed information (such as location, contact person, etc.) about the event is displayed. It is also possible to provide a feature for the owner to define different groups (user context) who may access different categories of the calendar. For example, assuming Alice is the owner of such a calendar. As a family member, her sister Karen can see "family activity" in detail but not the detailed information of events in other categories. This strict definition of groups is useful, but it does not fully satisfy Alice's needs. To make the

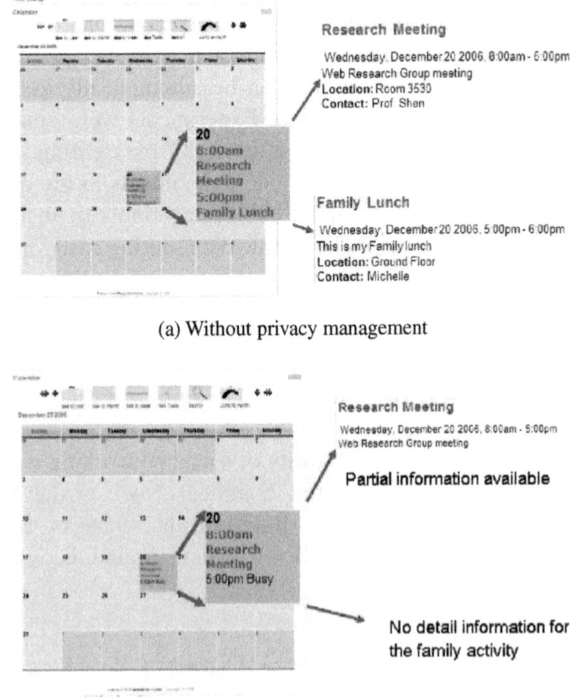

Fig. 1 Web calendar example

calendar more useful, some undefined visitors should also be allowed to see part of her calendar. Consider the following two scenarios:

- Bob, who is one of Alice's colleagues, can check her schedule and see the details of her "work activity". Carl, who is Bob's friend, hopes to make an appointment with Alice for some business discussion.
- Donald, who is Alice's travel agent, can check her schedule for the arrangement of a family vacation. Edward, who works for the car rental company which is a business partner of Donald's agency, needs the information regarding the family's arrival time.

The normal action for Carl is to ask his friend Bob to make the appointment for him. He may also write to Alice directly. This requires some amount of interactions between Carl and Bob, and may also involve Alice directly or indirectly. It will be more convenient if Carl can inherit some access right from Bob, who is Alice's colleague, and can check Alice's calendar directly for her "work activity" items when he visits her website. Donald (the travel agent) and Edward (the car rental agent) are in a similar situation; they should have the right to see the "family activity" category, but not the "work activity" category. Moreover, Alice's calendar can be checked by Donald and Edward based on additional context: Alice might only allow Donald to check her calendar after the final arrangement of her trip is settled and before the end of her trip (time context); and Edward is only allowed to check Alice's calendar information related to Edward's city (location context) and during the trip (time context, inherited from Donald).

In this example it is hard for Alice to assign a special group and access right to every potential user for different calendar categories. It is not possible to assign an access right to someone whom Alice does not even know, such as Carl and Edward. But a "trust network" can be used to derive specific access rights when needed. The network is a directed graph which represents the trust relationship among users in it. During the query process, some *private data owners* (PDOs) might be willing to share their private data with *private data requesters* (PDRs) through the network. We note that the trust relationship is transitive; i.e., Alice trusts Bob and Bob trusts Carl implies Alice trusts Carl to a certain extent. It is also directional; i.e., although Alice trusts Carl by implication, Carl may not trust Alice regarding his private data. Since the trusted PDR through transitive trust relationship might have less access right (Edward does not have the same right as Donald has in the above example), the information released to indirectly-trusted PDRs may need to be obfuscated according to the level of trust. The trust network therefore requires:

1. Trust relationship defined by PDOs
2. Obfuscation (Web data annotation) rules defined according to the nature of private data

With the help of obfuscation rules, the access right is no longer binary ("yes" or "no"). The access right for a private data item is considered a PERMISSION VALUE, which represents how much detail the private data item can be given to the PDR based on the level of trust. Figure 1(b) shows the result when Carl looks at Alice's calendar when he visits the website. From the figure we can find out that Carl can only see the "work activity" and for the "family activity" Carl only knows that Alice is busy. The ability to control the sharing of private data makes life easier since Carl does not need to ask Bob, who is Alice's colleague, to help checking Alice's calendar. And Alice can rest assured that no unauthorized person could gain access to all the details of her private data.

In this paper, we are not focusing on how to define Web data according to various levels of obfuscations. We solve the problem of assigning data access permission values when there is an existing social network. The contributions of this paper include the construction of a trust network from existing social networks. This network can be used to manage the sharing of private data in the Web environment. This trust network concept may be applied to data sharing in other ubiquitous computing environments.

The rest of the paper is organized as follows. Section 2 describes the related effort in improving privacy management. Section 3 describes how to bootstrap the trust network from an existing social network. Using the Web calendar as a case study, Section 4 demonstrates the process of trust network initialization and data sharing with obfuscation rules. Section 5 discusses possible improvements for the permission calculation process. A framework on how the components of the system manage private data sharing can be implemented is given in Sect. 6. Section 7 summarizes the experiments we have done using an existing social network (MSN.com and Facebook) to study the characteristics and significant issues of the trust network. Section 8 discusses possible refinements for the permission assignment techniques. Section 9 contains the conclusions.

2 Related Work

Private data management is not a new research topic. The Platform for Privacy Protection (P3P) Project [24] of the World Wide Web Consortium (W3C) is a standard for websites to publish their privacy policies semantically. Moreover, the APPEL [23], a language for describing collections of preferences regarding P3P policies between P3P agents, makes exchanging privacy preferences according to published privacy policies machine-processable. Unfortunately, P3P has not yet received much acceptance from Web users mainly due to its lack of enforcement, since current implementations do not include compliance of user preferences. Kolari et al. have pointed out that an enhanced P3P based on the Rei language can provide an improved trust model [16]. Since P3P does not provide any mechanism to ensure that these promises are consistent with internal data processing at the website, a purpose-based access control method can be used as an extension of P3P [5]. To address this issue we have proposed to extend the P3P protocol. We have successfully applied this extension to some context-aware applications [13]. The data privacy problem has also been noticed by database researchers who are trying to solve the problem with statistical databases through query restriction, data perturbation and output perturbation [1]. Such research focuses on hiding the relationship between the identity of the PDO and relevant private data [12, 21]. An example is that instead of giving the application an exact location, a regional context is used to satisfy the K-anonymity requirement. A list of candidates is returned to obfuscate private data [20].

In the mean time, social network analysis is a mature research area too. Much of the fundamental work in the analysis of social networks and the major advances in the past century have been carried out in the fields of sociology, psychology, and communications [9, 25]. The newly emergent social network applications, which enable individuals to connect with old friends and colleagues and form bridges to new individuals in areas ranging from business to socialization (e.g., Facebook and MySpace), need a new data management methodology [2].

Since most new social network applications is Web based, lots of researchers in the semantic Web area get interested in this problem. In order to identify Web users and their relationship with others, the Friend of a Friend (FOAF) [3] project creates a set of machine-readable data describing people online and offline, the links between them, and the things they create and do. Mika demonstrates how community-based semantics emerges from a tripartite model of ontologies through graph transformation and how to extract the ontologies from Web pages [18]. Researchers also want to cluster the online users into groups for easy user management and common interest discovery [19]. All these could be the basis used to construct trust networks by bootstrapping from existing social networks.

The first step to facilitate social networking is to have a definition of trust that captures the social features for both local and global scopes [27]. Trust management is quite well studied in P2P systems and semantic Web [14, 15, 17, 26, 27]. In [15], a definition that captures the nature of social trust relationships and an algorithm are proposed for computing the trust value in social networks using default logic. Kamvar et al. proposed EigenTrust for reputation management for file sharing in P2P systems [14]. Richardon proposed a trust value computation method using probability theory in global belief combination which can provide each user a personalized set of trust values [17]. Trust propagation is another important research topic. Guha et al. proposed a method for predicting trust between users [11]. The trust acquisition and propagation model is discussed in [6, 7, 27]. However, the relationship between trust and online private data is not well addressed.

Social networking can be considered a special ubiquitous application. Therefore, the extension we made in [13] can be used in social networks for private data protection. But the extension did not consider transitive trust relationships. PDOs still need to specify every potential PDR's access right based on the categories defined by P3P, which makes management of private data cumbersome.

3 From Social Network to Trust network

In the Web-based social network, the PDOs need to have some control on the management of their private data. However, it is not practical for a PDO to set a particular permission value for each private data category for every potential PDR.

The role-based access control (RBAC) has partially solved the problem [8]. In this approach, it is required to define all the potential users' into some groups. For example, in the UNIX file system, the file owner (user) can give each role (user, group, and other users) some specific permissions (read, write, execute). With the role-based access control, a PDO needs to define the permissions based on the roles of PDRs. But it still may be difficult to define the role of every potential PDR. Therefore it will be very nice if a transitive trust relationship exists among the potential PDRs.

It turns out that the transitive relationship does exist in our daily life. For example, if Carl wants to know how much is the toll to travel through the Cross Harbor Tunnel in Hong Kong, he may ask his friend Bob about it. If Bob does not have the answer, he may continue asking his friends by phone calls or by emails. Later from Alice, Bob finds out the toll charge and passes the information to Carl. Formally speaking, this transitive query continues until a satisfactory answer is obtained and returned to the originator along the query path.

When each person who is willing to share data in the community is represented by a vertex, and when how much a PDO trusts a PDR is represented by an edge, the whole community becomes a trust network. When users share private data in a community, the access decision is based on the trust relationship between the PDO and the PDR in the trust network.

Definition 1. The TRUST relationship between a PDO and one of its contacts is a permission value assigned by the PDO to a potential PDR:

$$permission = trust(a, g, c)$$

Where a is the PDO involved, g is a member within a group of contacts that the PDO has defined, and c is the context where the permission value applies.

The context in Definition 1 provides the application developer and the PDOs the ability to set constraints in data sharing. Context may be related to the time, location, nature, etc. of an event. For example, Alice only allows Bob to view his calendar on her "working" activity. The event type "working" in the calendar can be considered as one context. It is extensible based on the needs of the application or the PDOs.

PDOs are requested to define data access permissions for all the direct users using their privacy preferences. The permission value can be a decimal number ranging from [0,1], where 1 represents total trust and 0 represents no trust at all. The 0 permission value is seldom used in online social networks because a PDO joins the network for the purpose of sharing data with friends there. The context in Definition 1 refers to the particular situation a permission value is assigned. The context includes time context, location context, and query context (such as purpose, retention, etc.) When Web data annotation is available in the social network, the annotation can also be part of the query context.

For each kind of private data, the PDO can define several permission values to fit different contexts. A GROUP represents a group of PDOs who share the same permission value. A group can either be defined by a third party or by a PDO. One of the most popular Web-based social networks, Facebook, allows users to

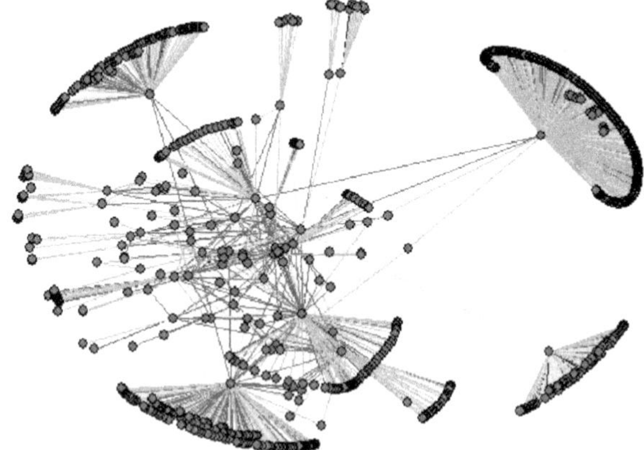

Fig. 2 Facebook network example (1190 nodes). The data includes friends of ID 655183482 and friends of friends

create private groups or to join the existing regional or alumni networks. Figure 2 shows "my friends" and "friends of my friends" relationship on Facebook for one of the authors. We can see that the relationship has been defined between Facebook users through the profile. When a PDO assigns his friends the permission which can be written in a preference file, the network becomes the trust network. The preference file can be stored as a single document or attached to the private FOAF document [3].

The trust relationship described above only supports the direct relationship. In the Web calendar application, the transitive trust relationship also needs to be considered. Carl, who is not directly connected with Alice, links to Alice through Alice's colleague Bob. In order to achieve this, we define a new operation JOIN.

Definition 2. TRANSITIVITY determines whether a trust relationship can be extended outside of the directly-connected PDRs. A propagated trust (Ptrust) relationship based on transitivity can be used to extend the relationship to other users. The JOIN operation shows that the trust relationship is transitive; that is, if PDO A trusts PDR B, who in turn trusts PDR C, it implies that PDO A Ptrusts PDR C .

$$\forall a : \text{PDO}, i, j : \text{GROUP}, c : \text{CONTEXT}, \exists interim \in i$$
$$trust[a, i, c] = p_1, trust[interim, j, c] = p_2 \Rightarrow$$
$$Ptrust[a, j, c] = trust[a, i, c] \bowtie trust[interim, j, c] = min(p_1, p_2)$$

With the JOIN operation, the permission propagates along the trust network with the maximum possible value. Every potential PDR can be assigned a permission value automatically if he is within the community or from a related community. In a real application a PDO might set more restricted access. Additional operations will be proposed in the future.

4 Trust Network and Obfuscation

Privacy management is separated into four steps: context pruning, transitive trust network initialization, permission value computation and data obfuscation. The four steps are applied when appropriate. In this section, we use the example when

Edward sends a query on Alice's "family activities" in the calendar application to demonstrate these four steps.

4.1 Context Pruning

In a Web-based social network, users are allowed to define a lot of relationships with other users. For example, in Facebook users can define every relationship with all friends, such as "We went to school together" or "We took the course together". Moreover, a user can further specify which school and which course to establish the link between two users. As a result, group definition is quite complicated. Each PDO might need to define permission values for an individual person or a group based on different contexts.

The goal for context pruning is that trust relationship only propagates within the same group of people. For example, Alice would like to share her "work activity" with Bob. But she may not wish to share the information with Bob's family doctor, whom Bob trusts totally. Therefore the trust network should be restricted by context. We zoom in Fig. 2 and extract part of the real Facebook network as shown in Fig. 3. The church events in the calendar can be exchanged among all members of this network since all these five people are from the same Clearwater Bay International Baptist Church (CBIBC). But the work event is just shared between Michelle and Cammy since they "worked together" and no other user in the network has a similar context. Here "church" or "work", which might be an attribute of the event, can be considered a context. Suppose there are two groups of users trusted by a PDO and a PDR is in both of the groups. If the PDR requests information from the PDO then it might be reasonable for the PDO to provide the larger permission value derived from each of the two groups. Another task for context pruning is to find out the maximum permission value for every direct trust relationship on the condition of satisfying the context requirement. In the previous example, during the trip time the travel agent

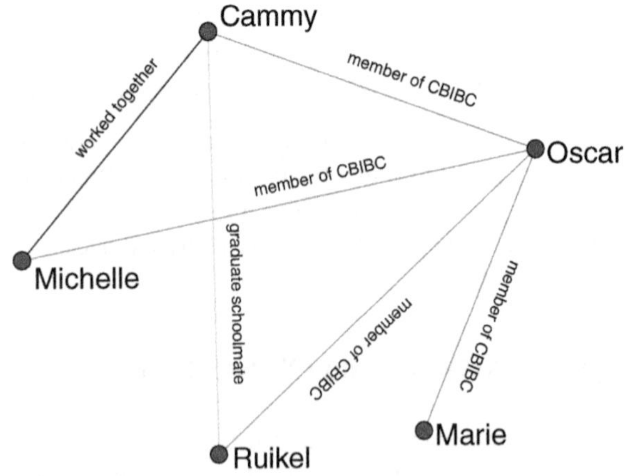

Fig. 3 FaceBook multiple relationship example. All information about religion can be sharing due to connections of "Member of CBIBC". Other sharing activities might be restricted

Donald is trusted by Alice based on RECIPIENT "ours"(see the definition in [24]). For other times, since the query context is not satisfied, Donald is not trusted.

4.2 Transitive Trust Network Initialization

Even if a PDO defines only a small portion of the whole community, data can still be shared based on the PDO's preferences. The users a PDO trusts may also have their own trust relationships (e.g., Donald trusts Edward due to partnership). We need to merge all the relationships together to build the trust network. For the example discussed in 1, after context pruning we know the direct trust relationships form a tree. Figure 4 shows the result after merging all direct trust relationship trees of Alice, Bob, Edward and Donald.

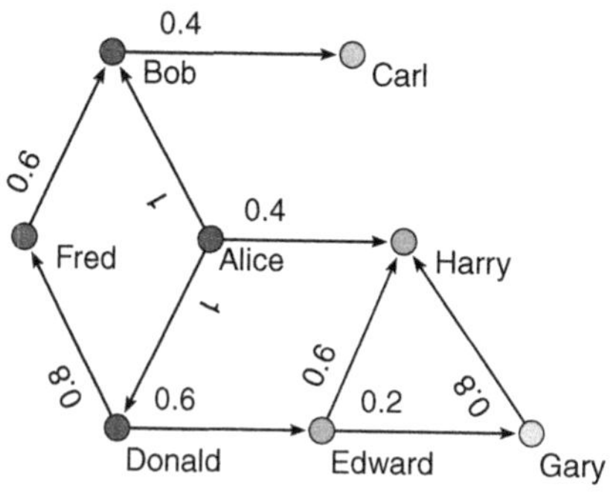

Fig. 4 Trust network based on the case discussed in Sect. 1 with transitive relationship. The different color shades represent different permission

Definition 3. In a trust network, the *hops* of a PDR is the number of vertices to traverse along the shortest path from the PDO to this PDR.

Even if the complexity of privacy preference files has been decreased by using group-based permission assignments, to define the permission values of every potential PDR is still plenty of work. With the transitive relationship, a PDO only needs to define the permission values of those PDRs who have a "close" relationship, or are directly connected in the trust network. Based on the privacy preferences defined for each of these PDRs, the trust relationship can be computed and propagated to the rest of the trust network. Since there are various types of private data on the Web, we need to consider the data categories, sharing contexts during the trust network merging process.

4.3 Permission Value Computation

Note that to apply the transitive relationship, all the trust relationships during the propagation process need to have the same context. Before computation of the permission value for a PDR, context pruning will ensure the network initialized in

Sect. 4.2 is extendable. Algorithm 1 can be applied to implement the JOIN operation in order to compute the shortest path from the PDO (source) to a PDR (destination). Given a social network graph $G(V, E)$, where V is the vertices set and E is the trust relationship set. $p(u, v)$ is user v's permission value given by user u. *Extract_MAX(Q)* is used to extract the vertex with the maximum permission value which is not in the finished set S. We use another function *CheckContent(u, v, c)* to search in the context database if this permission can be propagated in this context c. Through Algorithm 1, a user can get the most private data from a PDO based on the permission value assigned. Algorithm 1 is only one simple and possible solution to compute the permission value. The pageRank [4] or Max-Flow might be used to defined and compute the Ptrust. When Algorithm 1 is applied to Fig. 4, it first puts Donald and Bob into the waiting queue Q. Then the *Extract_MAX* function extracts Donald from the queue and puts Edward and Fred into Q. Then Bob is extracted and Carl is put into Q, too. The *Extract_MAX* function processes Fred and Edward in order. When Edward is handled, the algorithm knows Edward's permission value. Therefore the trust is propagated from Alice to Donald and finally to Edward. We compute the permission value of every potential user (all users except Alice herself), and use a gradient color to represent the value as shown in Fig. 4. The darker the vertex's color, the higher permission value it holds. We can see the effects of trust propagation by the changing color shades.

4.4 Data Obfuscation

There are lots of data items that can be represented in a hierarchical way. For example, the "current location" is a frequently-used private data in different applications. Room 4208, Floor 4, HKUST, Hong Kong, China is a common address to define a

```
input  : A weighted directed graph G(V,E);
edge weight, p(u,v), is the permission from u to v;
PDO, PDR, Context c
output: Permission Value
forall vertex v in V do
    permission[v]=0;
    previous[v]=undefined;
permission[PDO]= 1;
S= empty set;
Q= V[G];
while Q is not an empty set do
    u= ExtractMAX (Q);
    if u equals PDR then
        return permission[u]
    S= S union u;
    forall edge (u,v) outgoing from u and CheckContext (u,v,c)=true do
        if min(permission[u], p(u, v)) > permission[v] then
            permission[v] = min(permission[u], p(u, v));
            previous[v] = u;
```

Algorithm 1: Permission value computation

location precisely. To protect privacy, for some PDRs in some applications, a PDO may want different information shown on the PDR's screen. Detailed information (room number, etc.) is given to close friends and general information (Hong Kong) is given to unknown PDRs. Based on the transitive relationship, the permission value can be used to control the degree of obfuscation for a certain private data item based on either the default value or the user's preference. For example, Alice knows Edwards is in HKUST since the calculated permission is 0.6 (based on Algorithm 1).

5 Improvement of the Trust Network

5.1 Improvement 1: By Control Factors

From Fig. 4, we see that when the trust network becomes complex it is quite possible for an unknown PDR to obtain private data after several data passing actions. In order to make sure the private data passing scale is controllable, a PDO needs to set up some controls:

1. Maximum propagation hops, hop_{max}: how many hops private data can be passed along the network. This is helpful to stop data propagation to PDRs who are too far away.
2. Damping factor, ϖ: How much data is obfuscated through every hop. This method gradually reduces the information available and makes sure that an unknown PDR cannot get too much detailed information through several trustable intermediary users.

Therefore we can replace line 13–15 of Algorithm 1 by:

if $min(permission[u], p(u, v)) \times \varpi > permission[v] \cap hop[v] \le hop_{max} \wedge$ *u is not PDO* **then**
  $permission[v] = min(permission[u], p(u, v)) \times \varpi$;
  $previous[v] = u$;

Algorithm 2: Improvement with control factors

With the help of hop_{max} and the damping factor ϖ, the private data is controlled to spread only within a certain number of hops. Moreover, the farther a PDR is away from a PDO, the less private data he receives. For the previous example, Edward can know Alice is in HKUST without the damping factor. But if the damping factor is set to 0.7 (i.e., $\varpi = 0.7$), then the permission for Edward is 0.42. Edward can only know that Alice is in Hong Kong. The permission value might be hard for the PDO to understand. It is helpful to visualize the social network by painting users in the network with colors of different shades based on the permission values assigned as shown in Fig. 4. And it is also very helpful to assign the critical person, who has lots of connections the PDO is not familiar with, a small ϖ in order to keep the data private.

5.2 Improvement 2: By User Importance

In Algorithm 2, we consider every user in the social network to be equal. However, the users in social networks are usually not identical in importance. The importance of a user is similar to the importance of a single webpage in Web search, which is affected by the number of webpages which have the "in" or "out" hyperlinks connected to the page. One of the famous algorithms to decide the importance of a single page is Google PageRank [4]. We could apply the idea to rank the importance of users in a social network.

Definition 4. Given a user t and its friend set $F(t)$, we define

$$Importance(t) = (1 - d) + d \times \sum_{friend_i \in F(t)} \frac{Importance(friend_i)}{Num(friend_i)} \tag{1}$$

where $F(friend_i)$ is the friend set defined by the $friend_i$, $Num(friend_i)$ is the number of the friend defined by user i, and d is a damping factor to balance the initial importance value and inherited importance value from friends.

In order to simplify the process of the user preference calculation and make sure every new user is assigned an "Importance" value after joining, we use an approximate approach instead of the PageRank algorithm used in Web searches since PageRank assumes that the number of links in and out for a webpage is rather stable. Suppose $G = (V, E)$ is the current social network with N existing users and we already have the user importance for every user in G. Let t be a new user who just joins G and connects to $T = (t_1, t_2, \ldots, t_n)$, where $T \subseteq V$. Then we have

$$Importance(t) = 1 - d \tag{2}$$

This is because friend links connected to user t are all outgoing links. The inherited importance value is therefore zero. At the same time, the friend $m \in T$ needs to update his importance

$$Importance'(m) = Importance(m) + d \times \frac{Importance(t)}{Num(t)} \tag{3}$$

User m gets the information from the Web that user t has added him as a friend. If he decides to confirm the friendship, then user t can update his own importance to

$$Importance'(t) = Importance(t) + d \times \frac{Importance(m)}{Num(m)} \tag{4}$$

Equation (4) is the simplest format for Eq. (1) where $F(t)$ contains only one user m. When t becomes an "old" member of the social network, he can directly add a new friend k who is an existing user in G, then user t updates his user importance using Eq. (4) after user k has updated his value by Eq. (3). When user t wants to remove one friend l from his friend list,

$$Importance'(l) = Importance(l) - d \times \frac{Importance(t)}{Num(t)} \tag{5}$$

Comparing the above method with the PageRank algorithm, we can see that the computation for a social network website is very similar to the computation for ranking pages on a Web search engine. The importance of a user changes when he imports friends, adds or confirms a friend, or deletes a friend. The user importance is initialized when he joins the network. We also notice, however, that with the above method the user importance is not propagated to other users automatically. Such a situation is not critical for search engines since the effect of link changes needs not be reflected in search results immediately. It could be picked up next time the crawler visits the page. But the addition and deletion of friends in a social network should affect the propagation of private data immediately. One possible solution for a practical social network website is to schedule a periodical PageRank-like user importance computation for all users at non-peak times. Figure 5 demonstrates the user importance calculation with different update methods. Figure 5(a) keeps on updating user importance until all the user importance values become stable and the user importance only affects friends' user importance when it is updated in Fig. 5(b). The sequence to add friends in the network is alphabetical by user name and is marked as numbered circles. The more friendships haven been confirmed, the more important the user is no matter which update method is used. Comparing Fig. 5(a) with Fig. 5(b), we can see that the user importance is slightly different for a single user. We also admit that the single update method depends on the user joining sequence. However, the single update method is still a good solution considering the quick response to network changes and good matching for user actions on the social network.

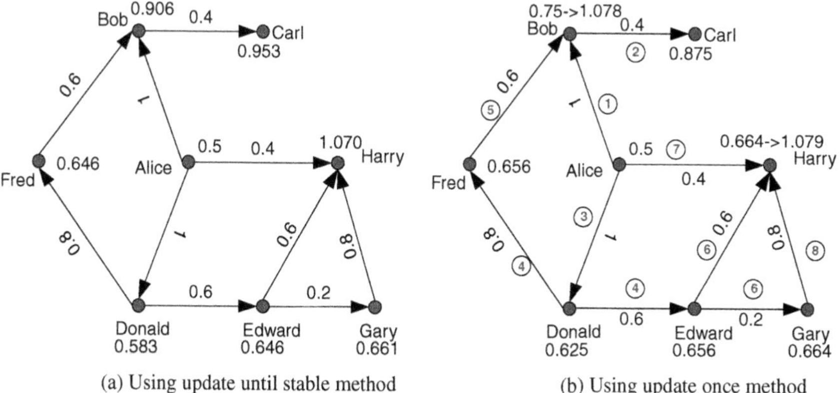

Fig. 5 Calculation of the user importance ($d = 0.5$)

Based on the user importance defined above, Algorithm 2 can be modified as

if $min(permission[u], p(u,v)) \times \varpi \times Importance(u) > permission[v] \cap hop[v] \leq hop_{max} \wedge$ *u is not PDO* **then**
  $permission[v] = min(permission[u], p(u,v)) \times \varpi \times Importance(u)$;
  $previous[v] = u$;

Algorithm 3: Improvement with user importance

5.3 Improvement 3: By Query Property

Algorithm 1 makes sure that the calculated permission is the maximum permission a PDR can get from the network. However, its running time grows exponentially as the size of the network grows. For some of the applications, it is helpful to shrink the network based on the query property. For example, a friend search application provides the function for finding friends who live in a specific city. A possible query to find one hundred friends or friends of friends who live in Hong Kong is

```
select FROM FRIEND
WHERE location='Hong Kong'
AND user1='Alice'
AND hop<5 LIMIT 0, 100
```

When we try to use Algorithm 1 to construct the network, every friend's location information might be visited until one hundred friends are found. We can solve the problem in a faster way by taking advantage of the query's property. Since the query is related to location information, for each user we can construct a table to list his friend's locations. The friend location information could be exchanged with the directly connected friends and become a query forwarding table (as in Fig. 6).

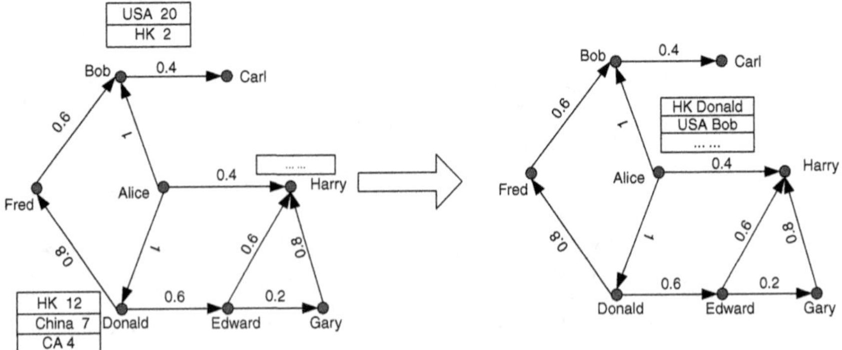

Fig. 6 Exchange the user profile information

When there is a query about a friend's location from Alice, the system does not need to randomly pick one candidate from the waiting list when there is a tie. The query forwarding table is used based on how many friends that Bob or Donald has in Hong Kong. We process Donald first since he has more such friends. For different applications, different query properties can be used to break ties. For the previous example, the forwarding table takes advantage of the user location information. In an application that recommends consumer products, we can use the user preferred brand to sort the reviews from friends who are interested in that particular product. Therefore, this improvement is application-oriented, which is based on the set of applications a social network website provides. In such cases the permission setting can be computed faster. In Algorithm 1, we can see that in the process of computing a permission value from User u to User v, we can also get the permission from User u to some other Users in the network. Algorithm 1 is very efficient when the query requires more than one user permission at the same time. When there is a request for the permission value for $v_1,v_2,\ldots,v_n$ from User u, we only need to modify the termination condition (line 9 in Algorithm 1) to

```
if all PDR has a permission then
    return permissions;
```

We can see that if we only request a single permission, then Algorithm 1 might waste a lot of resources for the computation of other users. Query properties can be used to change the network construction process. In real life suppose Alice wants to know some information about Hong Kong. Then in her mind, she knows that Donald is from Hong Kong and should have lots of friends there. As a result, she calls Donald to present the query directly, whether he is the most trustworthy person in her list or not. When Donald gets the query from Alice, he either answers the question or forwards the query to a friend who is the person who most likely knows the answer. This is quite similar to the procedure to set the permission value. We can simulate this "answer-or-forward" process for the permission calculation which may not provide the maximum permission value, but may traverse fewer edges in the social network.

In Algorithm 4, the function `CheckForwardTable` compares the forwarding table and tells the system which node is the next to visit. The forwarding table is maintained by the system. When a user adds or deletes a friend, information should be pushed to directly-connected friends to update their forwarding tables. There is much existing research on updating the routing tables for Internet. Those mature methods for routing table maintenance could be applied here, too. Function `CalculatePermission` computes the permission of user *next* based on the permission of user u. This function could use the control factors and user importance to adjust the final permission value. When a result from `CheckForwardTable` is the PDR, we calculate the permission and returns it as a result. If the result is another person other than the PDR, we calculate this person's permission and try to use this

```
input : A weighted directed graph G(V,E);
edge weight, p(u,v), is the permission from u to v;
PDO, PDR
output: Permission Value
forall vertex v in V do
    permission[v]=0;
    previous[v]=undefined;
permission[PDO]= 1;
u=PDO;
while u ≠ PDO ∩ CheckForwardTable (PDO)≠ ∅ do
    next= CheckForwardTable (u);
    if next equals ∅ then
        u=previous[u];
        continue;
    else if next equals PDR then
        return CalculatePermission (u,next);
    else
        permission[next]= CalculatePermission (u,next);
        previous[next]=u;
        u=next;
```

Algorithm 4: Permission value computation-answer and forward

person as a starting point to continue our search for the PDR. If the result is an empty set, it means this path cannot return any result, and we go back to previous user to check another possibility. Even though Algorithm 4 does not promise the maximum permission value, it is a good heuristic rule for finding a path between the PDO and the PDR. The popular AJAX technology is a good solution for this non-maximum problem. We can deliver some results to the PDR when Algorithm 4 gets a result and when Algorithm 1 provides a higher permission value, the webpage could be automatically updated to the PDR without a refresh button click. Moreover, when Algorithm 4 fails sometimes, AJAX still makes sure the PDR can get the desired result after waiting.

6 Framework Overview

If we consider the information posted online by users as context information, then queries about private data in the social network is similar to queries in ubiquitous computing. We applied the framework in [13] to social networks and the Privacy Server framework, which is used in the Web calendar example; the result is shown in Fig. 7. This framework is not specially defined for the Web calendar; other applications can also connect to the Privacy Server through an HTTP connection for the current CGI version. In the framework, PDO Preference Manager is an interactive component for PDOs to define the user preference. There are two databases in the framework:

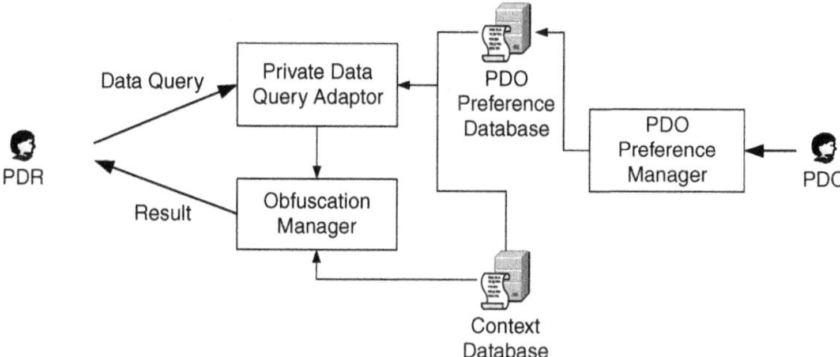

Fig. 7 Privacy server implementation framework

- PDO Preference Database: stores PDOs preference. PDOs manage preferences through the PDO Preference Manager.
- Context Database: stores private user data. The data is posted by the PDO to the social network directly. Context data can often be represented in many ways and forms.

When there is a data query initiated by a PDR, the Private Data Query Adapter acts as an interpreter for the query, which should include all the context information (e.g., the reason to access the data, how to forward data to third parties and the application user's name). After that, based on a PDO's preference definitions, the Private Data Query Adapter sets up the trust network using the transitive relationships defined by each PDO. These relationships are derived from the online community information. Users in a whole community who are willing to share private data become vertices in the network while the trust relationships between each other become edges. The strength of the trust relationship becomes the private data permission value which denotes the edge weight in the trust network. In this process, the Context Database might be needed since it is possible that some of the PDOs preferences are related. The Adapter computes the permission value and passes the value to the Obfuscation Manager.

After the permission value is obtained, the Obfuscation Manager blurs the private data according to the value and still returns some information to the PDR (unless the permission value is zero, indicating that the PDR is forbidden from accessing the data). For example, the location context can be represented at a particular point geographically, or in regions of various sizes which contain that point. Alice's location, in the previous example, could be represented as <Alice, at, Cross Harbor Tunnel, Hong Kong, China>, showing that Alice's location information at a certain time is one of the Cross Harbor Tunnel, Hong Kong, or China depending on the permission value. The Obfuscation Manager returns different results for different queries based on the relationship between the PDO and the PDR.

The transitive relationship and obfuscation rules break the current binary private data access characteristic and make context sharing easier. We modify an open source Web calendar component, JEvent, and connect it with the Privacy

Management Framework. Figure 1(a) is the original JEvent service. Users are allowed to check all the detailed calendar information by clicking on the event. With the privacy management as shown in Fig. 1(b) only registered users can check the calendar and in a certain case the "Family activities" is not available based on the data category the calendar owner (PDO) has defined. The successful hacking of the code for JEvent shows that the transitive trust relationship does work in a real application.

7 Experiment

7.1 General Characteristics of the Trust Network

Our study is focused on the "trust network" where edge (u, v) means u trusts v with a labeled permission value. There are lots of online communities available currently, such as MSN, Facebook, Blogger, etc. We picked MSN due to its popularity to test the implementation of permission value assignment scheme. Starting from one of the authors' friends who posts her friends list on the Web,[1] we used a crawler to trace the friends lists. We visited 187 users who are connected with the friend within four hops and obtained another 1,181 related users. None is more than four hops away from the friend. Since there was no permission value supported by MSN, we randomly assigned different permission values for every relationship. Figure 8 contains the trust propagation results after we randomly assigned permission values using Math.random (range [0,1)). The permission values became very small after four hops as shown in Fig. 8(a), since most peripheral nodes are

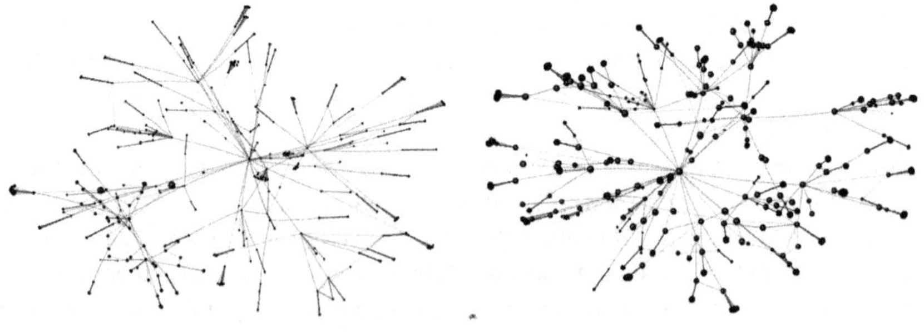

(a) Random permission value assignment (b) High permission value assignment

Fig. 8 Transitive network efficiencies. The node sizes represent the permission values it is granted based on transitive network. Figure 8(a) and (b) are based on the same social network connections but with different initial trust values. We use the same scale in 8(a) and 8(b) in that if a user in 8(a) is 40% of its size in 8(b), it means the user gets 2.5 of the permission value than before

[1] MSN URL:http://rp20040619.spaces.live/friends

in very small sizes. If these peripheral nodes wish to access the central node's information, their requests will not be successful. Since friend lists on MSN are defined by the users manually, the trust relationships should be higher than random assignments in the range of [0,1). By changing the range to [0.6,1), the results are shown in Fig. 8(b). Comparing Figs. 8(a) and (b), we see that the node sizes in Fig. 8(b) are bigger, which means that the permission values are higher after trust propagation when higher permission values are assigned initially. Therefore the permission values defined by PDOs are indeed affecting the private data propagation process.

7.2 Control Factors

Figure 8 demonstrates that it is possible to construct a trust network from an existing social network for managed data sharing, if the social network supports the setting of permission levels. We then explore how a PDO can control the transitive relationship with partial trust.

The maximum number of hops hop_{max} can be set by a PDO in order to control how far the private data can be forwarded. We again use the MSN social network as a test base. We randomly assigned permission values to every trust relationship and then kept this directed graph unchanged in the following experiment.

When no transitive relationship was allowed ($hop_{max} = 0$), 1,350 queries got no permission during data sharing in Fig. 9(a). When the transitive relationship was allowed, the non-empty query number was dramatically increased when $hop_{max} = 3$. This is because there are few users on the first one or two hops of the trust network. The bigger hop_{max} was, the more detailed result could be obtained. Moreover, we noted that blanket permission was not granted since only a small number of queries could get access to the private data. We can also see that even if the friend has only defined three close friends, if she allows three hops of data sharing, then around 700 users can see her obfuscated data.

Figure 9(b) demonstrates how the damping factor discussed in Sect. 4.4 affected the permission value. If the damping factor ϖ is zero, it meant that there was no transitive relationship. If ϖ is very small (e.g., 0.1 or 0.2), it strongly restricted the access permission of private data. Even when ϖ became 0.6, most users got permission value less than 0.2. When ϖ became bigger, the influence of ϖ significantly affected the permission value to access private data.

We understand that the number of users who get permission might be different due to different social network topologies. For example, if the PDO defines a lot of close friends, there will be a number of users who get permission to access private data even when $hop_{max} = 0$. The selection of ϖ and hop_{max} will indeed affect the topology of the trust network. But the trend of trust propagation will not change too much. In practice the damping factor should be used with maximum hop number together in order to achieve the desired access control. Moreover, the PDO can set up different damping factors to different groups or specific users if he wishes.

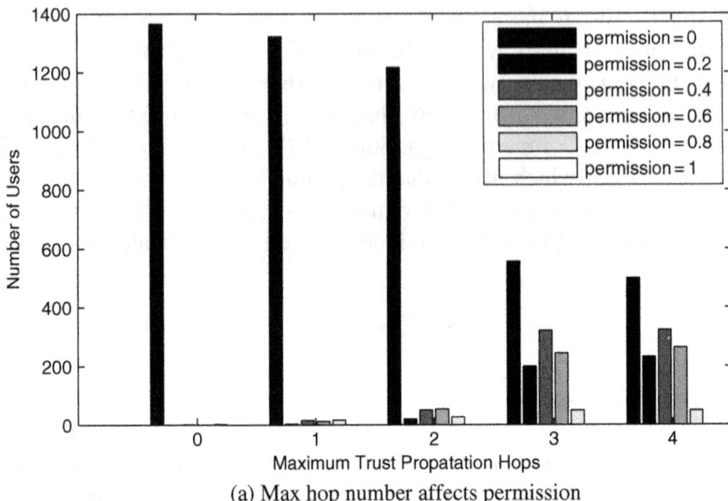

(a) Max hop number affects permission

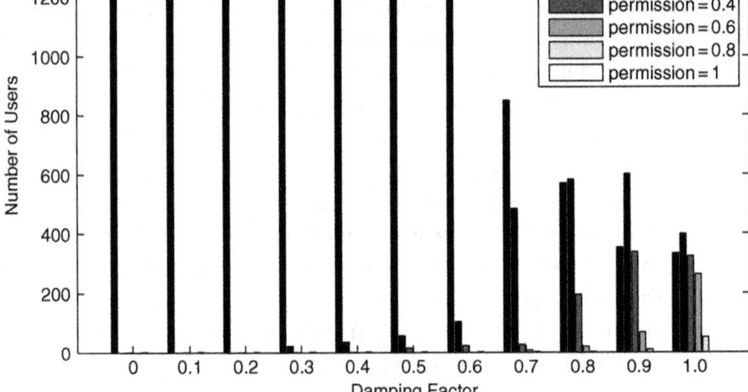

(b) Damping factor affects permission

Fig. 9 Control factors influence on the permission value

7.3 User Importance

We applied the "update once method" in the computation of the user importance to Fig. 10.

From Fig. 10 we can see that the grey users in medium size are those who share lots of friends in the society and inherit lots of user importance from others. From user 65513482's view, the grey users are the frequently contacted friends who should be trusted more even when they are not directly connected. Different from the grey users who are highly connected with each other, the big black users have lots of

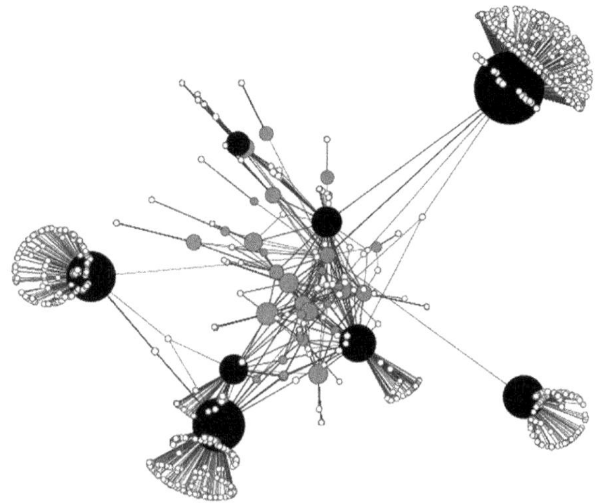

Fig. 10 User importance calculation of the Facebook sample data using the "update once" method ($d = 0.5$). The node size represents the user importance calculated by the method. The users with the user importance value more than 10 are marked in *black* and the users with importance between 1 and 10 are marked in *grey*. The rest of the users are marked in *white*

friends who are not connected with any other friends except themselves. These black users are the users who know someone in the available network by chance but are not really active in the community. The black users are useful for the community expansion. We admit that since Fig. 10 only has information on two hops within the network, the user importance will be different when the network expands and other new tightly connected community or friends may appear. However, the user importance trends should be the same.

The user importance is also very useful for permission control. The PDO can get the personalized user importance by limiting the maximum hop of friends who could appear on his personal view of the social network (i.e., Fig. 10 is a personalized user importance since it only has the friends and friends of friends of 65513482). A threshold can be set up to eliminate the big yellow users from the network from personal view and make sure that his personal data is not shared with some totally fresh people.

8 Discussions

8.1 Trust Priority

In a trust network, it is possible that a PDR may obtain more private data through transitive relationships. For example Fig. 11 is the result after running Algorithm 1. The gray line represents the trust propagation path when Harry queries Alice's information. Through a full transitive relationship, Harry can get 0.6 permission value through the path: Alice ⇀ Donald ⇀ Edward ⇀ Harry. However, Harry is directly defined in Alice's trust tree with permission value 0.4 (green line). There is now a conflict between the direct trust and trust derived from transitive relationships. Since trust based on multiple recommendations from a single source should not be higher

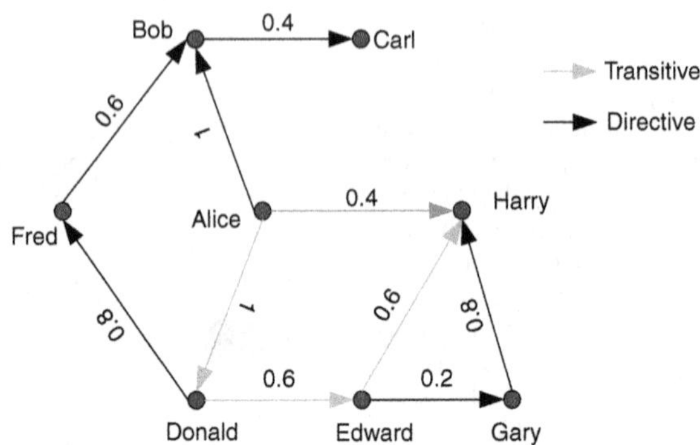

Fig. 11 Trust Priority: Directed vs. Transitive

than that from independent sources, if the PDR is one of the directly-connected vertices with the PDO then the permission for this PDR cannot be higher than the permission value originally assigned by the PDO.

8.2 Standardized Private Data Levels

It is often hard for users to assign accurate decimal permission values to others. Therefore, we should provide a visualization of the data. The user can directly select the data level they would like to share and the program can easily convert the level into a decimal number.

The levels of a private data item are either defined by a PDO or by a public ontology. Then different PDOs might have different data levels in real applications. For example, Alice defines her location in 5 levels, such as "Room 4208, Floor 4, HKUST, Hong Kong, China". Her secretary only uses "HKUST, Hong Kong, China". When the secretary grants Bob with permission value 0.67, Bob can only know "Hong Kong". If Alice gives a 0.8 permission value to her secretary, then with the transitive relationship Bob gets 0.67 (the maximum of 0.8 and 0.67) permission value and consequently a more specific area name (HKUST) of Alice's location. This could be a big privacy hole.

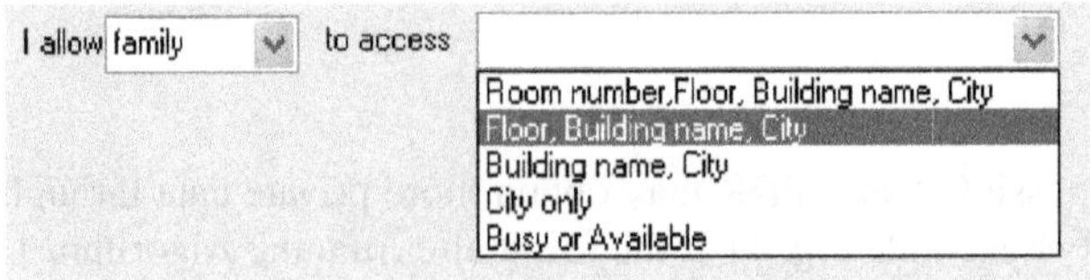

A possible solution is that for each category a standardized private context data level is set up and shared by all PDOs through a separate central information directory which provides all kinds of information level descriptions. The PDO Preference Manager connects to that directory and automatically helps users to search what other preferences the PDO has defined. Initially, there are only a few default levels for the data. When a PDO wants to have more specific context levels, he can insert a level himself and record the new level in the central information directory. For example, if Alice wants to identify the current building as a new context level, she finds that this information is between the floor information and the area name. Alice can then insert the building name between them and set the permission value for this new context level to be ($\frac{0.6+0.8}{2} = 0.7$). When other PDOs define their location information, this new level can also be used by them. Since the permission value is a decimal number between 0 and 1, an infinite number of context levels can be supported. Another advantage of using standard levels is that a PDO can see and directly choose the information level he wishes to share with other users instead of assigning a permission value which may not be meaningful to the PDO.

8.3 Other Applications

With the development of ubiquitous computing, more and more private data is available to the public either on the Web or through other applications. For example, a mobile service provider has already started friend location service. Users can dial a special number to trace their friends' location. Users might lose privacy control in that situation because he may not know what information about him is shared, compared with the social network situation that the user is the publisher of his own data on the Web. It is possible that through such a service, a thief can find out a user's regular schedule, such as the time to go home, by tracking the user's location for a period of time before breaking into his home when he is not there. The convenience of ubiquitous computing applications will not be enjoyed unless users can control what private data to share with whom at what time. Our privacy server framework can be helpful in these applications.

9 Conclusions

In this paper we propose a transitive trust network for private data sharing in social networks. We believe the lack of privacy protection is a major hindrance to the continued development of social networking websites. Taking advantage of the transitive property of trust relationship, it is possible for an owner of private data to restrict access to direct contacts. Through the trust network the indirect contacts of the private data owner can also access some of the private data in a controlled fashion. The Web calendar application with such an enhancement could make the calendar more useful than it is today. The characteristics of such a trust network are analyzed which may be applied to data sharing in ubiquitous computing environments. Further development of the trust network to reduce the data owner's involvement is possible and is currently being pursued.

Acknowledgments This research is supported in part by Hong Kong Research Grant Council Project 619507.

References

1. N. R. Adam and J. C. Worthmann. Security-control methods for statistical databases: a comparative study. *ACM Computing Survey*, 21(4):515–556, 1989.
2. E. Adar and C. R. Managing uncertainty in social networks. *IEEE Data Engineering Bulletin*, 30(2):15–22, 2007.
3. D. Brickley and L. Miller. Foaf project. http://www.foaf-project.org/, 2007.
4. S. Brin and L. Page. The anatomy of a large-scale hypertextual web search engine. In *WWW7: Proceedings of the Seventh International Conference on World Wide Web 7*, pages 107–117, Amsterdam, The Netherlands, 1998. Elsevier Science Publishers B. V.
5. J.-W. Byun, E. Bertino, and N. Li. Purpose based access control of complex data for privacy protection. In *SACMAT '05: Proceedings of the Tenth ACM Symposium on Access Control Models and Technologies*, pages 102–110, New York, NY, USA, 2005. ACM Press.
6. M. Conrad, T. French, W. Huang, and C. Maple. A lightweight model of trust propagation in a multi-client network environment: To what extent does experience matter? In *ARES '06: Proceedings of the First International Conference on Availability, Reliability and Security (ARES'06)*, pages 482–487. Washington, DC, USA, 2006. IEEE Computer Society.
7. B. Esfandiari and S. Chandrasekharan. On how agents make friends: mechanisms for trust acquisition. In *Proceedings of the Fourth Workshop on Deception, Fraud and Trust in Agent Societies 2001*, pages 27–34, 2001.
8. D. F. Ferraiolo, J. F. Barkley, and D. R. Kuhn. A role-based access control model and reference implementation within a corporate intranet. *ACM Transactions on Information and System Security*, 2(1):34–64, 1999.
9. L. Garton, C. Haythornthwaite, and B. Wellman. Studying online social networks. *Journal of Computer-Mediated Communication*, 3(1), June 1997.
10. Google. Google calendar. www.google.com/calendar.
11. R. Guha, R. Kumar, P. Raghavan, and A. Tomkins. Propagation of trust and distrust. In *WWW '04: Proceedings of the 13th International Conference on World Wide Web*, pages 403–412, New York, NY, USA, 2004. ACM Press.
12. A. Y. Halevy, A. Rajaraman, and J. J. Ordille. Data integration: The teenage years. In *VLDB*, pages 9–16, 2006.
13. D. Hong, M. Yuan, and V. Y. Shen. Dynamic privacy management: a plug-in service for the middleware in pervasive computing. In *MobileHCI 2005*, pages 1–8, Salzburg, Austria, September 2005. ACM.
14. S. D. Kamvar, M. T. Schlosser, and H. Garcia-Molina. The eigentrust algorithm for reputation management in p2p networks. In *WWW '03: Proceedings of the 12th International Conference on World Wide Web*, pages 640–651, New York, NY, USA, 2003. ACM Press.
15. Y. Katz and J. Golbeck. Using social network-based trust for default reasoning on the web. Available online http://www.cs.umd.edu/~golbeck/papers/jwsSocDefaults.pdf, 2007.
16. P. Kolari, L. Ding, S. G. A. Joshi, T. Finin, and L. Kagal. Enhancing web privacy protection through declarative policies. In *POLICY '05: Proceedings of the Sixth IEEE International Workshop on Policies for Distributed Systems and Networks (POLICY'05)*, pages 57–66, Washington, DC, USA, 2005. IEEE Computer Society.
17. R. Matthew, R. Agrawal, and P. Domingos. Trust management for the semantic web. In *Proceedings of the Second International Semantic Web Conference*, 2003.
18. P. Mika. Ontologies are us: A unified model of social networks and semantics. *Web Semantics*, 5(1):5–15, 2007.
19. N. Mishra, R. Schreiber, I. Stanton, and R. E. Tarjan. Clustering social networks. In *Workshop On Algorithms And Models For The Web-Graph (WAW2007)*, 2007.

20. M. F. Mokbel, C.-Y. Chow, and W. G. Aref. The new casper: Query processing for location services without compromising privacy. In *VLDB*, pages 763–774, 2006.
21. L. Sweeney. k-anonymity: A model for protecting privacy. *International Journal on Uncertainty, Fuzziness and Knowledge-based Systems*, 10(5):557–570, 2002.
22. Technorati. State of the blogosphere/state of the live web. http://www.sifry.com/stateoftheliveweb/, 2007.
23. W3C. A p3p preference exchange language 1.0 (appel1.0). http://www.w3.org/TR/P3P-preferences/.
24. W3C. Platform for privacy preferences (p3p) project. http://www.w3.org/TR/P3P/, April 2002.
25. S. Wasserman and K. Faust. *Social Network Analysis : Methods and Applications (Structural Analysis in the Social Sciences)*. Cambridge, 1994. Cambridge University Press.
26. C.-N. Ziegler and G. Lausen. Analyzing correlation between trust and user similarity in online communities. In C. Jensen, S. Poslad, and T. Dimitrakos, editors, *Proceedings of the 2nd International Conference on Trust Management*, volume 2995 of *LNCS*, pages 251–265, Oxford, UK, March 2004. Springer-Verlag.
27. C.-N. Ziegler and G. Lausen. Spreading activation models for trust propagation. In *EEE '04: Proceedings of the 2004 IEEE International Conference on e-Technology, e-Commerce and e-Service (EEE'04)*, pages 83–97, Washington, DC, USA, 2004. IEEE Computer Society.

Multiple Interests of Users in Collaborative Tagging Systems

Ching-man Au Yeung, Nicholas Gibbins and Nigel Shadbolt

Abstract Performance of recommender systems depends on whether the user profiles contain accurate information about the interests of the users, and this in turn relies on whether enough information about their interests can be collected. Collaborative tagging systems allow users to use their own words to describe their favourite resources, resulting in some user-generated categorisation schemes commonly known as folksonomies. Folksonomies thus contain rich information about the interests of the users, which can be used to support various recommender systems. Our analysis of the folksonomy in Delicious reveals that the interests of a single user can be very diverse. Traditional methods for representing interests of users are usually not able to reflect such diversity. We propose a method to construct user profiles of multiple interests from folksonomies based on a network clustering technique. Our evaluation shows that the proposed method is able to generate user profiles which reflect the diversity of user interests and can be used as a basis of providing more focused recommendation to the users.

1 Introduction

As the volume of information available on the Web continues to grow at a dramatic rate, recommender systems [1] are becoming increasingly desirable. While Web users find it difficult to locate information relevant to their needs, information providers also find it difficult to deliver their information to the target audience. A recommender system can be used to solve the problem by filtering information on behalf of the users and recommending potentially interesting resources to them.

A crucial element in a recommender system is the representation of user interests, which is usually referred to as a user profile [7]. The performance of a recommender system greatly depends on whether the user profiles truly reflect user interests.

C.M. Au Yeung (✉)
Intelligence, Agents, Multimedia Group, School of Electronics and Computer Science, University of Southampton, Southampton, SO17 1BJ, UK
e-mail: cmay06r@ecs.soton.ac.uk

I. King, R. Baeza-Yates (eds.), *Weaving Services and People on the World Wide Web*,
DOI 10.1007/978-3-642-00570-1_13,

While some research works attempt to construct user profiles based on the browsing history of the users [9, 27], some generate user profiles by analysing the documents collected by the users [4].

In recent years, the rising popularity of collaborative tagging systems such as Delicious provide new sources of information about the interests of Web users. Collaborative tagging systems [8] allow users to choose their own words (tags) to describe their favourite Web resources, resulting in an emerging classification scheme now commonly known as a ***folksonomy*** [28]. Given that the resources and the tags posted by Web users to these systems are highly dependent on their interests, folksonomies thus provide rich information for building more accurate and more specific user profiles for use in recommender systems.

There have been only a few studies in the literature which try to model user interests based on the information available in collaborative tagging systems [5, 17], and usually only a single set of frequently used tags are obtained to represent user interests. However, we observe that tags used by users are very diverse, implying that users have a wide range of interests. Hence, a single set of tags is not the most suitable representation of a user profile because it is not able to reflect the multiple interests of users. In this chapter, we propose a network analysis technique performed on the personomy [12] of a user to identify the different interests of the user, and to construct a more comprehensive user profile based on the results.

The remaining of this chapter is structured as follows. In Sect. 2 we briefly introduce folksonomies and personomies. Section 3 presents our analysis of the personomies obtained from Delicious. We describe our proposed method for generating user profiles from personomies in Sect. 4. Section 5 presents results of our evaluation and discusses the usefulness of the generated user profiles. We mention related works in Sect. 6 and finally give concluding remarks and future research directions in Sect. 7.

2 Folksonomies and Personomies

In a collaborative tagging system, users are allowed to choose any terms they like to describe their favourite Web resources. Folksonomies [28] represent user-contributed metadata aggregated in these systems. A folksonomy is generally considered to consist of at least three sets of elements, namely users, tags and documents [11, 16, 19].

Definition 1. A folksonomy $\mathbf{F}$ is a tuple $\mathbf{F} = (U, T, D, A)$, where U is a set of users, T is a set of tags, D is a set of Web documents, and $A \subseteq U \times T \times D$ is a set of annotations.

A folksonomy can be sliced into different sub-parts depending on which kind of elements one focuses on. In this chapter, we focus on the users and are interested in the collections of tags and documents possessed by individual users, which are given the name ***personomy*** [12].[1] In order to extract the set of tags and documents associated with a user, we can slice a folksonomy by narrowing our attention to a particular user.

Definition 2. A personomy $\mathbf{P}_u$ of a user u is a restriction of a folksonomy $\mathbf{F}$ to u: i.e. $\mathbf{P}_u = (T_u, D_u, A_u)$, where A_u is the set of annotations of the user: $A_u = \{(t,d)|(u,t,d) \in A\}$, T_u is the user's set of tags: $T_u = \{t|(t,d) \in A_u\}$, and D_u is the user's set of documents: $D_u = \{d|(t,d) \in A_u\}$.

A personomy can be represented in the form of a graph with nodes representing the tags and documents associated with this particular user. If folksonomy can be considered as a hypergraph with three disjoint sets of nodes (user, tags and documents), a personomy can be represented as a bipartite graph with two disjoint sets of nodes. The bipartite graph TD_u of a personomy of a user u is defined as follows.

$$TD_u = \langle T_u \cup D_u, E_{td} \rangle, E_{td} = \{(t,d)|(t,d) \in A_u\}$$

In other words, an edge exists between a tag and a document if the tag is assigned to the document by the user. The graph can be represented in matrix form, which we denote as $\mathbf{X} = \{x_{ij}\}$, $x_{ij} = 1$ if there is an edge connecting t_i and d_j, and $x_{ij} = 0$ otherwise.

We can further fold the bipartite graph into a one-mode network [19] of documents: $\mathbf{A} = \mathbf{X}^{\mathrm{T}}\mathbf{X}$. The adjacency matrix $\mathbf{A} = \{a_{ij}\}$ represents the personal repository of the user. a_{ij} represents the number of tags which have been assigned to both documents d_i and d_j. Thus, documents with higher weights on the edges between them can be considered as more closely related. On the other hand, a one-mode network of tags can be constructed in a similar fashion: $\mathbf{B} = \mathbf{X}\mathbf{X}^{\mathrm{T}}$. $\mathbf{B}$ represents a semantic network which consists of the associations between different tags. Tags in this network are connected by edges whose weights reflect how frequently the tags co-occur with each other. This can be considered as a simple ontology used by the particular user.

3 Analysis of Personomies

In order to understand the characteristics of personomies in collaborative tagging systems, we carry out some analyses on the personomies collected from Delicious.[2] Delicious is a social bookmarking site which allows users to assign tags to bookmarks. We use a crawler program written in Python to collect data of Delicious users in the period between December 2007 and February 2008. As there are some users who have assigned no tags to any of their bookmarks on the system, these users are

[1] In the blogosphere, the term personomy has also been used in a more general sense to represent the aggregated digit manifestation of a user on the Web. See http://personomies.com/what-are-personomies/.
[2] http://delicious.com

filtered out when performing the following analysis. The dataset after filtering contains a total of 9,185 unique users, with 514,929 unique tags and 3,281,306 unique bookmarks.

3.1 Number of Tags and Documents of a User

Firstly, we take a look at the number of tags and documents possessed by the users. On average a user has 285 unique tags and has 602 unique bookmarks on Delicious. Although some users have over 18,000 tags and over 34,000 bookmarks, only a very small number of users have more than 1,000 tags or bookmarks. Figure 1 shows graphs of the number of tags and bookmarks of the users. The graphs in logarithmic scale show that the distribution of frequencies of tags and bookmarks follows the power law. This finding agrees with what Golder and Huberman [8] report in one of the earliest papers on collaborative tagging systems, showing that there are a small number of users having a large number of tags and bookmarks, and a large number of users having a small number of tags and bookmarks.

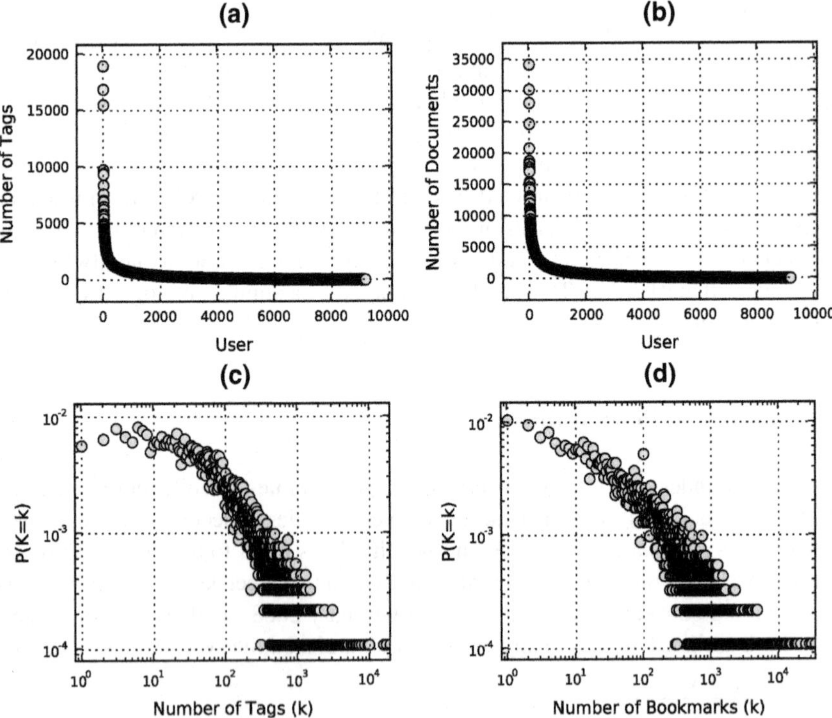

Fig. 1 Graphs showing the number of tags and bookmarks of the users in Delicious. (**a**) and (**b**) plots the data by sorting the users according to the number of tags and bookmarks they have. (**c**) and (**d**) are plots in logarithmic scale showing the distribution of the frequencies

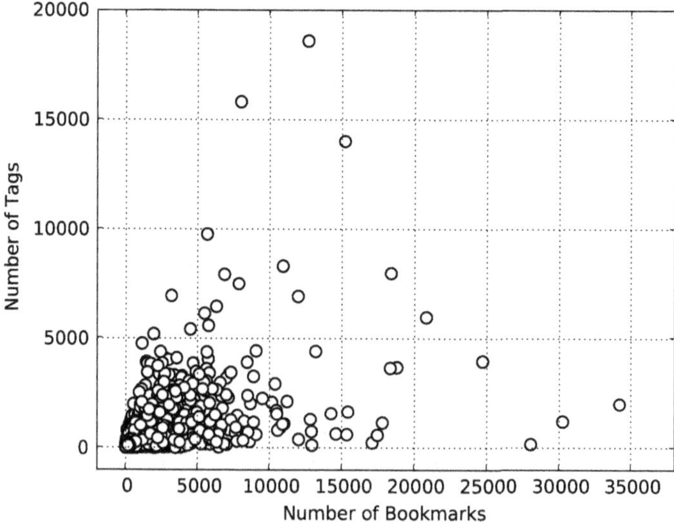

Fig. 2 Scatter plot of the number of distinct tags against the number of distinct bookmarks of the users

Secondly, we examine the correlation between the number of tags and the number of bookmarks of the users. Figure 2 shows a scatter plot of the data. It reveals a moderate relationship between the number of tags and the number of bookmarks, with a correlation coefficient of 0.55. Tagging can be considered as a kind of indexing. When there are more bookmarks in the collection of a user, the number of bookmarks appearing under any particular tag will also tend to increase. Hence it is natural to assume that the number of unique tags used by the user will also increase because it becomes necessary to use more tags to distinguish between different bookmarks by putting them into more specific categories.

However, tagging is also a very personal and subjective way of categorising bookmarks. The bookmarks and tags of the users are actually highly dependent on the interests of the users. If a user has a very specific interest, a small number of tags will be enough for even a large collection of bookmarks, because they will probably be about the same topic. On the other hand, if a user has diverse interests, more tags may be required to describe even a small number of bookmarks.

A further investigation of the data reveals that the correlation between the two numbers appears to be stronger for users with fewer bookmarks than those with many bookmarks. For users with fewer than 500 bookmarks, a correlation coefficient of 0.43 is obtained. For users with more than 5,000 bookmarks, the correlation coefficient is only 0.14. A similar result can also be found in [8]. This may suggest that users with many bookmarks can behave very differently: while some may stick to using a small number of tags on new bookmarks, others may continue to introduce new tags.

3.2 Measuring Diversity of Interests

The diversity of user interests is an important issue to be understood before we can accurately model user interests to provide recommendations. When users have multiple and diverse interests, the user profile should be able to reflect this diversity so that a recommender system will be able to provide recommendations which satisfy the different needs of the users.

Here, we propose two measures which are designed to reflect the diversity of interests of the users. We will give examples based on the two fictional users listed in Table 1, one with rather specific interests in Semantic Web related topics, while another has more diverse interests such as cooking and sports.

Our first measure involves examining how frequently a tag is used on the collection of resources of the users. Intuitively, if a user is only interested in only one or two topics, we would expect the tags used by this user to appear on most of the resources. On the other hand, if the interests of the user are very diverse, the tags are more likely to be used on only a small portion of the resources. This is because different tags are required to describe resources related to different interests of the user. To quantify this characteristic, we propose a measure called ***tag utilisation*** which is defined as follows.

Definition 3. Tag utilisation of a user u is the average of the fractions of bookmarks on which a tag is used:

$$TagUtil(u) = \frac{1}{|T_u|} \sum_{t \in T_u} \frac{|D_{u,t}|}{|D_u|} \tag{1}$$

where $D_{u,t}$ is the set of documents assigned the tag t: $D_{u,t} = \{d|(t,d) \in A_u\}$.

In addition, the diversity of a user's interest can also be understood by examining tag co-occurrence. If for a user the tags are always used together with each other, it is likely that the tags are about similar topics, and therefore it can be suggested that the user has a rather specific interest. If on the other hand the tags are mostly used separately, they are more likely to be about different topics, and thus reflect that the user has multiple interests which are quite distinctive from each other. Such characteristic can be measure by the ***average tag co-occurrence ratio***, which is defined as follows.

Table 1 Two example users with their personomies

User	Resource	Tags
u_1	r_1	web2.0, semanticweb, ontology, notes
	r_2	semanticweb, ontology
	r_3	semanticweb, ontology, rdf
u_2	r_4	semanticweb, folksonomy, tagging
	r_5	toread, cooking, recipe, food
	r_6	sports, football, news

Definition 4. Average tag co-occurrence ratio of a user measures how likely two tags are used together on the same bookmark by a user:

$$Avg\_Tag\_Co(u) = \sum_{t_i, t_j \in T_u, t_i \neq t_j} \frac{Co(t_i, t_j)}{2 \times C_2^{|T_u|}} \tag{2}$$

If we represent the co-occurrences between the tags as a network (by constructing the adjacency matrix **B**), we can see that the average tag co-occurrence ratio is actually equivalent to the density of the network of tags: $Co(t_i, t_j)$ counts the number of edges in the network, while $C_2^{|T_u|}$ calculates the number of possible edges based on the number of nodes. This agrees with the formula of the density of a network:

$$Density = \frac{2 \times |E|}{|V| \times (|V| - 1)} \tag{3}$$

where E is the set of edges and V is the set of nodes. Hence, the average tag co-occurrence ratio actually reflects the cohesion [29] of the network of tags, which in turn reflects whether the tags are related to a specific domain or a wide range of topics.

As an illustrating example, we apply these two measures to the two users listed in Table 1. The tag utilisation of u_1 is 0.60, while that of u_2 is 0.33. The average tag co-occurrence ratio of u_1 is 0.80, while that of u_2 is 0.27. For both measures, u_1 scores higher than u_2, this agrees with the fact that the interests of u_2 are more diverse as observed from this user's collection of resources.

We apply the calculations of tag utilisation and average tag co-occurrence ratio to the data collected from Delicious. The average values of these two measures of the users are plotted in Fig. 3.

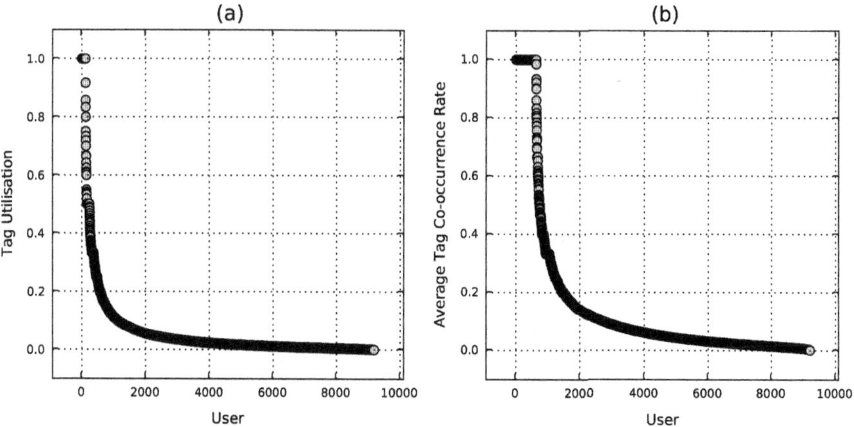

Fig. 3 Tag utilisation and average tag co-occurrence ratio of the personomies collected from Delicious. The x-axis represents the ranks of users sorted by their scores in descending order

Although the two measures consider different characteristics of the personomy of a user, the results are very similar. Firstly, there is a strong correlation between tag utilisation and average tag co-occurrence ratio, with a correlation coefficient of 0.71. The mean values of tag utilisation and average tag co-occurrence ratio are both very low, at 0.06 and 0.07 respectively, even though the values span across the whole range of 0–1 inclusively. This means that on average a tag is only used on 6% of the bookmarks in a user's collection, and that a tag is only used together with 7% of other tags. We can see that there is a small group of points in both graphs in Fig. 3(a) and (b) which attain a value of 1. These actually correspond to users who have only one bookmark in their collection. Other than these the values drop quickly, and the majority (93% in both cases) of personomies have values less than 0.2.

These figures suggest that for most users many tags are used only on a small portion of their bookmarks, and that these tags are not always used together. This shows that bookmarks collected by the users have topics which are very diverse such that a particular tag is only useful on a small portion of them and that the users keep tags which represent concepts in very different domains. Hence, this indicates that most users of Delicious have diverse interests instead of a single interest in a very specific domain.

4 Generating User Profiles of Multiple Interests

As the majority of users are observed to be interested in a wide range of topics from different domains, a user profile in the form of a single set of tags is definitely inadequate. Hence, for applications which provide different services based on user interests, it is very much desirable to have user profiles which can accommodate the multiple interests and present a more fine-grained representation of the users.

Identifying the different interests can be a challenging task as tags are freely chosen by users and their actual meaning is usually not clear. A solution to this problem is to exploit the associations between tags and documents in a folksonomy. As it is obvious that documents related to the same interest of a user would be assigned similar tags, clustering algorithms can be applied to group documents of similar topics together. We can then extract the sets of tags assigned to these documents and use them to represent the multiple interests of the users.

Based on this idea, we propose a method for constructing user profiles which involves constructing a network of documents out of a personomy, applying community-discovery algorithms to divide the nodes into clusters, and extracting sets of tags which act as signatures of the clusters to represent the interests of the users.

4.1 Community Discovery Algorithms

Clusters in a network are groups of nodes in which nodes have more connections among each other than with nodes in other clusters. The task of discovering clusters of nodes in a network is usually referred to as the problem of discovering community structures within networks [6]. Approaches to this problem generally fall into one of the two categories, namely agglomerative, which start from isolated nodes and group nodes which are similar or close to each other, and divisive, which operate by continuously dividing the network into smaller clusters [24].

To measure the "goodness" of the clusters discovered in a quantitative way, the measure of ***modularity*** [21] is usually used. The modularity of a particular division of a network is calculated based on the differences between the actual number of edges within a community in the division and the expected number of such edges if they were placed at random. Hence, discovering the underlying community structure in a network becomes a process of optimising the value of modularity over all possible divisions of the network.

Although modularity provides a quantitative method to determine how good a certain division of a network is, brute force search of the optimal value of modularity is not always possible due to the complexity of the networks and the large number of possible divisions. Several heuristics have been proposed for optimizing modularity, these include simulated annealing [10], and removing edges based on edge betweenness [21]. In addition, a faster agglomerative greedy algorithm for optimizing modularity, in which edges which contribute the most to the overall modularity are added one after another, has been proposed [20]. In this chapter, we will employ this fast greedy algorithm to perform clustering, as it is efficient and performs well on large networks.

4.2 User Profile Generation

Given a network of documents (which are bookmarks in our case), we apply the community-discovery algorithms to obtain clusters of documents. As the different clusters should contain documents which are related to similar topics, a cluster can be considered to correspond to one of the many interests of the user. A common way to represent user interests is to construct a set of tags or a tag vector. Similarly, we can obtain a set of most frequently used tags from each of the document clusters to represent the corresponding interest. As a summary of our method, the following list describes the whole process of constructing a user profile for user u.

1. Extract the personomy $\mathbf{P}_u$ of user u from the folksonomy $\mathbf{F}$, and construct the bipartite graph TD_u.
2. Construct a one-mode network of documents (by generating the adjacency matrix $\mathbf{A}$) out of TD_u, and perform modularity optimization over the network of documents using the fast greedy algorithm.
3. For each of the clusters (communities) c_i obtained in the final division of the network, obtained a set K_i of tags which appear on more than $f\%$ of the documents in the cluster. The set of tags of a cluster is treated as a signature of that cluster.
4. Finally, return a user profile P_u in the form of a set of $K_i's$: $P_u = \{K_i\}$.

Table 2 A resultant user profile

User A	
K_1	webdesign, web2.0, tutorial, blog, css
K_2	linux, opensource, ubuntu, software
K_3	webhosting, filesharing
K_4	grammar, english
K_5	digg, sharing, music, mp3

For the signatures of the clusters, one can include all the tags which are used on the bookmarks in the cluster, or include only the tags which are common to the bookmarks in the cluster. However, the set of tags chosen for a cluster will affect how accurate the profile is in modelling the user's interest. In general, for a large value of f only the most common tags in the cluster will be included in the signature, while a small value of f will include more tags in the signature. We will investigate the problem of choosing a right value for f in the following section. As an illustrating example, Table 2 shows the result of applying the proposed method on one personomy in our data set, with $f = 20\%$ (see also Fig. 4 for the visualisation of the network of documents).

5 Evaluation and Discussions

We believe that the use of multiple sets of tags in user profiles should give a more accurate representation of the interests of the users. It is also our hypothesis that user profiles generated by the proposed method will reveal the multiple interests of a user such that recommender systems using these profiles will be able to serve the different interests of the user better. Therefore we try to evaluate our proposed method by asking the following two questions. Firstly, are the sets of tags extracted from the clusters accurate descriptions of the bookmarks from which they are extracted?

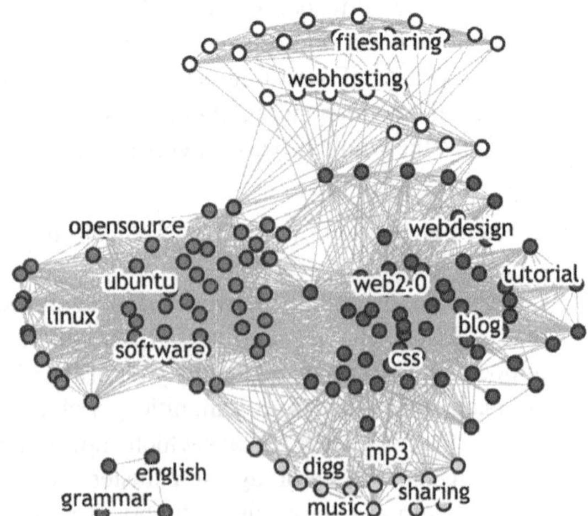

Fig. 4 An example of clustering of a personomy

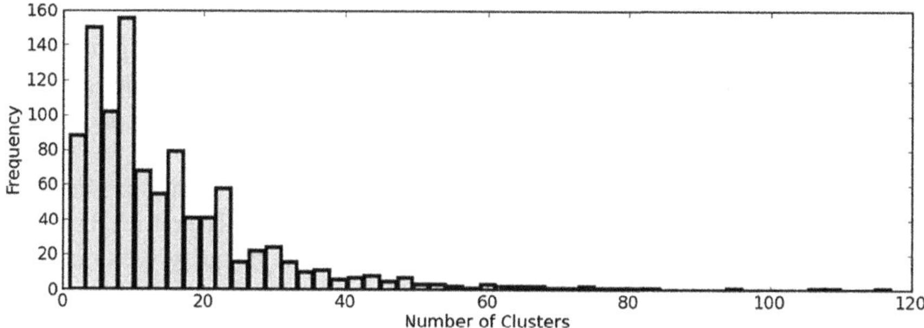

Fig. 5 Number of clusters discovered for the 1,000 personomies

If this is the case, then the user profiles should accurately represent the interests of the users. Secondly, can the generated user profiles be used to retrieve more relevant items than other user profiles which are generated without considering the multiple interests of the users? The two parts of our evaluation attempt to answer these two questions respectively.

To start with, we select at random 1,000 users from our dataset who have over 100 bookmarks in their personomies. The requirement of having at least 100 bookmarks is to ensure that there are enough bookmarks for clustering so that clearer results can be obtained. We apply our proposed method of generating user profiles on these personomies, and obtain a set of clusters of bookmarks and their signatures. We discover that there are a substantial number of clusters with only one bookmark. The bookmarks in these clusters are mostly not assigned any tags. Hence, we exclude these single-bookmark clusters in the following analysis. Figure 5 graphs the number of clusters discovered for each of the personomies. On average 15 clusters are discovered for a personomy in the dataset.

5.1 Representation of User Profiles

Our first question concerns with the issue of whether the sets of tags in the user profile are accurate descriptions of the bookmarks in the clusters. An appropriate method of evaluation is to approach this question from an information retrieval perspective. Given the signature of a cluster as a query, can we retrieve all the bookmarks within that cluster and avoid obtaining bookmarks in other clusters which are irrelevant? In addition, how many tags should be included in the signature in order to accurately describe a cluster? To answer such questions, we employ the measures of precision and recall [25] which are commonly used for evaluating information retrieval systems.

Precision and recall are two widely used measures for evaluating performance of information retrieval. Precision measures the fraction of documents in the retrieved set which are relevant to the query, while recall measures the fraction of relevant documents that the system is able to retrieve.

To employ the precision and recall measures, we treat the signatures of the clusters as queries, and use them to retrieve bookmarks by comparing the tags assigned to them to those in the queries. As for the representation of tags, we employ a vector space model of information retrieval. In other words, for each personomy, we construct a term vector $e = (e_1, e_2, \ldots, e_n)$ for each bookmark, with $e_i = 1$ if the bookmark is assigned the ith tag, and $e_i = 0$ otherwise. Similarly, the signature of a cluster is converted into a query in the form of a term vector q. The retrieval process is carried out by calculating the cosine similarity between the query vector and the bookmark vectors:

$$Sim(q, e) = \frac{q \cdot e}{|q||e|} \tag{4}$$

Those with similarity higher than a certain threshold t will be retrieved ($0 \leq t \leq 1$). For a cluster c, let the set of bookmarks in the cluster be D_c, and the set of bookmarks retrieved by the signature of the cluster be D_x. The precision and recall of the system on c are defined as follows. In addition, we also consider the F_1 measure [25] which is a combined measure of precision and recall.

$$Precision(c) = \frac{|D_x \cap D_c|}{|D_x|} \tag{5}$$

$$Recall(c) = \frac{|D_x \cap D_c|}{|D_c|} \tag{6}$$

$$F_1(c) = \frac{2 \times Precision(c) \times Recall(c)}{Precision(c) + Recall(c)} \tag{7}$$

We calculate the three measures for the user profiles generated from the 1,000 selected personomies. The results are presented in Fig. 6. We control two parameters in our evaluation. The first parameter is f (tag threshold in Fig. 6), the percentage of bookmarks above which a tag is assigned to in a cluster for it to be included in the signature. The second one is t, the threshold of cosine similarity.

Figure 6(a) shows that for most values of similarity threshold precision attains maximum for f in the range from 0.1 to 0.4, and thereafter it continues to decrease as f increases. The result suggests that if only the most common tags are included in the signatures, they will become less representative as summaries of the clusters. This is probably due to the fact that the most common tags are usually too general and a query constructed from these tags will tend to retrieve bookmarks from other clusters as well which are related to a different sub-topic under the common tags. On the other hand, when one includes all the tags which appear in a cluster (with $f = 0\%$), the signature will include too many tags such that it will not be similar to any of the signatures of the bookmarks, leading again to a low precision.

As for recall, we observe some differences for different values of similarity threshold. For small values of t (from 0.0 to 0.3), recall continues to decrease as f increases. However, for larger values of t (from 0.4 to 1.0), recall first increases and then decreases as t increases. This is probably due to the reason that when

Fig. 6 Precision, recall and F_1 measure. Different lines correspond to different values of similarity threshold

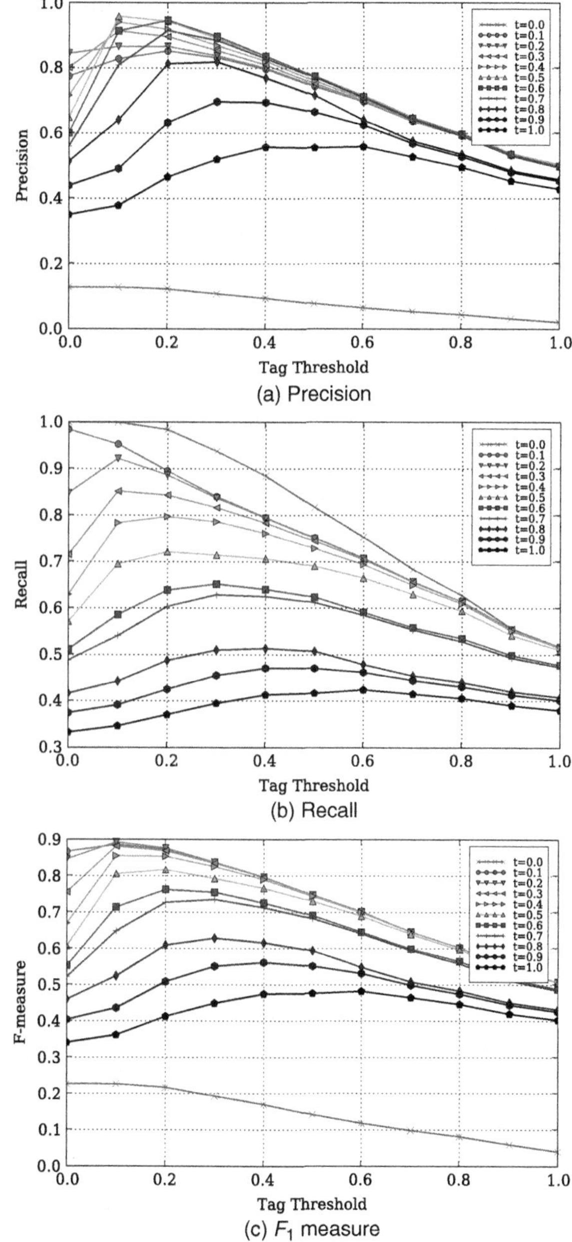

the similarity threshold is low, the number of tags in the cluster signature is less important as most of the bookmarks will be retrieved even if their similarity with the query is small. As f increases, fewer tags are included in the signature and therefore it becomes more difficult to retrieve relevant bookmarks. On the other hand, when

t becomes higher, signatures which include all the tags in a cluster or include only the most common tags are very dissimilar to any of the bookmarks in the cluster, therefore recall attains maximum somewhere between the two extremes.

For common values of similarity threshold between $t = 0.3$ and $t = 0.5$, precision and recall attain maximum for values of f between 0.1 and 0.2, with precision over 0.8 and recalls over 0.7. F_1 measures also attain maximum around these values of t and f. This suggests that it is better to include more tags in a cluster signature so as to make it specific enough for representing the topic of the cluster (and thus the interest of the user represented by the cluster). Given these results, we conclude that by choosing a suitable value of f the tags extracted do constitute good descriptions of the bookmarks within the clusters.

5.2 Usefulness of the Generated User Profiles

Our second question concerns whether the user profiles generated by our proposed method will provide better support to recommender systems. To answer this question, we divide our data into a training set and a test set. We extract the first 70% bookmarks and the tags associated with them, and use them to generate a profile for the user using our proposed method. The generated user profile is then used to retrieve the remaining 30% of the bookmarks in the user's personomy. The bookmarks are retrieved according to the similarity between the sets of tags in the user profile and the tags assigned to the bookmarks. In these experiments we employ the following similarity measure between two sets of tags. This measure is chosen because it gives more distinguishable values when the similarity is low, which is common when a bookmark is assigned a large number of tags.

$$Sim(X, Y) = \frac{2 \times |X \cap Y|}{|X| + |Y|} \tag{8}$$

We again adopt the notion of recall as a performance measure to judge the usefulness of the generated user profiles. Let D_i^α be the set of bookmarks retrieved by the user profiles at the similarity threshold α $(0 \le \alpha \le 1)$, and D_r be the set of bookmarks in the test set, recall is then defined as follows.

$$Recall(\alpha) = \frac{|D_i^\alpha \cap D_r|}{|D_r^\alpha|} \tag{9}$$

Our evaluation involves two experiments. In the first one is aimed at determining the optimal value of f, the fraction of tags to be included in the signature of a cluster, at which the user profiles are best at retrieving or recommending bookmarks which are interesting to the users. The result of this experiment is shown in Fig. 7(a).

Figure 7(a) plots recall against different values of similarity threshold for different values of f. The result shows that the user profiles do not help retrieve relevant bookmarks when too few tags, i.e. large values of f, are included in the signatures of

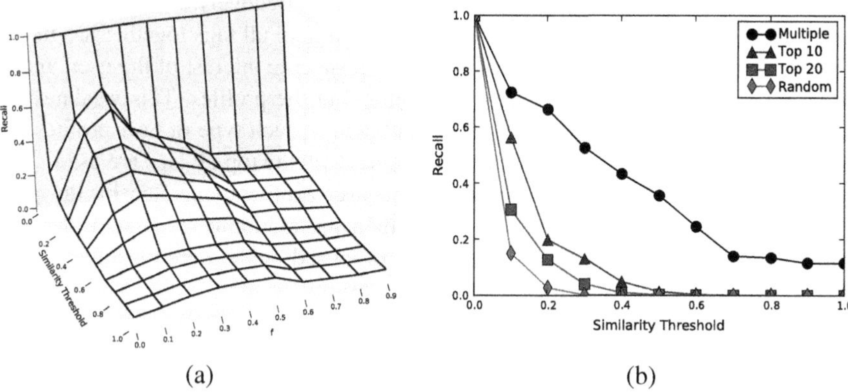

(a) (b)

Fig. 7 (**a**) Recall at different values of f. (**b**) Comparing the level of recall when different types of user profiles are used

the clusters. The optimal value of $f \simeq 0.2$ means that more tags should be included in the signature for better recall. This suggests that while each cluster might be characterised by one or two tags which represent the main topic of that cluster, there are also other tags which helps to describe bookmarks belonging to a sub-category. As a result, a signature should also include these tags such that it is able to retrieve more relevant bookmarks. This actually agrees with the results we presented in the previous section.

Figure 7(a) also shows that the graph flattens as the similarity threshold goes beyond 0.7. When we take a closer look at the results, we find that at these points most of the signatures only consist of one tag, meaning that they are only able to retrieve bookmarks which have been assigned that tag. Hence, recall experiences very few changes beyond that point.

In the second experiment, we compare the user profiles generated by our proposed method (with $f = 0.2$) with three baseline user profiles. The first type represents the interest of a user by a single set of the 10 most frequently used tags by the user. The second type is similar but includes the 20 most frequently used tags. The third type is in the form of multiple sets of tags like those generated by the proposed method, but the tags are randomly assigned to the sets. By using these baseline profiles, we aim to answer two questions: (1) Are the user profiles generated better than those single-set user profiles? (2) Does the cluster technique produce meaningful clusters for recommending interesting bookmarks to the users? The result of this experiment is plotted in Fig. 7(b).

Our results show that, when compared with the other baseline profiles, the profiles generated by the proposed method are able to retrieve more relevant bookmarks at the same similarity threshold. In other words, the user profiles allow a system to make better judgement regarding the relevance of a bookmark to the interests of a user. This suggests that the proposed method is able to break down a personomy into different meaningful sets of tags, so that a potentially interested bookmark can be matched with a particular interest of the user more effectively. On the other hand, single-set user profiles (Top 10 and Top 20) which pool all tags together are likely to miss some bookmarks which are relevant to a specific interest of the user, and it does not help even when more tags are included in the profiles. This weakness is actually exacerbated when more tags are included in such type of user profiles, as we can see in the recall levels when user profiles with the top 20 tags are used.

In addition, Fig. 7(b) also shows that the user profiles generated by the proposed method perform significantly better than the randomly generated profiles. This suggests the clusters discovered by the proposed method are meaningful and truly reflect the diversity of the interests of the users.

5.3 Potential Applications

Our proposed algorithm provides a new way for constructing better user profiles based on the data available from collaborative tagging. There are a number of areas in which such algorithms can be employed.

Firstly, as the user profiles provide a summary of the different interests of the users, it can be readily used to facilitate the management and organisation of personal Web resources. In addition, the user profiles can also be used in Web page recommendation. Currently, Delicious provides various methods which allow users to keep track of new bookmarks which they may find interesting such as by subscribing to the RSS feed of a tag. However, there are currently no mechanisms which directly recommend interesting bookmarks to users. With the user profiles constructed by our proposed method, recommender systems will be able to recommend more specific bookmarks to users by targeting a particular interest of the users.

The proposed method of generating user profiles from folksonomies can easily be extended to accommodate other desirable features in user profiling. For example, by weighting the different interests with the number of bookmarks in the corresponding clusters, we are able to differentiate the major interests from other minor interests of a user. In addition, since the time at which a bookmark is saved can easily be obtained from the collaborative tagging system, it is also possible to determine whether an interest is a short-term or a long-term one of a user. We plan to investigate these features in our future work.

6 Related Work

User profile representation and construction has been a key research area in the context of personal information agents and recommendation systems. The representation of user profiles concerns with how user interests and preferences are modelled in a structured way. Probably the simplest form of user profile is a term vector indicating which terms are interested by the user. The weights in the vector is usually determined by the *tf-idf* weighting scheme as terms are extracted from documents interested by the user or obtained by observing user behaviour [3, 15]. More sophisticated representations such as the use of a weighted network of n-grams [26] have also been proposed. However, a single user profile vector may not be enough when users have multiple interests in diverse areas [7], and several projects have employed multiple vectors to represent a user profile. For example, Pon et al. [23] use multiple profile vectors to represent user interests to assist recommendation of news articles. Kook [13] also proposes a Web user agent which represents user interests in multiple domains using multiple interest vectors.

In recent years, user-profiling approaches utilising the knowledge contained in ontologies have been proposed. In these approaches, a user profile is represented in terms of the concepts in an ontology which the user is interested in. For example, Middleton et al. [18] propose two experimental systems in which user profiles are represented in terms of a research paper topic ontology. Similar approaches have also been proposed to construct user profiles for assisting Web search [30] or enhancing recommendations made by collaborative filtering systems [2].

On the other hand, since the rise in popularity of collaborative tagging systems, some studies have also focused on generating user profiles from folksonomies. For example, in [5] a user profile is represented in the form of a tag vector, in which each element in the vector indicates the number of times a tag has been assigned to a document by the user. In [17], three different methods for constructing user profiles out of folksonomy data have been proposed. The first and simplest approach is to select the top k mostly used tags by a user as his profile. The second approach involves constructing a weighted network of co-occurrence of tags and selecting the top k pairs of tags which are connected by the edges with largest weights. The third method is an adaptive approach called the *Add-A-Tag* algorithm, which takes into account the time-based nature of tagging by reducing the weights on edges connecting two tags as time passes. In addition, Li et al. [14] introduce ISID, the Internet Social Interest Discovery system, which performs large scale clustering on tags and documents to group documents of similar topics together, thus finding out the common interests of the user community.

On the other hand, [22] discusses the issue of constructing a user profile from a folksonomy in the context of personalised Web search. In their approach, a user profile p_u is represented in the form of a weighted vector with m components (corresponding to the m tags used by the user). The use of $\mathbf{w}_d$ is to assign a weight between 0 and 1 to each of the n documents. While these attempts provide some possible methods for constructing user profiles based on data in folksonomies, the possibility of a user having multiple interests is not explicitly addressed in these works.

7 Conclusions

The emergence of collaborative tagging systems provide valuable sources of information for understanding user interests and constructing better user profiles. In this chapter, we investigate the characteristics of personomies extracted from folksonomies, and observe that the interests of many users are very diverse, and they cannot be modelled by simple methods such as a single set of tags. A novel method for constructing user profiles which take into account the diversity of interests of the users is proposed. We evaluate the user profiles by looking at whether they provide a good summary of the bookmarks of the users. We also show that the user profiles generated by using our method are able to provide better support to recommender systems.

We believe that this research work provides valuable insight into how user profiles of multiple interests can be constructed out of a folksonomy. From this point, we plan to carry out further research work in three main directions. Firstly, we will further investigate how the proposed method can be improved. In our study, a user profiles constructed treats every cluster of bookmarks and its signature as corresponding to a distinctive interest of the user. However, it may be true that two interests are related and are only sub-topics of a more general area. We will investigate if the introduction of a hierarchical structure is desirable. Secondly, we will investigate whether the introduction of weights of tags would help improve the usefulness of the generated user profiles. While the occurrence frequency of the tags is considered in this work, associating weights with the tags in the clusters may facilitate better matching between the signatures and relevant resources. Furthermore, we will also attempt to extend our method to accommodate features such as the relative importance of different interests and the differentiation between long-term and short-term interests. We hope this research will ultimately deliver useful algorithms and applications which utilise the power of user-contributed metadata in folksonomies.

Acknowledgments We would like to thank the Drs Richard Charles and Esther Yewpick Lee Charitable Foundation which has awarded the R C Lee Centenary Scholarship to the first author of this paper to support his doctoral study at the University of Southampton, where the research work described in this paper was carried out. We also thank the reviewers of this paper for their invaluable comments and suggestions.

References

1. Adomavicius, G., Tuzhilin, A.: Toward the next generation of recommender systems: A survey of the state-of-the-art and possible extensions. IEEE Trans. on Knowl. and Data Eng. **17**(6), 734–749 (2005)
2. Anand, S.S., Kearney, P., Shapcott, M.: Generating semantically enriched user profiles for web personalization. ACM Trans. Inter. Tech. **7**(4), 22 (2007)
3. Balabanovic, M., Shoham, Y.: Learning information retrieval agents: Experiments with automated web browsing. In: Proceedings of the AAAI Spring Symposium on Information Gathering from Heterogenous, Distributed Resources, March, 1995, Stanford, CA, USA, pp. 13–18 (1995)
4. Chirita, P.A., Damian, A., Nejdl, W., Siberski, W.: Search strategies for scientific collaboration networks. In: P2PIR '05: Proceedings of the 2005 ACM workshop on Information retrieval in peer-to-peer networks, pp. 33–40. ACM Press, New York, NY, USA (2005)

5. Diederich, J., Iofciu, T.: Finding communities of practice from user profiles based on folksonomies. In: Proceedings of the 1st International Workshop on Building Technology Enhanced Learning solutions for Communities of Practice (2006)
6. Girvan, M., Newman, M.E.J.: Community structure in social and biological networks. PROC.NATL.ACAD.SCI.USA **99**, 7821 (2002)
7. Godoy, D., Amandi, A.: User profiling in personal information agents: a survey. Knowl. Eng. Rev. **20**(4), 329–361 (2005)
8. Golder, S., Huberman, B.A.: Usage patterns of collaborative tagging systems. J. Inf. Sci. **32**(2), 198–208 (2006)
9. Grcar, M., Mladenić, D., Grobelnik, M.: User profiling for interest-focused browsing history. In: SIKDD 2005 at Multiconference IS 2005. Ljubljana, Slovenia (2005)
10. Guimera, R., Amaral, L.A.N.: Functional cartography of complex metabolic networks. Nature **433**, 895 (2005)
11. Hotho, A., Jäschke, R., Schmitz, C., Stumme, G.: Bibsonomy: A social bookmark and publication sharing system. In: A. de Moor, S. Polovina, H. Delugach (eds.) Proceedings of the Conceptual Structures Tool Interoperability Workshop at the 14th International Conference on Conceptual Structures. Aalborg University Press, Aalborg, Denmark (2006)
12. Hotho, A., Jäschke, R., Schmitz, C., Stumme, G.: Information retrieval in folksonomies: Search and ranking. In: Y. Sure, J. Domingue (eds.) The Semantic Web: Research and Applications, *LNCS*, vol. 4011, pp. 411–426. Springer Berlin (2006)
13. Kook, H.J.: Profiling multiple domains of user interests and using them for personalized web support. In: D.S. Huang, X.P. Zhang, G.B. Huang (eds.) Advances in Intelligent Computing, Proceedings of International Conference on Intelligent Computing (ICIC 2005), Part II, 23-26 August, 2005, Hefei, China, pp. 512–520. Springer-Verlag New York, Inc., Secaucus, NJ, USA (2005)
14. Li, X., Guo, L., Zhao, Y.E.: Tag-based social interest discovery. In: WWW '08: Proceeding of the 17th international conference on World Wide Web, Beijing, China, April 21–25, 2008, pp. 675–684. ACM, New York, NY, USA (2008)
15. Lieberman, H.: Letizia: An agent that assists web browsing. In: C.S. Mellish (ed.) Proceedings of the Fourteenth International Joint Conference on Artificial Intelligence (IJCAI-95), 20-25 August, 1995, Montreal, Quebec, Canada, pp. 924–929. Morgan Kaufmann Publishers Inc., San Mateo, CA, USA (1995)
16. Marlow, C., Naaman, M., Boyd, D., Davis, M.: Ht06, tagging paper, taxonomy, flickr, academic article, to read. In: HYPERTEXT '06: Proceedings of the Seventeenth Conference on Hypertext and Hypermedia, pp. 31–40. New York, NY, USA (2006)
17. Michlmayr, E., Cayzer, S.: Learning user profiles from tagging data and leveraging them for personal(ized) information access. In: Proceedings of the Workshop on Tagging and Metadata for Social Information Organization, Co-located with the 16th International World Wide Web Conference (WWW2007), 8–12 May, 2007, Banff, Alberta, Canada (2007)
18. Middleton, S.E., Shadbolt, N.R., Roure, D.C.D.: Ontological user profiling in recommender systems. ACM Trans. Inf. Syst. **22**(1), 54–88 (2004)
19. Mika, P.: Ontologies are us: A unified model of social networks and semantics. J. Web Semant. **5**(1), 5–15 (2007)
20. Newman, M.E.J.: Fast algorithm for detecting community structure in networks. Phy. Rev. E **69**, 066,133 (2004)
21. Newman, M.E.J., Girvan, M.: Finding and evaluating community structure in networks. Phy. Rev. E **69**, 026,113 (2004)
22. Noll, M., Meinel, C.: Web search personalization via social bookmarking and tagging. In: K. Aberer, K.S. Choi, N.F. Noy, D. Allemang, K.I. Lee, L.J.B. Nixon, J. Golbeck, P. Mika, D. Maynard, R. Mizoguchi, G. Schreiber, P. Cudré-Mauroux (eds.) Proceedings of the 6th International Semantic Web Conference and 2nd Asian Semantic Web Conference (ISWC/ASWC2007), LNCS 4825, Busan, South Korea, 11–15 November, 2007, pp. 365–378. Springer-Verlag, Berlin, Germany (2007)

23. Pon, R.K., Cardenas, A.F., Buttler, D., Critchlow, T.: Tracking multiple topics for finding interesting articles. In: KDD '07: Proceedings of the 13th ACM SIGKDD International Conference on Knowledge Discovery and Data Mining, pp. 560–569. ACM, New York, NY, USA (2007)
24. Radicchi, F., Castellano, C., Cecconi, F., Loreto, V., Parisi, D.: Defining and identifying communities in networks. PROC.NATL.ACAD.SCI.USA **101**, 2658 (2004)
25. van Rijsbergen, C.J.: Information Retrieval. Dept. of Computer Science, University of Glasgow (1979)
26. Sorensen, H., Mcelligot, M.: Psun: A profiling system for usenet news. In: CKIM'95 Workshop on Intelligent Information Agents (1995)
27. Sugiyama, K., Hatano, K., Yoshikawa, M.: Adaptive web search based on user profile constructed without any effort from users. In: WWW '04: Proceedings of the 13th International Conference on World Wide Web, pp. 675–684. ACM Press, New York, NY, USA (2004)
28. Vander Wal, T.: Folksonomy definition and wikipedia. *http://www.vanderwal.net/random /entrysel.php?blog=1750*, November 2, 2005. Accessed 13 Feb 2008.
29. Wasserman, S., Faust, K.: Social Network Analysis. Cambridge University Press, Cambridge (1994)
30. Zhou, X., Wu, S.T., Li, Y., Xu, Y., Lau, R.Y.K., Bruza, P.D.: Utilizing search intent in topic ontology-based user profile for web mining. In: WI '06: Proceedings of the 2006 IEEE/WIC/ACM International Conference on Web Intelligence, pp. 558–564. IEEE Computer Society, Washington, DC, USA (2006)

On the Effect of Group Structures on Ranking Strategies in Folksonomies

Fabian Abel, Nicola Henze, Daniel Krause and Matthias Kriesell

Abstract Folksonomies have shown interesting potential for improving information discovery and exploration. Recent folksonomy systems explore the use of tag assignments, which combine Web resources with annotations (tags), and the users that have created the annotations. This article investigates on the effect of grouping resources in folksonomies, i.e. creating sets of resources, and using this additional structure for the tasks of search & ranking, and for tag recommendations. We propose several group-sensitive extensions of graph-based search and recommendation algorithms, and compare them with non group-sensitive versions. Our experiments show that the quality of search result ranking can be significantly improved by introducing and exploiting the grouping of resources (one-tailed t-Test, level of significance $\alpha = 0.05$). Furthermore, tag recommendations profit from the group context, and it is possible to make very good recommendations even for untagged resources – which currently known tag recommendation algorithms cannot fulfill.

1 Introduction

The success of social systems in the Web is quite obvious, for example with popular systems like Flickr, YouTube, Blogger, and others more. Systems like these allow users to share photos, broadcast own videos, or blog about topics they are interested in. They document impressively that the active contribution of users to the creation process of content, and the possibility to share content immediately with (fellow) users, is highly requested by Web users. The *tagging* activity is one of the important characteristics of these systems: With tagging, a user adds freely chosen words that come into his or her mind when watching or using some content. The result of a single tagging activity is a binding between a user, a resource, and the respective keywords that this user assumes relevant for the resource. The evolving set of such

F. Abel (✉)
IVS – Semantic Web Group, Leibniz University Hannover, Appelstr. 4,
D-30167 Hannover, Germany
e-mail: abel@kbs.uni-hannover.de

I. King, R. Baeza-Yates (eds.), *Weaving Services and People on the World Wide Web*,
DOI 10.1007/978-3-642-00570-1_14, © Springer-Verlag Berlin Heidelberg 2009

bindings *user-resource-tag* is called a folksonomy [16]. By nature, the folksonomy is highly dynamic, and an important characteristic is that the tags assigned by users are not bound to any controlled vocabulary but contribute to a growing set of words.

The so-far developed folksonomy systems all have in common that the set of user-resource-tag bindings is hardly structured any further. Del.icio.us allows to structure tags by grouping them into so-called *bundles*, and BibSonomy [8] allows to structure users by formation of user groups. So far, nobody has investigated the effect of structuring the *resource dimension* in folksonomies, and, to the best of our knowledge, no present ranking algorithm takes further structure within the respective sets of users, tags or resources into account in order to improve the performance.

We have realized an appealing Web 2.0 application that enables users to easily construct groups of Web content that they consider interesting for some topic. GroupMe! users can group arbitrary Web resources like videos, news feeds, images, etc. Within a GroupMe! group these resources are visualized according to their media type – e.g. videos can directly be played within a group, news feeds list their latest items, etc. – so that content of groups is easy to grasp. GroupMe!'s tagging functionality allows users to annotate both, resources and groups. Hence, whenever resources are annotated, this is done in context of a group.

The immediate benefit of the GroupMe! approach is that we are now able to see Web resources in a context, namely the group context: Web resources which were previously not related at all now have in common that they belong to some group which defines a common context. Together with tagging, we can even further specify this relation between the members of a group: The group's tags are likely to be relevant for the members of the group, and vice versa. This is particularly interesting for the discovery of Web resources: the resource's context gives us means to find relevant tags even if the resource itself has not been tagged at all. We were able to show that the GroupMe! approach improves the recall of retrieval (see [2]).

Groups of content provide us with a database of *hand-picked resources* for certain topics, which are specified by the group and its tags. Presumably, these resources are of high relevance for the topic – in comparison to search results lists – as a subject is screening the search results and decides which to add to the group, and which not.

In this article, we investigate how to make use of this database of hand-picked resources, and how to exploit the grouping structure on resources in order to improve the quality of search & ranking strategies, and on tag recommendation strategies. The main contributions of our work can be summarized as follows.

- GroupMe! We introduce the GroupMe! system, which extends the idea of traditional tagging systems with the paradigm of grouping resources.
- GRank We propose the GRank algorithm, which exploits the context gained by grouping resources and which improves search for resources.
- Group-sensitive FolkRank We present different group-sensitive FolkRank adaptions and prove that the quality of search result ranking can be significantly improved by introducing and exploiting the grouping of resources (one-tailed t-Test, level of significance $\alpha = 0.05$).

Comparison We compare different ranking algorithms for folksonomies: GRank, FolkRank, group-sensitive FolkRank strategies, SocialPageRank, and SocialSimRank, and evaluate their quality with respect to (i) search and (ii) tag recommendation tasks.

The article is organized as follows: In the next section, we describe the GroupMe! system in more detail, and introduce folksonomy systems and the GroupMe! folksonomy in a formal way. Search and ranking strategies, for both the folksonomy model with and without groups, are discussed in Sect. 3. The analysis of our experimental findings are presented thereafter. The paper ends with a comparison to related work, and the conclusion.

2 Folksonomy Systems

2.1 GroupMe! Folksonomy System

The GroupMe! system[1] [1, 2], online since July 2007, is a tagging system similar to del.icio.us or BibSonomy as it allows users to search for resources or tag their own resources as well as the resources of other users. However, GroupMe! has a novel function that, as far as we know, no other present tagging system offers: Organizing resources by arranging them in groups. Users can use groups to structure their resources according to different topics, or to get a better overview of multiple resources as every resource is visualized in a multimedia-based fashion: Pictures are displayed as thumbnails, videos can be played immediately "within the group", and RSS feeds are previewed by displaying the recent headlines. Hence, users can get a quick overview of multiple resources by using the GroupMe! system. An example is given in Fig. 1 where a group *Travel to the WWW 2008 conference* is displayed. All relevant information, like a link to the official website, an image of some conference hotel, a short video tutorial for Chinese language, and other content can be seen at a glance without visiting each resource separately.

GroupMe! handles groups just like other resources, i.e. groups can be tagged like ordinary resources and groups can be included in other groups, allowing to build a hierarchical group structure. E.g. in Fig. 1, the WWW conference group also contains another group called *Business trip to Beijing*, which informs about common useful issues regarding business trips to Beijing.

Creating groups is very easy as users can put new resources into a group via simple *drag & drop* operations. GroupMe! includes interfaces for some major sources of resources. Currently, we provide search interfaces for Google, Flickr, and GroupMe! resources. Compared to tagging activities, which require a user to think of an appropriate keyword and entering this, grouping of resources does not require any typing and can be performed very fast. A remarkable feature of GroupMe! is that all

[1] http://groupme.org

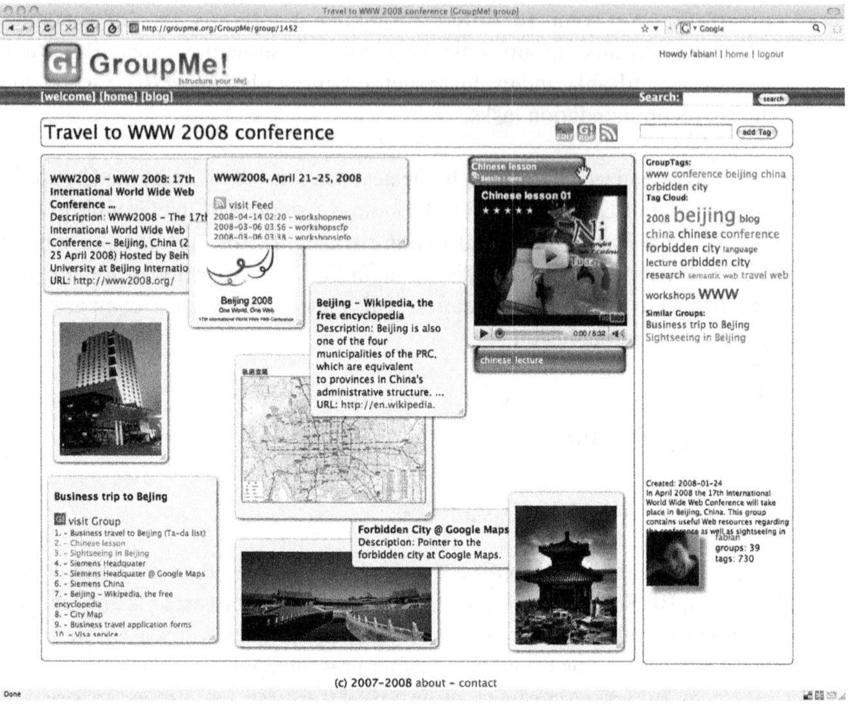

Fig. 1 Screenshot of the GroupMe! system: Constructing groups via *drag & drop*

user interactions are captured as RDF, which is made available according to the principles of Linked Data [4]. In that way Semantic Web applications are enabled to navigate through the whole GroupMe! data corpus. The GroupMe! ontology[2] ensures that such applications can interpret the additional semantics gained by the grouping activities of the users.

2.2 GroupMe! Tagging & Grouping Characteristics

In this section we have a look at the characteristics of the GroupMe! data corpus. The GroupMe! folksonomy, which was created by the community within a period of 6 months, contains 234 users, 974 tags, 1351 resources, 273 groups, and 1758 tag assignments. In the given data set, 49.3% of the resources do not have any tag assignment.

In Fig. 2(a) we evaluated the distribution of media types within the resources. Due to our architecture, GroupMe! groups are resources and make 20.2% of all resources. The remaining 79.8 % of resources are Web resources, which divide

[2] http://groupme.org/rdf/groupme.owl

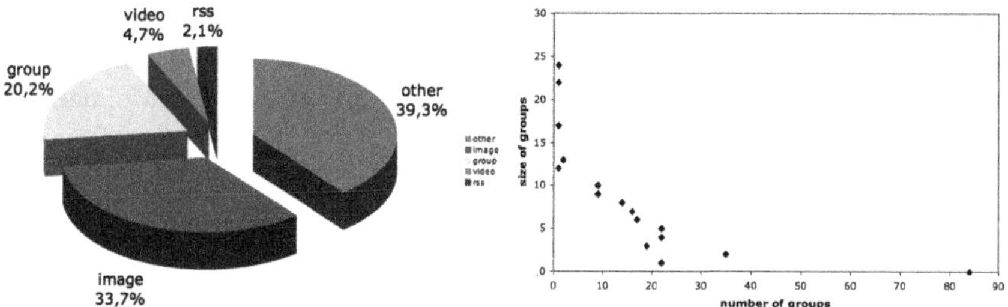

(a) Distribution of the media types of the resources

(b) Distribution of the number of resources per group

Fig. 2 GroupMe! characteristics

equally into normal websites or links (39.3% of all resources) and multimedia resources like videos, images, or RSS feeds (40.5% of all resources). This balanced distribution among the different media types, which is also present within the groups, is an evidence that users make use of the GroupMe! feature to bundle resources of different media types together.

Having a closer look at the groups, we checked the distribution of the number of resources in a group (see Fig. 2(b)). 94.89% of the groups contain less than 10 resources. This can be explained by the user interface, which limits the space of a group against the screen size. Therefore, only a limited number of resources can be placed in a group in a way that all resources are visible and accessible.

To make our outcomes applicable in other folksonomy systems we inspect whether the GroupMe! data set bears the characteristics that have been observed in other folksonomy systems like Flickr [19]. Therefore, we measured the distribution of tag assignments per resource (see Fig. 3(a)). The maximum number of tags that are assigned to a single resource is 15, which is lower than in other systems. However, on a log-log scale the scatterplot shows a distribution, which is observed in other folksonomy systems as well [19], and indicates a power law distribution. For the distribution of tags, we measured how often a tag was used by the users. The most popular tag is *semantic web*, being used 44 times, the next most frequent tag was used 24 times. Together with the distribution of the number of tags per

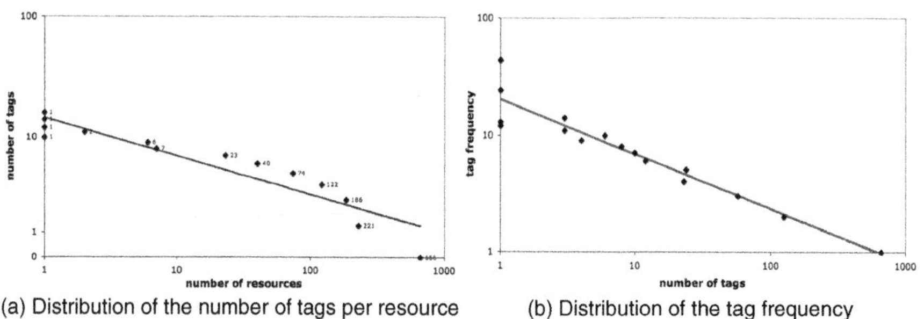

(a) Distribution of the number of tags per resource

(b) Distribution of the tag frequency

Fig. 3 Tag related characteristics

resource, we deduce that the GroupMe! folksonomy – even it is much smaller than folksonomies evolved in other systems – bears similar characteristics like common folksonomy systems. Hence, the results gained from the given GroupMe! data set are also relevant to other folksonomy systems.

2.3 Folksonomies

The term *folksonomy*, introduced by Thomas Vander Wal in 2004 [16], defines a taxonomy, which evolves over time when users (the *folks*) annotate resources with freely chosen keywords. Folksonomies can be divided into *broad* folksonomies, which allow different users to assign the same tag to the same resource, and *narrow* folksonomies, in which the same tag can be assigned to a resource only once [15]. Formal models of a folksonomy are e.g. presented in [6, 17]. They are based on bindings between users, tags, and resources. According to [8] a folksonomy is defined as follows:

Definition 1. A *folksonomy* is a quadruple $\mathbb{F} := (U, T, R, Y)$, where:

- U, T, R are finite sets of instances of *users*, *tags*, and *resources*, respectively, and
- Y defines a relation, the *tag assignment*, between these sets, that is, $Y \subseteq U \times T \times R$.

In [20], tag assignments are furthermore attributed with a timestamp and Hotho et al. also embed relations between tags into the formal folksonomy model [8]. In order to simplify the formalization we do not include these features. GroupMe! introduces groups as a new dimension in folksonomies.

Definition 2. A *group* is a finite set of resources.

A group is a resource as well. Groups can be tagged or arranged in groups, which effects hierarchies among resources. These hierarchies need not to form tree structures, which would e.g. result when organizing items into folders, but can also be cyclic, because groups can be contained in an arbitrary number of groups at the same time. In general, tagging of resources within the GroupMe! system is done in context of a group. Figure 4 presents a basic GroupMe! tagging scenario, in which users u_1 and u_2 have grouped resources r_{1-3} into g_1 and g_2, and have tagged both, resources and groups with keywords t_{1-3}. The tag assignment (u_1, t_2, r_2, g_1) in Fig. 4 describes that user u_1 has annotated resource r_2 in context of group g_1 with tag t_2. If users assign tags to a group, which is itself not contained in a group, then the group context information is not available ($\rightarrow$ $(u_2, t_2, g_2, \varepsilon)$). Hence, a GroupMe! folksonomy is formally characterized via Definition 3 (cf. [1]).

Definition 3. A GroupMe! folksonomy is a 5-tuple $\mathbb{F} := (U, T, \check{R}, G, \check{Y})$, where:

- U, T, R, G are finite sets that contain instances of users, tags, resources, and groups, respectively,
- $\check{R} = R \cup G$ is the union of the set of resources and the set of groups, and

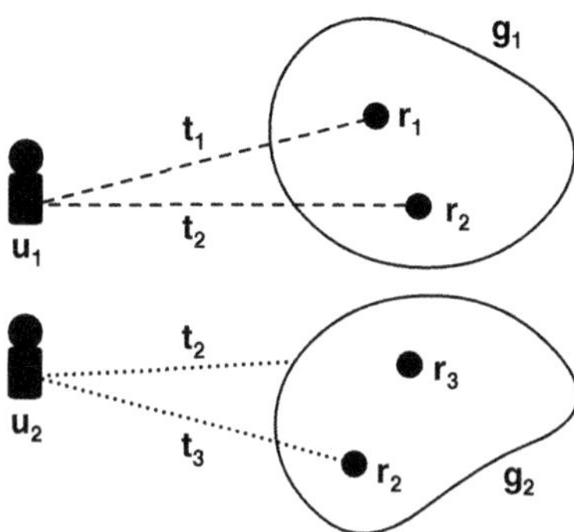

Fig. 4 Scenario in which two users assign tags to resources in context of different groups

- $\check{Y}$ defines a *GroupMe! tag assignment*: $\check{Y} \subseteq U \times T \times \check{R} \times (G \cup \{\varepsilon\})$, where ε is a reserved symbol for the *empty group context*, i.e. a group that is not contained in another group when it gets tagged by a user.

In comparison to traditional folksonomies (see Definition 1), in which relations between tags mainly rely on their co-occurrences (i.e. two tags are assigned to the same resource), a GroupMe! folksonomy gains new relations between tags:

1. A relation between tags assigned from (possibly) different users to different resources, where the resources are contained in the same group.
2. A relation between tags assigned to a group g and tags assigned to resources that are contained in g.

Relations between resources become in GroupMe! folksonomies more explicit than in traditional folksonomies. The latter allow to derive such relations if, for example, the same tag was assigned to different resources, or if the same user has annotated different resources. In the GroupMe! system users create groups with respect to a specific topic. Resources that are arranged together in a same GroupMe! group are therewith related to each other.

In the following section we present ranking algorithms, which exploit some of these new relations.

3 Ranking Strategies

In this section we present different algorithms, which target on ranking folksonomy entities. We first introduce graph-based algorithms that can be applied to arbitrary folksonomy entities (users, tags, and resources). In Sects. 3.3–3.5 we describe algorithms, which specifically focus on ranking resources and tags respectively.

Our contributions, i.e. ranking algorithms we developed, can be summarized as follows:

GFolkRank & CFolkRank Graph-based ranking algorithms, which extend FolkRank [9] and turn it into a group-sensitive algorithm in order to exploit GroupMe! folksonomies (see Sect. 3.2).

GRank A search and ranking algorithm optimized for GroupMe! folksonomies.

3.1 FolkRank

The core idea of the FolkRank algorithm [9] is to transform the hypergraph formed by the traditional tag assignments (see Definition 1) into an undirected, weighted tripartite graph $\mathbb{G}_{\mathbb{F}} = (V_{\mathbb{F}}, E_{\mathbb{F}})$, which serves as input for an adaption of PageRank [18]. At this, the set of nodes is $V_{\mathbb{F}} = U \cup T \cup R$ and the set of edges is given via $E_{\mathbb{F}} = \{\{u,t\},\{t,r\},\{u,r\} | (u, t, r) \in Y\}\}$ (cf. Definition 1). The weight w of each edge is determined according to its frequency within the set of tag assignments, i.e. $w(u,t) = |\{r \in R : (u,t,r) \in Y\}|$ is the number of resources the user u tagged with keyword t. Accordingly, $w(t,r)$ counts the number of users who annotated resource r with tag t, and $w(u,r)$ determines the number of tags a user u assigned to a resource r. With $\mathbb{G}_{\mathbb{F}}$ represented by the real matrix A, which is obtained from the adjacency matrix by normalizing each row to have 1-norm equal to 1, and starting with any vector $\mathbf{w}$ of non-negative reals, PageRank iterates as follows:

$$\mathbf{w} \leftarrow dA\mathbf{w} + (1-d)\mathbf{p}. \tag{1}$$

PageRank utilizes vector $\mathbf{p}$ as a preference vector, fulfilling the condition $||\mathbf{w}||_1 = ||\mathbf{p}||_1$. Its influence can be adjusted by $d \in [0, 1]$. Based on this, FolkRank is defined as follows [9]:

Definition 4. The *FolkRank algorithm* computes a topic-specific ranking in folksonomies by executing the following steps:

1. $\mathbf{p}$ specifies the preference in a topic (e.g. preference for a given tag).
2. $\mathbf{w}_0$ is the result of applying the adapted PageRank with $d = 1$.
3. $\mathbf{w}_1$ is the result of applying the adapted PageRank with some $d < 1$.
4. $\mathbf{w} = \mathbf{w}_1 - \mathbf{w}_0$ is the final weight vector. $\mathbf{w}[x]$ denotes the *FolkRank* of $x \in V$.

When applying FolkRank to GroupMe! folksonomies (see Definition 3) a straightforward approach is to ignore the group dimension of GroupMe! tag assignments. Therewith, the construction of the folksonomy graph $\mathbb{G}_{\mathbb{F}} = (V_{\mathbb{F}}, E_{\mathbb{F}})$ has to be adapted slightly. The set of nodes is given by $V_{\mathbb{F}} = U \cup T \cup \check{R}$ and $E_{\mathbb{F}} = \{\{u,t\},\{t,r\},\{u,r\} | u \in U, t \in T, r \in \check{R}, g \in G \cup \{\varepsilon\}, (u,t,r,g) \in \check{Y}\}$ defines the set of edges. Computation of weights is done correspondingly to the traditional FolkRank algorithm, e.g. $w(t,r) = |\{u \in U : g \in G \cup \{\varepsilon\}, (u,t,r,g) \in \check{Y}\}|$ is the number of users, who annotated resource r with tag t in any group.

3.2 Group-Sensitive FolkRank Algorithms

The traditional FolkRank does not make use of the additional structure of GroupMe! groups. In order to make the FolkRank algorithm aware of the novel group context gained by GroupMe! folksonomies, we adapt the process of constructing the graph $\mathbb{G}_{\mathbb{F}}$ from the hypergraph formed by the GroupMe! tag assignments. Therefore, we introduce two main strategies.

GFolkRank GFolkRank interprets groups as artificial, unique tags. If a user u adds a resource r to a group g then GFolkRank interprets this as a tag assignment (u, t_g, r, ε), where $t_g \in T_G$ is the artificial tag that identifies the group. The folksonomy graph $\mathbb{G}_{\mathbb{F}}$ is extended with additional vertices and edges. The set of vertices is expanded with the set of artificial tags T_G: $V_{\mathbb{G}} = V_{\mathbb{F}} \cup T_G$. Furthermore, the set of edges $E_{\mathbb{F}}$ is augmented by $E_{\mathbb{G}} = E_{\mathbb{F}} \cup \{\{u, t_g\}, \{t_g, r\}, \{u, r\} | u \in U, t_g \in T_G, r \in \check{R}, u \text{ has added } r \text{ to group } g\}$. The new edges are weighted with a constant value w_c as a resource is usually added only once to a certain group. We select $w_c = 5.0 \approx max(|w(t, r)|)$ because we believe that grouping a resource is, in general, more valuable than tagging it. GFolkRank is consequently the FolkRank algorithm (cf. Sect. 3.1), which operates on basis of $\mathbb{G}_{\mathbb{G}} = (V_{\mathbb{G}}, E_{\mathbb{G}})$.

CFolkRank If users assign a certain tag to resources in context of different groups then the meaning of the tag may differ. CFolkRank attaches the group *context* of tag assignments to the tags. In particular, CFolkRank replaces every tag t with a tag t_{tg}, which indicates that tag t was used in group g. It then transforms all GroupMe! tag assignments into traditional tag assignments. For example, the GroupMe! tag assignment (u_1, t_2, r_2, g_1), presented in Fig. 4, is interpreted as $(u_1, t_{t_2 g_1}, r_2)$ $(= tas_1)$. Assume we also have a tag assignment (u_1, t_2, r_2, g_2) then this would be converted into $(u_2, t_{t_2 g_2}, r_2)$ $(= tas_2)$. Thus, a 3-uniform hypergraph is built, which serves as input for the construction of the folksonomy graph $\mathbb{G}_{\mathbb{C}}$. The construction of $\mathbb{G}_{\mathbb{C}}$ is done as in the normal FolkRank algorithm, described in Sect. 3.1. Detecting equality of tags differs from FolkRank and GFolkRank, e.g. given tas_1 and tas_2 from above, the weight $w(u_1, t_{t_2 g_1})$ is not only determined by tas_1 but also partially by tas_2, although the tag $t_{t_2 g_1}$ in tas_1 is not exactly equal to $t_{t_2 g_2}$ in tas_2. We compute the similarity between two tags $t_{t_x g_y}$ and $t_{t_v g_w}$ and therewith the influence of a tag assignment to a weight as follows:

$\wedge$	$t_x = t_v$	$t_x \neq t_v$
$g_y = g_w$	1.0	0.2
$g_y \neq g_w$	0.4	0

Hence, based on tas_1 and tas_2 it is $w(u_1, t_{t_2 g_1}) = 1.4$.

In addition to GFolkRank and CFolkRank, we present two further extensions that help to exploit GroupMe! folksonomies. They can be applied to

GFolkRank, CFolkRank, and FolkRank as well. The core idea of both extensions is to propagate tags assigned to one resource/group to other resources/-groups. Such techniques synthetically increase the amount of input data and do not require to change the algorithms described above substantially.

(G/C)FolkRank$^+$ – Propagation of Group Tags. GroupMe! users annotate groups about 1.75 times more often than common resources [2]. By propagating tags which have been assigned to a group (*group tags*) to its resources we try to counteract this situation. For example in Fig. 4, tag t_2, which is assigned to group g_2, can be propagated to all resources contained in g_2. An obvious benefit of this procedure is that untagged resources like r_3 obtain tag assignments (here: (u_2, t_2, r_3, g_2)). In order to adjust the influence of inherited tag assignments, we weight these assignments by a dampen factor $df \in [0, 1]$. In our evaluations in Sect. 4 we set $df = 0.2$. FolkRank$^+$, GFolkRank$^+$, and CFolkRank$^+$ denote the strategies that make use of group tag propagation.

(G/C)FolkRank^{++} – Propagation of all Tags. Tags can correspondingly be propagated among resources that are contained in the same group. This extension induces propagation of (i) group tags to resources within the group, (ii) resource tags of one resource to other resources within a group, and (iii) resource tags to the group itself. Propagation is damped with factor df from above. Note that only tag assignments that have been carried out within the context of the corresponding group are considered for propagation. FolkRank^{++}, GFolkRank^{++}, and CFolkRank^{++} denote the algorithms that propagate all tags.

3.3 GRank

With GRank we propose a search and ranking algorithm specialized on GroupMe! folksonomies. GRank is defined as follows.

Definition 5. The *GRank* algorithm computes a ranking for all resources, which are related to a tag t_q with respect to the group structure of GroupMe! folksonomies (see Definition 3). It executes the following steps:

1. **Input:** keyword query tag t_q.
2. $\breve{R}_q = \breve{R}_a \cup \breve{R}_b \cup \breve{R}_c \cup \breve{R}_d$, where:

   a. $\breve{R}_a$ contains resources $r \in \breve{R}$ with $w(t_q, r) > 0$
   b. $\breve{R}_b$ contains resources $r \in \breve{R}$, which are contained in a group $g \in G$ with $w(t_q, g) > 0$
   c. $\breve{R}_c$ contains resources $r \in \breve{R}$ that are contained in a group $g \in G$, which contains at least one resource $r' \in \breve{R}$ with $w(t_q, r') > 0$ and $r \neq r'$
   d. $\breve{R}_d$ contains groups $g \in G$ containing resources $r' \in \breve{R}$ with $w(t_q, r') > 0$

3. $\mathbf{w}_{\check{R}_q}$ is the ranking vector of size $|\check{R}_q|$, where $\mathbf{w}_{\check{R}_q}(r)$ returns the *GRank* of resource $r \in \check{R}_q$
4. **for each** $r \in \check{R}_q$ **do:**
   (a) $\mathbf{w}_{\check{R}_q}(r) = w(t_q, r) \cdot d_a$
   (b) **for each** group $g \in G \cap \check{R}_a$ **do:**
   $\mathbf{w}_{\check{R}_q}(r) += w(t_q, g) \cdot d_b$
   (c) **for each** $r' \in \check{R}_a$ where r' is contained in a same group as r and $r \neq r'$ **do:**
   $\mathbf{w}_{\check{R}_q}(r) += w(t_q, r') \cdot d_c$
   (d) **if**($r \in G$) **then:**
   for each $r' \in \check{R}_a$ where r' is contained in r **do:**
   $\mathbf{w}_{\check{R}_q}(r) += w(t_q, r') \cdot d_d$
5. **Output:** GRank vector $\mathbf{w}_{\check{R}_q}$

$w(t_q, r)$ counts the number of users, who have annotated resource $r \in \check{R}$ with tag $t_q$in any group. When dealing with multi-keyword queries, GRank accumulates the different GRank vectors. The factors d_a, d_b, d_c, and d_d allow to emphasize the weights gained by (a) directly assigned tags, (b) tags assigned to a group the resource is contained in, (c) tags assigned to neighboring resources, and (d) tags assigned to resources of a group. In our evaluations we set $d_a = 10$, $d_b = 4$, $d_c = 2$, and $d_d = 4$.

3.4 SocialPageRank

The SocialPageRank algorithm [3] is motivated by the observation that there is a strong interdependency between the popularity of users, tags, and resources within a folksonomy. For example, resources become popular when they are annotated by many users with popular tags, while tags, on the other hand, become popular when many users attach them to popular resources.

SocialPageRank constructs the folksonomy graph $\mathbb{G_F}$ similarly to FolkRank. However, $\mathbb{G_F}$ is modeled within three different adjacency matrices. A_{TR} models the edges between tags and resources. The weight $w(t, r)$ is computed as done in the FolkRank algorithm (cf. Sect. 3.1): $w(t, r) = |\{u \in U : (u, t, r) \in Y\}|$. The matrices A_{RU} and A_{UT} describe the edges between resources and users, and users and tags respectively. $w(r, u)$ and $w(u, t)$ are again determined correspondingly. The SocialPageRank algorithm results in a vector $\mathbf{r}$, whose items indicate the *social PageRank* of a resource.

Definition 6. The *SocialPageRank algorithm* (see [3]) computes a ranking of resources in folksonomies by executing the following steps:

1. **Input:** Association matrices A_{TR}, A_{RU}, A_{UT}, and a randomly chosen SocialPageRank vector $\mathbf{r}_0$.

2. **until** $\mathbf{r}_i$ converges **do**:

   a. $\mathbf{u}_i = A_{RU}^T \cdot \mathbf{r}_i$
   b. $\mathbf{t}_i = A_{UT}^T \cdot \mathbf{u}_i$
   c. $\mathbf{r'}_i = A_{TR}^T \cdot \mathbf{t}_i$
   d. $\mathbf{t'}_i = A_{TR} \cdot \mathbf{r'}_i$
   e. $\mathbf{u'}_i = A_{UT} \cdot \mathbf{t'}_i$
   f. $\mathbf{r}_{i+1} = A_{RU} \cdot \mathbf{u'}_i$

3. **Output:** SocialPageRank vector $\mathbf{r}$.

SocialPageRank and FolkRank both base on the PageRank algorithm. Regarding the underlying *random surfer model* of PageRank [18], a remarkable difference between the algorithms relies on the types of links that can be followed by the "random surfer". SocialPageRank restricts the "random surfer" to paths in the form of resource-user-tag-resource-tag-user, whereas FolkRank is more flexible and allows e.g. also paths like resource-tag-resource.

3.5 SocialSimRank

The SocialSimRank algorithm [3] computes the similarity between two tags of a folksonomy. SocialSimRank adapts the idea of SimRank [11] and states that similar tags are usually assigned to similar resources. Definition 7 outlines the SocialSimRank algorithm as proposed in [3].

Definition 7. The *SocialSimRank* algorithm computes a ranking of tags in folksonomies by executing the following steps:

1. **Input:** Association matrix A_{TR}, tag similarity matrix S_T^0, and resource similarity matrix S_R^0
2. **Init:** $S_T^0(t_i, t_j) = 1$ for each $t_i = t_j$, otherwise 0
   $S_R^0(r_i, r_j) = 1$ for each $t_i = t_j$, otherwise 0
3. **until** S_T converges **do**:
   for each annotation pair (t_i, t_j) **do**:

$$S_T^{k+1}(t_i, t_j) = \frac{C_T}{|R(t_i)||R(t_j)|} \cdot \sum_{m \in R(a_i)} \sum_{n \in R(a_j)} \frac{min(A_{TR}(t_i,m), A_{TR}(t_j,n))}{max(A_{T|1R}(t_i,m), A_{TR}(t_j,n))} S_R^k(m, n)$$

   for each resource pair (r_i, r_j) **do**:

$$S_R^{k+1}(r_i, r_j) = \frac{C_R}{|T(r_i)||T(r_j)|} \cdot \sum_{m \in T(r_i)} \sum_{n \in T(r_j)} \frac{min(A_{TR}(m,r_i), A_{TR}(n,r_j))}{max(A_{TR}(m,r_i), A_{TR}(n,r_j))} S_T^k(m, n)$$

4. **Output:** SocialSimRank matrix S_T

SocialSimRank utilizes the association matrix A_{TR} for tags and resources, which is also part of the SocialPageRank algorithm. The weight $w(t, r)$, which is needed to fill the matrix, is computed as done in the FolkRank algorithm (cf. Sect. 3.1):

$w(t,r) = |\{u \in U : (u,t,r) \in Y\}|$. $A_{TR}(t_i, r_j)$ therewith corresponds to the number of users, who have annotated resource r_j with tag t_i. $R(t_i)$ is the set of resources that are tagged with t_i and $T(r_j)$ correspondingly defines the set of tags that are assigned to r_j. C_T and C_R are constant damping factors, which allow to adjust the similarity propagation of tags and resources respectively. In our experiments we set C_T and C_R to 0.7 as done in [3].

3.6 Synopsis

Table 1 summarizes some features of the ranking strategies presented in the previous sections. The FolkRank-based algorithms – except for CFolkRank that operates on artificial tags – are applicable for ranking of arbitrary folksonomy entities, i.e. users (u), tags (t), and resources (r). Furthermore, they are, as well as GRank and SocialSimRank, topic-sensitive, which claims that they do not compute a static ranking but allow to adapt rankings to a certain context. SocialPageRank computes static, global rankings independent of the context. For example, given a keyword query, SocialPageRank depends on an algorithms that detects (possibly) relevant resources, which are then re-ranked. GFolkRank, CFolkRank, and GRank denote search and ranking strategies, which exploit group structures of GroupMe! folksonomies (cf. Definition 3) and are therewith *group-sensitive*. FolkRank-based algorithms that make use of the tag propagation strategies (e.g. FolkRank^{+}), presented in Sect. 3.2, are group-sensitive as well.

Table 1 Feature overview of the different ranking strategies presented in Sects. 3.1–4

Ranking strategy	Applicable for	Topic-sensitive	Group-sensitive
FolkRank [9]	u, t, r	Yes	No
GFolkRank	u, t, r	Yes	Yes
CFolkRank	u, r	Yes	Yes
GRank	r	Yes	Yes
SocialPageRank [3]	r	No	No
SocialSimRank [3]	t	Yes	No

4 Evaluations

We evaluate the algorithms presented in Sect. 3 with respect to two popular applications: (1) search for resources and (2) tag recommendation. All experiments were run on the GroupMe! data set described in Sect. 2.2.

4.1 Search Evaluations

Topic-sensitive ranking strategies can directly be applied to the task of searching for resources, e.g. FolkRank-based algorithms can model the search query within the preference vector (see Equation (1) in Sect. 3.1) in order to compute a ranked search result list. Non-topic-sensitive ranking strategies – like SocialPageRank – compute global, static rankings and therewith need a search algorithm, which delivers a base set of possibly relevant resources, which serve as input for the ranking algorithm. We therefore split our search evaluations into two experiments. The first experiment analyzes the behavior of topic-sensitive ranking strategies while the second experiment also evaluates non-topic-sensitive strategies.

4.1.1 Metrics and Test Set

In order to measure the quality of our ranking strategies we used the *OSim* and *KSim* metrics as proposed in [7]. $OSim(\tau_1, \tau_2)$ enables us to determine the overlap between the top k resources of two rankings, τ_1 and τ_2.

$$OSim(\tau_1, \tau_2) = \frac{|R_1 \cap R_2|}{k}, \tag{2}$$

where $R_1, R_2 \subset \check{R}$ are the sets of resources that are contained in the top k of ranking τ_1 and τ_2 respectively, and $|R_1| = |R_2| = k$.

$KSim(\tau_1, \tau_2)$, which is based on Kendall's τ distance measure, indicates the degree of pairwise distinct resources, r_u and r_v, within the top k that have the same relative order in both rankings.

$$KSim(\tau_1, \tau_2) = \frac{|\{(u, v) : \tau_1, \tau_2 \text{ agree on order of}(u, v), u \neq v\}|}{|U| * (|U| - 1)} \tag{3}$$

U is the union of resources of both top k rankings. τ_1' corresponds to ranking τ_1 extended with resources R_1' that are contained in the top k of τ_2 and not contained in τ_1. We do not make any statements about the order of resources $r \in R_1'$ within ranking τ_1'. τ_2' is constructed correspondingly.

Together, *OSim* and *KSim* are suited to measure the quality of a ranking with respect to an optimal (possibly hand-selected) ranking. Our evaluations are based on 50 hand-selected rankings: Given 10 keywords, which were out of T, and the entire GroupMe! data set, 5 experts independently created rankings for each of the keywords, which represented from their perspective the most precise top 20 ranking. By building the average ranking for each keyword, we gained 10 optimal rankings. Among the 10 keywords, there are frequently used tags as well as seldom used ones.

4.1.2 Search and Ranking Experiment

For the first search experiment we formulate the task to be performed by the ranking strategies as follows.

Search and Ranking Task. *Given a tag as a query, the task of the ranking algorithm is to put these resources into an order so that the resources, which are most relevant to the query, appear at the very top of the ranking.*

The success of achieving the goal of this task is measured by means of the metrics defined in the section above. Figure 5 gives an overview on the measured results for the ranking strategies introduced in Sects. 3.1–3.3 with respect to OSim and KSim metrics. The strategies are ordered according to their OSim performance, whereas both, OSim and KSim values are averaged out of 10 test series (for the 10 different keywords and corresponding hand-selected rankings). In terms of the OSim, GRank clearly outperforms the other ranking algorithms and can be identified as best strategy: It computes rankings, which contain 82% of the resources that also occur in the corresponding hand-selected ranking lists. However, with respect to KSim, GRank is worse than, for example, CFolkRank^{++}, which is the best FolkRank-based strategy in terms of OSim.

FolkRank, which does not exploit the group structure, is outperformed by most of the group-sensitive ranking algorithms. Also the extensions of FolkRank, FolkRank^{+} and FolkRank^{++}, which rudimentary exploit GroupMe! folksonomies, do not improve the overlapping similarity of 0.405 but rather degrade the quality of FolkRank. We assume that the approach of propagating tags without modeling the group dimension within the graph, which serves as input for the ranking algorithm, primarily increases the recall but has a negative effect on the precision.

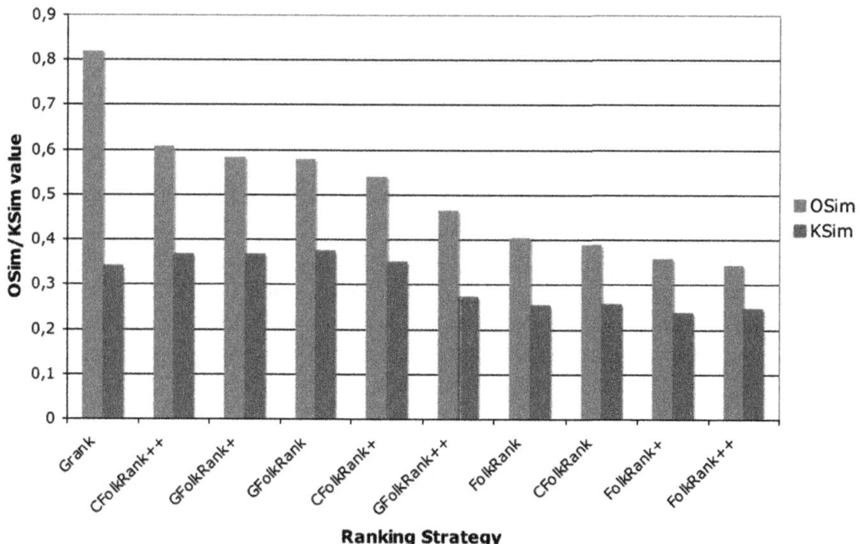

Fig. 5 Overview of OSim and KSim for different ranking strategies, presented in Sects. 3.1–3.3, ordered by OSim, where the dampen factor for propagating tags is 0.2

Results

To give proof on our hypothesis that grouping improves the quality of search, it is necessary to compare the search strategies which explore the grouping context to those search strategies which do not. As benchmark, we have chosen the FolkRank algorithm. All algorithms, FolkRank as well as the group-aware ranking strategies, were tested under the same conditions, i.e. the same set of data, hardware, etc.

We tested our hypothesis with a one-tailed *t*-Test. The null hypothesis H_0 is that some group-sensitive ranking algorithm is as good as a the normal FolkRank without group-awareness, while H_1 states that some group-sensitive ranking algorithm is better than normal FolkRank. We tested it with a significance level of $\alpha = 0.05$. Tests were performed for the two measures OSim and KSim (see Sect. 4.1.1).

OSim With respect to OSim, GRank is significantly better than all FolkRank-based algorithms. Furthermore, GFolkRank and CFolkRank^{++} are significantly better than FolkRank, FolkRank^{+}, and FolkRank^{++}. GFolkRank is not remarkably influenced by the propagation of tags (GFolkRank^{+} or GFolkRank^{++}). From our test data, we hypothesize that strategy CFolkRank benefits from the propagation of tags while GFolkRank does not. Our actual data did not give statistically significant results on this, and we will investigate the impact on tag propagation in our future work.

KSim With respect to KSim, the strategy GFolkRank is significantly better than normal FolkRank, whether or not the latter uses any tag propagation strategy. Also the strategy CFolkRank^{+}, where group tags are propagated, is significantly better than FolkRank.

OSim *and* KSim GRank is definitely the best strategy with respect to OSim. However, GFolkRank and GFolkRank^{+} are the only strategies that are significantly better with respect to both measures, OSim and KSim, than the normal FolkRank (whether or not the latter uses any tag propagation strategy).

Hence, the results of our search and ranking evaluations show that the grouping of resources significantly improves the quality of search in folksonomies. GRank is the most successful search algorithm as it gains the highest OSim and therewith detects a set of highly relevant resources. GFolkRank and GFolkRank^{+} also gain high results for KSim, which makes them particularly useful for applications that are interested in comparing the relevance of resources relative to one another.

4.1.3 (Re-)Ranking Experiment

Our second experiment evaluates non-topic-sensitive strategies. In particular, we compare SocialPageRank with the FolkRank-based ranking algorithms (without tag propagation). SocialPageRank requires an algorithm that delivers a base set of (possibly) relevant resources, which are then ranked by SocialPageRank. We therefore formulate the task performed by the ranking algorithms as follows.

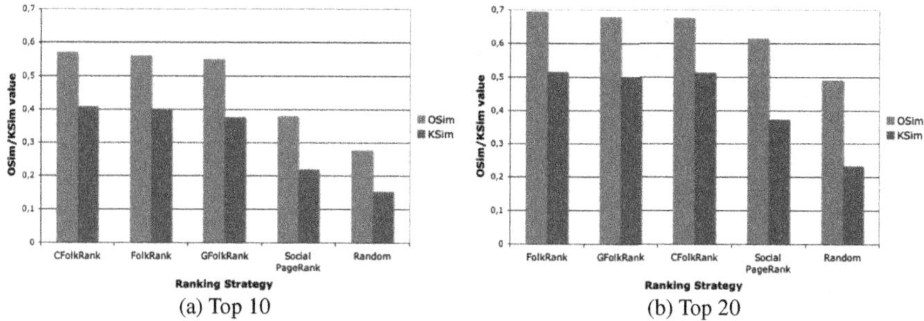

(a) Top 10 (b) Top 20

Fig. 6 Ranking Top k search results delivered by the GRank algorithm

Ranking Task. *Given a base set of possibly relevant resources, the task of the ranking algorithm is to put these resources into an order so that the most relevant resources appear at the very top of the ranking.*

In our experiment we detected the base set of (possibly) relevant resources via GRank, because GRank ensures a higher recall than the other ranking algorithms, as shown in the first experiment (see Sect. 4.1.2). Figure 6 lists the outcomes of the experiment, which was again performed on the GroupMe! data set described in Sect. 2.2. The results can be summarized as follows: Regarding KSim, the ranking quality of FolkRank and CFolkRank is significantly (one-tailed t-test, significance level $\alpha = 0.05$) better than the one of SocialPageRank (with respect to both, top 10 as well as top 20). Furthermore, the KSim score of GFolkRank is also significantly higher then the one of SocialPageRank within the top 10. Regarding OSim, CFolkRank algorithm is the only algorithm, which significantly outperforms SocialPageRank within the top 10. As expected, the strategy, which ranks resources randomly performs worth. However, due to the high quality of GRank, which is applied to detect the base set of (possibly) relevant resources, the performance of the random strategy is still acceptable.

4.2 Tag Recommendation Evaluations

SocialSimRank [3] (see Sect. 3.5) focusses on computing the similarity between tags, which makes SocialSimRank primarily applicable for tag recommendation. Supporting users during the process of tagging resources is an important application as folksonomy systems like Flickr, delicio.us, or GroupMe! suffer from the fact that eventually resources are not sufficiently annotated with descriptive tags. In our evaluations the tag recommendation task to be performed by the ranking algorithms can be specified as follows.

Tag Recommendation Task. *Given a resource, the task of the ranking algorithm is to compute a ranking of tags so that tags, which are most relevant to the resource, appear at the very top of the ranking.*

The tag recommendation process, which can be interpreted as a prediction of links between tags, resources, and (possibly) users, requires a high precision at the first positions of the ranking. In some application scenarios it might even be improper if the first relevant tag occurs at rank 2. In the following section we present metrics, which satisfy these requirements when evaluating the ranking quality.

4.2.1 Metrics and Test Set

The metrics that measure the success of the *tag recommendation task* correspond to those used in [19].

Mean Reciprocal Rank (MRR) The MRR metrics indicates at which rank the first *relevant* tag occurs on average.
Success at rank k (S@k) S@k stands for the mean probability that a *relevant* tag occurs within the top k of the tag recommendations.
Precision at rank k (P@k) The average proportion of *relevant* tags within the top k.

The *relevance* of a tag t to a given resource r is detected by two different modalities.

a. natural relevance t is the tag that was removed from resource r during the experiment, where we remove tags to evaluate if the ranking strategies are able to recommend exactly these removed tags to the resource again.
b. user-judged relevance t is a tag that was – in average – judged to be a *very good* or *good* description for the resource r.

The detection of *user-judged relevance* is executed on basis of a test set of user-judged tag recommendations. We randomly selected a test set of 52 resources, where each resource is equipped with at least two tags. The media type distribution within the test set corresponds to Fig. 2(a) except for groups, which are not covered by the test set. We asked assessors to evaluate tag recommendations for each of the 52 resources. Therefore, we presented the assessors each resource together with a set of tags, which was gained agglomeratively by adding the respective top 10 tag recommendations of our different recommendation strategies (duplicates were eliminated). In correspondence to [19], for each tag the assessors judged the descriptiveness of the tag on a four-point scale: *very good*, *good*, *not good*, and *bad / don't know*. The set of user-generated judgements contains overall 3715 judgements, in particular 843 *very good*, 759 *good*, 617 *not good*, and 1496 *bad / don't know* judgements.

4.2.2 Tag Recommendation Strategies

The ranking algorithms we evaluate regarding the tag recommendation task are FolkRank [9], GFolkRank, GFolkRank^{+}, and SocialSimRank [3]. CFolkRank,

GRank, and SocialPageRank cannot be applied for ranking of tags without modifications. For the others, we utilize the following generic tag recommendation to apply these algorithms to the recommendation problem.

Definition 8. The generic algorithm for recommending tags to a resource r performs the following steps.

1. Select a preference vector $\mathbf{p}$ according to the context of r.
2. Compute the ranking of tags with respect to $\mathbf{p}$.
3. Optional: remove tags from the ranking that are already associated with r.
4. Recommend the top k tags of the ranking.

In the first step of the algorithm the preference vector $\mathbf{p}$ weights tags that are relevant to the context of the given resource. We propose three different types of preference vectors, of which TC_G and TC_G^+ are group-sensitive.

Resource Tag Cloud (TC_R) The tag cloud of a resource r is a weighted list of tags t, which are assigned to the resource. We determine the weight $w(r,t)$ according to the number of users, who assigned t to r.

Group Tag Cloud (TC_G) The tag cloud of a group g is a weighted list of tags t, which have been assigned within the context of the group g. Hence, the weight of a tag t for a group g corresponds to the frequency t has been assigned to the group or a resource of the group: $w(g,t) = |\{(u,t,r,g) \in \check{Y} : r \in \check{R}, u \in U\}|$. In this paper we work with the top k tags of the group tag cloud, because too many tags in the preference vector are likely to cause noise. In particular, we set $k = 5$.

Group Tags (GT) When using the tags, which are directly assigned to a group g, as preference vector $\mathbf{p}$ for a resource $r \in g$, we refer to this strategy as GT. Here, weighting is done correspondingly to TC_R.

In context of the FolkRank-based algorithms the preference vector $\mathbf{p}$ directly conforms to the preference vector in Definition 4 so that computation of the ranking of tags is simply done via executing the FolkRank-based algorithm. In a recommendation process for resource r, which applies SocialSimRank (cf. Definition 7), we compute similarity rankings $S_T(t_i, t_j)$ for each tag t_i, which is part of the preference vector $\mathbf{p}$, and compute the weighted mean of these rankings according to the weights, which are specified in the preference vector.

After computing the ranking of tags, the generic algorithm for recommending tags (see Definition 8) allows to remove those tags from the ranking that are already assigned to the resource. In our evaluations we perform this step and recommend only tags, which have not been assigned to the resource before. Finally, the top k entities of the computed (and possibly filtered) ranking are recommended.

By combining the ranking and preference selection strategies we gain twelve recommendation strategies ($FolkRank\ (TC_R)$, $FolkRank(TC_G)$, etc.), which we evaluate in the next sections.

4.2.3 Experiments

In our evaluations of tag recommendation strategies, we run two kinds of experiments: *leave-one-out* [14] and *leave-many-out* [5] cross-validation.

Leave-One-Out Experiment

The leave-one-out method is convenient for small datasets [14] and is described in Fig. 7. The removal of some tag t from a resource r has direct impact on the computation of the tag recommendations. It effects the characteristics of the preference vector, and it has an impact on the association matrices, which are utilized by the ranking algorithms (see Sects. 3.1, 3.2, and 3.5). For example, it effects the construction of FolkRank's association matrix (cf. Definition 4) as the removed tag (assignment) is not considered for the folksonomy graph construction.

for each resource r of the test set:
  for each tag t assigned to r:
    1. remove t from r;
    2. **compute tag recommendations:**
       run *generic recommendation algorithm* (Definition 8)
       for strategy s;
    3. **evaluate tag recommendation ranking:**
       apply metrics of Section 1.4.2.1 to actual ranking;

average metrics values based on all computed rankings;

Fig. 7 Applying *leave-one-out* method for evaluation of tag recommendations of strategy s

We run the leave-one-out method for each resource of the test set, which is described in Sect. 4.2.1. The average metrics scores are used to describe the quality of a certain recommendation strategy. For each ranking strategy, we repeat the experiment two times, using either the *natural relevance* or the *user-judged relevance* to decide if the recommended tag is appropriate or not appropriate.

Leave-Many-Out Experiment

As outlined in Sect. 2.2, about 50% of the resources within the GroupMe! data set are not annotated with any tag. Therewith, the ability of recommending tags for resources, which are not tagged, becomes very important.

We evaluate the quality of our recommendation strategies with respect to untagged resources by applying *leave-many-out* validation [5], which is comparable to the leave-one-out method specified in Fig. 7. However, instead of removing only one tag, all tags are removed from the resource, for which the tag recommendation is computed. The *natural relevance* of a tag t is given if t is one of the tags that was removed from resource r during the leave-many-out validation. Strategies, which exploit TC_R as preferences, do not work for untagged resources and are thus not listed in Table 3.

Only the group-sensitive strategies are able to recommend tags to untagged resources, because untagged resources provide an empty resource tag cloud, and therewith an empty preference vector **p**.

4.2.4 Results

By nature of the experiments, evaluations based on the *user-judged relevance* gain better results than the ones, which base on *natural relevance*, because in the latter approach the recommendation is only successful if exactly that tag, which was from the resource, is recommended back to the resource. Therewith, the precision values listed e.g. in Table 2a, P@3 and P@5, are limited to $0.\bar{3}$ and 0.2, respectively.

Leave-One-Out Evaluation

Table 2 lists the outcomes of the *leave-one-out* experiment. With respect to Table 2a, $F(TC_R)$ turns out to be the most successful recommendation strategy. However, the performance of the top 6 strategies does not differ significantly. The strategies, which employ group tags as preferences (GT), perform worse than strategies that make use of the tag cloud of resources.

In Table 2b we also list the results achieved in [19], where the authors proposed tag recommendation strategies, which are based on tag co-occurence. Although the results in [19] were obtained in the same way as done in our experiment corresponding to Table 2b, a one-to-one comparison is not feasible as the authors used another data set for their experiments. However, the graph-based algorithms seem to outperform the tag recommendation strategy proposed in [19]. Our recommendation strategies do especially well at the top ranks (S@1 and S@3) and regarding the average rank of the first relevant tag (MRR). For some resources within the GroupMe! dataset there hardly exist 5 relevant tags,[3] which explains that the precision scores P@5 are not as high as the ones obtained from [19]. The strategies that apply SocialSimRank to rank the tag recommendations are clearly outperformed by the FolkRank-based approaches, e.g. considering S@1, $F(TC_R)$ leads to an improvement of more than 39% compared to $S(TC_R)$ (Table 2b).

Leave-Many-Out Evaluation

The leave-many-out experiment evaluates the important task of recommending tags to resources, which do not have any tag. This task can only be solved by the group-sensitive ranking strategies. Table 3 lists the results of the corresponding experiment. Here, the results of the natural-relevance analysis are nearly as high as the ones of the user-judged relevance analysis, which is caused by the fact that all tags of a resource are removed and therewith the number of available, relevant tags in the data set increases. This especially impacts the precision of the tag recommendation.

[3] Note that tags, which are already assigned to a resource, are not considered as tag recommendations.

Table 2 Evaluation results for tag recommendation strategies measured via *leave-one-out validation* with respect to (a) *natural relevance* and (b) *user-judged relevance* (ordered by MRR). Results of benchmark strategies are obtained from [19]. F, G, G^+, and S denote FolkRank, GFolkRank, GFolkRank$^+$, and SocialSimRank respectively, which use TC_R, TC_G, or GT as preferences (see Sect. 4.2.2). MRR, S@k, and P@k are the metrics described in Sect. 4.2.1

Strategy	MRR	S@1	S@3	S@5	P@3	P@5
F(TC_R)	0.7776	0.7290	0.7871	0.8194	0.2623	0.1638
G$^+$(TC_R)	0.7392	0.7034	0.7288	0.7797	0.2429	0.1559
G(TC_R)	0.7352	0.6949	0.7288	0.7542	0.2429	0.1508
G(TC_G)	0.7076	0.6271	0.7712	0.8136	0.2570	0.1627
G$^+$(TC_G)	0.6950	0.6017	0.7627	0.8220	0.2542	0.1644
F(TC_G)	0.6034	0.4903	0.7161	0.7677	0.2387	0.1535
S(TC_R)	0.5477	0.4153	0.6271	0.7627	0.2057	0.1513
G(GT)	0.4328	0.3814	0.4322	0.4831	0.1440	0.0966
G$^+$(GT)	0.4151	0.3475	0.4237	0.4746	0.1412	0.0949
F(GT)	0.3371	0.2323	0.4000	0.4645	0.1333	0.0929
S(GT)	0.1766	0.0619	0.1416	0.2920	0.0463	0.0573
S(TC_G)	0.1707	0.0593	0.1271	0.2373	0.0434	0.0452

(a)

Strategy	MRR	S@1	S@3	S@5	P@3	P@5
F(TC_R)	0.8777	0.8387	0.8903	0.9290	0.4172	0.3187
G(GT)	0.8673	0.8220	0.9153	0.9322	0.5762	0.4491
G$^+$(TC_R)	0.8365	0.8051	0.8390	0.8729	0.4237	0.3203
G(TC_R)	0.8390	0.7966	0.8559	0.8814	0.3813	0.2762
G$^+$(GT)	0.8477	0.7881	0.9068	0.9322	0.5734	0.4440
G(TC_G)	0.8572	0.7712	0.9576	0.9746	0.5367	0.4169
G$^+$(TC_G)	0.8490	0.7542	0.9492	0.9746	0.5734	0.4355
F(GT)	0.8146	0.7419	0.8645	0.9226	0.5333	0.4245
F(TC_G)	0.8086	0.6968	0.9290	0.9613	0.5505	0.4451
S(TC_R)	0.7447	0.6017	0.8559	0.9322	0.4637	0.3878
S(TC_G)	0.5560	0.3913	0.6413	0.7935	0.3483	0.3370
S(GT)	0.5556	0.3621	0.7069	0.8448	0.3594	0.3739
Results of strategies as proposed in [19]:						
Sum	0.7628	0.6550	–	0.9200	–	0.4930
Vote	0.6755	0.4550	–	0.8750	–	0.4730
Sum$^+$	0.7718	0.6600	–	0.9450	–	0.5080
Vote$^+$	0.7883	0.6750	–	0.9400	–	0.5420

(b)

Table 3 Evaluation results for tag recommendation strategies measured via *leave-many-out validation* with respect to (a) *natural relevance* and (b) *user-judged relevance* (ordered by MRR)

Strategy	MRR	S@1	S@3	S@5	P@3	P@5
G(TC_G)	0.9426	0.9268	0.9268	1.0000	0.5528	0.3756
G$^+$(TC_G)	0.9426	0.9268	0.9268	1.0000	0.5528	0.3756
F(TC_G)	0.8959	0.8537	0.9024	1.0000	0.5365	0.3756
G$^+$(GT)	0.6591	0.5610	0.6829	0.8537	0.2926	0.2243
G(GT)	0.6278	0.5122	0.6341	0.8537	0.2845	0.2341
F(GT)	0.5733	0.4390	0.6341	0.8049	0.2845	0.2439
S(TC_G)	0.3523	0.1951	0.3902	0.5122	0.2051	0.2051
S(GT)	0.2763	0.1000	0.3250	0.5000	0.1452	0.1692

(a)

Strategy	MRR	S@1	S@3	S@5	P@3	P@5
G(TC_G)	0.9682	0.9512	0.9756	1.0000	0.6991	0.5951
G$^+$(TC_G)	0.9682	0.9512	0.9756	1.0000	0.7398	0.5951
F(TC_G)	0.9520	0.9268	0.9756	1.0000	0.6991	0.5951
G(GT)	0.9174	0.8780	0.9512	1.0000	0.6504	0.5414
G$^+$(GT)	0.9052	0.8537	0.9512	1.0000	0.6504	0.5219
F(GT)	0.8776	0.8293	0.9024	0.9756	0.6260	0.5414
S(GT)	0.6300	0.4500	0.7750	0.8750	0.4358	0.4461
S(TC_G)	0.5899	0.4146	0.6829	0.8293	0.4615	0.4358

(b)

In general, the ranking strategies, which utilize the tag cloud of a group (TC_G) are the most successful strategies.

Synopsis

The SocialSimRank strategies are outperformed by the FolkRank-based algorithms. SocialSimRank merely exploits the relations between resources and tags, whereas the FolkRank-based approaches additionally utilize user-tag and resource-user relations. Relations gained by the group context are essential when tag recommendations should be determined for untagged resources. For untagged resources the group-sensitive ranking strategies provide outstanding results, e.g. GFolkRank utilizing the tag cloud of a group as preferences is, with MRR of 0.9682, the most successful strategy with respect to the mean rank of the first relevant tag (see Table 3b).

5 Related Work

In this article, our main motivation was whether additional context information – relating resources with each other, namely the group context – can be exploited to improve search and ranking performance in folksonomies. For this comparison we found that the FolkRank [9] algorithm, which is used in the BibSonomy system [8], is a perfect base to be extended. The algorithm mainly consists of two parts: First, the algorithm reduces the hypergraph to a two-dimensional graph which afterwards is processed by a PageRank variant. This enables us to adapt to the FolkRank in different extends: (a) adapting the construction of the input graph from the hypergraph spanned by the tag assignments or (b) modifying the adapted PageRank and FolkRank algorithm respectively. As any adaption of the part (b) would make it hard to prove that the performance gain was resulted by the new group structure instead of the tuning of the FolkRank algorithm itself, we decided to adapt only the process of transforming the hypergraph into a graph. Hence, we can study the group effect clearly.

In [19] the authors propose an approach for recommending tags, which is based on co-occurences of tags. Our evaluations indicate that graph-based recommender algorithms are more appropriate for folksonomies than strategies as described in [19]. Therewith, we confirm the outcomes of [10], where the authors show the advantage of graph-based FolkRank algorithm in comparison to collaborative filtering methods.

We tested our ranking strategies with a snapshot of the GroupMe! data set because there are, to the best of our knowledge, no other tagging systems that gain data comparable to the GroupMe! folksonomy. Flickr enables users to create groups of images but does not allow to tag those groups. Social bookmarking systems like BibSonomy or Connotea[4] provide functionality to create groups of

[4] http://connotea.org

users, however they do not offer functionality to structure bookmarks into groups. Creating a GroupMe!-like data set synthetically, e.g. based on del.icio.us bundles, is not appropriate because grouping as well as tagging is an activity done by users.

The design of a tagging systems has an important impact on resulting folksonomies. In [13] Marlow et al. propose a formal model (*tagging design taxonomy*) to classify tagging systems. According to the tagging design taxonomy, GroupMe! and BibSonomy are similar in many aspects (e.g. regarding the *tagging rights*: every user is allowed to tag everything), which was another motivation to adapt the FolkRank algorithm. The impact of the tagging system design on resulting folksonomies as well as the performance of ranking strategies with respect to different kind of folksonomies – e.g. broad vs. narrow folksonomies [15] – are open issues to analyze.

When designing algorithms for folksonomy systems, the basic assumption is that tags describe the content of resources very well. In [12] the authors prove this assumption by comparing the actual content of web pages with tags assigned to these websites in the del.icio.us system.

6 Conclusions

Folksonomies are characterized by a bottom-up approach to knowledge creation: Many people leave their traces, annotate resources, share annotations with others, browse via annotations, annotate again, etc. They are an interesting and highly dynamic source of information, and bear great potential for information discovery and retrieval. With the GroupMe! system we have created an intuitive Web 2.0 system that allows users to organize and maintain Web resources very easily. The system offers – like other current resource sharing systems – the tagging feature, but in addition enables users to group Web resources they consider interesting together, and tag also the groups. We capture the semantics of user interactions with the GroupMe! system, and exploit the dynamic and evolving grouping information for search. To verify that the grouping information improves the quality of ranking in folksonomy systems, we compared the results of ranking algorithms which can reflect the group information to those which cannot. To realize such a comparison, we benchmarked our algorithms against FolkRank and SocialPagRank, and are able to prove that grouping of resources in folksonomies significantly improves the quality of search result ranking. We furthermore show that the group context has great impact on the performance of tag recommendation strategies as group-sensitive strategies provide excellent results for the task of recommending tags even to untagged resources.

Acknowledgments We thank Nicole Ullmann, Mischa Frank, and Patrick Siehndel for their contribution and engagement in realizing the GroupMe! system.

References

1. Abel, F., Frank, M., Henze, N., Krause, D., Plappert, D., and Siehndel, P. GroupMe! – Where Semantic Web meets Web 2.0. In *Int. Semantic Web Conference (ISWC 2007)* (November 2007).
2. Abel, F., Henze, N., and Krause, D. A Novel Approach to Social Tagging: GroupMe! In *4th Int. Conf. on Web Information Systems and Technologies (WEBIST)* (May 2008).
3. Bao, S., Xue, G., Wu, X., Yu, Y., Fei, B., and Su, Z. Optimizing Web Search using Social Annotations. In *Proc. of 16th Int. World Wide Web Conference (WWW '07)* (2007), ACM Press, pp. 501–510.
4. Berners-Lee, T. Linked Data – Design Issues. Tech. Rep., W3C, May 2007. http://www.w3.org/DesignIssues/LinkedData.html.
5. Geisser, S. The Predictive Sample Reuse Method with Applications. In *Journal of the American Statistical Association* (June 1975), American Statistical Association, pp. 320–328.
6. Halpin, H., Robu, V., and Shepherd, H. The Complex Dynamics of Collaborative Tagging. In *Proc. of 16th Int. World Wide Web Conference (WWW '07)* (New York, NY, USA, 2007), ACM Press, pp. 211–220.
7. Haveliwala, T. H. Topic-Sensitive PageRank: A Context-Sensitive Ranking Algorithm for Web Search. *IEEE Transactions on Knowledge and Data Engineering 15*, 4 (2003), 784–796.
8. Hotho, A., Jäschke, R., Schmitz, C., and Stumme, G. BibSonomy: A Social Bookmark and Publication Sharing System. In *Proc. First Conceptual Structures Tool Interoperability Workshop* (Aalborg, 2006), pp. 87–102.
9. Hotho, A., Jäschke, R., Schmitz, C., and Stumme, G. FolkRank: A Ranking Algorithm for Folksonomies. In *Proc. of Workshop on Information Retrieval (FGIR)* (Germany, 2006).
10. Jäschke, R., Marinho, L. B., Hotho, A., Schmidt-Thieme, L., and Stumme, G. Tag recommendations in folksonomies. In *Proc. 11th Europ. Conf. on Principles and Practice of Knowledge Discovery in Databases (PKDD)* (2007), pp. 506–514.
11. Jeh, G., and Widom, J. SimRank: A Measure of Structural-Context Similarity. In *Proc. of Int. Conf. on Knowledge Discovery and Data Mining (SIGKDD)* (Edmonton, Alberta, Canada, July 2002), ACM Press.
12. Li, X., Guo, L., and Zhao, Y. E. Tag-Based Social Interest Discovery. In *Proc. of the 17th Int. World Wide Web Conference (WWW'08)* (New York, NY, USA, 2008), ACM Press, pp. 675–684.
13. Marlow, C., Naaman, M., Boyd, D., and Davis, M. HT06, Tagging Paper, Taxonomy, Flickr, Academic Article, to read. In *Proc. of the 17th Conf. on Hypertext and Hypermedia* (2006), ACM Press, pp. 31–40.
14. Martens, H. A., and Dardenne, P. Validation and Verification of Regression in Small Data Sets. In *Chemometrics and Intelligent Laboratory Systems* (December 1998), Elsevier, pp. 99–121.
15. Vander Wal, T. Explaining and Showing Broad and Narrow Folksonomies. *http://www.personalinfocloud.com/2005/02/explain ing_and_html* (February 2005).
16. Vander Wal, T. Folksonomy. *http://vanderwal.net/folksonomy.html* (July 2007).
17. Mika, P. Ontologies are Us: A Unified Model of Social Networks and Semantics. In *Proc. Int. Semantic Web Conference (ISWC 2005)* (November 2005), pp. 522–536.
18. Page, L., Brin, S., Motwani, R., and Winograd, T. The PageRank Citation Ranking: Bringing Order to the Web. Tech. Rep., Stanford Digital Library Technologies Project, 1998.
19. Sigurbjörnsson, B., and van Zwol, R. Flickr Tag Recommendation Based on Collective Knowledge. In *Proc. of 17th Int. World Wide Web Conference (WWW '08)* (New York, NY, USA, 2008), ACM Press, pp. 327–336.
20. Wu, X., Zhang, L., and Yu, Y. Exploring Social Annotations for the Semantic Web. In *Proc. of 15th Int. World Wide Web Conference (WWW '06)* (New York, NY, USA, 2006), ACM Press, pp. 417–426.

Resolving Person Names in Web People Search

Krisztian Balog, Leif Azzopardi and Maarten de Rijke

Abstract Disambiguating person names in a set of documents (such as a set of web pages returned in response to a person name) is a key task for the presentation of results and the automatic profiling of experts. With largely unstructured documents and an unknown number of people with the same name the problem presents many difficulties and challenges. This chapter treats the task of person name disambiguation as a document clustering problem, where it is assumed that the documents represent particular people. This leads to the person cluster hypothesis, which states that similar documents tend to represent the same person. Single Pass Clustering, k-Means Clustering, Agglomerative Clustering and Probabilistic Latent Semantic Analysis are employed and empirically evaluated in this context. On the SemEval 2007 Web People Search it is shown that the person cluster hypothesis holds reasonably well and that the Single Pass Clustering and Agglomerative Clustering methods provide the best performance.

1 Introduction

A field of growing importance and popularity is people search which deals with the presentation, representation, organization and retrieval of information items pertaining to people. For instance, searching for expertise within an organization is a rapidly growing research area (also known as expert finding), and its importance is underlined by the introduction of an expert finding task at TREC in 2005 [10]. However, there are many other related people search tasks (such as entity extraction, building descriptions of expertise, creating biographies, identifying social networks, etc). A more general task that helps facilitate such tasks is what we call people-document associations [5, 6]. This is the task of associating documents with

K. Balog (✉)
ISLA, University of Amsterdam, The Netherlands
e-mail: kbalog@science.uva.nl

This chapter is a revised and expanded version of [7].

I. King, R. Baeza-Yates (eds.), *Weaving Services and People on the World Wide Web*,
DOI 10.1007/978-3-642-00570-1_15,

particular people. For instance, within an organization in order to build profiles of employees the collection of documents needs to processed for such associations.

One particular case of this people-document association task is referred to as personal name resolution [23, 26, 27] (also referred to as personal name disambiguation/discrimination [9, 22], and cross-document co-reference [4, 12]). The task is as follows: given a set of documents all of which refer to a particular person name but not necessarily to a single individual (usually called *referent*), identify which documents are associated with each referent by that name. Recently, a test collection has been developed [3] to study this problem in a web setting; the scenario is this: given a list of documents retrieved by a web search engine using a person's name as a query, group documents that are associated to the same referent. This is a particularly relevant task because searching for people is one of the most popular types of web searches (around 5–10% of searches contain person names [27]). Given the popularity of people names in web queries, the problem of ambiguous person names is encountered frequently as a person name may have hundreds of distinct referents. Indeed, according to US Census Bureau figures approximately 90,000 different names are shared by around 100 million people (as cited by [2]). On the web, a query for a common name often yields thousands of pages referring to different namesakes [9]. Grouping the documents together by referent has been shown to be particularly useful in this scenario as a means of reducing the burden on the user to sort through the results [27].

In this chapter, we focus on the task of personal name resolution, a problem that has generally been considered as a clustering task: cluster the extracted representations of referents from the source documents so that each cluster contains all the documents associated with each referent. Essentially all work on the personal name resolution task has framed the problem in this way. However, we consider the problem from an Information Retrieval point of view, in the context of the cluster hypothesis [16]. The cluster hypothesis states that similar documents tend to be relevant to the same request. Re-stated in the context of the personal name resolution task, similar documents tend to represent the same person (referent). And thus, the task is reduced to document clustering.

Here, we explicitly examine the "person cluster hypothesis," making no assumptions about the underlying documents, i.e., their structure, format, style, type, and so forth (unlike the bulk of past work). While we recognize that considering the semantic attributes and features within documents can help in the disambiguation of names, it is the purpose of this chapter to examine the extent to which the hypothesis holds under the most general conditions using only the distribution of terms in a document as features. To this end, we consider several clustering algorithms: Single Pass, k-Means, and Agglomerative Clustering along with Probabilistic Latent Semantic Analysis, where we address a number of research questions based on the assumption of the "person cluster hypothesis." Since, under this view the person name resolution task boils down to clustering the document space where each cluster is assumed to be a particular person (referent), there is an obvious limitation. If the same person is described or involved in very disparate ways or things, then similarity-based methods will suffer. But, how much of a limitation is this? More generally, how good are clustering techniques for this task? And to what extent does the assumption/hypothesis hold?

In addition to these high-level questions, we also have a set of more low level issues that we aim to make progress on: What factors affect performance? How stable is the performance? When is the best performance obtained? And, what is the best number of clusters to use? Also, we are interested in more contrastive and reflective questions: Is term-based clustering better than semantic-based clustering, or vice versa? And, how can we improve the current methods?

The remainder of the chapter is organized as follows. In Sect. 2 we review related work. Then, in Sect. 3, we discuss ways of modelling the personal name disambiguation problem. Section 4 is devoted to a discussion of our evaluation platform, and we present the results of our experimental evaluation in Sect. 5. Finally, we conclude by zooming out to discuss our more general research questions surrounding the person cluster hypothesis in Sect. 6.

2 Related Work

The task of personal name resolution has been considered in many different ways; as (personal) name disambiguation, cross document co-reference and name resolution.

Name discrimination or name disambiguation is similar to word sense discrimination and generally relies upon the contextual hypothesis [21]: words with similar meaning are often used in similar contexts. Importantly, in word sense disambiguation the number of possible senses are known and limited to around 2–20; moreover, they are typically all known a priori—in name disambiguation the situation can be considerably more difficult as the numbers quoted in Sect. 1 suggest.

Cross document co-reference refers to the situation where an entity such as a person, place, event, etc. is discussed across a number of source documents [1]: if there are two instances of the same name from different documents, determine whether they refer to the same individual or not [9]. Essentially, cross document co-reference and personal name resolution/disambiguation are two sides of the same coin, where cross document personal name resolution is the process of identifying whether or not a person name mentioned in different documents refers to the same individual [23]. The problem can be broken down into two distinct sub-problems resulting from the types of ambiguity that manifest themselves in resolving person names [26]:

- multi-referent ambiguity: there are many people that share the same name; and
- multi-morphic ambiguity: one name may be referred to in different forms.

Past work has largely concentrated on the former problem, which has been addressed by clustering different types of representations extracted from the documents using different clustering techniques [4, 11, 12, 20, 23]. Different methods have been used to represent documents that mention a candidate, including snippets, text around the person name, entire documents, extracted phrases, etc. For instance, Bagga and Baldwin [4] first produce a summary of each person within each document (local person resolution). This summary is produced by extracting the text surrounding the person's name, which forms a bag of words representation. These, then, are clustered, using the cosine distance to determine similarity. Gooi and Allan [12] try a similar approach using snippets and perform agglomerative clustering with different similarity measures (cosine, KL-divergence). A possible criticism of such approaches is that the simplicity of the representation may not provide a rich enough representation of the person as the semantic relationships present within the document are ignored. However, in Information Retrieval, using a bag of words representation is common practice, because it is simple and effective. And it is a very powerful representation because it makes no specific assumptions about the underlying document structure and the content that it contains. It is more likely that the sparseness of the representations in the aforementioned techniques is more problematic.

An alternative approach that makes specific assumptions about the data was pursued by Mann and Yarowsky [20] who build a profile from each document based on learned and hand-coded patterns which are designed to extract (where present) the birth year, occupation, birth location, spouse, nationality, etc. Documents are matched based on matching the extracted factoids. A similar approach is taken by Phan et al. [23] who first create personal summaries consisting of a series of sentences; each summary is assigned a semantic label (such as *birthdate*, *nationality*, *parent*, etc); corresponding facts of each personal summary are then clustered using a notion of semantic similarity that is based on the relatedness of words. Fleischman and Hovy [11] use a maximum entropy classifier trained on the ACL data set to give the probability that two names refer to the same referent. This technique requires large amounts of training data which are usually not available in practical settings. Another approach which uses an alternative representation and approach to the problem of personal name resolution is based on social networks and co-citations to group/cluster the documents. Bekkerman and McCallum [8] use the link structure in web pages as a way to disambiguate the referents, while Malin [19] use actor co-citations within the Internet Movie DB. It should be noted that the approaches just outlined are limited as they make very strong assumptions about the data—which in web search, cannot always be met or guaranteed.

Several semantics-based approaches have been proposed in the literature. E.g., Pedersen et al. [22] propose a method based on clustering using second-order context vectors derived from singular value decomposition (SVD) on a bigram-document co-occurrence matrix. And Al-Kamha and Embley [1] study combinations of three different representation methods—attribute (factoid) based representations like those used in [20, 23], link/citation-based, and content-based.

In this chapter, we use a standard IR representation of each document (i.e., bag of words) because we want to examine the person cluster hypothesis and make as few assumptions about the data as possible. Then, we examine this hypothesis using multiple clustering approaches, ranging from naive, but intuitive, methods such as single pass clustering, agglomerative clustering, and k-means clustering, that focus on term similarity, to a more sophisticated approach, Probabilistic Latent Semantic

Analysis (similar to performing SVD) which focuses on semantic similarity. Since the goal of this work is aimed towards evaluating the person clustering hypothesis in a very general setting, we have selected these clustering methods because they are representative of the types already tried. For instance, Artiles et al. [2] use a similar representation of documents with agglomerative clustering technique to obtain a baseline for a pilot test collection for this task. However, our work differs because we focus on exploring how document clustering performs for this task.

While there has been growing interest in studying the person name disambiguation task, past work has used different test collections with significantly different characteristics (i.e., web pages or Internet Movie DB data or journal publications), which makes it hard to compare previous approaches. An important recent development has been the introduction of a common and publicly available test collection for testing personal name resolution [3]. Consequently, this is one of the first studies conducted of this nature using such a resource (see Sect. 4 for details).

3 Data Modeling and Clustering Approaches

In this section we describe the clustering approaches that we shall use in order to evaluate the person clustering hypothesis. Before doing so, it is important to explicitly state the assumptions we have about the data, which will allow us to contextualize how well the clustering methods fit the task of resolving person names. The main modeling assumptions engaged along with the person cluster hypothesis are as follows:

1. One document is associated with one referent. While this may not always be the case in practice, i.e., a page might contain several senses of the same personal name, there are only few instances of this within the test collection.[1]
2. The distribution of documents assigned to referents follows a power law, i.e., many referents have few documents associated with them, while few referents have many documents associated with them.
3. Every document refers to a distinct person sense, unless there is evidence to the contrary.
4. The number of distinct person senses is not known a priori. However, the number of possible person senses is limited by the number of documents available as a result of assumption (1) and (3).
5. The documents are assumed to be textual, and unstructured in nature with no predefined format, i.e., there are no guarantees about the format or structure within the documents.

Now, given these assumptions about the data, we evaluate how well the person cluster hypothesis holds under these conditions using four different clustering methods:

[1] This is a simplifying assumption often employed.

Single Pass, k-Means and Agglomerative clustering along with Probabilistic Latent Semantic Analysis. The first three methods provide different variations of traditional clustering methods (varying in terms of efficiency and quality). These methods also explicitly rely on the documents associated to a particular referent sharing common terms to describe the individual. We also contrast these clustering methods with PLSA, which does not have such an explicit reliance on the terms because transitive connections between terms can be identified through the latent space, although sharing common terms would certainly improve the method's effectiveness. Each of the chosen methods is described in more detail below before we perform the evaluation.

3.1 Single Pass Clustering

The first and simplest clustering method we employed is single pass clustering (SPC) [14] to automatically assign pages to clusters. SPC provides not only an efficient clustering algorithm, but also mimics a reasonable heuristic that a user might employ (i.e., start at the top and work down the list associating documents to different person senses). SPC does exactly this: each document is considered in turn starting with the top ranked document, if a cluster representing that person already exists, then the document is assigned to that cluster, otherwise the document is assigned to a new cluster, to represent the new person sense. In fact, this is very similar to the process taken by the annotators of the collection we use for evaluation; see [3] and Sect. 4. Also, since web search results are often ranked proportional to the number of in-links which represents the "popularity" of the page, it is reasonable to assume that the most dominant (popular) senses of the person name are highly ranked. So by starting with the highest ranked document, the SPC algorithm may capitalize on this external but implicit, knowledge. Finally, SPC is a very efficient algorithm and classification/clustering can be performed online, i.e., as the documents are downloaded.

The process for assignment is performed as follows: The first document is taken and assigned to the first cluster. Then each subsequent document is compared against each cluster with a similarity measure. A document is assigned to the most likely cluster, as long as the similarity score is higher than a threshold γ (this implements assumption 3); otherwise, the document is assigned to a new cluster, unless the maximum number of desired clusters η has been reached; in that case the document is assigned to the last cluster (i.e., the left overs).

We employ two similarity measures ($\text{sim}(D, C)$): Naive Bayes and a standard cosine measure using a TF.IDF weighting scheme.

3.1.1 Naive Bayes

The Naive Bayes similarity measure uses the log odds ratio to decide whether the document is more likely to be generated from that cluster or not ($\text{sim}(D, C) = O(D, C)$). This approach follows Kalt [17]'s work on document classification using the document likelihood by representing the cluster as a multinomial term distribution (i.e., a cluster language model) and predicting the probability of a document D, given the cluster language model, i.e., $p(D|\theta_C)$. It is assumed that the terms t in a document are sampled *independently and identically*, so the odds ratio is calculated as follows:

$$O(D, C) = \frac{p(D|\theta_C)}{p(D|\theta_{\bar{C}})} = \frac{\prod_{t \in D} p(t|\theta_C)^{n(t,D)}}{\prod_{t \in D} p(t|\theta_{\bar{C}})^{n(t,D)}}, \tag{1}$$

where $n(t, D)$ is the number of times term t appears in document D, and $\theta_{\bar{C}}$ is the language model that represents "not being in the cluster." Note that this is similar to the well-known relevance modeling approach [18] except that, here, it is applied in the context of classification, as done in [17]. The cluster language model is estimated by performing a linear interpolation between the empirical probability of a term occurring in the cluster $p(t|C)$ and the background model $p(t)$, the probability of a term occurring at random in the collection, i.e., $p(t|\theta_C) = \lambda \cdot p(t|C) + (1 - \lambda) \cdot p(t)$. The "not in the cluster" language model $\theta_{\bar{C}}$ is approximated by using the background model $p(t)$.

3.1.2 Cosine Similarity with TF.IDF

The other similarity measure we consider for single pass clustering is the cosine distance. Let $\mathbf{t}(D)$ and $\mathbf{t}(C)$ be term frequency vectors, weighted by the TF.IDF formula, representing document D and cluster C, respectively. Similarity is then estimated using the cosine distance of the two vectors:

$$\text{sim}(D, C) = \cos(\mathbf{t}(D), \mathbf{t}(C)) = \frac{\mathbf{t}(D) \cdot \mathbf{t}(C)}{\|\mathbf{t}(D)\| \cdot \|\mathbf{t}(C)\|}. \tag{2}$$

3.2 K-Means Clustering

K-means is a clustering technique [13], that creates a partitioning of data (i.e., the documents) given a desired number of clusters, K. K-means is based on the idea that a center point (centroid) can adequately represent a cluster. The basic K-means clustering algorithm for finding K clusters is as follows:

1. Select K points as the initial centroids
2. Assign all points to the closest centroid
3. Recompute the centroid of each cluster
4. Repeat steps 2 and 3 until centroids do not change

Again, we use the cosine similarity measure to compute which cluster centroid is closest to the given document. Following standard practice we calculate the centroid of clusters using the mean of the documents within the cluster. As advocated in [25] we use an incremental version of k-means clustering, i.e., centroids are updated as each point is assigned to a cluster, rather than at the end of an assignment pass as in the basic version. We set K based on the actual number of person name senses; see Sect. 5.2 for details.

3.3 Agglomerative Clustering

Agglomerative clustering [16] (AGGLOM) starts with documents as individual clusters and, at each step, merges the most similar pair of clusters. This is repeated until all clusters have been merged into a single cluster that contains all documents (thus, it is a hierarchical bottom-up approach). However, we want a partition of disjoint clusters, therefore, the hierarchy needs to be cut at some point. We use a pre-specified threshold γ for the level of similarity used to determine the cutting point. The distance between two clusters C_1 and C_2 is determined based on the maximum distance between elements of each cluster (also called complete linkage clustering). We use the cosine similarity to estimate the similarity of two pages. Formally:

$$sim(C_1, C_2) = \max\{\cos(\mathbf{t}(D_1), \mathbf{t}(D_2)) : D_1 \in C_1, D_2 \in C_2\}, \tag{3}$$

where $\mathbf{t}(D_1)$ and $\mathbf{t}(D_2)$ are TF.IDF weighted term frequency vectors representing documents D_1 and D_2, respectively.

Note that each agglomeration step occurs at a greater distance between clusters than the previous agglomeration. We decide to stop clustering when the clusters are too far apart to be merged, i.e., the distance criterion $sim(C_1, C_2) > \gamma$ is not met (and this implements assumption 3).

3.4 Probabilistic Latent Semantic Analysis

The final method for disambiguation we employ is probabilistic latent semantic analysis (PLSA) [15]. PLSA can be used to cluster documents based on the semantic decomposition of the term document matrix into a lower dimensional latent space. Formally, PLSA can be defined as:

$$p(t, d) = p(d) \sum_z p(t|z)p(z|d), \tag{4}$$

where $p(t, d)$ is the probability of term t and document d co-occurring, $p(t|z)$ is the probability of a term given a latent topic z and $p(z|d)$ is the probability of a latent topic in a document. The prior probability of the document, $p(d)$, is assumed to be uniform. This decomposition can be obtained automatically using the EM algorithm [15]. Once estimated, we make the simplifying assumption that each latent topic represents one of the different senses of the person name. The document d is assigned to one of the person-topics z if (i) $p(z|d)$ is the maximum argument, and

(ii) the odds of the document given z, i.e., $O(z,d)$, is greater than a threshold γ, where

$$O(z,d) = \frac{p(z|d)}{p(\bar{z}|d)} = \frac{p(z|d)}{\sum_{z',z'\neq z} p(z'|d)}. \tag{5}$$

Note that the requirement $O(z,d) > \gamma$ implements assumption 3: sufficient evidence must be found before assignment to a cluster can be made. All documents un-assigned are placed into their own cluster as per assumption 3.

In order to automatically select the number of person senses using PLSA, we perform the following process to decide when the appropriate number of person name-senses (defined by z) have been identified: (1) we set $z = 2$ and compute the log-likelihood of the decomposition on a held out sample of data; (2) we increment z and compute the log-likelihood again; if the log-likelihood has increased (by an amount larger than 0.001), then we repeat step 2, else (3) we stop as we have now maximized the log-likelihood of the decompositions with respect to the number of person name-senses. This point is assumed to be optimal with respect to the number of person name senses. Since we are focusing on identifying the true number of referents, this should result in higher inverse purity, whereas with the single pass and agglomerative clustering the number of clusters is not restricted, and so we would expect single pass and agglomerative clustering to produce more clusters but with a higher purity.

4 Evaluation Platform

In this section we describe the data set used, the evaluation metrics and methodology along with details concerning the preprocessing and representation of documents and estimation of PLSA.

4.1 Data Set

The data set we used for our experiments is from the Web People Search track at the Semantic Evaluation 2007 Workshop [3]. This data set consists of pages obtained from the top 100 results for a person name query to a web search engine.[2] Each web page from the result list is stored, as well as metadata, including the original URL, title, position in the ranking, and the snippet generated by the search engine. Annotators manually classified each web page to create a ground truth for evaluation. It is important to note that the original task statement allows a document to be assigned to multiple clusters, if it has multiple referents mentioned. However, because this was quite rare, we engaged a simplifying assumption and only perform

[2] Note that 100 is an upper bound, for some person names there are fewer documents.

hard classification (and leave fuzzy/soft classification for further work). Another caveat in this data set is that some web pages did not contain enough information about the person to make a decision (usually because the URL was out of date). These documents were discarded from the evaluation process (but not from the data set) and so we accept that a small amount of noise is introduced by the inclusion of these documents.

The collection is divided into training and test sets, comprising 49 and 30 person names, respectively.[3] In order to provide different ambiguity scenarios, the data set is made up of person names from different sources (the source of names was known in advance only for the training data):

US Census 42 names (32/10 in training/test set) picked randomly from the Web03 corpus [20];

Wikipedia 17 names (7/10 in training/test set) sampled from a list of ambiguous person names in the English Wikipedia;

ECDL06 10 names (training set only) randomly selected from the Program Committee listing of a Computer Science conference (ECDL 2006); and

ACL06 10 names (test set only) randomly selected from participants of a Computer Science conference (ACL 2006).

The statistics of the training/test sets and the different sources are shown in Table 1. Despite the fact that both were sampled from the same sources, the ambiguity in the test data (45.93 referents per person name, on average) is much higher than in the training data (where it is only 10.76). According to Artiles et al. [3], this shows that "there is a high (and unpredictable) variability, which would require much larger data sets to have reliable population samples." In order to measure performance as reliably as possible given the SemEval test suite, we conduct our experiments using

Table 1 Statistics of the data collection. The columns of the table are: data set (or source), number of person names (queries), average number of documents (per person name), average number of discarded documents (per person name), average number of referents (per person name)

Data set/source	#names	Docs	Discarded	Referents
Training set	49	71.02	26.00	10.76
US Census	32	47.20	18.00	5.90
Wikipedia	7	99.00	8.29	23.14
ECDL06	10	99.20	30.30	15.30
Test set	30	98.93	15.07	45.93
US Census	10	99.10	14.90	50.30
Wikipedia	10	99.30	17.50	56.50
ACL06	10	98.40	12.80	31.00

[3] The WePS organizers also released a trial data set, consisting of an adapted version of WePS corpus, described in [2]. We did not use this corpus in our experiments, but limited ourselves to the official SemEval training and test collections.

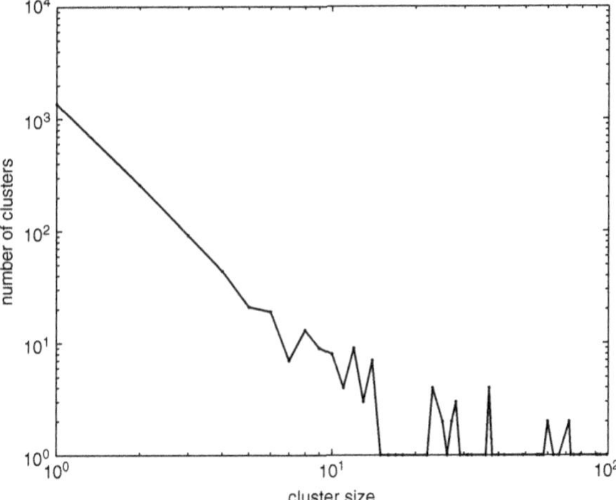

Fig. 1 Number of clusters for each cluster size on test+train data (log-log plot shown)

all names from both the training and the test sets; we will refer to it as *all names*. Unless stated otherwise results are reported on all names.

While there appears to be a high degree of ambiguity due to the large number of person name senses, we assumed that the distribution of documents to person name senses would follow a power law. Figure 1 shows that the size of the clusters follows a power law with an exponent of approximately 1.31 estimated using linear regression of the log-log plot. This confirms the second assumption of the data and is a novel finding regarding this task/data.

4.2 Performance Measures

Evaluation of the SemEval WePS task is performed using standard clustering measures: purity and inverse purity. Purity is related to the precision measure, well known in IR, and rewards methods that introduce less noise in each cluster. The overall purity of a clustering solution is expressed as a weighted average of maximal precision values:

$$purity = \sum_i \frac{|C_i|}{n} \max precision(C_i, L_j), \tag{6}$$

where n denotes the number of documents, and the precision of a cluster $|C_i|$ for a given category L_j is defined as:

$$precision(C_i, L_j) = \frac{|C_i \cap L_j|}{|C_i|}. \tag{7}$$

Inverse purity focuses on recall, i.e., rewards a clustering solution that gathers more elements of each class into a corresponding single cluster. Inverse purity is given by:

$$inv.purity = \sum_i \frac{|L_i|}{n} \max precision(L_i, C_j). \tag{8}$$

A weighted version of the F-measure is obtained by computing the weighted average of the purity and inverse purity scores:

$$F_\alpha = \frac{1}{\alpha \frac{1}{purity} + (1-\alpha) \frac{1}{inv.purity}}, \tag{9}$$

where $\alpha \in [0, 1]$ is a parameter to set the ratios between purity and inverse purity.

The harmonic mean ($\alpha = 0.5$) was used for the final ranking of systems at SemEval, and $F_{0.2}$ was also reported as an additional measure, which gives more importance to the inverse purity aspect ($\alpha = 0.2$). Artiles et al. [2] argue that the rationale for using $F_{0.2}$, from a user's point of view, is that "it is easier to discard a few incorrect web pages in a cluster which has all the information needed, than having to collect the relevant information across many different clusters." We decided to also report on $F_{0.8}$, a measure which gives more importance to the purity aspect ($\alpha = 0.8$). Our motivation for also reporting $F_{0.8}$ is that from a machine's point of view, it is more important to ensure that the precision/purity of the clusters are high (so that any subsequent task involving their use, like building a profile, does not contain any excessive noise).

4.3 Document Representation

A separate index was built for each person, using the Lemur toolkit.[4] We used a standard (English) stopword list but did not apply stemming. A document was represented using the *title* and *snippet* text from the search engine's output, and the *body text* of the page, extracted from the crawled HTML pages, using the method described below.

4.3.1 Acquiring Plain-Text Content from HTML

Our aim here is to extract the plain-text content from HTML pages and to leave out blocks or segments that contain little or no useful textual information (headers, footers, navigation menus, adverts, etc.). To this end, we exploit the fact that most web pages consist of blocks of text content with relatively little markup, interspersed

[4] URL: `http://www.lemurproject.org`

with navigation links, images with captions, etc. These segments of a page are usually separated by block-level HTML tags. Our extractor first generates a syntax tree from the HTML document. We then traverse this tree while bookkeeping the stretch of uninterrupted non-HTML text we have seen. Each time we encounter a block-level HTML tag we examine the buffer of text we have collected, and if it is longer than a threshold, we output it. The threshold for the minimal length of buffer text was empirically set to 10. In other words, we only consider segments of the page, separated by block-level HTML tags, that contain 10 or more words.

4.4 PLSA Estimation

We used the Lemur toolkit and the PennAspect implementation of PLSA [24] for our experiments, where the parameters for PLSA were set as follows. For each k we perform 10 initializations where the best initialization in terms of log-likelihood is selected. The EM algorithm is run using tempering with up to 100 EM Steps. For tempering, the setting suggested in [15] is used. The models are estimated on 90% of the data and 10% of the data is held out in order to compute the log-likelihood of the decompositions.

5 Experiments and Results

In this section, we present an experimental evaluation of the four clustering approaches. We address the following specific research questions, leaving the more general ones surrounding the person cluster hypothesis to Sect. 6:

- What factors affect performance? That is number of clusters, similarity threshold, similarity metric, etc.
- How stable is the performance?
- When is the best performance obtained?
- What is the best number of clusters to use? Can we determine this automatically?
- How do the different clustering approaches compare to each other?

We start by exploring the performance and behavior of the Single Pass Clustering, k-Means Clustering, Agglomerative Clustering, and Probabilistic Latent Semantic Analysis methods, separately. Then, we compare and contrast the various methods, before providing an analysis over different groups (as opposed to aggregated over all topics).

5.1 Single Pass Clustering

Figures 2 and 3 present the results of the SPC method along a number of dimensions, using the Naive Bayes (SPC-NB) and cosine similarity measures (SPC-COS),

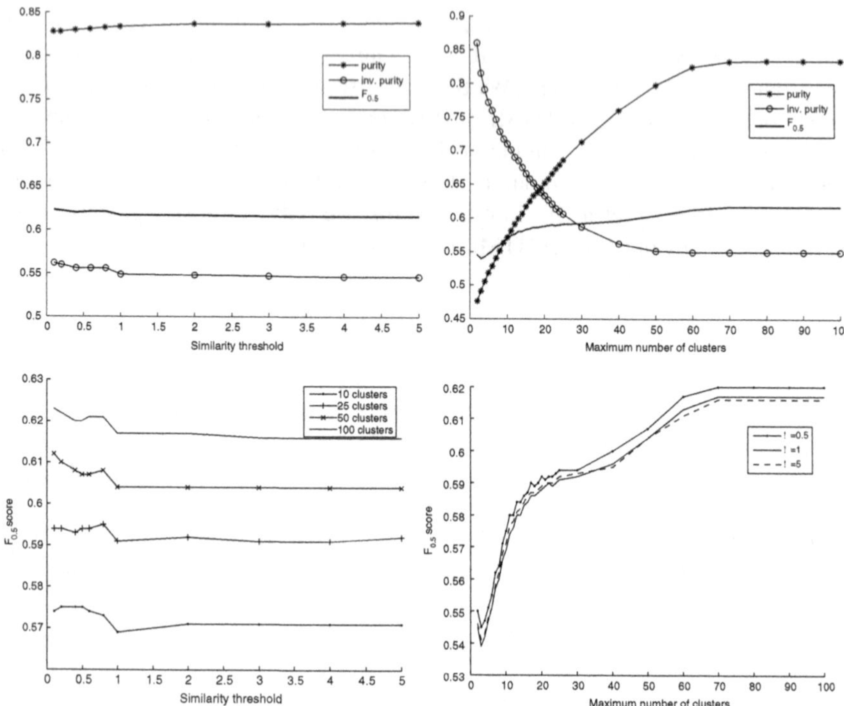

Fig. 2 Single pass clustering using the Naive Bayes similarity measure. (*Top Left*): varying the similarity threshold, maximum number of clusters is fixed. (*Top Right*): varying the maximum number of clusters, similarity threshold is fixed. (*Bottom Left*): varying the similarity threshold, using different cluster size configurations. (*Bottom Right*): varying the cluster sizes, using different similarity threshold configurations

respectively. Results are aggregated over all names (including both the training and test sets); the best scoring configurations are summarized in Tables 3 and 4. The top left plot shows performance given the maximum number of clusters is fixed ($\eta = 100$) as the similarity threshold is varied. The bottom left plots shows the harmonic F-score displayed for various similarity thresholds for η equal to a maximum of 10, 25, 50, and 100 clusters. These two plots across the similarity threshold show that the performance of either SPC is very stable w.r.t. the threshold, but the best performance obtained is with a lower threshold. This implies that the similarity between documents need not be very high (i.e., evidence to the contrary for assignment can be quite low, for assumption 3.).

In the top right plots, the similarity threshold is fixed ($\gamma = 0.1$) and performance is measured against different maximal cluster size limits. In the bottom right plots, the F-score is explored against the possible cluster sizes, using different similarity threshold configurations. In these two plots across the maximum number of clusters, we can see that enforcing a limit on the clustering is not appropriate—and actually violates the third assumption. However, this appears to be in contrast with the similarity threshold, which from above, does not need to be very high.

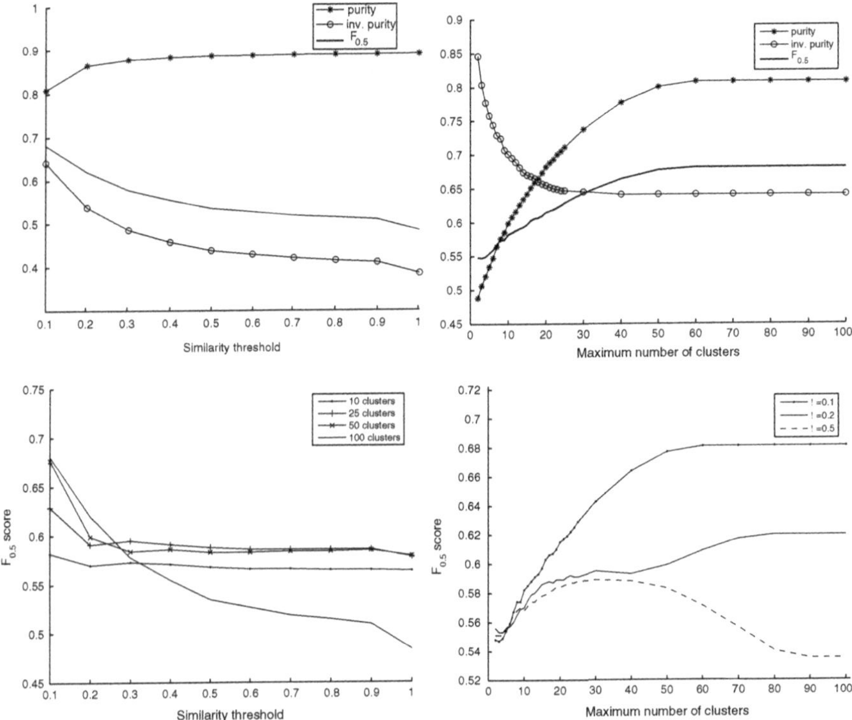

Fig. 3 Single pass clustering using the cosine similarity measure. (*Top Left*): varying the similarity threshold, maximum number of clusters is fixed. (*Top Right*): varying the maximum number of clusters, similarity threshold is fixed. (*Bottom Left*): varying the similarity threshold, using different cluster size configurations. (*Bottom Right*): varying the cluster sizes, using different similarity threshold configurations

Consequently, the best performance was achieved when the maximum number of clusters (η) was set to 100, and this was independent of the similarity measure. And while performance was quite stable given the similarity threshold, γ set to 0.1 was the threshold which delivered the highest F-score.

5.2 K-Means Clustering

Note that in order to perform k-Means Clustering, the number of desired clusters (K) has to be specified. We set K to be the actual number of person-senses based on the ground truth. This is a special—and arguably unrealistic—experimental condition, to determine the performance that could be achieved with this clustering method if the number of person-senses were known. While this violates assumption 4, we treat this experiment as an upper bound for the capability of k-Means clustering. As the performance of this method may vary depending on the initial assignments, the algorithm is run 100 times, and the scores are averaged over all 100 runs. The results are presented in Tables 3 and 4.

5.3 Agglomerative Clustering

Figure 4 shows the performance of Agglomerative Clustering as the similarity threshold (γ) is varied. We see from the plot that performance in terms of inverse purity and $F_{0.5}$ score decreases rapidly as the threshold hold increases (and conversely for purity). The best overall result (in terms of $F_{0.5}$ score) is obtained with a low γ value. This is in accordance with what we have seen for SPC; the evidence to the contrary for assignment can be quite low, for assumption 3. Results of the best scoring configuration are detailed in Tables 3 and 4.

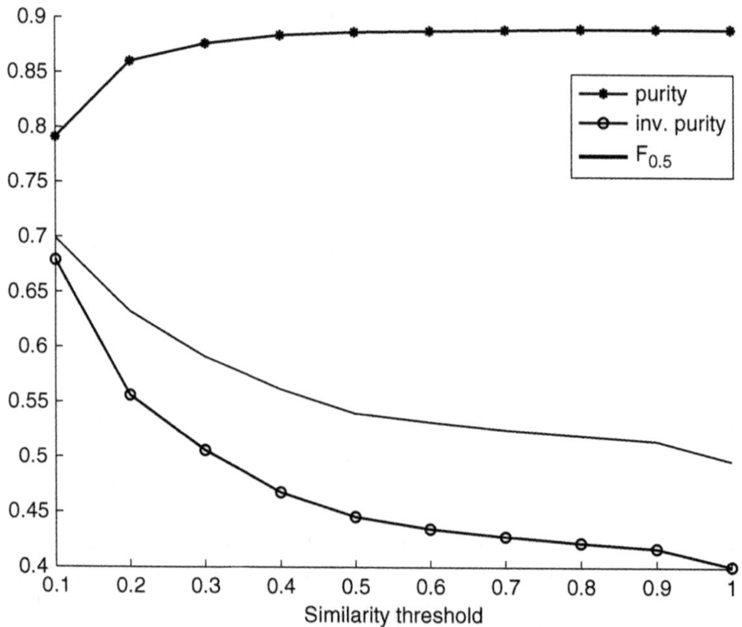

Fig. 4 The effect of varying the similarity threshold for agglomerative clustering

5.4 PLSA

Table 2 reports on the results we obtained from PLSA under two different experimental conditions. The first is a manual configuration of the number of latent topics which is set to be the actual number of person name-senses, based on the ground truth files. This is to determine an upper bound, which could be achieved if the number of latent topics could be identified, and assuming that each latent topic is actually representative of each person name-sense. The other, more realistic exper-

Table 2 Performance of PLSA

Experimental condition	Pur.	Invp.	$F_{0.5}$	$F_{0.2}$	$F_{0.8}$
Manual (truth)	0.530	0.647	0.547	0.591	0.530
Auto ($\gamma = 0.5$)	0.495	**0.800**	0.536	**0.624**	0.501
Auto ($\gamma = 1.0$)	0.517	0.782	0.543	0.622	0.515
Auto ($\gamma = 5.0$)	**0.662**	0.647	**0.561**	0.583	**0.584**

Best scores are in boldface.

imental setting uses unsupervised learning to determine the number of latent topics within the set of documents (as explained in Sect. 3.4). For this setting, we varied the similarity threshold. Surprisingly, the manual setting did not perform very well at all, and shows that the latent topics are not really that representative of the individual person name senses. We suspect this is because the distribution over the latent topics is dominated by only a few ("principal") components, so to speak; and so the number of resulting clusters is quite low (as we shall see in a following subsection); the automatic methods stop, in theory, when the overriding latent factors have been identified (because using any more would just introduce noise). Consequently, we find that the best performance for PLSA is obtained when the number of clusters is automatically estimated. In contrast to the SPC and AGGLOM methods, the number of clusters identified is very low, which results in high inverse purity scores, but lower purity (as we anticipated). Interestingly, for PLSA increasing the threshold means that more clusters are created, but at the expense of inverse purity.

5.5 Comparing Methods

Table 3 presents the results achieved by the best performing configuration of the different clustering approaches, while Table 4 presents a breakdown of scores to training and test sets. The parameters used are: $\lambda = 0.5$, $\eta = 100$, $\gamma = 0.1$ for SPC with Naive Bayes similarity (SPC-NB), $\eta = 100$, $\gamma = 0.1$ for SPC with cosine similarity (SPC-COS), $\gamma = 0.1$ for AGGLOM, and $\gamma = 1.0$ for PLSA.[5] Note that K is set to the actual number of person senses for k-Means Clustering.

Table 3 Results achieved by the best performing configurations of the different approaches

Method	Pur.	Invp.	$F_{0.5}$	$F_{0.2}$	$F_{0.8}$
SPC-NB	**0.828**	0.562	0.623	0.579	0.705
SPC-COS	0.808	0.641	0.681	0.651	0.736
K-MEANS	0.742	0.658	0.678	0.660	0.710
AGGLOM	0.791	0.679	**0.699**	**0.681**	**0.739**
PLSA	0.517	**0.782**	0.543	0.622	0.515

Best scores are in boldface.

[5] In the case of PLSA, there is no "best" γ, the setting we use is the one that performs well across the board.

Table 4 Breakdown of results achieved by the best performing configurations of the different approaches to training and test sets

	Training set					Test set				
Method	Pur.	Invp.	$F_{0.5}$	$F_{0.2}$	$F_{0.8}$	Pur.	Invp.	$F_{0.5}$	$F_{0.2}$	$F_{0.8}$
SPC-NB	**0.793**	0.484	0.547	0.501	0.641	**0.884**	0.688	0.747	0.707	0.809
SPC-COS	0.782	0.557	0.613	0.572	0.688	0.850	0.777	0.791	0.780	**0.815**
K-MEANS	0.694	0.632	0.634	0.625	0.662	0.820	0.701	0.750	0.718	0.789
AGGLOM	0.775	0.597	**0.640**	0.608	**0.700**	0.818	0.812	**0.796**	**0.802**	0.803
PLSA	0.607	**0.719**	0.605	**0.647**	0.596	0.370	**0.885**	0.442	0.581	0.382

Best scores are in boldface.

We can see the contrast between the methods when we consider the number of clusters each method creates against the actual number of person name-senses. Figure 5 plots the number of estimated clusters against the actual number of clusters, extracted from the truth files for each of the clustering methods. Clearly, the SPC and AGGLOM methods are providing a good estimate of the number of person name-senses. This is reflected by the strong correlation between clusters and person name senses. The Pearson's correlation coefficients for SPC-NB, SPC-COS, and

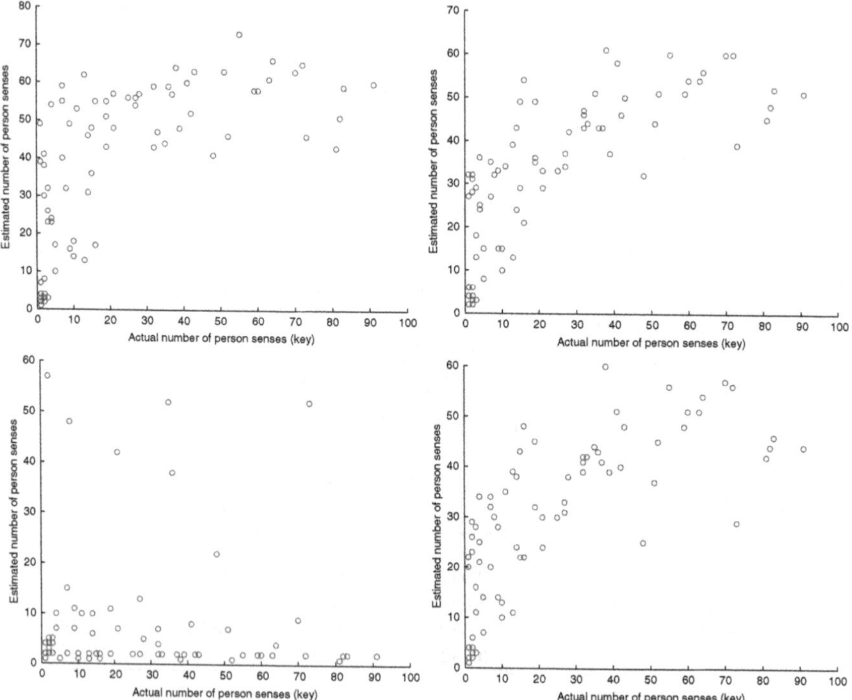

Fig. 5 Estimated versus actual number of person senses. (*Top Left*) SPC-NB, (*Top Right*) SPC-COS, (*Bottom Left*) PLSA, (*Bottom Right*) AGGLOM. The Pearson correlation coefficient r is 0.736, 0.634, 0.045, and 0.729 respectively

AGGLOM are $r = 0.736$, $r = 0.634$, and $r = 0.729$, respectively—where $r = 1$ would indicate that the method correctly identifies the true number of person name senses. On the other hand, the assignment to clusters based on the max $p(z|d)$ given the PLSA decomposition completely underestimates the number of person senses and the correlation is very weak ($r = 0.045$). Alternative assignment methods (such as clustering the latent space) could provide improvements but is left for future work.

These results clearly demonstrate the difference in the behaviors of the term-based approaches (SPC, K-MEANS, AGGLOM) and the semantic-based approach (PLSA), with the former outperforming the latter. Out of the term-based approaches, AGGLOM and SPC-COS deliver the best performance. We identify AGGLOM as the preferred method, as it gives a better estimation of the actual number of person name senses. The performance of K-MEANS is somewhat disappointing, as it delivers the worst results among the term-based methods. Overall, the term-based approaches assign people to the same cluster with high precision, as is reflected by the high purity scores. In contrast, the PLSA method produces far fewer clusters per person. These clusters may cover multiple referents of a name, as is witnessed by the low purity scores. On the other hand, inverse purity scores are very high, which means referents are usually not dispersed among clusters.

5.6 Group-Level Analysis

The results on which we have reported so far were aggregated over all people. Since the data is not homogeneous, it is interesting to see how performance varies on different groups of people. More specifically, we seek to answer: what is the performance of the methods like over (i) different data sources and (ii) different numbers of person name senses?

Figure 6 (Left) shows the performance of SPC, AGGLOM and PLSA across the different data sources. Note that we report only on the better performing SPC variation (SPC-COS) and we exclude K-MEANS (as it would not be a fair comparison given that information from the ground truth was used to set the value of K). All sources display high levels of variability, which seems independent of the size of the source. In case of SPC-COS and AGGLOM, the level of variance is more prominent for the US Census data than for the other three sets. The median F-scores of US Census and ECDL are in the same range (0.66–0.73), as are Wikipedia and ACL06 (0.78–0.81). However, for PLSA, the deviation is very high for all sources. The median F-scores of Wikipedia and ECDL are in the same range (0.64–0.66), but US Census and ACL06 are significantly lower (0.51 and 0.43, respectively).

Figure 6 (Right) shows the performance of the methods across the different cluster sizes, where the cluster size is the number of senses of a person name, based on the ground truth. Interestingly, as the number of senses goes up, so does the F-score achieved by the SPC-COS and AGGLOM algorithms. On the other hand, PLSA seems to have an orthogonal effect, the best F-score is achieved when the number

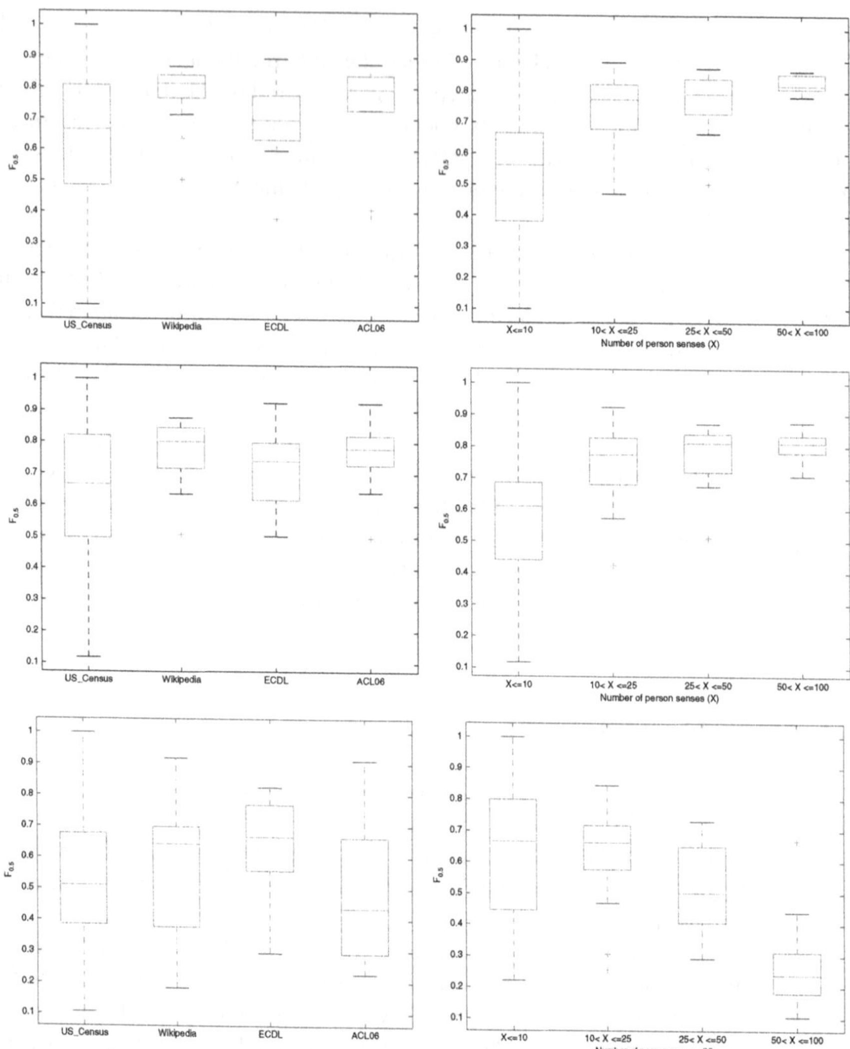

Fig. 6 Performance of (*Top*) SPC-COS, (*Middle*) AGGLOM, and (*Bottom*) PLSA. (*Left*) across different data sources, (*Right*) against different cluster sizes. The parameter settings for these methods correspond to the configurations reported in Table 3

of senses is low (≤ 10), and performance is gradually decreasing, as the number of senses increases. This behavior confirms our intuition, that the distribution of latent topics may be dominated by a few principal components, which are easier to associate with prominent person name senses, or when there are only a few referents. When only limited examples of the other referents are available (i.e., one or two documents, which is often the case according to assumption 2), PLSA seems unable to specifically identify such cases.

6 Discussion and Conclusion

In this chapter, we have explored the person cluster hypothesis for the person name resolution task in a web setting. As we have seen, SPC and AGGLOM with a standard bag of words representation provide excellent performance on this task. To put our results in context, Table 5 reports the results of our best performing methods, along with the top performing systems from SemEval [3] and two naive baselines: ONE-IN-ONE, which assumes that each document is a different referent (i.e., the worst case scenario of assumption 3, if we had no evidence), and ALL-IN-ONE, which assumes that all documents are associated with a single referent. While two of the top performing systems use richer features and more sophisticated clustering methods than we do, the performance of SPC-COS and AGGLOM are comparable to, if not better than the state of the art, and provides a strong baseline for this task. This is truly remarkable, and demonstrates that viewing the task of person name resolution as document clustering is quite effective. Furthermore, we contend that this result provides strong evidence to support the "person cluster hypothesis."

Table 5 Comparison of results to baselines and top performing systems at the SemEval 2007 WePS task [3]. Results are reported on the test set only

Method	Pur.	Invp.	$F_{0.5}$	$F_{0.2}$
SPC-NB	**0.884**	0.688	0.747	0.707
SPC-COS	0.850	0.777	0.791	0.780
K-MEANS	0.820	0.701	0.750	0.718
AGGLOM	0.818	0.812	**0.796**	**0.802**
PLSA	0.370	**0.885**	0.442	0.581
CU_COMSTEM	0.720	**0.880**	**0.780**	**0.830**
IRST-BP	**0.750**	0.800	0.750	0.770
PSNUS	0.730	0.820	0.750	0.780
ONE-IN-ONE	1.000	0.470	0.610	0.520
ALL-IN-ONE	0.290	1.000	0.400	0.580

While the way in which we used PLSA for this task has not performed as well as we expected, we have identified a number of possible reasons for this failure. We also noted that when there are only few person name senses, PLSA is more effective than the term-based approaches. An interesting line of future work would be to consider how the advantages of both methods could be combined in order to gain greater improvements. Other areas for future research where improvements could be gained include employing a richer feature set which includes named entities, etc., and pre-processing the documents to remove irrelevant content before the disambiguation process.

Acknowledgments We thank the participants in the NLPIX 2008 workshop at WWW 2008 for their helpful questions and suggestions.

This research was supported by the E.U. IST programme of the 6th FP for RTD under project MultiMATCH contract IST-033104, the DuOMAn project carried out within the STEVIN programme which is funded by the Dutch and Flemish Governments (http://www.stevin-tst.org) under project number STE-09-12, and by the Netherlands Organisation for Scientific Research (NWO) under project numbers 220-80-001, 017.001.190, 640.001.501, 640.002.501, 612.066.512, 612.061.814,612.061.815.

References

1. R. Al-Kamha and D. W. Embley. Grouping search-engine returned citations for person-name queries. In *WIDM '04: Proceedings of the 6th Annual ACM International Workshop on Web Information and Data Management*, pages 96–103, New York, NY, USA, 2004. ACM Press.
2. J. Artiles, J. Gonzalo, and S. Sekine. The SemEval-2007 WePS evaluation: establishing a benchmark for the Web people search task. In *Proceedings of Semeval 2007, Association for Computational Linguistics*, 2007.
3. J. Artiles, J. Gonzalo, and F. Verdejo. A testbed for people searching strategies in the www. In *SIGIR '05: Proceedings of the 28th Annual International ACM SIGIR Conference on Research and Development in Information Retrieval*, pages 569–570, New York, NY, USA, 2005. ACM Press.
4. A. Bagga and B. Baldwin. Entity-based cross-document coreferencing using the vector space model. In *Proceedings of the 36th Annual Meeting of the Association for Computational Linguistics (ACL) and 17th Conference on Computational Linguistics (COLING)*, pages 79–85, 1998.
5. K. Balog. *People Search in the Enterprise*. PhD thesis, University of Amsterdam, June 2008.
6. K. Balog, L. Azzopardi, and M. de Rijke. Personal name resolution of web people search. In *WWW2008 Workshop: NLP Challenges in the Information Explosion Era (NLPIX 2008)*, April 2008.
7. K. Balog and M. de Rijke. Associating people and documents. In *Proceedings of the 30th European Conference on Information Retrieval (ECIR 2008)*, pages 296–308, 2008.
8. R. Bekkerman and A. McCallum. Disambiguating web appearances of people in a social network. In *Proceedings of the 14th International World Wide Web (WWW) Conference*, pages 463–470, 2005.
9. D. Bollegala, Y. Matsuo, and M. Ishizuka. Extracting key phrases to disambiguate personal name queries in web search. In *Proceedings of the Workshop on How Can Computational Linguistics Improve Information Retrieval? At ACL'06*, pages 17–24, 2006.
10. N. Craswell, A. de Vries, and I. Soboroff. Overview of the TREC-2005 enterprise track. *The Fourteenth Text REtrieval Conference (TREC 2005) Proceedings*, 2006.
11. M. Fleischman and E. Hovy. Multi-document person name resolution. In *Proceedings of the 42nd Annual Meeting of the Association for Computational Linguistics (ACL), Reference Resolution Workshop*, 2004.
12. C. Gooi and J. Allan. Cross-document coreference on a large scale corpus. In *Proceedings of the Human Language Technology/North American Chapter of Association for Computational Linguistics Annual Meeting (HLT/NAACL)*, 2004.
13. J. A. Hartigan and M. A. Wong. A k-means clustering algorithm. *Applied Statistics*, 28: 100–108, 1979.
14. D. R. Hill. A vector clustering technique. In Samuelson, editor, *Mechanised Information Storage, Retrieval and Dissemination*, North-Holland, Amsterdam, 1968.
15. T. Hofmann. Probabilistic latent semantic analysis. In *Proceedings of Uncertainty in Artificial Intelligence, UAI'99*, Stockholm, 1999. URL `citeseer.ist.psu.edu/hofmann99probabilistic.html`.
16. N. Jardine and C. J. van Rijsbergen. The use of hierarchic clustering in information retrieval. *Information Storage and Retrieval*, 7:217–240, 1971.
17. T. Kalt. A new probabilistic model of text classification and retrieval. Technical Report CIIR TR98-18, University of Massachusetts, January 1996.

18. V. Lavrenko and W. B. Croft. Relevance-based language models. In *Proceedings of the 24th Annual International ACM SIGIR Conference*, pages 120–127, New Orleans, LA, 2001. ACM Press.
19. B. Malin. Unsupervised name disambiguation via social network similarity. In *Proceedings of the SIAM Workshop on Link Analysis, Counterterrorism, and Security*, pages 93–102, 2005.
20. G. Mann and D. Yarowsky. Unsupervised personal name disambiguation. In *Conference on Computational Natural Language Learning (CoNLL)*, 2003.
21. G. A. Miller and W. G. Charles. Contextual correlates of semantic similarity. *Language and Cognitive Processes*, 6:1–28, 1991.
22. T. Pedersen, A. Purandare, and A. Kulkarni. Name discrimination by clustering similar contexts. In *Computational Linguistics and Intelligent Text Processing*, pages 226–237. Springer Berlin - Heidelberg, 2005.
23. X. Phan, L. Nguyen, and S. Horiguchi. Personal name resolution crossover documents by a semantics-based approach. *IEICE Transactions on Information and Systems*, E89-D(2): 825–836, 2006.
24. A. I. Schein, A. Popescul, L. H. Ungar, and D. M. Pennock. Methods and metrics for cold-start recommendations. In *SIGIR '02: Proceedings of the 25th Annual International ACM SIGIR Conference on Research and Development in Information Retrieval*, pages 253–260, New York, NY, USA, 2002. ACM Press. See `http://www.cis.upenn.edu/datamining/software_dist/PennAspect/`.
25. M. Steinbach, G. Karypis, and V. Kumar. A comparison of document clustering techniques. *In Proceedings of Workshop on Text Mining, 6th ACM SIGKDD International Conference on Data Mining (KDD'00)*, pages 109–110, 2000.
26. M. Taffet. Looking ahead to person resolution. In *Proceedings of the 4th Annual Workshop on Technology for Family History and Genealogical Research*, pages 11–15, 2004.
27. X. Wan, J. Gao, M. Li, and B. Ding. Person resolution in person search results: Webhawk. In *CIKM '05: Proceedings of the 14th ACM international conference on Information and knowledge management*, pages 163–170, New York, NY, USA, 2005. ACM Press.

Studies on Editing Patterns in Large-Scale Wikis

Philip Boulain, Nigel Shadbolt and Nicholas Gibbins

Abstract Wiki systems have developed over the past years as lightweight, community-editable, web-based hypertext systems. With the emergence of Semantic Wikis, these collections of interlinked documents have also gained a dual role as ad-hoc RDF graphs. However, their roots lie at the limited hypertext capabilities of the World Wide Web: embedded links, without support for composite objects or transclusion. In this chapter, we present experimental evidence that hyperstructure changes, as opposed to content changes, form a substantial proportion of editing effort on a large-scale wiki. We then follow this with a in-detail experiment, studying how individual editors work to edit articles on the wiki. These experiments are set in the wider context of a study of how the technologies developed during decades of hypertext research may be applied to improve management of wiki document structure and, with semantic wikis, knowledge structure.

1 Introduction

In this chapter, we present a complementary pair of experiments on the way users edit Wikipedia. First, we look at the macro scale, quantitatively categorising the types of edits users made. Then, we look at the micro scale, qualitatively studying the rationale and process of individual editors. These experiments form part of a broader project looking into the potentially beneficial relationships between open hypermedia, the study of interconnected documents; Semantic Web, the study of interconnectable data; and "wikis", web-based communal editing systems.

Wikipedia is a communally-edited encyclopædia with over two and half million articles in the English version. Each article is a document with prose about an encyclopædic subject, usually supplemented with illustrations. Almost all articles are placed into at least one ad-hoc category, and linking between articles is common.

Hypermedia is a long-standing field of research into the ways in which documents can expand beyond the limitations of paper, generally in terms of greater

P. Boulain (✉)
Intelligence, Agents, Multimedia Group, School of Electronics and Computer Science, University of Southampton, Southampton SO17 1BJ, UK
e-mail: prb@ecs.soton.ac.uk

I. King, R. Baeza-Yates (eds.), *Weaving Services and People on the World Wide Web*, DOI 10.1007/978-3-642-00570-1_16, © Springer-Verlag Berlin Heidelberg 2009

cross-referencing and composition (reuse) capability. Bush's *As We May Think* [3] introduces the hypothetical early hypertext machine, the "memex", and defines the "essential feature" of it as "the process of tying two items together". This *linking* between documents is the common feature of hypertext systems, upon which other improvements are built.

As well as simple binary (two endpoint) links, hypertext systems have been developed with features including n-ary links (multiple documents linked to multiple other documents), typed links (links which indicate something about *why* or *how* documents are related), generic links (links whose endpoints are determined by matching criteria of the document content, such as particular words), and composite documents, which are formed by combining a set of other, linked, documents. Open Hypermedia extends this with interoperation, both with other hypermedia systems and users, and with non-hypermedia resources. A key concept in open hypermedia is that of the *non-embedded* link—links (and anchors) which are held external to the documents they connect. These allow links to be made to immutable documents, and to be added and removed in sets, often termed "linkbases". One of the earliest projects attempting to implement globally-distributed hypertext was Xanadu [9], a distinctive feature of the design of which was *transclusion*: including (sections of) a document into another by reference.

In related work, we are currently investigating the relationship between an exemplar semantic wiki, Semantic MediaWiki [7], and open hypermedia systems, as defined by the Dexter Hypertext Reference Model [6]. Our preliminary results based on a formal description of Semantic MediaWiki in terms of the Dexter model suggest that such semantic wikis can be treated as simple open hypermedia systems. While details are beyond the scope of this paper, some basic parallels are evident: a wiki node is akin to a hypermedia document, and a semantic web resource. Semantic wikis generally treat typed inter-node links as RDF statements relating the nodes, and these links are embedded and binary in hypermedia terms. From this we can see a meaningful similarity between a graph of documents connected by typed links, and a graph of resources connected by RDF statements. We can also see that wikis do not have features covering more advanced hypermedia links: such as those which are not embedded, or have more than two endpoints.

This then suggests that semantic wikis stand to gain from techniques developed within hypermedia, but we must first judge if there is any substantial cost to be reduced, hence these experiments. We found that twice as many edits changed links alone, not affecting the article text, and that edits which maintained manual indexes of pages constituted approximately a tenth of total edits. We also discovered that content re-use was not as desirable as hypermedia research has assumed, but that automatic linking and transclusion could still address problems with current technology.

2 Macro-Scale experiment

We carried out an experiment to estimate the proportion of effort expended maintaining the infrastructure around data, rather than the data itself, on a weak hypertext wiki system. We define a "weak" hypertext system here as one whose feature set is limited to embedded, unidirectional, binary links, as with the World Wide Web. Our hypothesis is that the manual editing of link structure, of a type which richer hypertext features could automate, will show to be a significant overhead versus changes to the text content. If supported, this indicates that further work on stronger hypertext wikis is potentially beneficial.

This experiment also seeks to partially recreate a related, informal experiment, discussed in an essay by Swartz [11].

2.1 Dataset

We chose English Wikipedia[1] as the experimental dataset, because it has both a considerably large and varied set of documents, and a complete history of the editing processes—performed by a wide range of Web users—between their first and current versions.[2] The wiki community keep the dataset fairly well inter-linked and categorised for cross-reference, but they do this via the cumulative efforts of a large body of part-time editors. As well as being statistically significant, demonstrating possible improvement of English Wikipedia is socially significant, as it is a widely-used and active resource.

It is important to stress the size of the English Wikipedia dataset. Wikipedia make available "dumps" of their database in an ad-hoc XML format; because this study is interested in the progression of page contents across revisions, it was necessary to use the largest of these dumps, containing both page full-text and history (unfortunately, also non-encyclopædic pages, such as discussions and user pages). This dump is provided compressed using the highly space-efficient (although time-complex) bzip2 algorithm; even then, it is 84.6GB. The total size of the XML file is estimated to be in the region of two terabytes.

2.2 Procedure

Figure 1 shows the simplified data flow of the processing of the dump performed for the experiment.

2.2.1 Reduction

First, we trimmed down the dataset to just those pages which are encyclopædic articles, as these are the pages of greatest significance to the Wikipedia project's goals, and thus the most important to study. Otherwise, the dataset would include a lot of "noise" in the form of discussion and user pages, which are likely to have different editing patterns, and be less connected to the hyperstructure. The most practical way to do this was to remove any page placed in a namespace. On English Wikipedia, this also has the effect of removing other page types, such as media and image descriptions, help pages copied from MetaWiki, front-page portal components, and

[1] `http://en.wikipedia.org/`

[2] MediaWiki, unlike many wikis, never deletes old revisions of a page.

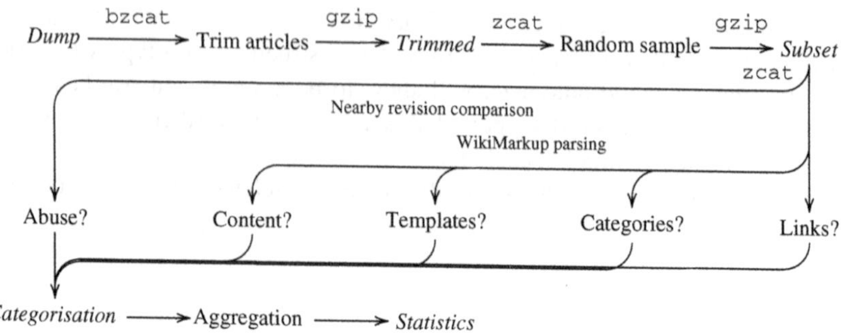

Fig. 1 Data flow of Wikipedia experiment

templates. As this stage also required decompressing the data, it ran over the course of several days on a multi-processor server.

We took a random subset of the data for processing. Samples of 0.04 and 0.01% of pages (approximately: see the description of the subset tool below; actual page counts 14,215 and 3,589 respectively) were selected, yielding a compressed dataset which would fit on a CD-ROM, and could be processed in a reasonable timeframe. Further iterations of the experiment may study larger subsets of the data.

2.2.2 Parsing

We performed categorisation on the revisions, into several edit types which would be automatically distinguished. In particular, a simple equality comparison between a revision, and the revision two edits previous, can detect the most common (anti-)abuse modification: the rollback, or revert (unfortunately, MediaWiki does not record such operations semantically). A sequence of reverts[3] is usually indicative of an "edit war", where two users continually undo each-others changes in favour of their own. Page blanking was also easy to detect, but identifying more complicated forms of vandalism (e.g. misinformation, spam) was not feasible—if reliable, automatic detection were possible, they would not be present in the data, as Wikipedia could prevent such changes from being applied. Identifying abuse (and abuse management) of the simpler types is important, as otherwise they would appear as very large changes.

In order to detect changes in the text content, templates used, MediaWiki categories, and links from a page, it was necessary to attempt to parse the MediaWiki markup format. Such "wikitext", as it is known, is not a formally defined language: there is no grammar for it, and it does not appear likely that an unambiguous grammar actually exists. MediaWiki does not have a parser in the same way as processing tools such as compilers and XML libraries; instead it just has a long and complicated set of text substitution procedures which convert parts of "wikitext" into display-oriented HTML. These substitutions often interact in a ill-defined manner, generally resulting in either more special-case substitutions, or as being defined as

[3] For example, `http://en.wikipedia.org/w/index.php?title=Anarchism&diff=next&oldid=320139`

a new, hybrid, feature, which editors then use. Because of these problems, and the lack of abstraction in MediaWiki's "parser", as much as the programming language boundary, a "scraping" parser was created which attempted to approximate partial processing of the wikitext format and return *mostly* correct results. This parser is a single-pass state machine (42 states) with a few additional side-effects. This yields excellent performance: testing showed that the time spent parsing is dominated by the time performing decompression.

2.2.3 Text Differences

To determine if an edit included a significant ("major") change to the text content, we required a difference metric between the plaintext of the revisions. This metric was then compared to a threshold to classify edits as being content changes or not (in particular, the imperfect parser generates "noise" from some non-content changes, as it cannot correctly remove all the markup). The default threshold was chosen as 5%: sentences in the English language are generally around 20 words in length, so this considers anything up to changing one word in each sentence as non-major (minor). MediaWiki also allows registered users to explicitly state than an edit is minor; this flag was respected where present.

We chose an approximation of Levenshtein distance [8], as it is a simple measure of insertions, deletions, and substitutions, fitting the kind of edit operations performed on the wiki. However, the algorithm for computing Levenshtein itself was far too time-complex, even with aggressive optimisation, taking 2 min on a tiny test set of just a few thousand revisions of a single page (before trimming away the identical parts at either end of both strings to take advantage of edit locality, this took 45 min). The problem was that the matrix-based approach is $O(n \times m)$, where n and m are the string lengths, in all cases: for n and m in the region of 16,000 characters, as found on many revisions, merely iterating through all 256 million matrix cells was prohibitively expensive.

Instead, we developed a new approach to computing such a distance, taking advantage of the domain-specific knowledge that the two strings being compared are likely very similar save for "local" edits: the difference is likely to be a new paragraph, or a removed sentence, or some changed punctuation. Instead of efficient search within the space of editing operations, as Levenshtein, it is based on the idea of "sliding windows": a pass is made over both strings in parallel; when characters begin to differ, a look-back "window" is opened between the point at which differences began, and continues until similarity is again found between these windows. At this point, the position through the strings resynchronises, the distance is increased by the offset required, and the windows are again "closed". When the end of either string is reached by the far edge of the window, the algorithm can terminate, as any remaining characters in the other string must be unmatched and thus add to the distance. As a result, the algorithm scales with regard to the shorter of the two strings, which is helpful when revisions may add whole paragraphs of new text to the end. To reduce inaccuracy in certain cases, the algorithm maintains a "processed point" cursor, to avoid double-counting of overlapping insertions and deletions. Pseudocode is presented as algorithm 1, which works on a pair of string buffers, and `upstr.c` in the tool source contains a C implementation. This

Algorithm 1: "Sliding window" string distance metric

```
procedure STRING-DISTANCE (A, B)
    proc ← 0                                          ▷ No. of chars. of string processed
    procstr ← NEITHER                                 ▷ Last string aligned upon
    dist ← 0                                          ▷ Difference accumulator
    nearA ← farA ← A                                  ▷ Near and far pointers
    nearB ← farB ← B
    Let endA be the beyond-last character of buffer A, and endB beyond B
    procedure SCAN (near, far)
        for scan ← near to before far do
            if Chars. at scan and far same then return scan
        return false
    while farA ≠ endA ∧ farB ≠ endB do
        synfarA ← SCAN(nearA, farA)
        synfarB ← SCAN(nearB, farB)
        if synfarA ∨ synfarB then                     ▷ Missed alignment
            if synfarA is further into A than synfarB is into B then
                farA ← synfarA
            else
                farB ← synfarB
        else if synfarA then farA ← synfarA
        else if synfarB then farB ← synfarB
        if Chars. at farA and farB same then
            ▷ Aligned; calc. nears after proc. point
            enA ← MIN(nearA, A + proc − 1)
            enB ← MIN(nearB, B + proc − 1)
            ▷ Unaligned lengths
            unA = positive dist. from enA to farA
            unB = positive dist. from enB to farB
            procedure ALIGN (un, far, buffer, other)
                distance ← distance + un
                proc = far's distance into buffer
                if procstr = other then proc ← proc + 1
                procstr ← buffer
            if unA > unB then
                ALIGN(unA, farA, A, B)
            else
                ALIGN(unB, farB, B, A)
            if farA = endA then                       ▷ Ending
                distance ← distance+ distance between farB and endB
            else if farA = endA then
                distance ← distance+ distance between farA and endA
            else                                      ▷ Advanced with closed window
                nearA ← farA ← farA + 1
                nearB ← farB ← farB + 1
                proc ← proc + 1
        else                                          ▷ Not aligned; widen windows
            if farA ≠ endA then farA ← farA + 1
            if farB ≠ endB then farB ← farB + 1
    return dist
```

approach is still O($n \times m$) worst-case, but is O(n) (where n is the shorter string) for identical strings, and degrades smoothly as *contiguous* differences increase in size: instead of 2 min, the tiny test set was compared in a little over 10 s.

Unfortunately, changes such as "ABCF" to "ADCDBCF" can return overestimates, as the localisation which explicitly prevents full lookback (and keeps computational cost below O(n^2)) causes the "C" in "BCF" to match with the "C" in "DCD": "ADC" is considered a substitution of "ABC" before the algorithm can realise that "BC" is still intact in the string, and "DCD" is merely an insertion. As a result, the later "B" is considered an insertion, as it no longer matches anything, and the distance is overestimated by one. Synthetic tests showed this overestimation to be minor; tests against Levenshtein on a tiny subset of Wikipedia data (a node's first few hundred revisions, thus under heavy editing) show it to be larger, with errors in the tens, and a peak error of over two-hundred. The reason for such large errors is unclear, as the resynchronisation approach should also keep *error* localised, but it does not greatly affect the result for the purpose of minor/major determination: the majority of changes were correctly classified.

2.2.4 Grouping

We identified the following non-mutually-exclusive groupings to usefully categorise edits:

Revert	Edit which simply undoes a previous edit.
Content	Major (nontrivial) edit of the page content.
Minor	Minor (trivial) edit of the page content.
Category	Edit to the categories of a page.
List of	Edit to a page which is an index to other pages.
Indexing	Edit to categories or listings, possibly both.
Template	Edit to the templates used by a page.
Page link	Edit to an internal page link.
URL link	Edit to a WWW URL link; usually external.
Links	Edit to page or URL links.
Link only	As "links", but excluding major edits.
Hyperstructure	Any hypermedia change: indexing, linking, or template.

These categorisations yielded simple information on which kinds of changes were made by each revision, and removed much of the "bulk" of the dataset (the revision texts); as a result, simple scripts could then handle the data to aggregate it into various groupings in memory, so as to produce graph data and statistics for analysis.

We expand upon the definition and significance of these groups as needed in Sect. 2.4.

2.3 Tools Developed

To process the sizable dataset, we created a set of small, robust, stream-based tools in C. Stream-based processing was a necessity, as manipulating the entire data in memory at once was simply infeasible; instead, the tools are intended to be combined arbitrarily using UNIX pipes. We used standard compression tools to de- and re-compress the data for storage on disk, else the verbosity of the XML format caused processing to be heavily I/O-bound.[4] The open source Libxml2[5] library was used to parse and regenerate the XML via its SAX interface. A selection of the more notable tools:

dumptitles	Converts a MediaWiki XML dump (henceforth, "MWXML") into a plain, newline-separated, list of page titles. Useful for diagnostics, e.g. confirming that the random subset contains an appropriate range of pages.
discardnonart	Reads in MWXML, and outputs MWXML, sans any pages which are in a namespace; pedantically, due to the poor semantics of MWXML, those with colons in the title. This implements the "trim to articles" step of Fig. 1.
randomsubset	Reads and writes MWXML, preserving a random subset of the input pages. In order for this to be O(1) in memory consumption, this does not strictly provide a given proportion of the input; instead, the control is the probability of including a given page in the output. As a result, asking for 50% of the input *may* actually yield anywhere between none and all of the pages: it is just far more likely that the output will be around 50% of the input.[6]
categorise	Reads MWXML and categorises the revisions, outputting results to a simple XML format.
cataggr	A Perl script which processes the categorisation XML to produce final statistical results and graph data. By this point, the data are small enough that a SAX parser is used to build a custom in-memory document tree, such that manipulation is easier.

The tools are available under the open source MIT license, and can be retrieved from `http://users.ecs.soton.ac.uk/prb/phd/wikipedia/` to recreate the experiment.

2.4 Results

Because of the known error margin of the approximation of Levenshtein distance, we computed results from both genuine and approximated distances on the

---

[4] Specifically, GNU Zip for intermediate; bzip2, as originally used by Wikipedia, made processing heavily CPU-bound.

[5] `http://xmlsoft.org/`

[6] A better algorithm, which is O(1) with regards to total data size, but O(n) with regards to subset size, is to store a buffer of up to n pages, and probabilistically replace them with different pages as they are encountered. However, even this would be prohibitively memory intensive on statistically significant subset sizes, as each page may have thousands of revisions, each with thousands of bytes of text, all of which must be copied into the buffer.

0.01% subset, so as to discover and illustrate the effects of approximation; the computational cost difference between the algorithms was significant: two-and-a-half hours for genuine, 8 min for approximated. Results were then generated from the more statistically significant 0.04% subset (27 h). This set contained some pages on contentious topics, which had seen large numbers of revisions as a result.

2.4.1 Index Management

Table 1 shows the proportions of edits in categories pertaining to index management. "Categories" are changes to the categories in which a page was placed. "Lists" are any change to any "List of" page; these pages serve as manually-maintained indices to other pages. "Overhead" are changes which fall into either of these categories: because they are not mutually exclusive (lists may be categorised), it is not a sum of the other two values. Because these metrics do not consider the change in "content" magnitude of a change, they are unaffected by the choice of distance algorithm.

The 10% overhead shows a strong case for the need for stronger semantics and querying on Wikipedia; this is one of the key goals, and expected benefits, of the Semantic MediaWiki project. While virtually every "list of" node could be replaced with a query on appropriate attributes, the gain in category efficiency is harder to measure. Any semantic wiki must still be provided with categorisation metadata such that the type of pages can be used to answer such queries. However, some improvement is to be expected, as there are current Wikipedia categories which could be inferred: either because they are a union of other categories (e.g. "Free software" and "Operating systems" cover the existing category "Free software operating systems") or because they are implied by a more specialised category, and no longer need to be explicitly applied to a page.

The increase in list overhead seen in the larger subset is likely a result of having a more representative proportion of "List of" pages. Otherwise, the results are largely consistent across sample sizes.

Table 1 Proportions of edits related to index management

(a) 0.01% subset

Edit type	Proportion
Categories	8.71%
Lists	1.97%
Overhead	10.56%

(b) 0.04% subset

Edit type	Proportion
Categories	8.75%
Lists	3.72%
Overhead	12.34%

2.4.2 Link Management

Table 2 shows categories related to the management of links. "Links" refers to edits which changed either page-to-page or page-to-URL links. "Links only" refers to such edits *excluding* those edits which also constituted a "major" content change: they are edits concerned only with links and other structure. "Hyperstructure" is the

Table 2 Proportions of edits related to link management

(a) 0.01% subset, Levenshtein		(b) 0.01% subset, Approximated		(c) 0.04% subset, Approximated	
Edit type	Proportion	Edit type	Proportion	Edit type	Proportion
Links	49.60%	Links	49.60%	Links	49.56%
Links only	35.53%	Links only	23.36%	Links only	25.24%
Hyperstructure	61.65%	Hyperstructure	61.65%	Hyperstructure	61.90%
Content	17.81%	Content	35.60%	Content	35.99%
Edit type	Ratio/content	Edit type	Ratio	Edit type	Ratio
Links	2.79	Links	1.39	Links	1.38
Links only	2.00	Links only	0.71	Links only	0.70
Hyperstructure	3.46	Hyperstructure	1.73	Hyperstructure	1.72

category of edits which changed any of the navigational capabilities of the wiki: either categories, "List of" pages, links, or templates. "Content" is simply the category of "major" edits.

The overestimating effect of the approximate string distance algorithm can be seen as a greater proportion of edits being considered "major", with a knock-on effect on reducing the ratios of edits over content edits. However, the results are consistent between the 0.01% subset with the approximated string distance, and the sample set four times the size. As a result, it would appear that the smaller size of the sample set has not introduced significant error in this case, and it is reasonable to assume that a Levenshtein distance comparison of the larger dataset would yield similar results to the 0.01% subset. Therefore, further discussion will focus on the 0.01% subset with Levenshtein distance results.

These figures show the significance of hyperstructure to Wikipedia, to a surprising degree. While we expected that link editing would prove a substantial proportion of edits compared to content, we did not anticipate that *twice as many edits change links alone than those that change content.* Most link changes were page links—those to other pages on the wiki, or metawiki—as opposed to URL links to arbitrary webpages (in some cases, pages on the wiki with special arguments). 36,076 edits modified the former, but only 8,525 the latter.

With such a proportion of editing effort being expended on modifying links on Wikipedia, there is a clear need to improve this process. Introducing richer hypermedia features to wikis, such as generic links, should prove one possible improvement. Generic links are links whose endpoints are defined by matching on criteria of the document content: a basic example being matching on a particular substring. A generic link can specify that a page's title should link to that page, rather than requiring users to manually annotate it: some early wiki systems offered this capability, but only for page titles which were written in the unnatural "CamelCase" capitalisation. Advanced examples such as local links, present in Microcosm [4, 5], can specify scope limits on the matching. This would help with ambiguous terms on Wikipedia, such as "Interval", which should be linked to a specific meaning, such as "Interval (music)".

2.4.3 Overall Editing Distribution

Table 3 shows the categorisation of all edits in the 0.01% dataset, using Levenshtein for string distance, for registered and unregistered users. Note that the edit categories are not mutually exclusive, thus will not sum to the total number of edits by that class of user. "Minor" is the category of edits which did not appear to change anything substantial: either the information extracted from the markup remains the same, and the plaintext very similar; or a registered user annotated the edit as minor. Notably, over 5% of edits are reverts: edits completely rolling back the previous edit; this implies that a further 5% of edits are being reverted (presumably as they are deemed unsuitable).[7] A substantial amount of effort is being expended merely keeping Wikipedia "stationary".

Figure 2 demonstrates the distribution of users over the total number of edits they have made, in the vein of the Swartz study [11]. There is a sharp falloff of number of users as the number of edits increases (note the logarithmic scale on both axes): by far, most users only ever make very few edits, whether registered or not. Unsurprisingly, registered users tend to make more edits overall, and unregistered users are dominant at the scale of fewer than ten edits.

Figure 3 breaks the low-edit end of this distribution down by basic categories. It is interesting to note that, other than being in close proximity (e.g. "content" and "page link"), the lines do not have any definitive overlaps: the breakdown of edits is consistent regardless of the number of edits the user has made. Users who have made 70 edits have made edits in the same relative proportions (i.e., more "revert" than "list of") as those who have only made five.

Figure 4 shows how the magnitude of edits breaks down by the number of edits of that magnitude, again in the vein of Swartz [11]. Because this is clearly sensitive

Table 3 Categorisation of edits for 0.01% subset, Levenshtein

Category	Registered	Unregistered	Total
List of	1,146	453	1,599
Revert	4,069	679	4,748
Category	6,121	954	7,075
URL link	5,548	2,977	8,525
Indexing	7,174	1,397	8,571
Template	7,992	1,330	9,322
Content	10,275	4,182	14,457
Minor	13,776	9,961	23,737
Link only	20,969	7,877	28,846
Page link	27,205	8,871	36,076
Links	29,671	10,606	40,277
Hyperstructure	38,358	11,701	50,059
Total	57,463	23,733	81,196

[7] Actual figures may vary in either direction: this does not detect rollbacks to versions earlier than the immediately preceding version, and "edit wars" of consecutive rollbacks *will* be entirely included in the first 5%, not belonging in the latter.

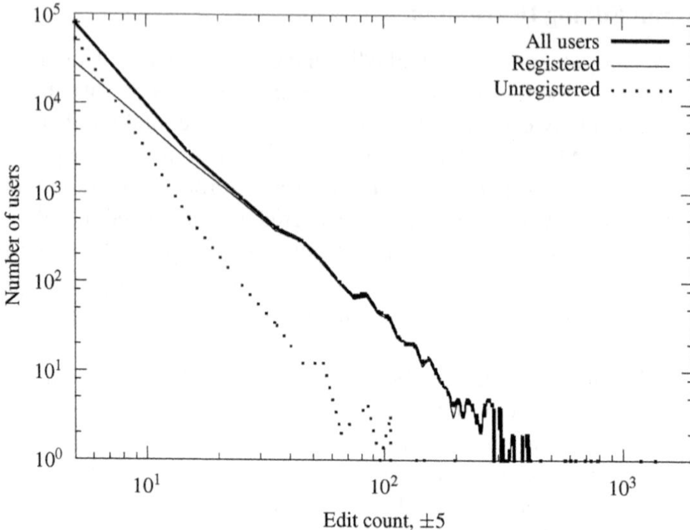

Fig. 2 User distribution over total number of edits made; 0.04% subset

to the string distancing algorithm, the 0.01% subset was used, with a focus on Levenshtein: the approximate distance for all users is shown as a sparsely dotted line with a consistent overestimate. These results are largely unsurprising: registered users make larger edits, and most edits are small, with the count rapidly falling off as magnitude increases.

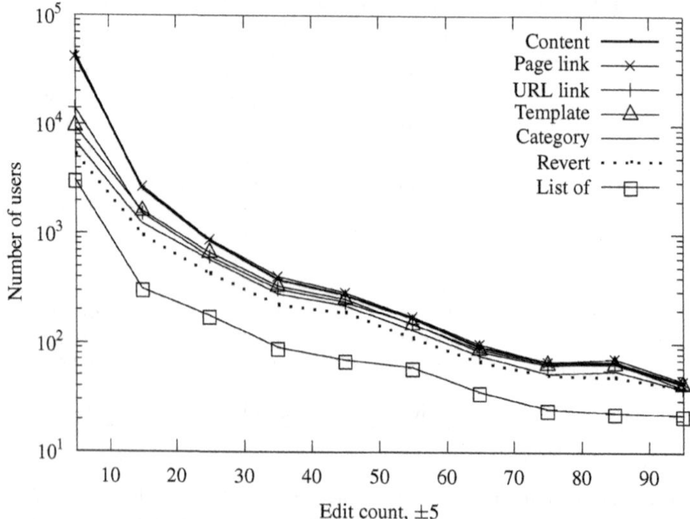

Fig. 3 User distribution over total number of edits made, by category; 0.04% subset

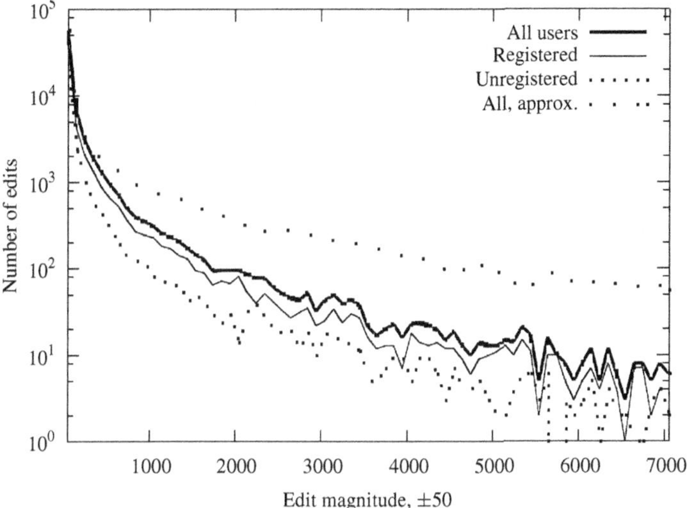

Fig. 4 Edit distribution over magnitude of edit; 0.01% subset

2.4.4 Limitations of Detection

There are, unfortunately, several kinds of "overhead" costs which simply cannot be detected in a computationally feasible manner by this approach. For example, MediaWiki supports a feature called template "substitution", which actually imports the template, with parameter substitution performed (with some caveats), into the source text of the including node. It is important to note that the relationship between the including and included nodes is lost, and that the benefits of re-use (such as storage efficiency and later corrections) are not available. The information regarding the origin of the text is also lost without manual documentation effort, including any parameters required for the more complicated templates. Because use of this feature is not semantically recorded by MediaWiki, it is largely indistinguishable from the addition of a paragraph of wikitext. As a result, it is not then possible to evaluate the cost of maintaining or documenting these substitutions once the link to the original template has been lost.

It is also not computationally feasible to detect the pattern of a user performing the same fix on multiple pages, which would identify the cost of inadequate, or underused, transclusion. Transclusion is an inclusion-by-reference mechanism, where a selected (fragment of a) document is included "live" into another, greatly facilitating re-use.

In Wikipedia, it is often desirable to accompany a link to a page with a short summary of that page's topic. In particular, Wikipedia has many cases where articles include a summary of another article, along with a "main article" link. The "London" page,[8] for example, has many sections which consist primarily

[8] `http://en.wikipedia.org/w/index.php?title=London&oldid=155695080`

of summaries of more detailed pages, such as "Education in London". However, without some form of transclusion or composition to share text, if the main article's summary changes—possibly because its subject changes—this change must be replicated manually out to any page which also summarises it. A transclusion mechanism would allow a single summary of the subject to be shared by all pages which reference it, including the main article on the subject, if desired.

For example, the "Education in London" page may begin with a summary of its topic, highlighting the most notable institutions and successful research areas. The article on "London" may then, within its "Education" section, transclude this summary from the "Education in London" page. Should the summary be updated, perhaps because a University gains significant notability in a new research area, this change would be automatically reflected in the "London" page, as it is using the same text.

While MediaWiki's templates do function as transclusion, they are not employed for this role: common usage and development effort focus on their use as preprocessing macros.

2.5 Summary

The experiment consisted of the non-exclusive classification of edits made throughout the history of Wikipedia, a large and public wiki system. Classifications included both the areas of "text editing" (assumed to primarily be maintaining the *information content* of Wikipedia: its encyclopædic articles), and "link editing" (maintaining the *navigational structure* of the content). The hypothesis, that link editing formed a substantial proportion of total editing effort, which may potentially be automated, was supported by the results. Twice as many edits changed links alone, not affecting the article text. Edits which maintained manual indexes of pages constituted approximately a tenth of total edits.

3 Micro-Scale Experiment

The macro-scale experiment shows that scope exists for hypermedia-based improvements to wiki editing. To better understand the relative usefulness of these improvements, formal study must be made of current editing practices on large-scale wiki systems. This is a form of knowledge elicitation task, and thus has no particular hypothesis to test. However, the domain of possible actions, and the steps entailed in performing them, are already known as aspects of the software.

The objective of this experiment is to identify the mental processes behind wiki editing: information on the tasks editors set themselves, and how their actions are used to achieve them. This will then be used to prioritise efforts to develop hypermedia features to assist with these tasks.

3.1 Procedure

The experiment consisted of two main parts: a week of data collection while the participant used Wikipedia, or a functionally similar system, normally, followed by a meeting of less than an hour, covering a pair of protocol analysis sessions [1, 10]. A small questionnaire preceded the week of collection to record the prior experience of the subject and ensure that we covered a wide range, as well as to obtain informed consent of their willingness to participate.

The first protocol analysis was an off-line review using logged editing information from Wikipedia. Off-line study is necessary in order to work with real-world problems in a real-world environment: the reduced accuracy of recall for the reasoning behind decisions and actions is balanced against the validity of those actions. Wikipedia helps provide partial compensation here by encouraging the participant to record a short motivation for any action, which may prompt their memory.

The second protocol analysis supplemented this with an on-line self-report session in a high-fidelity simulated environment (another MediaWiki install with a tiny sample of Wikipedia's content), and a set of synthetic problems, presented in a randomised order. This then trades validity of the actions for the benefits of immediate, more accurate, feedback regarding the participant's thought processes. The investigator is also present at the time of the decision to observe any other details of the process of which the participant does not make explicit note.

Information was retrieved from the Wikipedia database about the participant's editing within the span of the study: which pages were edited, and how the source text changed. This information was publicly available as part of normal Wikipedia activity. It was not, however, directly analysed: instead, it provided material for the off-line review. The data collected were anonymised transcripts from this, and the on-line self-report, for verbal protocol analysis.

Participants were taken from geographically close wiki editors, as a practical limitation of the in-person nature of the data collection. We sought people who already had some experience with wikis, so as to capture the editing process, rather than the initial user interface experiences of a beginner. While this limited the set of potential candidates, the method of analysis is not statistical, and can work at small sample sizes [2].

The tasks for the self-report were designed around the knowledge elicitation goal, to attempt to capture the user's reasoning, and also to solicit their opinions on the perceived effort required for each task.

Edit description of same villain in two movies. Discovers how the user handles having to update a section of text which is used by two articles. The history of the page shows rough synchronisation by manual copying, but is desynchronised at the point captured for the test. Transclusion could be used to share this text.

Add fact to specific article, and to summary in general article. A similar case to the above, but this time with a level-of-detail angle. Because the latter is summary of the former article, there is less scope for text to be shared outright. The domain is the London Underground. Adaptation and transclusion could form a solution.

Refine links pointing to the disambiguation node for "shelf". Requires the ability to traverse (or edit, but MediaWiki does not support this) links in the reverse direction. The ability to edit links from any of their endpoints, which is facilitated by first-class links, could help with this.

Create page summarising two other articles about type of train. Requires aggregation of summaries, which are suggested to be taken from the pages' introductory overview. This again touches on the issues of synchronising shared content, and also the task of updating the list as new train articles are written. Transclusion of query-endpoint fat links could achieve this.

Add links where appropriate to plain text of "cake" article. This task attempts to capture the reasoning behind which words in an article are hyperlinked, which then informs us where use of generic links may, or may not, be appropriate.

Add fact to infobox of "Belgium" article. Tests resource property editing, which is hidden within template code. Provides information on how users approach what is abstractly a very simple operation. Richer support for semantics, such as forms to edit known class properties, could improve this.

All of the tasks were created from content taken from Wikipedia, for authenticity of the simulated environment. Minimal errors and omissions were introduced where necessary to set up the required problem.

3.2 Results

Six subjects participated, with a range of experience levels from casual editors with only passing knowledge of the wiki system's complicated markup, to experience with administrative tasks. All participants considered themselves to make fewer than ten major edits a week, and only participants five and six considered themselves in the 10–30 band of overall edits per week.

3.2.1 Off-Line Reviews

All participants had made general text edits to a range of articles: correcting typographical, spelling, and grammatical errors. One even tended to use the "random article" feature to find articles to correct, and would perform more extensive editing to ensure that articles were suitably encylocopædic in style. Half also attempted to find supporting citations for articles that were lacking them: usually via web search, although in one case the participant found suitable sources at the bottom of the article which had simply not been linked in the appropriate places.

Two participants looked at other articles as examples when fixing markup during general editing; another two had learnt from the documentation. The preview feature was useful to refine from-example markup through trial-and-error. One participant showed signs of also learning Wikipedia policy through example: they improved the indexing of articles by adding redirects from acronyms which they expected people to use to the appropriate article. They also added an article to a disambigation page after being unable to find it via that page, and having to resort to a search; added an article to a category it had been omitted from, having seen the category used elsewhere for the same class of items; and added a "recently died" template to a person's article after hearing about the death on the news, having seen it done elsewhere. Another converted an external link to the website for a piece of software to a link to that software's Wikipedia article, as such a link should offer information which is more encyclopædic.

Some edits were removals, rather than additions. One participant reverted vandalism, using the "undo" feature of the page history, because it was quicker than editing out the maliciously added word, and added a warning template to the page of the user responsible. They also removed a dangling link from navigational templates, reasoning that the page used to exist but has been deleted, and this template overlooked. Another participant found a section marked with a long-standing citation problem template, and removed the marker and still-unsupported text.

A participant had taken a photograph for the purpose of illustrating a notable person's Wikipedia article, which they added by using modified markup from another included image. Conversely, one of the participants decided that an article needed illustration, and sought suitable images via a web search.

One participant worked on articles for things they were particularly related to outside of the wiki: their home town and place of study. They made structural changes and, in one case, deliberately left empty subsections for some of the transport facilities in their town which they intended to fill in later, or to prompt some other editor to provide more information.

Another two participants corrected errors they discovered in the process of looking to see what information Wikipedia had on a subject they were familiar with. One commented that they didn't "particularly [go] out to go and edit something; it's just that I happened to come across it". One of these edits was to remove a recurrent piece of incorrect information, so the participant left a note about it on the article's discussion page to justify its removal and try to dissuade its re-addition.

Two participants transferred information from Wikipedia variants in their native language to the English Wikipedia. Neither performed a straightforward translation: one modified it as they went, and the other largely rewrote the articles.

Large-Scale Edits

One of the experienced participants performed two large sets of edits: a continuation of some previously-started work on an article about a section of railway which they were preparing in a personal sandbox under their user account's namespace, and a cleanup of a series of computer games. We now cover these edits in detail.

The railway article contains a diagram of the rail network for this section of track, which is constructed out of a grid of icons using templates. With this, the participant adds some text, and references taken from web searches. The text contains a "citation needed" claim, as the participant knew the fact but couldn't find a satisfactory citation for it, so they decided to "get the gist in" and let someone else fix it.

They found out how to construct the rail network diagrams by spotting other diagrams in rail articles and looking at how they were constructed. They then searched for the templates used to find the documentation, which includes a catalogue of icons. The participant constructs the diagrams within a sandbox because they do not want to leave "public" nodes in a half-finished or broken state. The preview feature is unsuitable because the diagram templates are very complex and time-consuming to build up; if they make a mistake, they want to have an edit history available to revert to, else they have effectively lost their work as an incomprehensible mess.

Once it is in a "reasonable" state, the participant moves the sandbox article to its intended page about the railway station. First they prepare the links to the target page. They find articles which should be linking to it by physical properties—for a rail network, this is station adjacency—and make all the link names consistent, as dangling links can often suffer from co-reference problems.They then view the backlinks of the still-non-existent target page to ensure that all pages they expect to be linking inwards are now doing so. Finally, they copy-and-paste from the sandbox to the target, and set the sandbox pages to redirect to the new, "public" page.

For another railway section, the participant had some information left over in their prepared notes while writing about the station which they could not work into the text of the article. Rather than leave these notes unused as a local file on their computer, they put them on the discussion page for the article, with sources, so that other editors may use them if they see fit.

The participant also found some historical pictures of a railway while browsing, and wondered if Wikipedia would have any. They discovered that Wikipedia did not, so added the pictures, and a reference.

The other major set of edits, about twenty in number, affected a series of computer games. There was one article for the series overall, and one article for the second game in the series; the participant felt that the first game should also be split out, the third was not yet up to quality—it should be copy-edited before it is moved—and that the fourth game's section was too small. First, the participant added a template proposing to split the series article apart. They found the template via cheat-sheet documentation, which they access via a shortcut term in the search box. They added the reasoning for the proposed split to the talk page, and received positive feedback from a previous editor, identified from the page history.

The participant added an "in use" template, seen in the documentation, to the series, which acts as an advisory lock to warn other editors that their changes may be lost in conflicts, and to avoid editing now. They cut down the second game's section within the series article because it already had an article. They then factored out the first game to a separate article, created by following a dangling link, although they changed plan slightly during the process: rather than avoiding an existing disambiguation page, they replaced it with this article and added the template for "for less common meaning X, see article Y" to the top. This did lose the very short history of the new first game article up to that point, because only administrators can move pages while preserving or merging histories. They also moved out categories and external links to the game-specific articles. After a lot of adjustments, they removed the "in use" and "split apart" templates.

3.2.2 On-Line Self-Reports

Edit Duplicated Villain

The participants had to add a fact about a villain to his section in the articles for two films he appeared in.

Two participants simply edited both appearances of the villain; another contemplated splitting the villain out into a separate article, but didn't know how, so resorted to editing both. Two would split the article, although one suggested first looking for other examples of characters with multiple appearances to see if this case has been tackled elsewhere.

The participant most experienced with Wikipedia would make the edit in both places due to the relatively small change against the complexity of refactoring the articles, but would add templates and discussion page comment to propose a split. They consider it important to seek consensus before making a large change, so as to avoid "upsetting" other editors.

Edit Summary and Main Article

The participants had to add an important fact to the "London Underground" article, then to the "London Underground" section of the "Transport in London" article.

All but one participant completed the task successfully. None of the participants made any consideration of sharing text. One noted that the edits were "major", as they had "added a new fact, which might be under debate".

Disambiguate Shelf Links

The participants had to find links to the disambiguation page for "Shelf", and correct them to point at the specific meaning of "shelf" intended.

All but one participant were able to traverse links in reverse without problems, and all participants were able to disambiguate links successfully once they arrived at the place where the link was embedded.

Summarise Trains

The participants had to create a page summarising several trains from different countries.

All participants did, or declared that they would, use different text for the summary article. Only two directly derived the summary text from the text for a specific country's train, and one of these said that they would want to work on improving the quality and consistency of the per-country articles first to avoid duplicated work. The other four wanted different summary text due to the different context: one stressed the need for simpler terminology.

One participant considered sharing some text via templates, but said that such would be complex and confusing, as the text would not then actually be in either page when editing.

With regards to keeping this summary page updated as new regional variations of the train were added, most participants simply stated that the page would need another subheading or list item. One suggested categories as a possible approach, although noted the caveat that category pages on Wikipedia can only have an overall summary of the category, not a small summary for each item listed within it. Another suggested "see also" links, to keep people aware of the interdependencies of these pages, or a navigation box template if there were more than four or five types of train, which would be more visible.

Link Terms in Cake

The participants had to add what they felt were appropriate links to the introductory, plain text paragraph of the "cake" article.

All participants focused on nouns, and limited the amount of links they created; one commented that "all the things can be really linked to", and another wanted to avoid "overloading the user". They differed in which words they selected: two selected toward simpler terms and more fundamental ingredients (e.g. "flour", "sugar"), while the others chose those they considered to be uncommon or ambiguous terms (e.g. "buttercream", "sweetening agent").

One participant ensured that link targets existed and were suitable (e.g. not disambiguation pages); another did this for most links, but deliberately left simpler targets, such as "marzipan", unchecked as they should be created if they did not yet exist. No participant linked a term more than once, and two explicitly stated that this was a deliberate effort.

Add Fact to Infobox

The participants had to add the date of EU membership to the infobox in the "Belgium" article.

Two participants were unable to complete the task, with one expressing surprise that adding information to an infobox was harder than adding to a table. Two improvised a solution which did not use the specific template key for the date of EU membership, but instead a general-purpose one for chronological events. The other two found the template documentation, and added the information with the correct key, although one had problems due the number of adjacent templates in the source, the syntax of which they found "nasty".

3.3 Summary

We set out to determine the goals editors set themselves, and how they act to achieve them.

Several of the participants edited articles to correct errors they encountered while following a primary goal of looking up some information. While this is not particularly surprising for cases of simple, non-content corrections, such as markup or typographical errors, it is counter-intuitive that people who are looking up information, and thus are presumably not experts in that field, will make more significant edits, such as finding and providing references. However, some participants looked up articles on subjects about which they are knowledgeable, either as a reference, or out of curiosity as to what information Wikipedia would have.

There are three ways shown that editors will select images to add to an article. They may deliberately seek to create them with the intent to then add them to Wikipedia; they may discover them while browsing on unrelated tasks, then decide to add them to Wikipedia; or they may be editing an article, decide that it needs illustration, and search for suitable images. There is therefore a range of premeditation to major edits such as this; an extreme case for textual editing is the major railway work, with preparation of an entire node in a semi-private area of the wiki, and a local collection of resources.

Learning by example is a common practice to all of the participants, even those who are also adept at using the documentation. Editors often tried to keep their articles, and meta-activities such as edit comments, consistent with those of other editors. They were actively aware that other editors were at work, and in cases implicitly delegated tasks to whichever editor is inclined to address any outstanding issues, by leaving incomplete sections, dangling links, or marker templates (such as "citation needed"). Dangling links also provided a common mechanism to create new pages, as the wiki has no explicit UI feature to do this.

Even relatively advanced features which do not offer additional capabilities over simpler ones, such as the "undo" links in the history, may be used if they save the editor time.

In the tasks where participants were asked to share text between articles, most of them decided that they would use different text on the different articles, because of the different contexts. For the specific article/general overview case, they edited the information into the existing contexts with no outward consideration of synchronising the summaries. For the trains, several explicitly stated that different text was needed. Hence, there are cases where what is abstractly the same semantic information in multiple places may still not be sharable, because of differing presentation needs. Conversely, the "villain" task shows that sharing is suitable in some situations, where there is a larger, mostly self-contained section of content. This task also highlights the need for better knowledge modelling on Wikipedia, as the current articles do not clearly divide the concepts of actors, characters, and films.

Templates were generally troublesome, even to the more experienced editors. While they would technically permit content sharing, as one participant observed, this has the detrimental property of "hiding" away the text while editing, requiring the editor to follow a possible chain of templates to find where the text they wish to change actually exists. Infobox templates made what should be a simple task of adding a statement about a property of a resource a complicated procedure which some participants could not complete without prompting. While Wikipedia, and hence the synthetic environment, currently runs on a non-semantic wiki, we must stress the risks in not breaking away from this templating-for-properties paradigm as one moves on to systems such as Semantic MediaWiki.

The general problem is that templates on Wikipedia, due to their macro limitations, are presentational, not declarative. This is problematic with regard to their usage for straightforward semantic properties, but the rail network diagram activities highlight this as a more general problem. The complexity of these templates stems from their need to specify exact layout and rendering of arbitrarily complex graphs, here composited from tiled images, when the actual semantic content is a relatively straightforward set of connections. In this case, simple text display of the relation data is insufficient: there is a more complex transform required to generate appropriate presentation. Other example problem domains are molecular diagrams and family trees. Wikipedia currently primarily uses manually-created images for the former, and the community are investigating approaches to entering and displaying the latter,[9] but all are presentational. Solving this in the general case may be impractical without providing the facility to define Turing-complete transforms, which then introduces security and performance problems.

Both in the "cake" task, and in general editing behaviour, all participants felt that things that exist should generally be linked, but that there is a optimal link density to maintain. The threshold to which they would link terms varies significantly between participants, from most of the nouns, to just a few phrases (nouns and noun phrases being those most likely to be article titles). They also prioritised links differently: some chose the simpler terms as their few; others the more obscure terms. All participants only linked a single instance of each term, and several commented explicitly on this decision.

4 Conclusion

We now consider how these observations apply to a hypothetical, richer hypertext system, to determine the desired ordering of feature importance.

4.1 Current Strengths

We should note the importance of keeping two common wiki features, despite our push towards stronger hypertext. First, the editors made use of "broken" hyperstructure, such as empty sections and dangling links, so we should *not* attempt to prevent this, as many classic hypertext systems did. This is somewhat of a unique point of wikis, in that their mutable nature means that navigating to a non-existent target can have useful behaviour: creating the node. Second, the editors often learn by example, so must be able to view the source of pages to see how some

[9] http://en.wikipedia.org/w/index.php?title=Wikipedia:Family_trees&oldid=212894318

construct is achieved, even if they are not permitted to modify the source. Some wikis entangle the source view with the editing operation such that this is not possible, which then deprives the editors of this valuable source of real-world example usage.

These incomplete states are being used as a form of passive communication between editors. The message is implicit and, interestingly, the recipient is often simply the next editor to encounter the page who has the motivation and experience to act upon it. Because these incomplete states are co-ordination between editing users, they are potentially of no interest to reading users. However, the complexity with hiding them from non-editors is that, on a normal wiki, every user is potentially an editor, even if not logged in. While users which have not created accounts are potentially less likely to undertake major editing tasks (see "Overall editing distribution" for the macro-scale experiment), this is heuristic at best, and may discourage editors from getting involved if only because they are not aware of the incomplete changes. The current approach of using different styles of link—by colour, in MediaWiki—has the advantage of leaving the decision, if also workload, of ignoring dangling links to the user.

4.2 Current Weaknesses

The ability to edit links from any of their anchors is a relatively simple step from first-class linking, but we did not reveal any compelling evidence that there is a pressing need for this. All the participants, once they had found the functionality in the user interface, were able to use the wiki backlinks tool to find the endpoint at which the link was embedded, and correct it there. This capability may yet prove useful as wikis transition towards semantic links, as many semantic relations are meaningful in either direction (i.e. many properties have inverses), but is not currently a priority.

Level of detail, part of adaptation, may not be as useful as one may theoretically suppose. Abstractly, it would seem sensible that a low-detail version of a page could be used as a summary about that page when linking to it from elsewhere, as with the specific/general task. However, we have found that the surrounding context affects, if not the semantics of the content, the appropriate wording, such that these summaries are not particularly re-usable.

This also affects the use of transclusion with fat and computed links for aggregation. The most obvious application of this functionality in our synthetic tests would be the types of train, aggregating the low-detail summaries of each train type into a general page on the subject. However, this is also the case where we have identified that context affects the re-usability of the content.

Transclusive re-use of content in general, however, has useful cases. Content which is sufficiently self-contained, not a summary in the context of another page, is a potential candidate for sharing.

Edit-time transclusion solves one of the problems identified by a participant: templates hide the text away. This opacity then greatly limits the usefulness of templates for re-use. As such, we consider the transparency that would be afforded by edit-time transclusion worth prototyping.

The template mechanism also greatly overcomplicates property editing. Instance property editing based on class descriptions, where an HTML form is generated based on RDFS or OWL knowledge of property ranges and domains, would provide a much cleaner interface to this. We consider this feature highly important due to the significant problems with the current approach, but note that similar, non-research implementation is already underway in the Semantic Forms extension.[10]

The linking of terms, as stressed in the "cake" task, is effectively a manual form of generic linking. Outside of the synthetic tasks, this was a common "minor edit" behaviour, and as such there should be enough benefit from automating it that we consider this a strong priority to develop. However, we must be aware that the task is not as trivial as pattern matching. Editors have varying heuristics to determine if a "manual" generic link should be applied to a given instance of a term, and while the lack of such variation in a deterministic algorithm may improve consistency, we must ensure that the link density is kept manageable by some comparable means. At least one restriction is reasonably clear: only one instance of a term per document should be linked.

4.3 Toward Solutions

We have continued this work with the development of a model for a system which overlaps the open hypermedia and semantic web areas, with focus informed by these experiments. Our long-term goal is to continue this research by means of implementation and evaluation of a prototype system, which can be used to test the hypothesis that increased hypermedia features actually result in benefits such as a decrease of editing overhead.

References

1. Bainbridge, L.: Verbal protocol analysis. In: J.R. Wilson, E.N. Corlett (eds.) Evaluation of Human Work, chap. 7. Taylor & Francis Ltd, London (1990)
2. Borenstein, N.S.: Programming as if People Mattered, chap. 19. Princeton University Press, Princeton, N (1991)
3. Bush, V.: As we may think. The Atlantic Monthly **176**, 101–108 (1945). `http://www.theatlantic.com/doc/194507/bush`
4. Davis, H., Hall, W., Heath, I., Hill, G., Wilkins, R.: Towards an integrated information environment with open hypermedia systems. In: ECHT '92: Proceedings of the ACM Conference on Hypertext, pp. 181–190. ACM Press, New York, NY, USA (1992)
5. Fountain, A.M., Hall, W., Heath, I., Davis, H.: MICROCOSM: An open model for hypermedia with dynamic linking. In: European Conference on Hypertext, pp. 298–311 (1990). `http://citeseer.ist.psu.edu/fountain90microcosm.html`

[10] `http://www.mediawiki.org/wiki/Extension:Semantic_Forms`

6. Halasz, F., Schwartz, M.: The Dexter hypertext reference model. Communications of the ACM **37**(2), 30–39 (1994)
7. Krötzsch, M., Vrandečić, D., Völkel, M.: Wikipedia and the semantic web – the missing links. In: Proceedings of the WikiMania2005 (2005). `http://www.aifb.uni-karlsruhe.de/WBS/mak/pub/wikimania.pdf`
8. Levenshtein, V.: Binary codes capable of correcting deletions, insertions and reversals. Soviet Physics Doklady **10**, 707 (1966)
9. Nelson, T.: Literary Machines, 93.1 edn. Mindful Press, Sausalito, California (1993)
10. Shadbolt, N., Burton, M.: Knowledge elicitation. In: J.R. Wilson, E.N. Corlett (eds.) Evaluation of Human Work, chap. 13. Taylor & Francis Ltd London (1990)
11. Swartz, A.: Who writes Wikipedia? (2006). `http://www.aaronsw.com/weblog/whowriteswikipedia`. Online only

Index

X

Y